The Ideology of Democratic Athens

New Approaches to Ancient Greek Institutional History

Series editors: Mirko Canevaro, University of Edinburgh; Edward Harris, Durham University; David Lewis, University of Edinburgh

This series will showcase new trends in the study of Greek political, legal, social and economic institutions and institutional history. It will create a fruitful dialogue between Greek institutional historians and the political and social sciences – and in particular the New Institutionalisms.

Books in the series will go beyond a traditional approach to offer theoretical and methodological reflection on the importance of institutions and on how we should study them. They will appeal to Greek historians and to political and social scientists alike.

Books available in the series
The Ideology of Democratic Athens: Institutions, Orators and the Mythical Past
Matteo Barbato

Forthcoming books in the series
The Politics of Association in Hellenistic Rhodes
Christian A. Thomsen

Visit the series web page at: edinburghuniversitypress.com/series-new-approaches-to-ancient-greek-institutional-history.html

The Ideology of Democratic Athens
Institutions, Orators and the Mythical Past

Matteo Barbato

Edinburgh University Press is one of the leading university presses in the UK. We publish academic books and journals in our selected subject areas across the humanities and social sciences, combining cutting-edge scholarship with high editorial and production values to produce academic works of lasting importance. For more information visit our website: edinburghuniversitypress.com

© Matteo Barbato, 2020, 2022

Edinburgh University Press Ltd
The Tun – Holyrood Road, 12(2f) Jackson's Entry, Edinburgh EH8 8PJ

First published in hardback by Edinburgh University Press 2020

Typeset in 11/13 Bembo Std by
IDSUK (DataConnection) Ltd

A CIP record for this book is available from the British Library

ISBN 978 1 4744 6642 4 (hardback)
ISBN 978 1 4744 6643 1 (paperback)
ISBN 978 1 4744 6644 8 (webready PDF)
ISBN 978 1 4744 6645 5 (epub)

The right of Matteo Barbato to be identified as the author of this work has been asserted in accordance with the Copyright, Designs and Patents Act 1988, and the Copyright and Related Rights Regulations 2003 (SI No. 2498).

Contents

List of Tables and Illustrations		vii
Preface		ix
Abbreviations		xi
1	Introduction	1
	A Brief History of Ideology	3
	Ideology and Democratic Athens	5
	Ideology, New Institutionalism and Social Memory	10
	Myth, Memory and Institutions in Democratic Athens	17
	Outline of the Book	21
2	Myth and Athenian Democracy	24
	The Dramatic Festivals and the Panathenaea	25
	The Institutional Settings of Attic Oratory	38
	Myth in Private Contexts	48
	Myths and Variants in Democratic Athens	52
	Conclusions	56
3	The Discursive Parameters of Athenian Democratic Institutions	57
	The State Funeral for the War Dead	58
	The Lawcourts	66
	The Assembly and the Council	69
	The Dramatic Festivals	76
	Conclusions	80
4	Exclusiveness and *Eugeneia* in the Myth of Autochthony	82
	Autochthony, Exclusiveness and *Eugeneia*	88
	Eugeneia: From Homeric Society to Democratic Athens	91

	Autochthony and Collective *Eugeneia* at the State Funeral	96
	Deconstructing Autochthony on the Tragic Stage	104
	Autochthony and Exclusiveness in Apollodorus' *Against Neaera*	109
	Conclusions	113
5	Between *Charis* and *Philanthrōpia*: The Heraclidae	115
	Athens and the Heraclidae: *Charis* or *Philanthrōpia*?	118
	Between *Charis* and *Philanthrōpia*	120
	Euripidean Tragedy and Reciprocity	126
	Lysias and Athenian *Philanthrōpia*	133
	Charis and *Philanthrōpia* in Isocrates' *Panegyricus*	140
	Conclusions	142
6	Fading Shades of *Hybris*: The Attic Amazonomachy	144
	Hybris and the Causes of the Attic Amazonomachy	147
	Hybris: An Introduction	149
	Lysias: The State Funeral and the Discourse of *Hybris*	152
	Theseus and the Amazons in Aeschylus' *Eumenides*	161
	An Allusion to the Abduction in a Private Setting?	165
	Theseus' Abduction of Antiope in the Figurative Arts	167
	The Abduction of Antiope in Mythographers and Atthidographers	170
	The Abduction of Antiope in Isocrates' Private Rhetoric	175
	Conclusions	178
7	Combining *Hybris* and *Philanthrōpia*: The Myth of Adrastus	182
	Philanthrōpia and *Hybris*: Values in Interaction	185
	Athenian *Philanthrōpia*, Theban *Hybris*: Lysias' *Funeral Oration*	186
	Philanthrōpia, *Hybris* and Advantage in Euripides' *Suppliant Women*	193
	The Myth of Adrastus in Procles' Speech to the Assembly	202
	The Myth of Adrastus in a Fictional Assembly	205
	Questioning Theban *Hybris* in a Private Context	209
	Conclusions	213
8	Conclusions	215

Bibliography	221
Index locorum	240
General index	248

List of Tables and Illustrations

Table 2.1	Myths in tragedies and satyr plays	30
Table 2.2	Myths in the extant funeral speeches	41
Table 2.3	Myths in the extant forensic speeches	44
Figure 2.1	Achilles and Patroclus. Red-figure cup from Vulci (c. 500 BC). Berlin, Antikensammlung F 2278. Image © Antikensammlung, Staatliche Museen zu Berlin – Preussischer Kulturbesitz (J. Laurentius).	54
Figure 4.1	Birth of Erichthonius. Red-figure hydria by the Oinanthe Painter (c. 470–460 BC). London, British Museum E 182. Image © Trustees of the British Museum.	84
Figure 4.2	Birth of Erichthonius. Red-figure cup by the Codros Painter (c. 440–430 BC), Side A. Berlin, Antikensammlung F 2537. Image © Antikensammlung, Staatliche Museen zu Berlin – Preussischer Kulturbesitz (J. Laurentius).	85
Figure 4.3	Athenian kings and the Cecropids. Red-figure cup by the Codros Painter (c. 440–430 BC), Side B. Berlin, Antikensammlung F 2537. Image © Antikensammlung, Staatliche Museen zu Berlin – Preussischer Kulturbesitz (J. Laurentius).	85
Figure 6.1	Theseus abducts Antiope. Black-figure amphora from Cumae (c. 510–500 BC). Napoli, Museo Archeologico Nazionale 128333. Image © Museo Archeologico Nazionale di Napoli.	168

Figure 6.2	Theseus abducts Antiope. Red-figure cup (c. 510 BC). Oxford, Ashmolean Museum AN1927.4065 Oltos, 'Attic red-figure stemmed pottery cup depicting a mythological scene'. Image © Ashmolean Museum, University of Oxford.	169
Figure 6.3	Theseus and Antiope step together onto a chariot. Black-figure amphora from Vulci (c. 510–500 BC). München, Staatliche Antikensammlungen und Glyptothek 1414. Image © Staatliche Antikensammlungen und Glyptothek München (R. Kühling).	169

Preface

This book is a revised version of my doctoral thesis, which I wrote under the supervision of Mirko Canevaro and Douglas Cairns at the University of Edinburgh. It investigates the construction of Athenian democratic ideology through a study of the social memory of Athens' mythical past. The debate on Athenian democratic ideology has long been polarised around two extremes. A Marxist tradition has propounded a negative view of ideology as a cover-up for Athens' internal divisions. Another tradition, sometimes referred to as culturalist, has provided a neutral interpretation of ideology as the fixed set of ideas shared by the members of the Athenian community. This book remedies this dichotomy by providing a unitary and comprehensive approach to Athenian democratic ideology. Through four case studies that compare different versions of selected myths in Athenian public discourse, it demonstrates that Athenian democratic ideology was a fluid set of ideas, values and beliefs shared by the Athenians as a result of a constant ideological practice influenced by the institutions of the democracy. This process entailed the active participation of both the mass and the elite, and enabled the Athenians to produce multiple and compatible ideas about their community and its mythical past.

    This work originated as a study of the use and manipulation of myth in Athenian funeral speeches. It was the natural continuation of my MA dissertation, written at the University of Bologna and supervised by Simonetta Nannini. To her I am grateful for encouraging me to start a doctorate and advising me during the first stages of the application process. As I moved on to working on my PhD, my focus shifted from rhetoric to history. Under the patient and inspiring guidance of Mirko Canevaro, I started experimenting with social memory and Athenian public discourse at large and finally landed on ideology and the New Institutionalism. My gratitude to Mirko cannot be stressed enough. He believed in me even when I did not, encouraged me to explore new themes and methodologies, and supported me in all my academic endeavours. I am equally thankful to Douglas Cairns, whose insightful comments and thoughtful criticism have been fundamental to refining my methodology, strengthening my argument and broadening my perspective. I have been lucky to work with such excellent scholars, and this book would not have been possible without their precious input.

Many other academics contributed to this book and need to be acknowledged. My Viva examiners, Paola Ceccarelli and Richard Rawles, provided me with detailed and constructive criticism on my thesis and encouraged me to expand it into a much more ambitious work. Edward Harris deserves a special mention for kindly offering invaluable advice on this and other projects and sharing with me several forthcoming essays throughout the years. At the University of Edinburgh, I had the opportunity to meet many outstanding scholars who offered me feedback, advice and bibliographical suggestions. It is impossible to mention them all here, but I would especially like to thank Ben Gray, who provided precious feedback on several drafts of my thesis, and Alberto Esu, who shared with me his knowledge of Athenian democracy in countless conversations. I am also grateful to Sarah Cassidy, Alison John, Alana Newman and Belinda Washington for proofreading previous versions of this work, and to Will Mack and my colleagues at the University of Birmingham for offering insightful suggestions on the final drafts of several chapters.

Finally, I would like to thank the University of Edinburgh for funding my doctorate, as well as the University of Birmingham and the Leverhulme Trust for enabling me to complete this book during the first months of my research fellowship. I am also grateful to EUP's commissioning editor and series editors for assisting me during the publication process, and to the anonymous peer reviewers for allowing me to improve my manuscript significantly. Any remaining mistakes are of course my own.

Matteo Barbato
Birmingham, October 2019

Abbreviations

Ancient works are abbreviated according to the fourth edition of the *Oxford Classical Dictionary*. References to the fragments of Aeschylus, Sophocles and Euripides use the numbering of the relevant volumes of *Tragicorum Graecorum Fragmenta*. Journal abbreviations follow *L'Année philologique*. All other abbreviations are listed below.

Bernabé	A. Bernabé, ed., *Poetae Epici Graeci. Testimonia et Fragmenta. Pars I* (Leipzig 1987).
BNJ	I. Worthington, ed., *Brill's New Jacoby* (Leiden 2006–).
DK	H. Diels and W. Kranz, eds, *Die Fragmente der Vorsokratiker* (Berlin 1951–2).
FGrHist	F. Jacoby, ed., *Die Fragmente der griechischen Historiker* (Berlin and Leiden 1923–58).
IG	*Inscriptiones Graecae* (Berlin 1872–).
IPrien	F. Hiller von Gaertringen, ed., *Inschriften von Priene* (Berlin and Boston 1906).
K.-A.	R. Kassel and C. Austin, eds, *Poetae Comici Graeci* (Berlin and New York 1983–2001).
LIMC	*Lexicon Iconographicum Mythologiae Classicae* (Zürich 1981–2009).
LSJ	H. G. Liddell and R. Scott, *A Greek–English Lexicon*, 9th edn, revised and augmented by H. S. Jones (Oxford 1940).
Maehler	H. Maehler, ed., *Pindari Carmina cum Fragmentis. Pars II: Fragmenta. Indices* (Leipzig 1989).
Miletos	D. F. McCabe, ed., *Miletos Inscriptions. Texts and List* (Princeton 1984).
OED	J. A. Simpson and E. S. C. Weiner, *Oxford English Dictionary*, 2nd edn (Oxford 1989).

PMG D. L. Page, ed., *Poetae Melici Graeci* (Oxford 1962).
PMGF M. Davies, ed., *Poetarum Melicorum Graecorum Fragmenta. Volumen I: Alcman, Stesichorus, Ibicus* (Oxford 1991).
SEG *Supplementum epigraphicum Graecum* (Leiden 1923–).
Smyth H. W. Smyth, *A Greek Grammar for Colleges* (New York 1920).
Suda A. Adler, ed., *Suidae lexicon* (Leipzig 1928–35).
TrGF B. Snell, R. Kannicht and S. Radt, eds, *Tragicorum Graecorum Fragmenta* (Göttingen 1971–2004).
Voigt E.-M. Voigt, ed., *Sappho et Alcaeus: Fragmenta* (Amsterdam 1971).
West M. L. West, ed., *Iambi et Elegi Graeci ante Alexandrum Cantati*, 2nd edn (Oxford 1989–92).

CHAPTER I

Introduction

The evidence of public discourse provides modern scholars with a window onto the ideology of democratic Athens during the fifth and fourth centuries BC. At the state funeral for the war dead, an orator chosen to deliver the customary funeral speech would praise the Athenians' equality within the community, their devotion to Greek freedom or their selfless pursuit of justice in the relations with other states. Speakers in the lawcourts would address boards of popular judges and appeal to the values of justice and the rule of law. The orators deliberating on public policy in the Assembly would advise what was best and advantageous for the city. Speakers addressing the Council would appeal to both considerations of justice and advantage. Even the dramatic festivals provided an arena for discussing a wide range of values significant for the community, from religious piety to the belief in the autochthony of the Athenians, and from the protection of suppliants to the appropriate attitudes towards honour, *hybris* or the law.

These are only some of the ideas, values and beliefs that underpinned Athens' political life and have given rise to a fruitful scholarly tradition that has investigated Athenian democratic ideology. The works of Nicole Loraux and Josiah Ober are indisputably the most representative and influential products of such a tradition. Both have greatly enriched our knowledge of Athenian democracy, but they were based on different sets of sources and reached rather contrasting conclusions. Loraux explored the funeral speech for the war dead and determined that the genre was an ideological mask for Athens' internal divisions and the exploitative reality of the Empire.[1] Ober focused mostly on forensic

[1] Loraux 1981.

and deliberative speeches and adopted a neutral, if not positive approach. He interpreted Athenian democratic ideology as the fixed set of ideas and values of the mass which were passively endorsed by the elite to vie for political influence, and concluded that this ideological compromise between mass and elite ensured the stability of the democracy for about two hundred years.[2]

The contrast between Loraux's and Ober's views of Athenian democratic ideology is symptomatic of a broader dichotomy in the scholarship about ideology in the social sciences. Loraux's work, despite taking a slightly different direction, was inspired by the Marxist tradition, which provides a negative interpretation of ideology as false consciousness and as the ideas of the dominant class in a given historical period. Ober, on the other hand, can be associated with a tradition (sometimes labelled as 'culturalist') that proposes a neutral interpretation of ideology as the set of ideas shared by the members of a given community. This book aims to reconcile these contrasting approaches and offer a more nuanced understanding of Athenian democratic ideology, one that combines the descriptive aspect and neutral notion of ideology held by the culturalist tradition with the normative aspect and evolving nature of ideology typical of the Marxist tradition. I therefore seek to advance the debate on ideology in democratic Athens while at the same time making a wider contribution to the research agenda of the social sciences.[3]

I suggest that the study of Athenian democratic ideology would benefit from an increased attention to institutions. Ancient historians interested in ideology have usually neglected the study of institutions, and the two realms have often been perceived as alternative and incompatible tools for the investigation of Athenian democracy.[4] Yet, a recent trend in political science known as New Institutionalism has successfully challenged extra-institutionalist approaches and made a convincing case for considering the mutual interaction between the formal institutions of the state and the ideological and discursive practices of political actors.[5] I argue that the New Institutionalism offers a fruitful and yet unexplored perspective to overcome the opposition between the Marxist and the culturalist traditions on ideology. Accordingly, this book defines Athenian democratic ideology as a fluid set of ideas shared by the majority of the Athenians as a result of a constant process of ideological practice influenced by the institutions of the

---

[2] Ober 1989a.
[3] The reconciliation of the Marxist and the culturalist approaches to ideology is a recurrent topic in the social sciences. For some attempts in this direction, see Ricoeur 1986: 1–18; van Dijk 1998; Chiapello 2003.
[4] See, for example, the exchange between Ober 1989b and Hansen 1989a on the importance of institutional analysis for our understanding of Athenian democracy. For an excellent overview of the institutionalist and non-institutionalist approaches to Athenian democracy, see Azoulay and Ismard 2007.
[5] See March and Olsen 1984; Schmidt 2008; Lowndes and Roberts 2013.

democracy. This view is tested against the use of the social memory of the mythical past in Athenian public discourse. Four case studies (Chapters 4 to 7) analyse a set of mythical variants (the myth of autochthony; Athens' help for the Heraclidae; the Attic Amazonomachy; the myth of Adrastus) within the institutions that produced them, and determine the discursive parameters which conditioned political actors in each institution and enabled them to construct multiple and compatible ideas about their community and its past.

This book complements and significantly advances previous interpretations of Athenian democratic ideology. While Loraux held a negative view of ideology as a means to conceal internal divisions and conflict within the *polis*, I lay greater stress upon the constructive power of ideology and public discourse (especially in specific institutions) to foster civic cohesion through the creation of an 'imagined community'.[6] At the same time, I build upon yet modify Ober's view of ideology as a fixed set of ideas by acknowledging the dynamic nature of Athenian democratic ideology. By this I mean that ideology could evolve and incorporate newly developed ideas and values, and that ideas and values were themselves flexible and could interact with one another differently depending on each institutional context. Finally, my view challenges our understanding of Athenian ideological practice as either a top-down or bottom-up process. I argue that ideology was neither a form of brainwashing imposed by Athens' dominant class on the subordinate classes in the Marxist sense,[7] nor a system that allowed the Athenian masses to exert their hegemony and control the elites as argued by Ober.[8] Instead, I suggest that Athenian democratic ideology was produced by the combined agency of mass and elite through discourse within the institutions of the democracy. This book therefore paints a more complete picture of Athenian democratic ideology through a synthesis of the features of the Marxist and the culturalist approaches that are most appropriate to the nature of Athenian democracy.

A BRIEF HISTORY OF IDEOLOGY

The term ideology was coined in the eighteenth century by Enlightenment philosopher Antoine Destutt de Tracy. Ideology originally held the positive meaning of 'science of ideas', and was set in opposition to religion and the system of thought which sustained the *ancien régime*.[9] The concept of ideology has since been the object of constant debate and analysis. Taken up by Marx

---

[6] For the notion of 'imagined community' see B. Anderson [1983] 2006.
[7] See de Ste Croix 1981: 409–16; but this view was notably rejected by Loraux 1981: 348.
[8] Ober 1989a: 332–9.
[9] Eagleton 1991: 63–70; F. Jameson 2009: 323.

and Engels during the nineteenth century, the term went through a considerable shift in meaning and lost its original positive sense. In his reflection on ideology, Marx oscillated between an epistemological and a political interpretation of the notion. The epistemological interpretation is expressed in *The German Ideology*, where Marx and Engels elaborated the theory of ideology as false consciousness.[10] Against German Idealism, which they considered guilty of privileging consciousness and ideas over what they perceived as real life, Marx and Engels promoted a materialistic approach. They advocated a shift of focus from ideas to the actual life-processes that produce them, and reacted against the illusion created by ideology, which they described as inverting the causal relationship between the real world and consciousness.[11] *The German Ideology*, however, also contains the kernel of a political interpretation which Marx further elaborated in his subsequent writings and which views ideology as the ideas of the ruling class, and therefore the ruling ideas of a given historical period. These ideas are the direct expression and legitimisation of the material relations of production within society and are not necessarily judged as true or false.[12]

A significant (and institutionalist) development of the Marxist theory of ideology was offered by French philosopher Louis Althusser in his essay 'Ideology and Ideological State Apparatuses'. Althusser defined ideology as a representation of the 'imaginary relationship of individuals to their real conditions of existence' and envisioned it as an instrument for the reproduction of the relations of production. Such reproduction is achieved through the Ideological State Apparatuses (ISAs). These are a set of institutions (e.g., cultural, religious, educational) that mould the individual according to the ruling ideology and ensure the continuation of the domination of the ruling class over the subordinated classes.[13] Not only did Althusser further develop Marx's political interpretation of ideology as the ideas of the ruling class, but he also highlighted the evolving nature of ideology as a result of class struggle. He stressed in particular that 'the ideology of the ruling class does not become the ruling ideology by the grace of God, nor even by virtue of the seizure of state power alone. It is by the installation of the ISAs in which this ideology is realized and realizes itself that it becomes the ruling ideology. But this installation [. . .] is the stake in a very bitter and continuous class struggle'.[14]

---

[10] The interpretation of ideology as false consciousness is commonly held as the standard Marxist theory of ideology; however, as Chiapello 2003: 156 rightly points out, this interpretation is not shared by all Marxist thinkers.
[11] Marx and Engels [1932] 1938: 13–16; Eagleton 1991: 70–9; F. Jameson 2009: 323–4.
[12] Marx and Engels [1932] 1938: 39; Eagleton 1991: 79–80; F. Jameson 2009: 325–8.
[13] Althusser [1971] 1984: 1–60.
[14] Althusser [1971] 1984: esp. 58–9; see also Rose 2012: 44–6.

In response to the evaluative, and mostly pejorative, interpretation of ideology endorsed by Marxism, a more neutral approach has been advanced by a tradition that is sometimes labelled as 'culturalist'.[15] The culturalist tradition stems from Mannheim's attempt to develop a non-evaluative concept of ideology in his book *Ideology and Utopia*. Building on Mannheim's paradox that, since all thought is socially mediated, all thought about ideology (including Marxism) must itself be ideological,[16] anthropologist Clifford Geertz relied on semiotics to investigate the realm of ideology. Since all human thought, not unlike ideological thought, is symbolically mediated, ideology should be considered no more false or distortive than cognitive processes themselves.[17] Geertz therefore emphasised the integrative aspect of ideology, whose function he compared to a map which orients people's actions and makes 'an autonomous politics possible by providing the authoritative concepts that render it meaningful'.[18] In this line of thought, ideology neutrally denotes 'the general material process of production of ideas, beliefs and values in social life', and tends to be assimilated to the broader anthropological concept of culture.[19] Mannheim's paradox similarly inspired political theorist Martin Seliger to criticise the Marxist view of ideology and propose a neutral, 'inclusive' definition of ideology as 'a set of ideas by which men posit, explain, and justify ends and means of organised social action, irrespective of whether such action aims to preserve, amend, uproot, or rebuild a given order'.[20]

IDEOLOGY AND DEMOCRATIC ATHENS

From the social sciences, the gulf between Marxist and culturalist approaches to ideology moved to the scholarship on Athenian democracy. The Marxist theory of ideology has been notably applied to ancient Greece by G. E. M. de Ste Croix in *The Class Struggle in the Ancient Greek World: From the Archaic Age to the Arab Conquests*. De Ste Croix envisioned ideological class struggle as the

---

[15] The 'culturalist' label is employed, for example, in Chiapello 2003: 157–9 and Meyer et al. 2009: 4–5.
[16] Mannheim [1929] 1936: 88–90; Ricoeur 1986: 159–80.
[17] Geertz 1973: 208–18; Ricoeur 1986: 254–66.
[18] Geertz 1973: esp. 218–19.
[19] Eagleton 1991: 28–9; Chiapello 2003: 157–9. Another culturalist definition of ideology was provided by French anthropologist Luis Dumont, who highlighted the character of ideology as the sum of the social representations produced by a given country at a given time in history: Dumont 1977: 26–31. On the concept of culture in anthropology, see Geertz 1973: 4–5; J. B. Thompson 1990: 127–35.
[20] Seliger 1976: 14. Since it does not belong to the domain of anthropology, Seliger's definition of ideology cannot be strictly counted as culturalist. Yet, it shares Geertz's neutral, non-derogative approach to ideology, and for this reason it is listed under the same category.

attempt of the dominant classes (i.e., the propertied classes), through propaganda or brainwashing, to persuade the exploited classes (i.e., slaves and other providers of unfree labour) to accept their own condition of exploitation.[21] De Ste Croix, however, aimed to recognise the exploitation of unfree labour as the source of the economic surplus enjoyed by the propertied class. Such an approach imposed a significant limit on his analysis of ideology, which as a result mainly focused on slavery and class struggle. De Ste Croix's discussion was based on the writings of Plato, Xenophon and other elite authors and did not consider public discourse, which was an extremely significant site of ideological practice in Athenian democracy. De Ste Croix similarly neglected the important role of several intermediate categories between slaves and the propertied elite (e.g., peasants, traders and artisans) in the ideological dynamics of democratic Athens.[22] Instead, I argue that the citizen masses, which were made up of people belonging to these categories, played an important role in the construction of Athenian democratic ideology. They participated in Athenian public discourse as judges in the lawcourts, members of the Assembly or the Council, mourners at the state funeral or members of the audience at the dramatic festivals. They expected political actors (mostly orators and playwrights) to act in accordance with the discursive parameters of each institution, and their expectations influenced the behaviour of those actors and the ideas they would convey.[23]

The Marxist approach to ideology has been questioned by other ancient historians. Like de Ste Croix, Finley considered ideology in connection with slave economy, but he came to the opposite conclusion that 'in ancient Greece, with its open exploitation of slaves and foreign subjects, there would be little scope for ideology in the Marxist sense'.[24] The influence of class struggle on the ideological dynamics of democratic Athens was partly contested by David Whitehead in *The Ideology of the Athenian Metic*. Whitehead defined the ideology of the metic as 'a portmanteau phrase encompassing not only the sum of opinions, prejudices, and tensions, recorded or deducible, in [the Athenian] *polis* but the actual reciprocal relations between *politai* and *metoikoi* coexisting in a political and social environment controlled exclusively by the *politai*'.[25] Despite recognising the citizens' control of democratic institutions and the possible existence of class conflict within Athens' citizen body, Whitehead explicitly refused

---

[21] De Ste Croix 1981: 409–16.
[22] The limited scope of de Ste Croix's discussion of ideology has been highlighted even by a Marxist classicist such as Rose 2006: 104, who points out how this analysis was overly dependent on Plato.
[23] On the agency and respective roles of the mass and the elite in Athenian ideological practice, see Chapter 3.
[24] Finley [1973] 1985: 104.
[25] Whitehead 1977: 3–4.

to consider the relationship between citizens and metics as a '"class struggle" in the normal sense of the term, or indeed any kind of struggle at all'.²⁶

If these scholars attest to a debate around the applicability of the Marxist notion of ideology to Athens, the best illustration of the dichotomy between the Marxist and the culturalist approaches to ideology in Athenian democracy lies in the works of Nicole Loraux and Josiah Ober in the 1980s. In her influential book *L'invention d'Athènes: Histoire de l'oraison funèbre dans la cité classique*, Nicole Loraux asserted the ideological nature of Athenian public discourse and applied a revised version of the Marxist approach to ideology to the funeral oration for the war dead (*epitaphios logos*). Loraux discarded as simplistic the idea that the *epitaphios logos* may have been the result of a conscious mystificatory action enacted by Athens' dominant class in order to pursue their class interests.²⁷ Yet, she questioned the generic usage of the word 'ideology' with the meaning of 'system of ideas' and explicitly endorsed the Marxist view of ideology as dissimulation. Arguing against Finley that such a notion can indeed be applied to ancient Greece, Loraux concluded that the *epitaphios logos* was ideological in so far as it denied the internal divisions of the *polis* and misrepresented the Empire as a benevolent hegemony.²⁸ Despite trying to tone down the nuance of illusion in her conception of ideology by resorting to the notion of *imaginaire*,²⁹ Loraux therefore could not appreciate the positive and even necessary character of the funeral oration in creating civic bonds and making up for private losses on behalf of the city.³⁰

The *epitaphios logos* did have an ideological function, but I argue that this function should more productively be read in the light of Benedict Anderson's notion of 'imagined community', which was not yet available to Loraux. In his study *Imagined Communities: Reflections on the Origin and Spread of Nationalism*, Anderson posited that any community whose members do not know the majority of their fellow-members is an imagined community. Such an act of imagining is conceived of in positive terms as a necessary construction. Not only does it enable people to die for their country, but it also binds them together and constitutes the foundation of reciprocal obligations in relations

---

²⁶ Whitehead 1977: 174–5.
²⁷ Loraux 1981: 348. One could add that the Athenians did share some class-neutral ideas, including e.g. the rule of law: see Harris 2013b: 3–4. The Marxist notion of ideology as mystification enacted by the dominant class (albeit in a broad sense) is implicit in Loraux [1981] 1993: 13–21, who interpreted the myth of autochthony as men's attempt to deny the reality of reproduction and the significance of the feminine.
²⁸ Loraux 1981: 340–7.
²⁹ Loraux 1981: 347–9.
³⁰ Loraux 1981: esp. 206–7 did highlight the function of the *epitaphios logos* as an expression of the cohesion of the Athenian community, but interpreted it mainly as a means to conceal the reality of civil strife.

that are no longer face-to-face.³¹ The notion of imagined community fits the case of classical Athens, which was not a face-to-face society and relied on public discourse to build a community.³² The main function of the *epitaphios logos* was thus to construct an imagined community. The speech turned the state funeral from a potential occasion of private resentment towards the *polis* into a source of social cohesion. By giving the Athenians a city worth dying for, the funeral oration justified the sacrifice of their relatives and inspired them to follow their example.³³

The positive aspects of ideology were highlighted by Josiah Ober in *Mass and Elite in Democratic Athens: Rhetoric, Ideology, and the Power of the People*. Ober's study provides a culturalist definition of ideology, and is still to this day the standard account of Athenian democratic ideology.³⁴ Ober posited a fundamental division of the Athenian population between an elite of wealth, education and birth, and the mass of ordinary citizens which constituted the Athenian *dēmos*. In doing so, he aimed to understand how the Athenian democracy managed to survive and achieve stability for almost two hundred years without *de facto* relinquishing all power to the hands of a ruling elite.³⁵ Ober concluded that stability was achieved through ideological negotiation, and emphasised the importance of rhetoric for the functioning of Athenian democracy. In his view, public discourse (especially in the lawcourts) was the arena where mass and elite negotiated ideological compromises that created a balance between socio-economic inequality and political equality.³⁶

Ober defined ideology as the set of 'assumptions, opinions, and principles which are common to the great majority of th[e] members [of any given community]', and suggested that ideology, intended as a system of symbols,

---

[31] B. Anderson [1983] 2006: 5–7. The applicability of the notion of imagined community to classical Athens has been endorsed by G. Anderson 2003 and Shear 2011: 10–11.

[32] The idea that Athens was a face-to-face society, originally endorsed by Finley [1973] 1985: 17–20, has been convincingly challenged by R. Osborne 1985: 64–5 and Ober 1989a: 31–3. While face-to-face dynamics cannot be detected at the *polis* level, some degree of such dynamics is conceivable at the deme level or in the case of the Council. In the speech *Against Pancleon*, for example, Lysias claims that Pancleon had misappropriated citizen status based on the fact that his alleged fellow demesmen did not know him (Lys. 23.3). As for the Council, its 500 members (fifty per tribe) met almost on a daily basis (Rhodes 1972: 1–48, 30; Hansen [1991] 1999: 247–55). This led them to engage in constant personal interactions and face-to-face dynamics: see Ober 2008: 142–51.

[33] The importance of the dead in the *epitaphios logos* was emphasised by Longo 2000: 9–27.

[34] Ober himself has recently emphasised the relevance of *Mass and Elite* for current scholarship as well as the necessity to update and extend the picture of Athenian democracy provided by his book: see Ober 2016.

[35] Ober 1989a: 11–20.

[36] Ober 1989a: esp. 304–6. This view has been criticised by Harris 2006: 134–9, who argues that social stability was achieved more through material means than ideological negotiation.

determines social and political decisions to a large extent.[37] In his concluding remarks, Ober pointed out how his thesis challenged not only the view of those who consider Athenian democracy ultimately as dominated by a ruling elite, but also the traditional Marxist approach that conceives ideology as the set of ideas used by the dominant class to mask its domination over the lower classes.[38] Ober had the merit of uncoupling ideology from the negative associations that had accrued to the term under the influence of much Marxist tradition, and emphasised instead the positive and integrative function of ideology.[39] Yet, his view of ideology appears rather static and descriptive, as it does not account for the ideological practice of classical Athens and the normative aspect it entails.

While Ober envisioned the Athenians' assumptions, opinions and principles as a fixed, monolithic set of ideas shared by the *dēmos* and passively accepted by the elite, I argue that these assumptions, opinions and principles were in fact the result of constant ideological practice, a continuous process of creating and re-creating which took place in an array of institutional settings and involved both the mass and the elite. Ober rightly noted the centrality of rhetoric and public discourse in this process, but did not fully appreciate the role played by the orators. He viewed the orators as mere negotiators between the ideology of the elite, of which they were often members, and that of the mass, who held supreme power and ideological hegemony in the democratic *polis*. In *Mass and Elite*, in other words, the orators passively interpreted the community's democratic ideology, in a sort of play of which the masses were the beneficiaries and ultimate judges.[40] I argue that the role of the orators in the ideological dynamics of democratic Athens was instead more active and multifaceted, and largely depended on the institutional settings in which they operated. This is especially evident in the case of the state funeral for the war dead. This institution allowed the orators to play an active part in creating and perpetuating the shared ideas of the community, but received only limited discussion in *Mass and Elite*.

Ober's claim that public discourse was the *locus* of a negotiation between the opposing ideologies of mass and elite also needs to be addressed. I do not deny that the systems of beliefs of the Athenian mass and elite could sometimes differ or conflict, but oratory is not the ideal place to look for traces of

---

[37] Ober 1989a: 38–42; he is followed by Steinbock 2013a: 13–14. See also Canevaro forthcoming a.
[38] Ober 1989a: 339. Ober 1989a: 38–40 emphasised that the Marxist view of ideology as a product of the ruling elite is not applicable to the Athenian democracy.
[39] But the conception of ideology as false consciousness is not common to all Marxist thinkers and was subject to evolution even in Marx's own thought: see pp. 3–4 and n. 10.
[40] Ober envisions the Athenian lawcourts as an arena for elite competition under the regulation of the *dēmos*; see also D. Cohen 1995. For a criticism of this view, see Harris 2013b: 60–98 and Canevaro 2016b: 48 n. 39.

elite ideology.[41] Public discourse was instead the expression of a wide-ranging democratic ideology that the orators themselves endorsed and contributed to produce, and which invested Athenian democratic institutions according to their specific discursive parameters. This book argues that the study of Athenian ideological practice will benefit from a greater attention to the institutions of Athenian democracy, which Ober's analysis relegated to the background.[42] My approach to the ancient evidence is based on the principles of the New Institutionalism, and its additional aim is to bridge the gap between the study of ancient history and current trends in political science. The next section illustrates these principles and how I intend to use them to advance our understanding of Athenian democratic ideology through the analysis of the social memory of Athens' mythical past.

IDEOLOGY, NEW INSTITUTIONALISM AND SOCIAL MEMORY

The New Institutionalism emerged in the late 1970s as a reaction to the focus on individual actions propounded by behaviouralism and rational choice theory, and advocated a return to the study of institutions as independent factors in political life.[43] The New Institutionalism envisions institutions as ensembles of rules, practices and narratives which condition the behaviour of individual political actors by both empowering them and compelling them to act according to a logic of appropriateness.[44] Mostly ignored and even rejected by institutionalist scholars until the 1990s, ideas and discourse have recently enjoyed increasing attention as methodological tools particularly suitable for explaining institutional change. They have originated a variant sometimes labelled as Discursive Institutionalism and distinct from the main traditions of Historical Institutionalism, Sociological Institutionalism and Rational Choice Institutionalism. Discursive Institutionalism sees ideas and discourse simultaneously as a product and as constitutive of institutions, and highlights the importance of studying them within their institutional context.[45] Vivien Schmidt, for example, correlates a country's

---

[41] Such traces are rather to be found in the private writings of the Athenian elite which Ober himself has analysed in a more recent monograph: see Ober 1998.

[42] See Hansen 1990: 351–2.

[43] For an example of the behaviouralist approach to democratic Athens, see Herman 2006.

[44] The first enunciation of the principles of the New Institutionalism is found in March and Olsen 1984; see also March and Olsen 2006 and Lowndes and Roberts 2013.

[45] On Discursive Institutionalism, see Schmidt 2006, 2008 and 2010. As noted by Schmidt 2008: 304, not all institutionalists interested in ideas posit a distinct fourth New Institutionalism, and those who do sometimes refer to it with different labels, such as 'Ideational Institutionalism', 'Constructivist Institutionalism', and 'Strategic Constructivism'. On the 'turn to ideas' in the New Institutionalism see also Hay 2006 and Blyth et al. 2016.

discourse with its institutional structure. She suggests that, while polities where governing activity is exercised by a single authority (e.g., Britain and France) develop a more elaborate discourse to the general public, polities where governing activity is shared among multiple authorities (e.g., Germany and Italy) develop a more elaborate discourse among policy actors.[46] John Campbell investigates the impact of ideas on policy-making by analysing the role of ideas and institutions in the rise of supply-side economics in the macroeconomic policy-making of the United States in the late 1970s and early 1980s.[47] Colin Hay similarly uses the crisis of Keynesianism and the rise of neoliberalism in Britain during the 1970s as a case study to explore how new politico-economic paradigms are institutionalised and replace old paradigms.[48]

I suggest that a renewed focus on institutions based on these recent trends in political science can provide a fruitful and yet mostly unexplored angle for the advancement of the study of Athenian democracy and the Greek *polis* in general.[49] The New Institutionalism has been successfully employed by Edward Harris to show that the Athenians were aware of the etiquette of the Assembly as opposed to that of the lawcourts, and consequently expected public speakers to respect it.[50] In *Proxeny and Polis: Institutional Networks in the Ancient Greek World*, William Mack draws on the New Institutionalism to establish how *proxenoi* were expected to carry out their function according to a logic of appropriateness.[51] Mirko Canevaro has applied an institutionalist approach to the realm of Athenian popular culture. He argues that, since Athenian institutions were controlled by the masses, 'authorised' cultural forms in Athens that were produced within the formal institutions of the state were an expression of the ideas of those masses, whereas 'unauthorised' cultural forms produced in informal contexts were often the expression of the ideas of the elite.[52] The New Institutionalism is thus gaining increasing popularity among ancient historians,[53] and can be extremely beneficial for our understanding of Athenian democratic ideology beyond the traditional

---

[46] Schmidt 2002: chs 5–6.
[47] Campbell 1998.
[48] Hay 2001.
[49] A fruitful tradition has investigated the formal aspects of Athenian democratic institutions: see e.g. Rhodes 1972; Hansen 1974, 1978, 1983, 1987 and [1991] 1999; Rhodes and Lewis 1997. This book complements these studies by investigating the influence of those institutions on the behaviour of the individuals acting within them.
[50] Harris 2013a; see also the general remarks in Harris 2013b: 3–18.
[51] Mack 2015.
[52] Canevaro 2016b.
[53] See also Esu 2017, who analyses Spartan deliberative institutions from the perspective of the Historical Institutionalism, and Simonton 2017, who argues that the stability of Greek oligarchies was based on institutions that prevented intra-elite conflict and popular uprisings against the ruling elite.

divide between Marxist and culturalist approaches. This book therefore looks at Athenian ideological practice from a discursive institutionalist perspective, and makes the case that Athenian democratic institutions conditioned the construction of the shared ideas of the community.

I shall focus on a specific facet of Athenian ideological practice, and investigate how a shared image of the city's mythical past was constructed within Athenian democratic institutions and according to the discursive parameters of each institutional setting. Such an analysis interweaves with and builds upon existing scholarship on Athenian social memory.[54] Rosalind Thomas's *Oral Tradition and Written Record in Classical Athens*, for example, identifies various traditions about Athens' past and reveals the existence of a subterranean struggle and cooperation between different mnemonic communities.[55] Her depiction of Athens as mainly an oral society, however, leads Thomas to underestimate the influence of writing in the processes of memory formation and negotiation, which has been convincingly argued by Maurizio Giangiulio in the case of colonial traditions in Cyrene.[56] Thomas concludes that in Athenian social

---

[54] The concept of social (or collective) memory was originally elaborated by Maurice Halbwachs, who highlighted the social dimension of memory. Halbwachs considered memory impossible to achieve as a purely individual effort, and pointed out that the reconstruction of the past is based on the present: see Halbwachs 1925 and 1950. For an outline of Halbwachs's thought and influence, see Giangiulio 2010 and Proietti 2012: 13–19. Fentress and Wickham 1992 appropriated the concept of social memory for historiography and insisted on its active nature, where details tend to be adapted to present social and performative contexts. Assmann 1992 emphasised the role of memory in preserving a group's identity, and introduced a distinction between communicative memory (i.e., memories of the recent past that cover a span of three or four generations and are shared by individuals in informal interactions) and cultural memory (i.e., memories about mythical origins transmitted in formal and ceremonial occasions through a fixed set of symbols). Gehrke 2001: 298 has elaborated the concept of 'intentional history', i.e. 'history in a group's own understanding, especially in so far as it is significant for the make-up and identity of the group'; see also Gehrke 2010: 16. Alcock 2002 investigates the role of monuments and landscape (the so-called *cadre matériel*) in the social memory of ancient Greece; on the same topic for the Hellenistic period see Ma 2009.

[55] Thomas 1989.

[56] See Giangiulio 2001. Recent studies have shown that writing was much more central to Athenian society than acknowledged by Thomas: see Pébarthe 2006 for an extensive study on literacy and writing in Athenian society, and Faraguna 2009 specifically on the role of writing in the Athenian legal system. See also Missiou 2011, although her hypothesis that Athenian democratic institutions facilitated the development of mass literacy is only partially convincing. On the development of writing and, specifically, letter writing, see Ceccarelli 2013: 23–53. The large body of archaic rupestral graffiti inscribed by shepherds in the Attic countryside analysed by Langdon 2015 suggests that literacy might have been relatively widespread even outside the elites since an early stage. Vansina 1985: 120–3 recognised the influence of writing on oral traditions and acknowledged that, in societies where orality and literacy coexist, homeostasis (i.e., the tendency of traditions to change and be congruent with the present state of the society that produces them) is not complete.

memory, 'where contemporary written evidence either does not exist or is ignored, there is almost no check on the accumulating changes and distortions'.[57] This view does not grant enough credit not only to written sources, but also to the several channels available to the Athenians for the transmission of the past, such as monuments or drama.[58]

Thomas's conclusions about oral traditions and mnemonic communities have been taken up by Bernd Steinbock in his book *Social Memory in Athenian Public Discourse*. Steinbock investigates the role of the orators in Athenian social memory, and convincingly argues that arguments from social memory were not mere rhetorical cover-ups for *Realpolitik* but had an actual impact on Athenian decision-making.[59] Like Thomas, however, Steinbock envisions Athenian social memory as a sum of parallel traditions elaborated by separate mnemonic communities, and the orators as simply picking each time the tradition that best suited their needs.[60] This view is problematic for several reasons. First, it overlooks the role of institutions in conditioning the choice of appropriate historical narratives. Second, it is risky to conceive of distinct memory communities (and specifically purely private family traditions) in a society where the past of the city was constantly recalled and discussed in public arenas.[61] In such a context, traditions about the city's past were unlikely to develop in complete independence from one another and without mutual interference. Finally, by viewing the orators as passively drawing memories from pre-existing mnemonic communities, Steinbock underestimates their role in shaping the memory dynamics of classical Athens. That this role was instead active and consisted in creating and not just preserving memory has been rightly suggested by Julia Shear in a recent article on the *epitaphios logos*,[62] where she also stresses the malleability of memory depending on specific contexts.[63]

The notion that the orators actively created shared memories for the Athenian community is instead one of the premises of Andrew Wolpert's *Remembering Defeat: Civil War and Civic Memory in Ancient Athens*. In his study of the democratic restoration and Amnesty of 403 BC, Wolpert analyses the speeches of the orators in order to determine how they helped the Athenians to negotiate an image of their defeat in the Peloponnesian War and of the subsequent civil war which could prevent oligarchy and civil

---

[57] Thomas 1989: 284.
[58] See Harris 2018.
[59] See Steinbock 2013a; also Steinbock 2013b.
[60] See in particular Steinbock 2013a: 96–9.
[61] On the importance of remembering the past in classical Athens, see Canevaro 2019.
[62] Shear 2013: 531.
[63] Shear 2013: 535.

strife from arising again.⁶⁴ Like Steinbock, however, Wolpert overlooks the institutional settings in which memory was created and preserved, their specific discursive parameters and their impact on what the orators could do with the past. As a result, he uses forensic and funeral speeches interchangeably and does not fully appreciate the different ideological function of recalling the past in these two rhetorical genres.

The institutions of Athenian democracy and their discursive parameters shall inform this study of Athenian ideological practice and social memory. My case studies dissect the variants of four very significant myths for the Athenian community (the myth of autochthony; Athens' help for the Heraclidae; the Attic Amazonomachy; the myth of Adrastus) and place a strong focus on the institutional settings that conditioned each mythical version. This will in turn shed light on the dynamics of Athenian ideological practice, and illuminate the role of the orators in different institutions of Athenian democracy.⁶⁵ By using the memory of Athens' mythical past as a case study, this book will advance our understanding of Athenian democratic ideology and consider Athens' ideological practice dynamically. I shall highlight the integrative function of ideology as a means to construct an imagined community in the institutional setting of the state funeral for the war dead,⁶⁶ and show that the ideas and values of the Athenians were not a fixed and monolithic set but were in fact constantly moulded by the ideological practice taking place within the institutions of the state.⁶⁷

Athenian democratic institutions all coherently participated in the city's democratic ideology, but each of them was characterised by specific discursive parameters.⁶⁸ The role of the orators was not simply that of passive recipients of democratic ideology and mere negotiators in the ideological dynamics between the elite, of which they were often members, and the mass, which held the power in the democratic city.⁶⁹ Their function depended on the institutional context in which they operated. More generally, institutions had a profound impact on how the past (both mythical and historical) was recalled.

---

⁶⁴ See Wolpert 2002. The regime of the Thirty and the democratic restoration have also been analysed from the perspective of social memory by Shear 2011, who has compared Athenian memory strategies following the fall of the Thirty to those following the democratic restoration in 411. See also Loraux [1997] 2002.

⁶⁵ See Gehrke 2001: 286, who has highlighted the 'ideological significance of references to the past'.

⁶⁶ *Pace* Loraux 1981.

⁶⁷ *Pace* Ober 1989a. Sobak 2015 suggests that this process of production and dispersal of political knowledge occurred also outside the formal institutions of the state, in the net of interactions among non-elite citizens taking place in 'free spaces' such as markets and workshops.

⁶⁸ The discursive parameters of Athenian democratic institutions are discussed in more detail in Chapter 3. What follows is only a brief summary to delineate the theoretical framework of the book.

⁶⁹ *Pace* Ober 1989a: esp. 304–6.

The state funeral for the war dead, where the funeral oration (*epitaphios logos*) was delivered, was an important arena for the recollection of the city's past. The *epitaphios logos* was devoted to the praise of the Athenians who had died in war, but also to the praise of the ancestors and the city itself.[70] In the funeral speeches, the orators created a version of Athenian history which did not simply adopt ideological *topoi*,[71] but actively shaped the memory of past events to construct and validate the identity and beliefs of the community.[72] The *epitaphios logos* fulfilled its function towards the dead by providing the survivors with an idealised image of the city, one which could justify the personal sacrifice of their relatives and inspire them to follow their example.[73] Funeral speeches thus produced shared memories and beliefs that Athens, which was not an archetypal face-to-face society, needed in order to create an imagined community and guarantee its unity and cohesion.[74]

The past was also frequently recalled in the Assembly and the lawcourts.[75] When alluding to the city's past, deliberative and forensic orators respected the beliefs of their democratic audience because they needed to avoid alienating their sympathies. Yet, their prime function was not that of creating an idealised image of the city's past. According to Aristotle, the aim of the deliberative orator was the advantageous and the harmful (τὸ συμφέρον καὶ βλαβερόν), whereas that of the forensic orator was the just and the unjust (τὸ δίκαιον καὶ τὸ ἄδικον) (Arist. *Rh.* 1358b21–8). Advantage and justice, in other words, were central in the discursive parameters of the Assembly and the lawcourts respectively, and the following chapters of this book will show that Aristotle's theorisation was based on the realities of Athenian speeches.[76] Expressing his respect for the idealised image of the city was therefore one of the means through which the deliberative orator could persuade his fellow citizens of the advantages of his policy and the forensic orator could convince the judges on matters of justice and the laws. Consequently, the ways speakers used events from the past varied depending on the institutional setting.

The scope of this book is not limited to the institutional settings of Athenian oratory. The past was extremely valuable for the Athenians and

---

[70] On the *epitaphios logos* and the commemoration of the Athenian war dead in general, see Thuc. 2.34; Walters 1980; Loraux 1981; Thomas 1989: 196–237; Low 2010; Shear 2013.
[71] *Pace* Loraux 1981: 340–1. See Balot 2013: 277.
[72] See the notion of intentional history developed by Gehrke 2001 and 2010.
[73] On the importance of the dead in the economy of the *epitaphios logos*, see Longo 2000: 9–27.
[74] On the notions of imagined community and face-to-face society and their applicability to classical Athens, see pp. 7–8 and n. 32.
[75] For a study of the past in the orators from a rhetorical perspective, see recently Westwood 2017 and 2018.
[76] See Harris 2013a, who has convincingly shown that the Athenians were aware of the rules of the different genres of rhetoric; see also Harris 2016a.

it was significant also to other institutions. The dramatic festivals were an important occasion where the (mostly but not exclusively) mythical past was recalled and re-enacted.[77] Compared to the contexts of oratory, the dramatic festivals had yet another impact on mythical narratives. This institution enabled tragedians to pose questions about and reaffirm the core values and ideas of the democratic city.[78] In Euripides' *Ion*, for example, Athens' earthborn royal family (and its last surviving member, Creusa), ignored in the renditions of the myth of autochthony in the funeral speeches, coexists with the Athenians' collective autochthony typical of the *epitaphios logos*. By focusing on Creusa's individual tragedy and Ion's difficult integration into the Athenian citizen body, Euripides brings onto the stage the contradictions within the idealised image of the city developed in funeral orations. The notion of nobility of birth (*eugeneia*), which in the *epitaphios logos* unites the Athenian people by virtue of their autochthony, in the play becomes the private attribute of Creusa's family. Autochthony shows its dark side through the conflict between the earthborn Creusa and her lost son, Ion, whom she believes to be a foreigner. By the end of the play, however, Athena reveals Ion's autochthonous nature and successfully integrates him into Athens' citizen body. What was not appropriate at the state funeral was therefore possible at the dramatic festivals.[79]

The ways Athenian political actors shaped the memory of the past were strongly conditioned by Athenian democratic institutions and their discursive parameters. This principle is illustrated by Aeschines' appeal to the ancestors in the speech *On the Embassy*. There, Aeschines, prompted by Demosthenes' accusation that he had exhorted the Athenians to forget about the victories of their ancestors (Dem. 19.15–16), reconstructs his own address to the Assembly from three years earlier and provides an unusual interpretation of the city's historical past. Aeschines states that he had in fact invited the Athenians to imitate the good judgement of the ancestors, embodied by the Persian Wars and the generalship of Tolmides, but had warned them against emulating their ill-timed love for victory. The latter was exemplified by the Sicilian expedition and the refusal of Sparta's peace proposal at the end of the Peloponnesian War (Aeschin. 2.74–7). Such a distinction between good and bad ancestors would have been inconceivable at the state funeral, where only the positive deeds of the ancestors were highlighted and recommended for imitation.[80] In this institutional setting, the orators contributed to the creation of an idealised image of Athens' past which was functional to the construction of an imagined community. In the lawcourts and the Assembly,

---

[77] For a survey of the mythical subjects of Greek tragedies, see Table 2.1.
[78] See Allan and Kelly 2013.
[79] For a detailed analysis of the myth of autochthony in Euripides' *Ion*, see Chapter 4, pp. 104–8.
[80] Cf. e.g. Thuc. 2.36.1–3; Lys. 2.3; Dem. 60.6.

however, recalling the example of the ancestors performed a different function. In such contexts, the orators exploited the ancestors' ideological weight to support the argument of their speeches, and couched their appeals to the memory of the ancestors respectively in terms of justice and advantage.[81] Aeschines was therefore able to provide a (partly) critical appeal to the memory of the ancestors thanks to the institutional setting of the Assembly. Uninterested in providing an idealised picture of the ancestors, Aeschines offered a set of historical examples which focused on the advantage and safety of the state and were appropriate to the discursive parameters of the Assembly.[82]

MYTH, MEMORY AND INSTITUTIONS IN DEMOCRATIC ATHENS

Aeschines' attempt at recalibrating his historical allusions to the deeds of the Athenian ancestors according to the discursive parameters of the Assembly demonstrates the potential of an institutionalist approach to Athenian ideological practice and social memory. But what can myth tell us about the ideological dynamics of classical Athens? This is the last question that needs to be answered before setting off to explore the domain of Athenian myths, institutions and ideology, and it first requires establishing a working definition of the word 'myth'.[83]

The Greek word μῦθος and its derivatives already appear in the Homeric poems, where they have the neutral meaning of 'word, speech'.[84] The word later evolves to have a more negative meaning of 'tale, fiction', and μῦθος (as opposed to λόγος) comes to be often associated with falsehood.[85] Herodotus and Thucydides, for example, use μῦθος and its derivatives to refer to stories for which no evidence is available (Hdt. 2.23, 45; Thuc. 1.21.1).[86] Despite this,

---

[81] For appeals to the memory of the ancestors in the lawcourts, cf. e.g. Din. 1.109–10; Dem. 23.204–6; in the Assembly, cf. e.g. Dem. 9.74; 18.66–8; 18.95–101.

[82] See Barbato 2017. See also Steinbock 2013b, who overlooks the ideological dynamics of democratic Athens and the influence of the Assembly in enabling Aeschines to reassess the image of the ancestors.

[83] As noted by Bremmer 1987, the nature of Greek myth is a complex and debated question, which has given rise to many unsatisfactory answers. I am not aiming at settling such an issue and I shall content myself with providing a few introductory remarks. For a survey of current and historical approaches to myth, see Vernant [1974] 1988: 226–60, Dowden 1992: 16–27 and Csapo 2005.

[84] LSJ s.v. μῦθος, I. 1. Cf. e.g. Hom. *Il.* 6.381–2; 9.431, 443. In the *Iliad*, according to R. P. Martin 1989: 1–42, the word μῦθος, as opposed to the generic ἔπος, denotes specifically an authoritative speech-act, which usually takes place in public in front of an audience.

[85] LSJ s.v. μῦθος, II.

[86] Gotteland 2001: 52–5; Dowden 1992: 3–4.

myth was no less valuable to the Greeks, who did not perceive a clear boundary between myth and history. Myth was mostly envisioned as very ancient history. The main difference between the domains of myth and history laid in the lesser amount of evidence available to reconstruct the former with confidence.[87] Herodotus, for example, when recounting the causes of the enmity between Greeks and barbarians, moves seamlessly from the mythical episodes of Io, Europa, Medea and Helen to the historical reign of Croesus, whom he pinpoints as the first barbarian ever to wrong the Greeks (Hdt. 1.1–6). Isocrates similarly establishes a chronological continuity between mythical and historical events when he narrates the Athenian achievements against the barbarians in his *Panegyricus*. The orator matches the older victories over the Amazons and the Thracians with the more recent ones against Darius and Xerxes, which he explicitly describes as akin (ἀδελφά) to the former (Isoc. 4.66–72). Even Lysias, who in his *Funeral Oration* separates Athens' mythical exploits from his account of the Persian Wars by including a digression on the immutable character conferred to the Athenians by their autochthonous origins, does not treat the two realms any differently (Lys. 2.3–47).[88]

If the distinction between myth and history was not very well drawn for the ancient Greeks, the same is not true from a modern perspective. To the modern scholar, Theseus' abduction of Antiope or Erichthonius' birth from the earth obviously bear no resemblance to historical facts. Their value for the ancient historian lies mostly in what these myths meant to their Athenian audiences. My research will thus focus on Athenian myths. By this expression, I refer to those stories that dealt with the legendary times which the Athenians considered their remote past. Such stories were deemed culturally and historically relevant to the present, and had been transmitted for generations through several media which included poetry, prose and the visual arts.[89] The modern distinction between myth and history, however, is one worth exploring further. A focus on the memory of Athens' mythical past offers significant advantages over a study of Athenian social memory of the historical past. First,

---

[87] On the Greeks' understanding of the relationship between myth and history, see in general Veyne [1983] 1988.
[88] Gotteland 2001: 89–102.
[89] See Gotteland 2001: 12, who defines myth as 'tout récit transmis par la tradition, mettant en scène des personnages divins ou héroïques, décrivant une suite d'actions dont le caractère historique ne peut être démontré, et inscrit dans un cadre temporel antérieur au retour des Héraclides ou contemporain de cet événement'. Csapo 2005: 9 defines myth as 'a narrative which is considered socially important, and is told in such a way as to allow the entire social collective to share a sense of this importance'. Tyrrell and Brown 1991: 6 in turn define myth as 'a tale rooted in Greek culture that recounts a sequence of events chosen by the maker of the tale to accommodate his own medium and purpose and to achieve particular effects in his audience. As narratives that both exemplify and shape that culture, myths are words in action.'

whereas the orators' historical allusions are subject to the modern interpreter's evaluation of their trustworthiness, the same does not apply to the case of mythical accounts. To us, in other words, no version of a myth is more genuine than another. The same, however, was not necessarily true for an ancient audience. The Greeks were aware of the multiplicity and contradictory nature of their mythical traditions. Hecataeus criticises the stories of the Greeks for being many and ridiculous, and embarked on the task of writing a truthful account by rationalising some of those myths (*FGrHist* 1 F 1).[90] Isocrates, who in the *Panegyricus* had adopted the bellicose version of the myth of Adrastus (Isoc. 4.54–9), uses the peaceful version of the same myth in the *Panathenaicus* and openly admits to contradicting his previous account (Isoc. 12.168–74).[91] In Plato's *Symposium*, Phaedrus criticises Aeschylus' *Myrmidons* for depicting Achilles as Patroclus' older lover (*erastēs*). Phaedrus recalls how, according to Homer, Achilles was in fact much younger than Patroclus, and therefore necessarily his beloved (*eromenos*) (Pl. *Symp.* 180a).

One cannot expect every Greek to have the critical attitude of a Hecataeus.[92] Yet, an Athenian audience would have been familiar with different versions of the same myths from drama, epic and lyric poetry, oratory and the visual arts. The presence of myth at all levels of Athenian society and the Athenians' familiarity with their mythical tradition constitute another notable advantage offered by an analysis that privileges Athenian myths over the city's historical past.[93] Any variations on the part of the orator would have hardly gone unnoticed and would probably have been perceived as significant. Because his variations would have been patent to his audience, the role of the orator must be considered essential in the ideological dynamics of classical Athens. Far from merely picking a mythical variant from one or another memory community, the orators were active agents in Athenian ideological practice and the construction of the shared image of the city's past. The function of the past in turn varied according to the institutional settings of Athenian democracy. The myth of autochthony, for example, could be employed at the state funeral to create an image of Athens as a cohesive and egalitarian community. In a lawsuit over citizenship rights, in accordance with the focus on justice and the laws typical of the lawcourts, the same myth could instead provide the aetiology of an exclusive prerogative of a limited section of the citizen body which the defendant was accused of having misappropriated.[94] The orators had to accommodate their mythical narratives

---

[90] See Bertelli 2001: 80–4; Fowler 2001: 101.
[91] On this passage and its possible interpretations, see Nouhaud 1982: 18–19 and, more at length, Steinbock 2013a: 203–10.
[92] On Greek critical approaches to myths, see Veyne [1983] 1988: 41–57.
[93] For a survey of the mythical knowledge of the Athenians during the fifth and fourth centuries, see Chapter 2.
[94] See Chapter 4.

to the institutions of the democracy and create memories appropriate for the discursive parameters of each institutional setting.

Despite its significant advantages, the analysis of the mythical past has had to this day only a marginal place in studies on Athenian social memory.[95] A comparative study of mythical variants therefore offers a privileged, yet mostly unexplored perspective to the student of Athenian ideological practice and social memory. By following the ideological thread through the mythical narratives performed in different institutions of Athenian democracy, this book reconstructs the complex interaction between social memory and ideology in fifth- and fourth-century Athens. The texts of the Attic orators are the main (though not exclusive) focus of this investigation, but I shall also pay attention to other institutional settings and media through which memories of the mythical past were produced, such as tragedy at the dramatic festivals and the visual arts. Texts produced for private settings outside the formal institutions of the state, such as the speeches of Isocrates or the fragments of the Atthidographers, will also be employed. These will act as a foil to the ideological specificity of the institutional settings of the Athenian democracy.

My approach differs from previous approaches to mythology, and notably from structuralism, in that it does not aim at uncovering the underlying structure of a myth that determines its universal value.[96] I shall focus on specific versions produced within specific Athenian institutions, in order to investigate the concrete uses of myth in the ideological dynamics of Athenian democracy in the classical age. By reading myth from an ideologically minded and institutionalist perspective, I also intend to fill the gaps of the only extensive work devoted to the use of myth in the orators: Sophie Gotteland's *Mythe et Rhétorique. Les exemples mythiques dans le discours politique de l'Athènes classique*. Gotteland aims to develop a theory of the Greek mythical *exemplum*, and investigates its perception by the orators and its relation to the historical *exemplum*. She offers a detailed account of the orators' mythical allusions with the inclusion of relevant comparative material from other genres. Yet, her book does not pay sufficient attention to issues of social memory. More importantly, the institutional settings of the speeches of the Attic orators are mostly overlooked. Gotteland locates the speeches of the orators in an institutional vacuum, which does not allow her fully to appreciate the ideological specificity of – to mention just one example – Lysias' narrative of the causes of the Amazonomachy in his *Funeral Oration* (Lys. 2.4–6) as opposed to Isocrates' versions in the *Panegyricus* (Isoc. 4.66–70) and the *Panathenaicus* (Isoc. 12.193).[97]

---

[95] The main exception is the analysis of the myth of Adrastus in Steinbock 2013a: 155–210.
[96] For the programmatic enunciation of the structuralist approach to myth, see Lévi-Strauss [1958] 1963: 206–31, and esp. 213–18 for its application to the Oedipus myth. See also Kirk 1970: 42–83; Vernant [1974] 1988: 246–53; Csapo 2005: 181–261.
[97] Gotteland 2001: esp. 141–9.

To what extent did the orators contribute to the ideological practice of Athenian democracy? How did their contrasting versions of myths reflect the discursive parameters of different Athenian institutions? I shall endeavour to answer these questions by studying a selected set of mythical variants within the institutional settings that produced them. I shall pay attention to the ideological specificity of each version and investigate how Athenian political actors shaped and re-shaped the Greek mythical tradition to accommodate their narrative to different institutional settings of the Athenian democracy. This will in turn provide a constructive, dynamic and multifaceted picture of Athenian ideological practice that will reconcile and advance the Marxist and the culturalist interpretations of ideology.

OUTLINE OF THE BOOK

The Introduction has outlined the aims and methodology of this book in relation to existing scholarship on ideology and social memory. This study aims to reconcile and advance Nicole Loraux's and Josiah Ober's interpretations of Athenian democratic ideology. Loraux's Marxist interpretation of ideology has been reviewed in the light of Benedict Anderson's notion of imagined community to account for the constructive function of the *epitaphios logos* in creating civic bonds, rather than concealing conflict within the Athenian community. Ober's culturalist interpretation has been reconceptualised in terms of ideological practice to investigate the dynamics through which both the mass and the elite actively produced shared ideas and values under the influence of Athenian democratic institutions. I have restricted the topic of my investigation to Athenian social memory of the mythical past and explained the advantages of such a choice. Finally, I have outlined my methodology, which is based on the discursive tradition within the New Institutionalism. This book thus compares a selected set of mythical variants produced by Athenian political actors and analyses them within their respective institutional settings in order to highlight their ideological specificity.

Chapters 2 and 3 establish the general framework sustaining the four case studies analysed in Chapters 4 through 7. Chapter 2 shows that myth constitutes valuable evidence for the study of Athenian democratic ideology. It provides a survey of the myths deployed in the institutions of Athenian democracy, and specifically at the dramatic festivals, the Panathenaea, the state funeral for the war dead, the lawcourts, the Assembly and the Council. Contextually, it investigates the presence of myth in Athenian private settings, such as the family, the symposium and the writings of the Atthidographers. The chapter shows that the Athenians were continually engaging with myth in almost every aspect of their public and private lives. As a result, they were able to perceive changes and innovations in mythical narratives and allusions, which had the potential to carry ideological value. Chapter 3 assesses the influence of Athenian democratic institutions on the behaviour of individual political actors within Athenian ideological practice and reconstructs the discursive parameters of the state funeral for the war dead, the lawcourts, the Assembly and the Council, and the dramatic festivals. This discussion also illustrates some of the characteristics of Athenian democratic ideology described in the Introduction, namely its constructive function, its normative value and its bidirectional nature due to the active contribution of both the mass and the elite.

Chapters 4 to 7 show how the discursive parameters of Athenian democratic institutions conditioned specific mythical narratives by adapting them and using them to convey ideas and values appropriate to each institutional setting. Each case study is centred on one myth of cultural, historical and political relevance for the Athenian community, and on one or two values significant to that specific myth. These values serve as pivots to illuminate the impact of the discursive parameters of different institutions on how political actors recalled Athens' mythical past, while the mythical variants in turn show how the shared ideas and values of the Athenians were flexible and could interact dynamically with one another.

Chapter 4 deals with the myth of autochthony and the earthborn kings of Athens. The mythical variants found in Euripides' *Ion*, Apollodorus' *Against Neaera* and the surviving *epitaphioi* are read in connection to the theme of nobility of birth (*eugeneia*). Chapter 5 deals with the myth of Athens' help to the Heraclidae as told in Lysias' *Funeral Oration*, Euripides' *Children of Heracles* and Isocrates' *Panegyricus*, and is constructed around the notions of reciprocity (*charis*) and humaneness (*philanthrōpia*). Chapter 6 is devoted to the Attic Amazonomachy, and specifically to the variants found in Lysias' *Funeral Oration*, Aeschylus' *Eumenides*, Isocrates' *Panegyricus* and *Panathenaicus*, and in the fragments of Philochorus and Pherecydes transmitted in Plutarch's *Life of Theseus*. My analysis revolves around the notion of *hybris* and includes a discussion of relevant scenes in the visual arts. Chapter 7 discusses the accounts of the myth of Adrastus in Lysias' *Funeral Oration*, Euripides' *Supplicant Women*, Procles' speech to the Athenian Assembly in Book 6 of Xenophon's *Hellenica*, and Isocrates' *Plataicus* and *Panathenaicus*, and uses them to illuminate the interaction between *philanthrōpia* and *hybris*. Each case study starts with a brief history of the relevant myth in Athenian social memory, followed by an introduction of the case study. It then presents the values which are the focus of the discussion and explores their significance in Athenian democratic ideology.[98] Separate sections are devoted to the

---

[98] Such a section does not feature in Chapter 7, because the notions of *philanthrōpia* and *hybris* are already discussed respectively in Chapters 5 and 6.

mythical variants deployed in each institutional setting, while accounts produced for private contexts sometimes provide useful terms of comparison.

The book's findings are summarised in Chapter 8. This draws some general conclusions on Athenian democratic ideology, social memory and institutional history, illustrates the broader significance of my notion of Athenian democratic ideology within the social sciences, and suggests possible future research perspectives.

CHAPTER 2

Myth and Athenian Democracy

The Introduction has set out the aim of this book: to overcome the limits of the Marxist and the culturalist approaches to ideology and gain a fuller understanding of Athenian democratic ideology by setting ideology in the context of the institutions of the democracy. I have defined Athenian democratic ideology as a fluid set of ideas shared by the majority of the Athenians as a result of a process of ideological practice achieved by both mass and elite through discourse within the institutions of the democracy. In Chapters 4 to 7, I focus on one particular facet of Athenian ideological practice and explore how the discursive parameters of Athenian democratic institutions enabled the Athenians to construct multiple and compatible ideas and beliefs about their mythical past and their very community.

My approach rests on two basic assumptions. First, the choice of a specific mythical variant as opposed to another can be seen as carrying a distinctive ideological value only if the Athenians were able to appreciate variations in mythical narratives. In the Introduction, I discussed some textual evidence showing that this was the case.[1] This evidence needs to be complemented by an assessment of the mythical knowledge of the Athenians during the classical period in order to demonstrate myth's legitimacy as a source for the investigation of Athenian democratic ideology. Second, I have adopted the principles of the New Institutionalism, which posits that institutions have a strong and conditioning impact on the behaviour of political actors. This hypothesis needs to be checked against the evidence from classical Athens to determine the functioning of the institutions of Athenian democracy and their influence on individual behaviour. In other words, it is necessary to reconstruct the

[1] See pp. 18–19.

discursive parameters of Athenian democratic institutions and their impact on how individual Athenians acted, talked and discussed the past within these institutions.

While the discursive parameters of Athenian democratic institutions are explored in Chapter 3, the present chapter tackles the issue of the mythical knowledge of the Athenians and shows that myth constitutes valuable evidence for the study of Athenian democratic ideology. I thus review the array of myths employed inside and outside the formal institutions of Athenian democracy, and show that myth was virtually omnipresent in the lives of the Athenians and enabled them to appreciate the ideological value of different mythical variants. First, I look at the use of myth at the dramatic festivals and the Panathenaea. I then explore the myths deployed in the institutional settings of Athenian oratory: the state funeral for the war dead, the lawcourts, the Assembly and the Council. Another section investigates the presence of myth in private contexts, namely the family, the symposium and the writings of the Atthidographers. Finally, I analyse some examples of mythical variants available to fifth- and fourth-century Athenians to assess the Athenians' familiarity with the Greek mythical tradition in all its complexity.

THE DRAMATIC FESTIVALS AND THE PANATHENAEA

The dramatic festivals were key in providing the Athenians with a popular setting for the performance and re-discussion of their mythical tradition. During the course of the year, the Athenians had several opportunities to watch their myths brought to the stage. In Athens, dramatic contests took place at the Great Dionysia and at the Lenaea. Drama retained a special place in both festivals, which were held every year in honour of Dionysus. Dramatic contests are also attested for the Rural Dionysia, which provided the inhabitants of the whole of Attica with further opportunities to attend the theatre. In addition to the dramatic festivals, myth was also prominent at the Panathenaea, where it featured in the dithyrambic and rhapsodic contests as well as in the physical setting of the festival. This section describes Athens' dramatic festivals and assesses which myths (based on the available evidence) were most popular in tragedy and satyr drama (but also dithyramb) during the fifth and fourth centuries. The study underscores the popularity of the theatre in Athens and the vast range of the mythical themes deployed, and shows that the dramatic festivals provided the bulk of the Athenians' mythical knowledge. I then discuss the Panathenaea and show that this festival contributed to the Athenians' familiarity with specific myths, most notably the Gigantomachy and the Homeric poems.

The Great Dionysia took place in the spring, during the month of Elaphebolion, and was the most important of Athens' dramatic festivals. The dramatic contests were held at the Theatre of Dionysus and attracted a huge audience, made up of both Athenians and foreigners from all over Greece. Such contests are commonly thought to have started in the late sixth century in connection with the tyranny of Pisistratus.[2] This is based on two pieces of evidence. First, according to the *Suda* and the Parian Marble, Thespis performed at the festival at some time between 538 and 528 BC (*TrGF* I T 1–2). Second, the list of victors recorded in the 'Fasti' (*IG* II^2 2318), whose preserved section starts from 472 BC, is assumed to have gone back to 501 BC.[3] At least during most of the fifth century, three tragedians competed, each with three tragedies and a satyr play, while five comic poets competed with one comedy each. The celebrations also included competitions for dithyrambic choruses. Each Attic tribe trained one chorus of men and one of boys for a total of twenty dithyrambic choruses. During the Peloponnesian War, however, it seems that the number of comedies was cut down to three for economic reasons. As for the fourth century, epigraphic evidence (*IG* II^2 2320) seems to point to the conclusion that, starting some time before 341 BC, the tragic programme regularly included a single satyr play and a single old tragedy. The same evidence shows that each tragic contestant produced three plays, but only two tragedies per poet are attested in 340 BC. Regular performances of old comedies, on the other hand, are attested at the festivals from 311 BC (*IG* II^2 2323 a), while the number of comic contestants might have returned to the same as in the period before the Peloponnesian War.[4]

The Lenaea was a festival held in winter, during the month of Gamelion. It was run on a smaller scale than the Great Dionysia, since its audience was mainly constituted by Athens' population and did not include many foreigners (Ar. *Ach.* 504–6). The dramatic contests at the Lenaea, which originally took place in the Agora and were then transferred to the Theatre of Dionysus, were more oriented to comedy than to tragedy and probably originated in the second half of the fifth century.[5] During this period and probably also during the fourth century, only two tragedians competed, with two plays each, while

---

[2] See Pickard-Cambridge [1953] 1968: 57–8; Csapo and Slater 1995: 103–4; Rhodes 2003: 106. The traditional view has been challenged by Connor 1989, who dated the institution of the Great Dionysia after Cleisthenes' reforms and connected the festival with Athenian democracy.

[3] Pickard-Cambridge [1953] 1968: 71–2; Rhodes 2003: 106. But Scullion 2002: esp. 81–4 has cast doubts on the reliability of the sources about drama's early history and asserted that 'there is no longer any reason to suppose that it was in the 530s that tragic performances were first put on or some sort of tragic festival instituted at Athens'.

[4] Pickard-Cambridge [1953] 1968: 52–100; Parke 1977: 125–35; Csapo and Slater 1995: 103–21; Csapo and Wilson 2014: 293–6.

[5] On the dating of the tragic contests at the Lenaea, see Pickard-Cambridge [1953] 1968. He pointed out that there is no secure evidence for the traditional date of c. 432 BC (108), and suggested that the tragic contests were introduced around 440–30 BC, slightly later than the comic contests (125).

five comic poets produced for the occasion one play each. It is commonly acknowledged that the Lenaea, like the Great Dionysia, saw the number of comedies reduced to three during the Peloponnesian War. There is no secure evidence for the re-performance of old plays. As for satyr plays and dithyrambs, no performances seem to be attested for the period under analysis.[6]

In winter, during the month of Poseideon, individual demes organised the local festivals known as Rural Dionysia. Their status and ambition varied depending on the dimensions and prosperity of each deme. One such festival was held at Piraeus and featured tragedy and, from the fourth century, dithyrambic choruses (*IG* II² 380; 456; 1496.70; [Plut.] *X orat.* 842a; Ael. *VH* 2.13).[7] Dramatic contests taking place during the classical period are also attested for other Attic demes. These included Eleusis, where tragedy, comedy and dithyramb were performed (*IG* II² 1186; 3090; 3100), and Acharnai, where there is evidence for comedy and dithyramb (*IG* II² 3092; 3106). Dionysian festivals of some kind are attested for Myrrhinous (*IG* II² 1182; 1183.36), while Kollytos (Aeschin. 1.157; Dem. 18.180), Thorikos (*IG* I³ 258bis) and perhaps Ikarion (*IG* I² 186–7; *IG* II² 1178; 3094; 3095; 3099) hosted both tragic and comic contests. Comic performances took place during the festivals at Aixone (*IG* II² 1198; 1200; 1202) and Rhamnous (*IG* II² 3108; 3109), while only dithyramb is attested for Salamis (*IG* II² 3093).[8]

The vast array of dramatic festivals held every year shows that theatre played a central role in the life and mythical knowledge of the Athenians. If one only considers the Great Dionysia and the Lenaea, at least during the second half of the fifth century and with the exclusion of the Peloponnesian War, the Athenians had the opportunity to attend twenty dithyrambic choruses, thirteen tragedies, ten comedies and three satyr plays every year. The situation was not particularly different during the fourth century. At that time, the dramatic programme included twenty dithyrambic choruses, fourteen tragedies (including one old tragedy brought on the stage by an actor), ten comedies (and, starting from 311 BC, also one regular old comedy) and one satyr play. It is difficult to determine how many plays were performed at the Rural Dionysia, but it has been reasonably argued that, since the festivals were structured as contests, their programme included at least two plays for each genre.[9] Whatever the number of plays,

---

[6] Pickard-Cambridge [1953] 1968: 25–42; Parke 1977: 104–6. Csapo and Slater 1995: 123 recall evidence for two tragic poets at the contest in 418 BC and three in 363 BC, and conclude that 'it is impossible to know which represents the norm'. Csapo and Wilson 2014: 298 cast some doubts on the inclusion of the Lenaea in the 'controversy about the reductions in comedies at the Dionysia during the Peloponnesian War'.

[7] Comic performances at Piraeus are attested in the Law of Evagorus, quoted in Dem. 21.10, but the document should be considered a late forgery: see Harris in Canevaro 2013a: 216–23.

[8] Pickard-Cambridge [1953] 1968: 42–54; Parke 1977: 100–3; Csapo and Slater 1995: 121–32; Csapo and Wilson 2014: 296–7.

[9] Csapo and Slater 1995: 122.

however, the Rural Dionysia, taking place almost in every corner of Attica, probably contributed to increasing the geographic and social reach of drama.

The Theatre of Dionysus itself, with its several phases of construction, reflects the immense popularity of the dramatic festivals and their potential impact on the mythical knowledge of the Athenians. The building was originally a simple structure with a wooden auditorium and a primitive stage. As the interest in drama grew stronger, the Theatre of Dionysus underwent an intense reconstruction. This started during the Periclean age, when the stage was improved but the auditorium was still made of wooden seats. The theatre was then enlarged and completely rebuilt in stone during the fourth century by Lycurgus.[10] According to modern estimates, the size of the audience must have been between 3,700 and 7,000 spectators for the fifth-century building,[11] while the Lycurgan theatre is thought to have reached a capacity of 14,000 to 17,000.[12] Such numbers are impressive and suggest a massive participation in theatre events.[13] During the fourth, and possibly already in the fifth century, the *polis* also instituted the Theoric Fund.[14] This granted Athenian citizens a sum of money to attend the festivals and helped make dramatic performances accessible even to the poor.

The available data all point to the huge popularity of the dramatic festivals in classical Athens and show that drama was deeply rooted in Athenian culture and society.[15] If one correlates this with the fact that tragedy, satyr drama and dithyrambic poetry, unlike comedy, mainly focused on myth, one comes to the conclusion that the dramatic festivals had the potential for deeply influencing the mythical culture of the Athenians. Different accounts of the same myths are likely to have circulated thanks to the work of different playwrights, and one may guess that particularly powerful plays may have been able to impose specific versions of some myths in the collective memory of

---

[10] Pickard-Cambridge 1946: 265–8; Csapo and Slater 1995: 79–81; Csapo 2007: 98–9; Goette 2007.

[11] See Csapo 2007: 97, who also offers a summary of alternative estimates. Roselli 2011: 72–5 argues that during the fifth century the total size of the audience was the sum of the capacity of the *theatron* (around 6,000 spectators) with a couple of thousand extra viewers standing in free viewing spaces beyond the auditorium.

[12] See Pickard-Cambridge 1946: 141; Csapo 2007: 97. Roselli 2011: 64 notes that these same numbers have also been wrongly applied by many scholars to the fifth-century theatre.

[13] Pickard-Cambridge [1953] 1968: 263; Goldhill 1997: 58.

[14] There is no scholarly consensus on the date of introduction of the Theoric Fund: see Pickard-Cambridge [1953] 1968: 265–86; Csapo and Slater 1995: 287–8; Sommerstein 1997: 66–7; Goldhill 1997: 66–7; Csapo 2007: 100–3 and 114. Roselli 2011: 90–2 rejects the idea of a permanent Theoric Fund during the fifth century and suggests that *theōrika* at that time were 'ad hoc payments approved by the Assembly when deemed necessary'.

[15] On the social span of the theatre audience, see Pickard-Cambridge [1953] 1968: 263–5; Goldhill 1997: 60–6.

the Athenians.[16] It is also worth recalling that, starting from 386 BC and 339 BC, re-performances of old tragedies and old comedies respectively started to appear on an irregular basis, while this privilege had been already accorded to Aeschylus' plays sometime after the poet's death.[17] Such a habit may have helped reinforce the popularity of some stories and the Athenians' knowledge of particular versions to the detriment of others.

Now that we have described the institutional context of Attic drama and made clear how pervasive theatre was in Athenian society, we can move to an analysis of the myths that provided the subject for tragedies and satyr plays. The massive tragic production of the fifth and fourth centuries is mostly lost and only a small part survives to this day. Nevertheless, a brief survey of the plays can help us understand what myths were most often brought on stage. In order to reconstruct as widely as possible the contribution of the dramatic festivals to the mythical knowledge of the Athenians, it is important not to limit our study to the better known works of Aeschylus, Sophocles and Euripides. By taking into account also their fragmentary plays as well as the titles and fragments of the minor tragedians, we can draw a general outline of the tragic production of the fifth and fourth centuries. The outcome of such a study, presented in tabular form, is necessarily tentative. The analysis of the lost tragic production rests on very shaky foundations. This is mainly due to the fact that, especially in the case of the minor tragedians, the available evidence is not always sufficient to determine the content of the plays with any certainty. Moreover, the sources are not always consistent when they mention titles of lost or fragmentary plays. This makes it sometimes difficult to discern between alternative titles of a single tragedy, and titles that actually refer to different plays. For these reasons, when dividing the titles into thematic categories, I have chosen to round them down and list any additional plays or possible alternative titles in the footnotes.

The survey which follows is based on the titles and plots of the fragmentary plays as they have been reconstructed in the Loeb editions of the Great Tragedians, namely Sommerstein 2008 for Aeschylus, Lloyd-Jones 1996 for Sophocles, and Collard and Cropp 2008 for Euripides. As for the minor tragedians, I based my work on the titles collected in the first volume of *Tragicorum Graecorum Fragmenta*, edited by Bruno Snell in 1971. Table 2.1 is organised according to clusters of myths (e.g., myths about the Trojan Cycle; myths about the Argonauts), further divided into specific themes (e.g., Philoctetes; Medea) accompanied by references to the relative plays, and only includes clusters of myths which appear in at least five plays.

---

[16] On the diverse use of myth by the tragedians and their innovations, see e.g. Edmunds 2006: esp. 13–56 on Oedipus between the epic tradition and the tragedians; Cropp 1988: xliii–l on Electra in Euripides and his predecessors.

[17] Pickard-Cambridge [1953] 1968: 99–101; P. J. Wilson 2000: 22–4; Nervegna 2007: 15–18.

Table 2.1 Myths in tragedies and satyr plays

Myths (number of titles)	Themes and Plays
Cypria (22)	**Palamedes/Nauplius:** Aesch. F 180a–82; Soph. F 425–8; 429–31; 478–9; Eur. F 578–90; *TrGF* 24 ante F 1; 60 F 5; F 5a. **Paris/Helen:**[a] Soph. F. 181; 360–1; *TrGF* 72 F 3. **Iphigenia in Aulis:**[b] Soph. F 305–8; Eur. *IA*. **Achilles/Telephus:**[c] Aesch. F 238–9; Eur. F 696–727c. **Other episodes:** Soph. F. 33a–59; 176–80; 462–7; 497–521; 562–71; 618–35; Eur. F 681a–86
Aethiopis (4)[d]	**Memnon:** Aesch. F 126a–8; F 279–80a; Soph. F 28–9.[e] **Achilles/Thersites:** *TrGF* 71 F 1a–3.
Little Iliad (21)	**Ajax/Teucer:**[f] Aesch. F 83, 84a; 174–7a; 215a, 216; Soph. *Aj.*; F 576–8; *TrGF* 19 F 34–5; 52 F 1; 60 F 1a; 70 F 1; 72 F 1; 85 T 1. **Philoctetes:** Aesch. F 249–53, 255; Soph. *Phil.*; F 697–9, 701; Eur. F 787–803; *TrGF* 20 F 37; 24 post F 1; 72 F 5b. **Other episodes:** Soph. F 206–22b; 367–9a; 553–61.
Iliou Persis (12)	Soph. F 10a–18; 137; 370–1, 373–5; 522–6; 542–4; Eur. *Hec.*; *Tro.*; T 6; *TrGF* 17 T 1; 22 F 2b; 77 T 1.
Nostoi (22)	**Agamemnon/Orestes:** Aesch. *Ag.*; *Cho.*; *Eum.*; Soph. *El.*; F 235–6; Eur. *El.*; *Or.*; *TrGF* 19 F 1–5; 24 ante F 1; 77 F (6); 17 T 1; 70 F 1g; 72 F 5; 73 F 1. **Iphigenia in Tauris:** Soph. F 726–9; Eur. *IT*; *TrGF* 78 F 1.[g] **Other episodes:** Soph. F 202–3; 485–96; Eur. *Andr.*; *Hel.*;[h] *TrGF* 55 F 1
	Total titles about the Trojan Cycle: 81[i]
Oedipodia (18)	Aesch. F 121–2a; 173; 235–6; Soph. *OT*; *OC*; Eur. F 539a–57; *TrGF* 20 F 30–1; 24 ante F 1; 33 F 1; 36 F (T 1); 48 F 1 (tetralogy); 70 F 1f; 72 F 4; 86 T 3; 88 F 1f.
Thebaid (12)	**Seven vs Thebes:** Aesch. *Sept.*; F16–17; *149a; Soph. F 113–21; Eur. *Phoen.*; *TrGF* 60 F 5b; 70 F 1c; 72 F 5a; 77 T 1. **Antigone:** Soph. *Ant.*; Eur. F 157–76; *TrGF* 60 F 1e.
Epigoni/Alcmeonis (16)	**Epigoni:** Aesch. F 55. Soph. F 185–90. *TrGF* 60 F 2b. **Alcmeon:** Soph. F 108. Eur. F 65–73; 73a–87a. *TrGF* 20 F 12–5; 38 F (1); 39 F 2; 56 F 1; 60 F 1b–c; 72 F 1a–2; 85 T 2. **Diomedes/Oeneus:** Eur. F 554–70; *TrGF* 24 ante F 1; 71 F 14.
	Total titles about the Theban Cycle: 46[j]
Heracles (28)	**Alcmena/Heracles' birth:** Aesch. F 12; Eur. F 87b–104; *TrGF* 19 F 5a–8; 60 F 1d; 76 F 2. **Antaeus:** *TrGF* 3 F 3a; 9 F 1; 75 F 1. **Other episodes and labours:** Aesch. F 108–13; 123; Soph. *Trach.*; F 122–4; 223a–b; 225–6; Eur. *HF*; F 312b–15; 371–80; 473–9; 686a–94; *TrGF* 19 F 17a–33; 20 F 16a; 20 F 32–5; 33 F 2; 40 T 1; 43 F 1–14; 49 F (1); 60 F 4; 88 F 1c.

MYTH AND ATHENIAN DEMOCRACY   31

Myths (number of titles)	Themes and Plays
Dionysus (26)	**Lycurgus/Orpheus/Pentheus:** Aesch. F 22; 23–5; 57–67; 124–6; 146–9; 168–72b; 183; Soph. F 328–33; Eur. *Bacch.*; *TrGF* 1 F 1c; 7 F 1 (tetralogy); 22 F 2; 33 F 1; 71 F 4–7; 77 F (4); 86 T 2. **Semele:** Aesch. F 221–4; *TrGF* 40 T 1; 45 F 1; 70 F 2–3. **Other episodes:** Aesch. F 78a–82; 246a–d; Soph. F 171–2.
Theseus/Athens (23)	**Heraclidae:** Aesch. F 73b–7; Eur. *Heracl.*; *TrGF* 51 T 1. **Adrastus:** Aesch. F 53a–4; Eur. *Supp.*[k] **Eumolpus:** Eur. F 349–70. **Theseus' exploits:** Aesch. F 102–7; Soph. F 19–25a; Eur. F 1–13; 381–90; 674a–81; *TrGF* 37 F 1. **Phaedra:** Soph. F 677–93; Eur. *Hipp.*; F 428–47; *TrGF* 20 F 18 **Alope:** Eur. F 105–13; *TrGF* 2 F 1; 70 F 1b. **Ion:** Soph. F 319–22;[l] Eur. *Ion*. **Other episodes:** Aesch. F 281; Soph. F 596–617a.
Argonauts (22)	**Medea:** Eur. *Med.*; *TrGF* 15 F 1–3; 17 T 1; 23 T 4a; 29 F 1; 52 F 1a; 70 F 1e; 78a T 1; 88 F 1e. **Daughters of Pelias:** Eur. F 601–16; *TrGF* 73 F 1. **Hypsipyle/Lemnos:** Aesch. F 95–7a; 123a–b; 247–8; Soph. F 384–8; Eur. F 752–70; *TrGF* 84 T 4. **Other episodes:** Aesch. F 20–1; Soph. F 337–46; 534–5; 546, 549; *TrGF* 55 F 1a
Tantalus' family (21)	**Tantalus:** Soph. F 572–5; *TrGF* 3 F 7; 4 F 2; 14 F 1b. **Pelops:** Soph. 471–7; Eur. F. 571–7; 838a–44; *TrGF* 88 F 1g. **Pleisthenes:** Eur. F 460–70a; 625–33; *TrGF* 39 F 1; 70 F 1. **Atreus/Thyestes:** Soph. F 140–1; 247–69; Eur. F 391–7b; *TrGF* 39 F 3; 64 T 1; 71 F 8; 77 F (7); 88 F 1; 88 F 1d.
Iliad (7)	**Patroclus/Hector/Achilles:** Aesch. F 78–78a; 131–9; 150–3; 263–7; *TrGF* 60 F 1h–2a; 76 F 2a. **Dolon:** [Eur.] *Rhes*.
Odyssey (8)	**Slaying of the Suitors:** Aesch. F 179–80; 187; *TrGF* 24 post F 1. **Circe:** Aesch. F 113a; 273–5. **Polyphemus:** Eur. *Cyc.*; *TrGF* 9 F 4. **Nausicaa:** Soph. F 439–41.
	Total titles about the Homeric Poems: 15
Perseus (11)[m]	**Perseus' exposure:** Aesch. F 46a–47c; Soph. F 61–7; Eur. F 316–30a. **Medusa/Polydectes:** Aesch. T 78,15b; 261–2; Eur. F 330b–48; *TrGF* 86 T 4. **Andromeda:** Eur. F 114–56; Soph. F 126–33. **Other episodes:** Soph. F 378–83; *TrGF* 4 F 2.
Athamas (10)[n]	**Phrixus/Helle:** Aesch. F 1–4a; Soph. F 1–10; Eur. F 818c; 819–20b; *TrGF* 20 F 38; 86 T 3. **Other episodes:** Eur. F 398–423; *TrGF* 33 F 1; 60 F 1.
Danaids (8)	Aesch. *Supp.*; F 5; 13–15; 43–6; *TrGF* 3 F 1; 3 F 4; 36 F (T 2); 72 F 3a.
Caledonian Boar Hunt (6)	Aesch. T 78, 3a; Soph. F 401–6; Eur. F 515–39; *TrGF* 9 F 2; 55 F 1b; 92 F 1.
Telephus (6)	Aesch. F 143–5; Soph. F 77–91; 409–18; Eur. F 264a–81; *TrGF* 73 F 1.

(continued)

32 THE IDEOLOGY OF DEMOCRATIC ATHENS

Myths (number of titles)	Themes and Plays
Ixion (5)	Aesch. F 90–3; 184–6a; Soph. F 296; Eur. F 424–7; *TrGF* 38 f 1.
Minos (5)⁰	Aesch. F 116–20. Soph. F 323–7; 389a–400. Eur. F 471a–72f; 634–46.
Sisyphus (5)	Aesch. T 78, 16a; T 93b3. Eur. F 282–4; 673–4. *TrGF* 43 F 19.
Prometheus (5)ᵖ	Aesch. *PV*; F 190–204; 204a–8a; Soph. F 362–6; 482–6.

ᵃ Sophocles' *Rape of Helen* (no surviving fragments) and *Eris* (F 199) might be added to the list, if they are not alternative titles for *Helen's Wedding* (F 181) and *The Judgment* (F 360) respectively.
ᵇ Sophocles' *Clytemnestra* (F 334) might have been an alternative title for his *Iphigenia* (F 305–8). Aeschylus' *Iphigenia* (F 94) may be included in this category, but it cannot be established whether it was parallel to Euripides' *Iphigenia in Tauris* or *Iphigenia in Aulis*.
ᶜ There is evidence for three *Telephus* plays by minor tragedians (*TrGF* 22 F 2c; 39 F 4; 77 T 1), but whether they belonged to this category or dealt with earlier episodes of Telephus' life is hard to tell.
ᵈ One cannot rule out that some among seven *Achilles* plays by minor tragedians may have dealt with episodes of the *Aethiopis*: for the references, see note i.
ᵉ One could add Sophocles' *Memnon* (no surviving fragments) to the list, but this may be an alternative title for *Aethiopians* (F 28–9): see Lloyd-Jones 1996: 22.
ᶠ The titles about Ajax and Teucer may be twelve if Sophocles' *Eurysaces* (F 223) and *Teucer* (F 576–8) are two different plays.
ᵍ The story of Iphigenia in Tauris did not feature in the *Nostoi* and may have been Euripides' own invention: see Kyriakou 2006: 21–2. Yet, the myth is included in this category because it belongs to the same timeline as the *Nostoi*. On Aeschylus' *Iphigenia* (F 94), see note b.
ʰ The story of Euripides' *Helen* does not feature in the *Nostoi*, but the poem did include Menelaus' arrival in Egypt, which provides the background to the play.
ⁱ Several titles which may have dealt either with the Trojan Cycle or the Homeric poems might be added to this category, e.g. three *Odysseus* plays (*TrGF* 62 T 8; 64 T 1; 71 F 13) and seven *Achilles* plays (*TrGF* 14 F 1a; 22 F 1a; 60 F 1f; 70 F 1d; 77 F (3); 85 T 1; 88 F 1a).
ʲ The number of titles relating to the Theban Cycle may rise to forty-seven, if one considers Sophocles' *Epigoni* (F 185–90) and *Eriphyle* (F 201a–g) two distinct plays.
ᵏ The myth of Adrastus may have been the subject of Ion's *Argives* (*TrGF* 19 F 8a–9a), Achaeus' *Adrastus* and *Theseus* (*TrGF* 20 F 1, 18, 18a) and Apollodorus' *Suppliants* (*TrGF* 64 T 1–2): see Steinbock 2013a: 181–2.
ˡ One may add Sophocles' *Creusa* (F 350–7) to this group, if that is not an alternative title for *Ion* (F 319–22).
ᵐ The plays in this category may have been twelve, if Sophocles' *Danae* (F 165) is not an alternative title for *Acrisius* (F 61–7).
ⁿ According to schol. *ad* Ar. *Nub.* 257b, Sophocles produced two plays entitled *Athamas* (F 1–10). The plays in this category may be eleven, if Sophocles' *Phrixus* (F 721–2) is not identical with either of his *Athamas* plays.
ᵒ The amount of plays about Minos may be larger, if Sophocles' *Minos* (F 407) is not a corruption and *Daedalus* (F 158–62) is not identical with *Men of Camicus* (F 323–7).
ᵖ The plays about Prometheus may have been six, if Aeschylus' *Prometheus the Fire-Bearer* (F 208–a) and *Prometheus the Fire-Kindler* (F 204a–7a) refer to two separate plays: see Sommerstein 2008: 210–13.

A quick glance through the table immediately shows the sheer range of mythical themes developed in Athenian tragedies and satyr plays.[18] A substantial part of Athens' tragic production was inspired by cyclic epics. The Trojan Cycle provided at least eighty-one titles, while at least forty-six refer

---

[18] Myths that were only the object of allusions could expand this list further but are not included in the survey. The Attic Amazonomachy, for example, does not feature in any of the extant titles but is briefly mentioned in Aesch. *Eum.* 685–90. Some of Heracles' labours that do not feature in any of the surviving titles, such as Heracles' Amazonomachy or the slaying of the Lernaean Hydra, are alluded to at Eur. *HF* 348–435. On mythological *exempla* in tragedy, see Konstantinou 2015 with references.

to the Theban Cycle. With only fifteen titles, the Homeric poems are comparatively underrepresented but still feature among the popular categories. These include, for example, myths concerning Heracles (twenty-eight titles), the Argonauts (twenty-two) and the family of Tantalus (twenty-one). Myths about Athens and Theseus (twenty-three plays) also belong to this group. Yet, if one considers their civic value for the Athenian community, these stories are surprisingly underrepresented,[19] to the extent that a myth as significant as the Attic Amazonomachy does not feature in any of the surviving titles. Many other myths, such as stories about Prometheus, Ixion or Minos, had only limited currency at the dramatic festivals but still provided the subject of at least five plays each. The list could be expanded by mentioning some of the myths which received minor attention on the tragic stage and are not included in Table 2.1. The story of Alcestis, for example, was the subject not only of Euripides' *Alcestis* but also of a lost play by Phrynichus (*TrGF* 3 F 1c–3). The myths of Bellerophon (Soph. F 297–9; Eur. F 285–312; 661–71; *TrGF* 60 F 1g) and Actaeon (Aesch. F 241–6; *TrGF* 3 F 1b; 22 ante F 1; 77 F 1) were the subject of four plays each. Even smaller dramatic attention was devoted to the infinite constellation of other characters of the Greek tradition, such as Tereus (Soph. F 581–95b; *TrGF* 24 post F 1; 70 F 4), Niobe (Aesch. F 154a–67b; Soph. F 441–51), or Alphesiboea (*TrGF* 20 F 16; 56 F 1; 71 F 1).

Some myths seem to have been particularly popular on the stage during the fifth century, although this may be due to the uneven distribution of the extant sources, more evidence being available for fifth-century tragedy because of the popularity of Aeschylus, Sophocles and Euripides. Philoctetes, for example, features in seven titles of plays produced by fifth-century tragedians (Aesch. F 249–53, 255; Soph. *Phil.*; F 697–9, 701; Eur. F 787–803; *TrGF* 20 F 37; 24 post F 1), while only Theodectes seems to have dramatised this story during the fourth century (*TrGF* 72 F 5b). The fortune of Dionysus similarly decreased from the fifth to the fourth century, the distribution of the plays being twenty-two (Aesch. F 22; 23–5; 57–67; 78a–82; 124–6; 146–9; 168–72b; 183; 221–4; 246a–d; Soph. F 171–2; 328–33; Eur. *Bacch.*; *TrGF* 1 F 1c; 7 F 1 tetralogy; 22 F 2; 33 F 1; 40 T 1; 45 F 1) to four (*TrGF* 70 F 2–3; 71 F 4–7; 77 F (4); 86 T 2). Some playwrights seem to have been particularly fond of some categories of myths. Out of fourteen plays dealing with Homeric themes, for example, seven are ascribed to Aeschylus alone (Aesch. F 113a; 131–9; 150–3; 179–80; 187; 263–7; 273–5), whereas Athenian myths are particularly well represented in Euripides' production (Eur. *Heracl.*; *Hipp.*; *Supp.*; F 1–13; 105–13; 349–70; 381–90; 428–47; 674a–81).

---

[19] E. Stewart 2017: 22–7. The same tendency can be detected in Old Comedy, where Athenian myths were underrepresented compared to Panhellenic myths (see A. M. Bowie 2007: 194); Athenian myths were slightly more popular in Middle and New Comedy (see A. M. Bowie 2012: 149–50).

Despite the existence of trends and tendencies in the distribution of mythical themes, my survey shows that the dramatic festivals virtually covered the entire Greek mythical tradition.[20] The range of the mythical themes employed, especially if seen in conjunction with the popularity of the theatre and its centrality in Athens' cultural life, justifies the claim that the dramatic festivals provided the bulk of the Athenians' mythical knowledge.[21] Tragedy and satyr drama, however, were not the only components of the dramatic festivals to be involved with myth. In order to assess the role of the dramatic festivals fully, it is necessary to devote a few words to the dithyramb.

The name of the genre is itself a source of confusion and debate. Early sources (most notably Archilochus' fragment 120 West) use the word 'dithyramb' to allude to a song in honour of Dionysus performed in a ritual context and connected to wine consumption. Such denomination corresponded to an early system of classification of the genres of lyric poetry based on a functional criterion. During the fifth century, a new system based on formal criteria started to overlap with the pre-existing one. Performances of dithyrambs began to go under the name of *kyklioi choroi*, which allowed the circular chorus of the dithyramb to be distinguished from tragedy's quadrangular chorus. The expression *kyklioi choroi* also applied to generic round choirs performed in non-Dionysiac contexts, such as the Panathenaea, the Thargelia and the Prometheia. The overlap of the two systems is reflected in the work of the Alexandrian scholars, who eventually labelled songs performed by *kyklioi choroi* in both Dionysiac and non-Dionysiac festivals as 'dithyrambs', thus causing the modern interpreters' confusion.[22]

The uncertainty surrounding the name, together with the scanty amount of surviving dithyrambs, makes it hard to delineate the characteristics of this enigmatic genre, whose history has been commonly perceived as one of rise and

---

[20] This is even more evident if one also takes comedy into account. Despite the paucity of surviving evidence for mythological plays, mythological comedy constituted about a third of the total production of Old Comedy and about a quarter of the production of fourth-century comedy (comprising both Middle and New Comedy): see A. M. Bowie 2007: 190 n. 2 and 2012: 145–6 n. 7. The Trojan myth (including both Homeric and Cyclic poems) was the most popular theme; Heracles, Dionysus, Zeus, and the Centaurs were also recurring topics on the comic stage: see Carrière 1997: 414–18; A. M. Bowie 2012: 147–50. To the mythological plays, one could also add the mythical allusions found in extant, non-mythological comedies (cf. e.g. Ar. *Lys.* 781–828; *Nub.* 1047–70), on which see A. M. Bowie 2007: 198–9.

[21] Cf. Isoc. 12.168–9, where Isocrates assumes that his readers have heard the myth of Adrastus from the tragedians at the Dionysia (τῶν τραγῳδοδιδασκάλων Διονυσίοις).

[22] See Käppel 2000: 15–26; Fearn 2007: 165–74 and 205–12. Kowalzig and Wilson 2013: 16 state that the success of the dithyrambic contests at the Dionysia 'encouraged the spread of similar choral contests to festivals of gods other than Dionysos', but that such contests 'should probably not be thought of as dithyrambs' but as generic *kyklioi choroi*.

decline. According to many scholars, the dithyramb originated as a non-literary, anonymous composition in honour of Dionysus sung by a processional chorus led by a leader (*exarchos*), and received its literary 'codification' at the end of the seventh century thanks to Arion of Corinth (Hdt. 1.23). The dithyramb was then introduced in Athens probably under the tyrants or at the beginning of the democracy, and the institution of dithyrambic contests has been attributed to the poet Lasos of Hermione. The tradition credited dithyrambs (not necessarily designed for performance at Athens) to all three great lyric poets of the fifth century. Nothing survives of Simonides' production, while Pindar's dithyrambs have only been preserved in fragmentary form (Pind. frr. 70–86a Maehler). Recent papyrological discoveries have brought the Alexandrian edition of Bacchylides' *Dithyrambs* (Bacchyl. 15–20) back to light, but it is hard to tell if these were the kind of dithyrambs that would have been performed at the Great Dionysia. Some innovations seem to have occurred between the end of the fifth and the beginning of the fourth century, when poets such as Melanippus, Philoxenus and Timotheus started challenging the traditional dithyramb. The 'New Dithyramb' was characterised by experimental music, lyric solos and obscure and innovative language. Due to Plato's and Aristophanes' criticism (Pl. *Leg.* 3.700a–01a; Ar. *Av.* 1377–1409), this new trend has long been perceived as an elaborate and yet superficial kind of poetry, emptied of any real religious meaning.[23]

As for the themes, there is substantial agreement about the centrality of mythological narrative in the dithyramb. Doubts arise about the actual Dionysiac content of the poems, and the available evidence does not provide any secure answers. On the one hand, Pindar's fragments tend to appear as cult songs and show some connections to Dionysus even when they deal with completely different myths. Only two out of Bacchylides' six dithyrambs, on the other hand, can be clearly assigned to a Dionysiac context: Bacchyl. 16 and 19. The former dealt with the myth of Heracles and Deianira and belonged to the winter rituals held in Delphi in honour of Dionysus, while the latter, probably written for the Great Dionysia, was concerned with the myth of Io and included a genealogy of Dionysus. The remaining poems show a significant diversity of themes, which range from the demand of Helen's return (Bacchyl. 15) to episodes from Theseus' life (Bacchyl. 17; 18) and the story of Idas and Marpessa (Bacchyl. 20).[24]

---

[23] For a reconstruction of the history of the dithyramb see Pickard-Cambridge 1927: 5–75; Zimmermann 1992: 21–133. Fearn 2007: 181–205 and Kowalzig and Wilson 2013 argue against the theories of decline.

[24] See Pickard-Cambridge 1927: 5–75; Käppel 2000: 12–18 and 26; Maehler 2004: 157–222; Fearn 2007: 177–81 and 219–25; Kowalzig and Wilson 2013: 4–5; Calame 2013. Zimmermann 1992: 113–16 suggests that two tendencies existed in dithyrambic poetry: a non-Dionysiac current, represented by Bacchylides, and a Dionysiac counter-tendency, represented by Pindar, which aimed at the restoration of the original cultic character of the genre.

The dramatic festivals played a key role in the development of the Athenians' mythical knowledge, but they were by no means the only festival where the Athenians engaged with their mythical tradition. Another major religious festival in particular needs to be mentioned: the Panathenaea. Held in honour of Athens' patron goddess, Athena Polias, the event itself was rooted in myth. The Panathenaea celebrated Athena's birthday or her role in the Olympians' victory over the Giants. The foundation of the festival was placed in mythical times. The Athenians attributed it to Erichthonius (*FGrHist* 323a F 2; 324 F 2; schol. *ad* Aelius Aristides 1.362) and Theseus (Plut. *Thes.* 24.3; Paus. 8.2.1; schol. *ad* Pl. *Prm.* 127a; Phot. *Lex.* s.v. Παναθήναια; *Suda* s.v. Παναθήναια). As Athena's foster child and earthborn ancestor of the Athenians, Erichthonius was well suited to be the inventor of the Panathenaea and was specifically associated with some of the festival's individual components, such as the procession and some of the sporting events (*IG* XII, 5 444.17–18; *FGrHist* 328 F 8; [Eratosth.] *Cat.* 13). Theseus was thought to have been the festival's second founder, and ancient sources associate his reform of the Panathenaea with his synoecism. Because of its mythical *aition* and the identity of its founders, the Panathenaea had a martial flavour and celebrated Athens' greatness and special relationship with Athena.[25]

Two versions of the festival can be distinguished. The Small Panathenaea, which was celebrated every year, was a local event where only Athenians could participate. The Great Panathenaea, introduced in 566/5 BC possibly by Pisistratus, took place every four years and had an international character. The Panathenaea was held in the final part of the month of Hekatombeion, at the beginning of the Attic year.[26] The central moment in both versions of the festival was the procession, which started at the Ceramicus and followed the Panathenaic Way through the Agora and up to the Acropolis. There, the procession culminated in the sacrifices to Athena, which were followed by feasting and revelling. While in the Small Panathenaea only Athenian men and women took part in these events, the Great Panathenaea saw also the participation of metics, colonists and, only for the fifth century, allies. Myth also played a role in the procession, when a robe (*peplos*) depicting the Gigantomachy was dedicated to Athena on behalf of the Athenians. This offering was one of the main components of the celebration, and during the classical period it only took place at the Great Panathenaea.[27]

Competitions played a prominent role at the Panathenaea. Sporting events included gymnastic, equestrian and tribal competitions, some of which were

---

[25] Parke 1977: 33; Neils 1992: 14–15; Shear 2001: 29–71; Sourvinou-Inwood 2011: 270–80.
[26] Parke 1977: 33–4; Neils 1992: 14–15; Shear 2001: 5–8.
[27] Neils 1992: 23–4; Shear 2001: 72–230; Tracy 2007. Specifically on the *peplos*, see Barber 1992; Shear 2001: 173–86; Sourvinou-Inwood 2011: 267–70.

limited to Athenian contestants.[28] More relevant to this chapter are the musical and poetic contests. Tribal contests for *kyklioi choroi*, or 'dithyrambs', are attested for both the Small and Great Panathenaea, but nothing can be said about their mythical topics. The only well-preserved dithyramb that may be associated with the festival is Bacchyl. 15, which deals with the cyclic episode of Menelaus and Odysseus' embassy to demand Helen's return.[29] A wider range of events was offered at the Great Panathenaea. According to Plutarch, musical contests had been introduced by Pericles (Plut. *Per.* 13.5–6). Based on Attic vase painting, however, modern scholars agree that at least some of the events were already part of the festival's programme in the sixth century. In the classical period, such contests included competitions for *kitharōidoi*, *aulōidoi*, *kitharistai* and *aulētai*. The Great Panathenaea also hosted rhapsodic contests. These must have been part of the programme since the sixth century. This can be inferred by the fact that Solon or Hipparchus were credited with the rule that rhapsodes at the Panathenaea had to recite the Homeric epics in sequence, each taking up where the previous contestant had left off ([Pl.] *Hipparch.* 228b4–c3; Diog. Laert. 1.57). It is not clear whether these competitions implied adherence to a fixed text of the Homeric poems, nor can it be established if the contestants recited the poems in their entirety or only performed selected episodes in their narrative order. Whatever the format of the rhapsodic contests, however, their subject certainly came from the Homeric epics and (possibly, but less likely) the Trojan Cycle.[30]

Myth featured conspicuously in the figurative cycles adorning the buildings of the Agora and the Acropolis, which provided the physical setting for most of the events of the Panathenaea. The Gigantomachy used to appear on the east pediment of the archaic temple of Athena and later featured on the east metopes of the Parthenon, on the shield of the statue of Athena Parthenos and on the east pediment of the temple of Athena Nike. The fall of Troy was sculpted on the north metopes of the Parthenon and depicted in the Painted Stoa, whereas the Centauromachy featured on the south metopes of the Parthenon, on the sandals of the statue of Athena Parthenos and on the shield of Athena Promachos. The Amazonomachy appeared on the west metopes of the Parthenon, on the shield of Athena Parthenos, in the Painted Stoa and possibly on the west pediment of the temple of Athena Nike. Athena and her special relationship with Athens were celebrated on

---

[28] Kyle 1992; Boegehold 1996; Shear 2001: 231–350.
[29] On Bacchyl. 15, see Maehler 2004: 157–8; Fearn 2007: 257–337.
[30] Shapiro 1992; Shear 2001: 350–76; Nagy 2002: 9–35. The performance of cyclic epics at the Panathenaea has been posited by Burgess 2004–5. Recitation of non-epic poetry is attested for other Athenian festivals: according to Plato, for example, Athenian boys performed Solon's poetry, together with poems by other poets, at the festival of the Apatouria (Pl. *Ti.* 21b).

the pediments of the Parthenon, which depicted the birth of the goddess and the contest between Athena and Poseidon over the city.[31]

Overall, the impact of the Panathenaea on the mythical knowledge of the Athenians seems to have been far from negligible. Several myths physically unfolded in front of the participants when once a year they marched in the procession through the Agora and up to the Acropolis. Mythical narratives were also part of the competitions for *kyklioi choroi* at both Small and Great Panathenaea. The rhapsodic contests, held once every four years at the Great Panathenaea, probably contributed to the Athenians' familiarity with the mythical subjects of the *Iliad* and *Odyssey*. The mythical themes deployed at the Panathenaea cannot be delineated completely, but they spanned from the Gigantomachy to the Homeric epics and the Trojan Cycle, from the Centauromachy to Athenian myths such as the Attic Amazonomachy and the contest between Athena and Poseidon. Such range, relatively limited when compared to the thematic flourishing of the dramatic festivals, was by no means inferior to the one employed in other public contexts, to which it is now time to turn.

THE INSTITUTIONAL SETTINGS OF ATTIC ORATORY

Athenian orators made abundant use of the past. Whether they provide a point of comparison with the present or are used to praise the city, episodes from the past are often recalled in the extant speeches. Most allusions refer to the historical past, but many others derive their subject matter from myth.[32] The vast majority of the mythical allusions in the orators, however, come from the private speeches of Isocrates.[33] Only part of the preserved mythical allusions was therefore delivered in the institutions of Athenian democracy, or at least

---

[31] Castriota 1992: 33–89, 134–83; Shear 2001: 708–14, 724–42, 761–8, 773–8; Hurwit 2004: 123–33, 147–54, 181–91; Castriota 2005; Stansbury-O'Donnell 2005; Barringer 2008: 59–108. Brommer 1967: 191–5 rejected the identification of the west metopes of the Parthenon with the Amazonomachy and suggested scenes of Greeks fighting Persians. The sacrifice of the daughters of Erechtheus during Eumolpus' invasion of Athens may have featured on the Parthenon frieze, if one believes Connelly 1996, but her view has been disproven by Neils 2001: 178–80. Instead, most scholars agree that the frieze portrayed the Panathenaic procession itself: see Hurwit 1999: 222–8 and 2004: 133–46; Neils 2001: 173–201; Shear 2001: 742–61; Barringer 2008: 85–91. The frieze of the temple of Athena Nike may also have depicted mythical battles. Proposed identifications include the myth of Adrastus, the defence of the Heraclidae and the war against Eumolpus: see Shear 2001: 782–5.

[32] For a general study of the use of history in the orators, see Nouhaud 1982; for a similar study of the use of myth in the orators, see Gotteland 2001.

[33] For a table describing the distribution of mythical allusions among the Attic orators, see Nouhaud 1982: 19. On the private nature of the speeches of Isocrates, see Too 1995: 74–112; Mirhady and Too 2000: 5–6.

written with an institutional setting in mind. This section focuses on these institutions and explores the range of myths deployed in each of these contexts. As we shall see, myth featured almost regularly in the funeral speeches delivered at the state funeral for the war dead and influenced to some extent the Athenians' knowledge of specific episodes from the city's past. Myths were less central in the forensic speeches delivered at the lawcourts. No specific story was especially popular in this context, but myth provided forensic orators with a useful tool to build their arguments. Finally, myth played a minor role in the Assembly and, possibly, the Council, and neither of these institutions fulfilled their potential to influence the Athenians' mythical knowledge.

The state funeral for the war dead provided the Athenians with a public, emotionally charged occasion at which to recall and construct the city's past.[34] As a part of the burial rituals, an orator chosen by the city would deliver a funeral speech (*epitaphios logos*) to commemorate the war dead. Such speeches often included narratives about the historical and mythical exploits of the Athenian ancestors. Thucydides describes the state funeral when he introduces the funeral speech delivered by Pericles in the winter of 431/0 BC. Before the ceremony, the bones of the dead were laid out in a tent for three days and received offerings from the mourners. There followed a procession during which the bones, placed into coffins according to tribes, were transported to the public burial ground (*dēmosion sēma*),[35] while an empty bier was prepared for the dead who had not been recovered. Anyone who wished, both Athenians and foreigners, could participate in the procession, and women were there to lament the dead. The bones were then laid out and buried, and a man chosen by the city delivered a funeral speech in honour of the dead (Thuc. 2.34.2–6).

The place of myth at the state funeral was in the *epitaphios logos*. This genre is not well represented in our sources, as only six funeral speeches survive. Two fragments (DK Gorg. B 5a–6) of one such speech composed by the

---

[34] The collective burial of the war dead was also practised in other Greek *poleis*: see Low 2003; Fournier and Hamon 2007.

[35] The expression δημόσιον σῆμα is only attested in Thucydides. For other expressions used to refer to the public cemetery, see Arrington 2014: 66–7. The *dēmosion sēma* was located in the Ceramicus (schol. ABFGc₂ *ad* Thuc. 2.34.5), in the north-western part of Athens. The graves were distributed along the road that connected the Dipylon Gate with the Academy (Paus. 1.29.4; Cic. *Fin.* 5.1.1–5.2.5; Philostr. *V S* 2.22). According to Stupperich 1977: 22, 26 and Clairmont 1983: 32, the graves strictly lined the road, but Arrington 2014: 67–8 (further elaborating Goette 2009: 188) has convincingly argued that some of them were scattered on a series of cross-streets. The *dēmosion sēma* was not an enclosed area exclusively devoted to the war dead: see Patterson 2006: 53–6; Low 2012: 23–32; Arrington 2010: 500 n. 4 and 2014: 73–6. Pausanias (1.29.3–15) mentions several public graves of individuals, cavalrymen and allies, and archaeological evidence reveals that the area also hosted private burials: see Clairmont 1983: 3–4, 38, 40–1, 44; Low 2012: 31–2; Arrington 2014: 86–8. From a juridical point of view, the area of the Ceramicus included both public and private lands: see Faraguna 2012: 177–80.

sophist Gorgias, probably a literary exercise, are attested.[36] Pericles delivered the *epitaphios* for the dead of the first year of the Peloponnesian War. The speech is reported by Thucydides (2.34–46), and whether it was a (more or less) faithful reproduction of Pericles' real speech or Thucydides' free composition is a matter of debate.[37] Lysias' *Funeral Oration* commemorated the dead of the Corinthian War (395–386 BC), but its exact date cannot be determined with any certainty. The speech's authenticity has often been questioned because of Lysias' status as a metic, and scholars have similarly debated whether the text was meant for private circulation.[38] Whatever one's view on this issue, Lysias' speech reflects the themes and discursive parameters of a real *epitaphios logos* and is a highly valuable source. Demosthenes is known to have delivered the funeral speech for the fallen at the Battle of Chaeronea in 338 BC (Dem. 18.285; Plut. *Dem.* 21.2), but the authenticity of the preserved text of the speech has been the object of debate.[39] In Plato's *Menexenus*, Socrates recounts a funeral speech that he had allegedly heard from Aspasia. The dialogue is generally regarded as authentic, and the speech is usually seen as a parody of the genre of the *epitaphios logos*.[40] Finally, Hyperides' *Funeral Speech* commemorated the dead of the Lamian War (323/2 BC) and is commonly considered unusual because of its focus on the fallen general Leosthenes.[41]

The *epitaphios logos* is unique in offering a continuous, albeit selective narrative of Athenian history. Funeral speeches commemorate a relatively fixed set of myths and historical events. As Table 2.2 shows, four out of six funeral speeches allude to Athenian autochthony. Athens' mythical wars were also a common epitaphic *topos*. The Amazonomachy, the war against Thebes for

---

[36] Todd 2007: 151.
[37] See Kakridis 1961: 5; Flashar 1969: 28 n. 54; Ziolkowski 1981: 188–95, 202; Hornblower 1991: 294–6; Pritchard 1996: 141–4; Bosworth 2000: 1. More in general on the speeches in Thucydides, see J. Wilson 1982; Walbank 1985: 244–6; Hornblower 1991: 59–60; Marincola 2010: 298–303. Plutarch attests that Pericles also delivered the funeral speech for the fallen of the Samian War in 440/39 BC (Plut. *Per.* 28.3–5), and preserves the only surviving fragment of the speech (Plut. *Per.* 8.6).
[38] Todd 2007: 157–64.
[39] On the issue of authenticity, see Worthington 2003 and Herrman 2008.
[40] See Coventry 1989; Loraux 1981: 321–37; Thomas 1989: 210–11; Trivigno 2009. Monoson 1998 sees Socrates' speech generically as critical towards Pericles' funeral speech. The parodic nature of Plato's *Menexenus* has been questioned by Kahn 1963 and recently by Pappas and Zelcer 2015: 77–93. Tsitsiridis 1998: 63–92 takes a middle ground between these two interpretations.
[41] Loraux 1981: 132–5 explains Hyperides' focus on Leosthenes as a result of the increasing importance of exceptional individuals in Greek politics during the fourth century. Herrman 2009: 61–2 and Petruzziello 2009: 83–7 connect this feature of the speech with the development of prose encomia. But Hesk 2013 rightly emphasises that praise of individuals or subgroups was not unusual in funeral speeches, and downplays the uniqueness of Hyperides' *Funeral Speech*. The authenticity of the speech, questioned by Canfora 2011, is generally accepted.

Table 2.2 Myths in the extant funeral speeches

Myth	Speech
Autochthony	Lys. 2.17; Pl. *Menex.* 237b1–c6, 237e, 238e5–239a7; Dem. 60.4; Hyp. 6.7.
Amazonomachy	Lys. 2.4–6; Pl. *Menex.* 239b; Dem. 60.8.
Adrastus	Lys. 2.7–10; Pl. *Menex.* 239b; Dem. 60.8.
Defence of the Heraclidae	Lys. 2.11–16; Pl. *Menex.* 239b; Dem. 60.8.
War against Eumolpus	Pl. *Menex.* 239b; Dem. 60.8.
Trojan War	Dem. 60.10; Hyp. 6.35–6.
Daughters of Erechtheus	Dem. 60.27.
Theseus establishes *isonomia*	Dem. 60.28.
Procne and Philomela	Dem. 60.28.
Daughters of Leo	Dem. 60.29.
Acamas at Troy	Dem. 60.29.
Birth of Oeneus from Dionysus	Dem. 60.30.
Double nature of Cecrops	Dem. 60.30.
Marriage of Alope	Dem. 60.31.
Ajax's suicide	Dem. 60.31.
Antiochus, son of Heracles	Dem. 60.31.

the recollection of the bodies of the Seven and the war against Eurystheus in defence of the Heraclidae, in particular, feature in all three *epitaphioi* which offer a narrative of the ancestral exploits: Lysias', Demosthenes' and Plato's funeral speeches. The Trojan War is twice mentioned as a point of comparison for the deeds of the Athenian ancestors, who surpassed the excellence of the Greek heroes who captured Troy.[42] Many other myths, including for example the sacrifice of Erechtheus' daughters, Ajax's suicide and the story of Procne and Philomela, are recalled exclusively in Demosthenes' catalogue of the eponymous heroes (Dem. 60.27–31). This catalogue prompts a discussion of the reasons that brought the Athenians of each tribe to strive for a noble death, but it is Demosthenes' own innovation and does not feature in any other extant funeral speech.[43] If one takes this detail into account, it is safe to conclude that the range of myths employed at the state funeral was limited to four or five episodes from the early history of the city.

The captivating power of the *epitaphios logos* over the audience is testified by Socrates in Plato's *Menexenus*. The philosopher ironically praises the orators' ability to bewitch the souls of the listeners (γοητεύουσιν ἡμῶν τὰς ψυχάς) and

---

[42] On the reception of the Trojan myth in classical Greece, see Erskine 2001: 61–92.
[43] On tradition and innovations in the funeral speeches, see Frangeskou 1998–9.

make them all feel ennobled (Pl. *Menex.* 234c–35c). As previous scholarship has pointed out, this may not be sufficient to support the assumption that the *epitaphios logos* always provided the dominant versions of the myths current in classical Athens.[44] The emotional weight of epitaphic narratives, however, together with the constant presence of a limited set of themes repeated with very few variations, probably caused the state funeral to contribute significantly to the mythical knowledge of the Athenians and to influence to some extent their ideas about specific episodes from the city's past.

The lawcourts (*dikastēria*), manned by ordinary Athenians, were an essential and defining feature of Athenian democracy (Arist. *Pol.* 1275a22–33; [Arist.] *Ath. Pol.* 41.2), and their institution was traditionally attributed to Solon (Arist. *Pol.* 1273b35–74a5; [Arist.] *Ath. Pol.* 9.1).[45] Several locations have been proposed as meeting places for the *dikastēria*. Five structures excavated under the Stoa of Attalus in the east side of the Agora were built from the end of the fifth century and are identified as lawcourts by the remains of dicastic equipment. Around 300 BC, these structures were replaced by a single building known as Square Peristyle, which offered the advantage of concentrating all trials in one location. Other sites hosting popular lawcourts during the fifth and fourth centuries are attested from literary and epigraphic sources. Such sites included the Periclean Odeon (Ar. *Vesp.* 1108–9; [Dem.] 59.52; Poll. 8.33) and the Painted Stoa (Dem. 45.17; *IG* II² 1641.25–33; 1670.34–5), whereas other courts such as the Parabyston (Ar. *Vesp.* 1108–9; Paus. 1.28.8; Harp. s.v. παράβυστον; *IG* II² 1646.12) and the Red and Green Courts (Paus. 1.28.8) have been associated with some of the buildings under the Stoa of Attalus.[46]

Every Athenian over thirty years of age who was not a debtor to the Treasury or disenfranchised had the right to serve in the lawcourts ([Arist.] *Ath.*

---

[44] See Brock 1998: 229–30 and Hanink 2013. The size of the audience would also be a significant variable, but it is one which is hard to quantify. Thucydides' reference to the elevated platform (βῆμα ὑψηλόν) set up in the *dēmosion sēma* to allow Pericles' funeral speech to be heard by as many members of the crowd as possible (ὅπως ἀκούοιτο ὡς ἐπὶ πλεῖστον τοῦ ὁμίλου) (Thuc. 2.34.8), together with Pericles' own remark about the multitude of Athenians and foreigners (τὸν πάντα ὅμιλον καὶ ἀστῶν καὶ ξένων) listening to his speech (Thuc. 2.26.4), may suggest that the audiences of the funeral orations were indeed large, but Bosworth 2000: 2 might be going too far when he argues that Pericles' funeral speech was better witnessed compared to most (non-epitaphic) speeches reported by Thucydides.

[45] This attribution is generally accepted, but modern scholars disagree on the nature of the judicial institution created by Solon, which is usually referred to as *hēliaia*. The traditional view, shared e.g. by Rhodes 1981: 160–2, 318–19 and Ostwald 1986: 9–12, is that Solon's *hēliaia* was a judicial session of the Assembly. Hansen 1989b: 237–49, 258–62 and Boegehold 1995: 17–20, on the other hand, argue that the Solonian *hēliaia* was an institution separate from the Assembly and divided into several courts.

[46] On the locations proposed as meeting places for the lawcourts, see Boegehold 1995: 3–16, 91–113 and Townsend 1995: 24–106.

Pol. 63.3). A total of 6,000 judges were selected by lot every year and had to swear the Heliastic Oath. This bound them, among other things, to cast their votes in accordance with the laws and decrees of the city.[47] The judges were then allocated to specific courts every morning. How this happened during the fifth century is unclear. From at least 410 BC, however, the judges were divided into ten sections and allocated to courts by lot. By the end of the fourth century this process was improved and came to include a second selection by lot that assigned judges to courts individually ([Arist.] *Ath. Pol.* 63–4). The size of judging panels varied from a minimum of 201 to a maximum of 501 judges depending on the nature of the procedure, but on some occasions two or three panels of 501 judges could be brought together ([Arist.] *Ath. Pol.* 53.3, 68.1). Daily pay for the judges was introduced by Pericles (Arist. *Pol.* 1274a8–9; [Arist.] *Ath. Pol.* 27.3–4) and its rate, which was originally two obols, was raised to three obols by Cleon (schol. *ad* Ar. *Vesp.* 88, 300; [Arist.] *Ath. Pol.* 62.2).[48]

Five special courts require some separate remarks. The Council of the Areopagus, the Palladion, the Delphinion, the Court at Phreatto and the Prytaneion each dealt with a specific type of homicide charge ([Arist.] *Ath. Pol.* 57.3). The mechanism for the selection of judges differed from the one employed in the popular courts. Only former Archons could serve in the Areopagus (Plut. *Sol.* 19.1; Dem. 24.22; [Arist.] *Ath. Pol.* 60.3) and they were appointed for life (Lys. 26.11; [Arist.] *Ath. Pol.* 3.6). The size of the Council of the Areopagus is not known, but suggested numbers range from 150 to 250 Areopagites. The other Homicide Courts were manned by judges called *ephetai*, who had to be at least fifty years old and formed panels of 51 (*IG* I³ 104.13–19; [Arist.] *Ath. Pol.* 57.4; Poll. *Onom.* 8.125; Phot. *Lex.* s.v. ἐφέται). Homicide charges were brought before the King Archon, who held three preliminary hearings (*prodikasiai*) in order to determine the appropriate court for the trial. At the hearing proper, the prosecutor spoke first and the defendant spoke second; both litigants were then allowed a second shorter speech. Finally, the judges voted and the King Archon, who was not allowed to vote, pronounced the verdict.[49]

---

[47] The text of the oath quoted in Dem. 24.149–51 is a forgery, but its contents can be reconstructed thanks to the many allusions in the orators: see Harris 2013b: 101–37, 353–7; Canevaro 2013a: 173–80.

[48] On the selection of the judges, the size of the panels and the pay for the judges, see Rhodes 1981: 697–716, 728–30, 734–5; Boegehold 1995: 21–42; Hansen [1991] 1999: 181–96.

[49] Rhodes 1981: 640–50; Wallace 1989: 94–127; Boegehold 1995: 43–50; Hansen [1991] 1999: 288–95; Leão 2010; Harris 2016b: 76–80. The identity and method of selection of the *ephetai* is highly debated. The sources state that they were elected by lot (λαχόντες) ([Arist.] *Ath. Pol.* 57.4) or selected according to birth (ἀριστίνδην) (*IG* I³ 104.19, partially restored based on Poll. *Onom.* 8.125). As a result, some scholars have reasonably (*pace* Kapparis 1999: 188) conjectured that the *ephetai* were selected by lot among the Areopagites. Scholarship is similarly divided on whether the *ephetai* were replaced by regular judges at the end of the fifth century. For a survey of these and other issues connected to the *ephetai*, see Kapparis 1999: 187–9 and Canevaro 2013a: 56–7.

Table 2.3 Myths in the extant forensic speeches

Myth	Speech
Autochthony	[Dem.] 59.74; Lycurg. 1.41, 47, 100
Trial of Orestes at the Areopagus	Dem. 23.66 and 74; Din. 1.87
Trial of Ares at the Areopagus	Dem. 23.66; Din. 1.87
Eumolpus/daughters of Erechtheus	Lycurg. 1.98–100; Demad. 1.37
Theseus and the synoecism	[Dem.] 59.75
Achilles and Patroclus	Aeschin. 1.144–50
Phoenix	Aeschin. 1.151–2
Acamas and Amphipolis	Aeschin. 2.31
Thersites	Aeschin. 3.231
Trojan War	Lycurg. 1.62
Death of king Codrus	Lycurg. 1.84–7
Hector	Lycurg. 1.102–4

As the data shows, the judicial system was deeply rooted in Athenian society. At least 6,000 Athenians served in the lawcourts every year, not to mention the additional number of Areopagites (and possibly *ephetai*) serving in the Homicide Courts. If one also considers that the lawcourts met between 150 to 200 days per year and that forensic speeches make up the vast majority of the surviving oratorical production of classical Athens,[50] the mythical allusions in such speeches are proportionately few. Table 2.3 shows that, especially compared to the state funeral, no specific myths were particularly associated with the lawcourts. Most mythical allusions in forensic speeches, however, deal with Athens' past. Some of these episodes, such as the Athenians' autochthonous origins and the war against Eumolpus, also feature in extant funeral speeches. Other Athenian myths, such as the mythical trials at the Areopagus and the death of king Codrus, are not part of typical epitaphic narratives. Episodes and characters from the Trojan War are also employed and sometimes feature together with poetic quotations. A significant example is Aeschines' use of quotations from the *Iliad* to illustrate the love between Achilles and Patroclus. Myth therefore was not a central element in the rhetoric of the lawcourts, but provided forensic orators with a useful tool for the construction of their arguments.

The Council and the Assembly were the deliberative bodies of the Athenian democracy. The Council (*boulē*) of the Five Hundred was introduced by Cleisthenes ([Arist.] *Ath. Pol.* 21.3), even though a previous

---

[50] On the frequency of the sessions of the lawcourts, see Hansen 1979 and [1991] 1999: 186.

Council of the Four Hundred was attributed to Solon ([Arist.] *Ath. Pol.* 8.4; Plut. *Sol.* 19.1).[51] The Council met in the Council house (*bouleutērion*) in the west side of the Agora. Its original meeting place, the Old Bouleuterion, had been built in the early fifth century. In the last quarter of the fifth century this building came to be used as the state archive, while the New Bouleuterion was constructed to host the meetings of the Council.[52] Extraordinary meeting places are also attested, including the dockyards at Piraeus, the Acropolis and, during the Persian invasion, even Salamis.[53] Another building associated with the Council was the Tholos. Circular in shape, it was built around 470 BC and hosted the members of the tribe that took turns presiding in the Council. These were called *prytaneis*, and they would all sleep and have their meals in the Tholos.[54]

All Athenian citizens over the age of thirty were eligible to serve in the Council unless debarred by specific circumstances. These included practising prostitution (Aeschin. 1.19–20) and having performed military service under the Four Hundred in 411 BC (And. 1.75), but other restrictions may have applied. It was possible for the same person to serve in the Council twice, although not two years in a row, but only a minority of Athenians seems to have exercised this right.[55] The Council was manned by 500 councillors who received a salary of five obols per day. Each tribe provided fifty councillors selected by lot among volunteers from Athens' 139 demes ([Arist.] *Ath. Pol.* 43.2). Each deme was allotted a number of seats in proportion to its size, but this number could vary depending on whether the smaller demes were able to provide enough councillors.[56] The Council met around 300 times a year.[57] As previously mentioned, each tribe's fifty councillors had to take turns in leading the Council as *prytaneis*. Their period of office lasted one prytany, i.e. one tenth of the Attic year. Their main task was to summon the Council and the Assembly, and they received an extra obol in addition to the councillors' normal salary. Every day a chairman (*epistatēs*) was selected by lot among the *prytaneis* to act as the head of state.[58]

Together with the lawcourts and the magistracies, the Assembly (*ekklēsia*) was one of the cornerstones of Athenian democracy (Arist. *Pol.* 1275a22–33; [Arist.] *Ath. Pol.* 41.2). The Assembly might have originally met in the Agora (Plut. *Sol.* 8.2, 30.1) or in the Lyceum (*IG* I³ 105.34), but its meetings were

---

[51] Rhodes 1972: 1 and 208–9; Hansen [1991] 1999: 247.
[52] Thompson and Wycherley 1972: 29–31; Rhodes 1972: 30–2; Hansen [1991] 1999: 251–2.
[53] Rhodes 1972: 35–6; Hansen [1991] 1999: 251.
[54] Thompson and Wycherley 1972: 41–6; Rhodes 1972: 16–23, 32; Hansen [1991] 1999: 250–2.
[55] Rhodes 1972: 1–4; Hansen 1985: 51–5; Hansen [1991] 1999: 249.
[56] Rhodes 1972: 8–12; Hansen [1991] 1999: 247–8.
[57] Rhodes 1985: 30; Ober 2008: 144.
[58] Rhodes 1972: 16–23; Hansen [1991] 1999: 250–1.

eventually moved onto the Pnyx. This hill, located south-west of the Agora, hosted the Assembly until the end of the fourth century, when the meetings were transferred to the Theatre of Dionysus (*IG* II² 389). Archaeological excavations have revealed three phases in the development of the Assembly site. Pnyx I (c. 460–400 BC) hosted about 5,000–6,000 people sitting directly on the rock in a semicircle and facing the speaker's platform (*bēma*) placed on the north side of the hill. Pnyx II (c. 400–345 BC) hosted about 6,000 people sitting, probably on benches, in a rebuilt auditorium facing south. Pnyx III (c. 345–300) was rebuilt, possibly by Lycurgus or Eubulus, with an enlarged auditorium and might have hosted over 10,000 people.[59]

All adult male Athenian citizens, except for those who had been disenfranchised or were public debtors, were entitled to attend, speak and vote in the Assembly, and there were no restrictions based on census or land ownership. The introduction of Assembly pay after the democratic restoration in 403 BC encouraged even the poorest citizens to take part in the meetings, and the reimbursement amounted to one drachma or a drachma and a half depending on the type of session. Based on literary and epigraphic sources, average attendance of the Assembly has been estimated at about 5,000 people during the fifth century (Thuc. 8.72; Ar. *Ach.* 1–25) and about 6,000 during the fourth, when a quorum of 6,000 voters was established for certain types of decisions to be valid (Dem. 24.45–6; [Dem.] 59.89–90; *IG* II² 103). Compared to population estimates, these numbers indicate that participation to the Assembly increased in the fourth century: while only one tenth of Athens' citizen population attended the *ekklēsia* during the fifth century, one fifth took part during the fourth.[60] There were two types of sessions of the Assembly: principal assemblies (*ekklēsiai kyriai*) and regular assemblies (*ekklēsiai nomimoi*). Principal assemblies took place once every prytany and were devoted to specific matters such as votes on the conduct of magistrates or *eisangeliai*, whereas regular assemblies were held three times per prytany. Therefore, the Assembly regularly met a total of four times per prytany and forty per year ([Arist.] *Ath. Pol.* 43.3–6).[61] This number, however, could be exceeded, because in case of emergency it was possible to summon extraordinary meetings called *ekklēsiai synklētoi* (Dem. 19.123; Aeschin. 2.72).[62]

---

[59] H. A. Thompson 1982; Hansen 1987: 12–14; Hansen [1991] 1999: 128–9.
[60] Hansen 1987: 14–19; Hansen [1991] 1999: 130–2.
[61] Rhodes 1981: 520–31; Hansen 1987: 19–24; Harris 2006: 81–120. According to Hansen 1983: 35–72, esp. 37, the number of four meetings per prytany and forty per year constituted a fixed limit that could not be exceeded, but Harris 2006: 85–90 has shown that such a limit did not exist.
[62] Harris 2006: 81–120. *Pace* Hansen 1983: 35–72, esp. 41–2, *ekklēsiai synklētoi* were not ordinary meetings summoned at short notice within a fixed limit of four meetings per prytany.

Both the Council and the Assembly had the potential to influence the mythical knowledge of the Athenians due to the frequency of the sessions (especially in the case of the Council) and the large number of citizens involved. It is therefore striking that no mythical allusions are attested in any of the extant Assembly speeches or in the ones recounted by Thucydides.[63] Myth is similarly absent from the speeches destined to the Council, but this can be partially ascribed to the small amount of preserved bouleutic speeches.[64] The only extant mythical allusions in deliberative oratory are found in Xenophon's account of a speech delivered by the ambassador Procles of Phlius in front of the Athenian Assembly.[65] Procles recalls how the Athenians fought against the Thebans over the bodies of the Seven, and against Eurystheus in defence of the Heraclidae (Xen. *Hell.* 6.5.46–8). Procles' use of myth in his embassy speech, however, may not have been an isolated case, as we can infer from a passage in Thucydides. There, Athenian envoys address the Spartan Assembly and declare that they will not mention the very ancient events (καὶ τὰ μὲν πάνυ παλαιὰ τί δεῖ λέγειν;) but rather focus on the Persian Wars (Thuc. 1.73.2).[66] Aeschines offers further proof in his speech *On the Embassy*, where he states that during an embassy to Macedon he once recalled how Theseus' son Acamas had acquired the area known as Ennea Hodoi (Aeschin. 2.31). It can then be argued that embassy speeches provided a possible occasion for the Athenians to engage with myth in the Council and the Assembly, where such speeches were normally delivered.

This survey of the institutional settings of Athenian oratory has shown that myth was certainly used at the state funeral, in the lawcourts and in the Assembly, and that it may have also been employed in the Council. The presence of myth and the range of the mythical themes deployed, however, are not comparable to those of the dramatic festivals, and they varied in each of the institutions considered. Despite the possible use of mythical *exempla* in embassy speeches, the available sources show that myth only played a minor role in the Council and the Assembly. Myth featured to a larger extent in the lawcourts. The mythical allusions attested in forensic oratory usually deal with

---

[63] The myth of Athens' defence of the Heraclidae is mentioned in a decree quoted in Demosthenes' *On the Crown* (Dem. 18.187), but the document is a later forgery: see Canevaro 2013a: 310–18.

[64] Only five bouleutic speeches survive: Lys. 16; 24; 26; 31; Dem. 51. Most of them deal with cases of *dokimasia* and can be ascribed to the forensic genre.

[65] On the reliability of the speeches in Xenophon, see Buckler 1982.

[66] Cf. also Hdt. 9.26–7, where Tegeans and Athenians each claim the command over the left wing of the Greek army at Plataea and construct their speeches on episodes from the mythical past. As noted by Brock 1998: 228–9, these passages may well have been Thucydides' and Herodotus' free compositions, but must have employed 'the sort of arguments that contemporary Athenians were presenting to outsiders'.

Athens' past or with the Trojan War, but no specific episodes seem to have been particularly popular in this setting. Compared to forensic rhetoric, the mythical allusions in extant funeral speeches are numerically and proportionately larger. This shows how central the past, both mythical and historical, was at the state funeral for the war dead. Funeral speeches usually dealt with a fixed set of myths, which were limited to Athens' mythical wars and Athenian autochthony, but their emotional and rhetorical charge probably had a significant impact on the Athenians' knowledge of those specific myths.

MYTH IN PRIVATE CONTEXTS

The previous sections have shown that the Athenians constantly engaged with the mythical past in virtually every aspect of their public life. Together with history, however, myth was also recalled and transmitted in private contexts outside the formal institutions of the state.[67] One such context was the family. Ancient sources mention older relatives passing down knowledge about the past to their descendants through casual conversation (Pl. *Lach.* 179a–80b; Aeschin. 3.191). The information remembered concerned the family itself or the history of the *polis* at large. Especially for the first type of memories, Rosalind Thomas has introduced the notion of 'family tradition', which implies an almost esoteric transmission of the past within the family.[68] Such a closed system of transmission is hardly conceivable in classical Athens,[69] but this does not detract from the importance of the family as a context for the recollection of the past. Orators often mention their own families as sources of historical information. In *On the Embassy*, for example, Aeschines attributes his knowledge of Athens' past mistakes to the testimony of his father and uncle (Aeschin. 2.74–8).[70] The specific

---

[67] Unlike much recent scholarship (Vlassopoulos 2007; Gottesman 2014; Taylor and Vlassopoulos 2015), I do not think that a dichotomy existed between Athenian democratic institutions and extra-institutional, 'free' spaces. I consider private contexts not to be diametrically opposed to but embedded in the structure of the democracy. I merely take such settings as additional *loci* of social interaction and transmission of memory, and claim that they were not necessarily conditioned by the discursive parameters of the democratic institutions. See also Canevaro 2017 for some criticism specifically on Gottesman's approach.

[68] See Thomas 1989: 95–154, esp. 98; Steinbock 2013a: 73–6.

[69] For a criticism of Thomas's approach, see pp. 12–13. Thomas herself acknowledges that the anthropological notion of 'esoteric tradition' is not entirely appropriate to the Athenian context: see Thomas 1989: 98 n. 8.

[70] On the Aeschines passage see Steinbock 2013b and Barbato 2017. On the habit of citing family as one's source of historical information see Canevaro 2019. According to Thomas 1989: 99, 110–23, historical information preserved through family traditions was often employed in the lawcourts to provide a 'family defence', i.e. 'a plea for voters' sympathy in which a speaker asserts his democratic ancestry, the service given by his ancestors for the city and its democracy'.

place of myth at the family level is hard to determine. Athenian families may have preserved the memory of their mythical ancestors. This is suggested by a passage in Plato's *Theaetetus* which mocks those people who trace their ancestry back to Heracles or other mythical forebears (Pl. *Tht.* 174e–75a).[71] The family might also have been the context where the Athenians were first exposed to myth. If we believe Plato's *Republic*, nurses and mothers told children tales similar to those sung by the poets, such as the story of Cronus and Uranus (Pl. *Resp.* 2. 377b–83c). This information is confirmed by later sources, with Philostratus stating that nurses were very skilled at telling stories such as Theseus' abandonment of Ariadne (Philostr. *Imag.* 1.15.1–5).[72]

Another important private context for the recollection of myth may have been the symposium. This social and cultural institution originated as an exclusively elite activity, but at least in Athens since the late fifth century it gradually became familiar to larger strata of society. In a typical symposium, a small group of friends would gather in a private house to enjoy wine, company and various forms of entertainment, usually after a dinner and before taking part in a revel out in the streets. The participants would recline on couches placed in a circle along the walls of the room. Such an arrangement allowed the fellow drinkers to engage in conversation with each other in an intimate and egalitarian atmosphere. A symposiarch was elected to decide the strength of the wine and supervise the night's entertainment. Wine was diluted with water in a krater according to Greek custom and poured to the symposiasts by servants. The participants were adult males, sometimes accompanied by younger relatives. The only women admitted were courtesans and flute players hired to provide entertainment. Sympotic pastimes included drinking games, toasts, mockeries, cultured discussions and performances of lyric poetry and drinking-songs (*skolia*), and they often had erotic implications.[73]

The intimate atmosphere of the symposium and its several forms of entertainment contributed to reinforce the group identity of the participants, which at least in the case of the *hetaireiai* could be associated with anti-democratic tendencies (Thuc. 3.82.5–6; 8.54.4; Lys. 12.43; 14.25).[74] Performance of songs and poetry provided an opportunity to recall meaningful episodes from the

---

[71] See Thomas 1989: 108–9. The other examples offered by Thomas cannot be securely associated with transmission within the family (Pl. *Lysis* 205b–e), do not attribute a claim of mythical ancestry to a family tradition (Hdt. 5.57) or do not mention mythical ancestors at all (Pl. *Alcib.* I 104a–c, 112c).

[72] Cf. also Pl. *Leg.* 10.887c–d. See Veyne [1983] 1988: 43.

[73] Murray [1980] 1993: 207–12 and 1990a: 5–7; Fisher 2000; Lynch 2013; Węcowski 2014: 27–55.

[74] Murray 1990b; Hobden 2013: 117–56, esp. 140–54; Canevaro 2016b: 61–3. But the institution of the symposium was not inherently anti-democratic, and, as shown by Fisher 2000: 356–61, sympotic practices in classical Athens were relatively widespread even outside the elite.

past.[75] Some fragments of elegiac poetry, a genre traditionally associated with the symposium, show an interest in the past. Xenophanes, for example, reflects on the importance for the symposiasts to recall noble actions (ἐσθλά) and avoid invented stories (πλάσματα), such as battles against Titans, Giants and Centaurs, as well as stories about civil strife (Xenophanes fr. 1.19–24 West). Tyrtaeus recalls episodes from Spartan history (Tyrtaeus frr. 2.12–15; 5 West); Mimnermus provides a brief narrative of the colonisation of Smyrna (Mimnermus fr. 9 West), and a poem on a battle between Smyrna and the Lydian king Gyges is also attributed to him (Paus. 9.29.4). A long fragment of the 'New Simonides', which might have been originally destined for public performance at a festival, provides a historical narrative of the Battle of Plataea and includes a comparison with Trojan myth (Simon. fr. 11 West). Athenian history was one of the themes of sympotic *skolia*. The Aristotelian *Constitution of the Athenians*, for example, quotes one such song devoted to the Battle of Leipsydrion ([Arist.] *Ath. Pol.* 19.3 = *PMG* 907), while several drinking-songs celebrating the Tyrannicides are attested from other sources (*PMG* 893–6).[76]

The mythical past also had a place in the symposium. Mythical scenes were often depicted on vase shapes traditionally associated with the symposium such as kraters and kylikes. Popular subjects included Heracles' labours, Theseus' exploits, and episodes from the Trojan War, but the thematic range was very broad.[77] Another medium for the recollection of myth at the symposium may have been epinician poetry. Scholars have now recognised the symposium as a possible context for the performance, or at least re-performance, of epinicia.[78] The re-performance of epinicia in Athenian symposia, in particular, is attested by a passage in Aristophanes' *Clouds* where Strepsiades blames his son, Pheidippides, for refusing to sing an epinicion by Simonides during a symposium (Ar. *Nub.* 1355–8). Myth was an important component of epinician poetry, and even though we do not know which epinicia were popular in Athenian symposia, it is safe to assume that they too showed some involvement with the mythical past. If one takes Pindar's victory odes as a standard for the genre, it appears that epinician poetry used myth to several ends. These ranged from providing

---

[75] For an overview of poetry in the symposium, see E. L. Bowie 1986: 15–21 and 1993: 358–66; Gerber 1997: 7; Carey 2009: 30–8.

[76] Rösler 1990; Grethlein 2010: 54–72; Steinbock 2013a: 76–80.

[77] For examples of mythical scenes depicted on Greek pottery, including Attic shapes associated with the symposium, see in general Carpenter 1991 and Lissarrague 2001. A significant portion of the evidence, however, was made for the export market, and according to Lynch 2011: 103 the Athenian market tended to avoid domestic pottery with mythical themes. Even if that was the case, the fact that Athenian potters produced vases depicting some specific myths demonstrates, if not use, at least knowledge of such myths.

[78] Kurke 1991: 5; Currie 2004; Morrison 2007; Grethlein 2010: 41. This view has been partly challenged by Budelmann 2012.

the victor with a heroic equivalent (Pind. Ol. 1.75–111; Pyth. 6.28–46) to illustrating a maxim through a mythical example (Pind. Pyth. 1.50–7; 2.20–30).[79] Finally, Plato's *Symposium* attests that myth was also a possible topic of conversation among symposiasts. Upon Eryximachus' advice, the characters in the dialogue decide to each give a speech in praise of love. In his speech, Phaedrus illustrates the power of love with the help of some mythical *exempla*. He recalls the stories of Alcestis, who chose to die for her husband Admetus, and Achilles, who went to the rescue of his lover Patroclus despite knowing that this would lead to his own death. While Alcestis and Achilles were rewarded by the gods for their actions, Phaedrus states that Orpheus was punished because he did not have the courage to die for Eurydice (Pl. *Symp.* 179b–80b).

Some Athenians would also have been familiar with the mythical past of the city through the writings of the Atthidographers. These were the authors of the local histories of Attica known as *Atthides* and now only available in fragmentary form. The Atthidographers recorded (mainly, but not exclusively oral) traditions about the history, topography, religion and institutions of Athens and Attica, which they transmitted in chronicle format. Hellanicus of Lesbos (*FGrHist* 323a), author of several mythographic and ethnographic works during the late fifth century, is usually considered the initiator of the genre. His example was followed by a series of Athenian authors active during the fourth and third centuries, among whom Androtion (*FGrHist* 324) and Philochorus (*FGrHist* 328) are the best preserved.[80] Based on the evidence available on local historians from other areas of the Greek world, it can be suggested that the works of the Atthidographers acquired some level of popularity (Dion. Hal. *Thuc.* 6–7) through written consultation (*IPrien* 37.107–23; *Miletos* 27.5–12) and oral performances (Polyb. 9.1.2–5; Dion. Hal. *Ant. Rom.* 1.8.3; cf. Thuc. 1.22.4).[81]

Athens' mythical past featured heavily in the *Atthides*. Based on the available evidence, Theseus was unsurprisingly the most popular character. The myth of the Minotaur, for example, was narrated by Hellanicus (*FGrHist* 323a F 14), Cleidemus (*FGrHist* 323 F 17), Demon (*FGrHist* 327 F 5) and Philochorus (*FGrHist* 328 F 17a–c, 111), who provided disagreeing versions of the story. Theseus' abduction of Antiope and the Attic Amazonomachy similarly featured in Hellanicus (*FGrHist* 323a F 16a; 17a–c), Cleidemus (*FGrHist* 323 F 18) and

---

[79] On the functions of myth in epinician poetry, see Rutherford 2011.
[80] Jacoby 1949: 86–107; Harding 2008: 1–10; Clarke 2008: 175–93; Thomas 2019: 321–53.
[81] Tober 2017; Thomas 2019: 29–73. Clarke 2008: 313–54 suggests that local histories (including the *Atthides*) were performed publicly at the *polis* level, but her argument depends mostly on a series of Hellenistic honorific inscriptions for local historians. It is therefore unlikely (though not impossible) that the works of the Atthidographers were recited in the public, institutional settings of the democracy during the Classical period.

Philochorus (*FGrHist* 328 F 110), while several Atthidographers told stories about Theseus' abductions of several women (*FGrHist* 323a F 18–20; 325 F 27; 328 F 18a–c; cf. also *FGrHist* 334 F 10). Many other myths, however, are attested in the surviving fragments of the Atthidographers. The earlier mythical kings and their families are frequently attested: this is the case of, for instance, Cecrops (*FGrHist* 328 F 93–8) and his daughters (*FGrHist* 323a F 1; 324 F 1; 328 F 10, 105–6; cf. also *FGrHist* 334 F 27), Erichthonius (*FGrHist* 323a F 2; 324 F 2; 328 F 8–9), and Erechtheus (*FGrHist* 323 F 19; 325 F 4; 328 F 11, 13). Stories concerning the mythical origins of the Areopagus were transmitted by Hellanicus (*FGrHist* 323a F 1, 22a–b), Androtion (*FGrHist* 324 F 4b) and Philochorus (*FGrHist* 328 F 3, 20c),[82] but many other episodes and characters are attested up until the end of the monarchy.[83]

It can be concluded that myth was a significant presence in the private lives of many Athenians. It is plausible that the Athenians first came into contact with myth in the family thanks to nursery rhymes and stories that were passed down generations. Young and adult Athenians could also interact with myth at symposia through the scenes depicted on sympotic pottery, learned conversation among symposiasts, and possibly the re-performance of epinician poetry. Atthidography constituted a further medium for the preservation of traditions on Athens' mythical past. The impact of private contexts on the mythical knowledge of the Athenians cannot be precisely quantified, nor is it possible to identify particularly popular themes. The family, the symposium and the writings of the Atthidographers, however, along with the constant use of myth in public contexts, probably contributed to the Athenians' familiarity with the Greek mythical tradition at large.

MYTHS AND VARIANTS IN DEMOCRATIC ATHENS

The analysis of the use of myth in the institutions of Athenian democracy and in private contexts has shown that myth was a constant presence in the life of the Athenians during the classical period. The dramatic festivals combined great popularity with an exceptional thematic range and provided the bulk of the Athenians' mythical knowledge. Myth was central to the Panathenaea and featured not only on the façades of the public buildings which formed the landscape of the festival but also in the rhapsodic and dithyrambic contests within the programme. Orators often employed mythical allusions at the state funeral for the war dead and in the lawcourts, while myth had a rather

---

[82] Cf. also *FGrHist* 334 F 14.
[83] For an overview of Athens' mythical past in the Atthidographers, see Harding 2008: 13–85.

minor role in the Assembly and possibly in the Council. Finally, the Athenians also engaged with myth privately, through the family, the symposium and the writings of the Atthidographers. To acquire a fuller understanding of the mythical knowledge of the Athenians, however, it is necessary to determine the range of mythical variants deployed in the institutions and private contexts of classical Athens. This section therefore looks at some myths which appear in multiple versions in sources available to fifth- and fourth-century Athenians. These examples are evidence of the Athenians' significant familiarity with the Greek mythical tradition in all its complexity, which is in turn indicative of their ability to appreciate the ideological value of different mythical variants.

In the *Panathenaicus*, Isocrates defends his choice of the peaceful over the bellicose version of the myth of Adrastus (Isoc. 12.168–74). In the peaceful version, the Athenians sent ambassadors to Thebes and obtained the return of the bodies of the Seven through diplomacy. In the bellicose version, which Isocrates admits to having used in the *Panegyricus*, the Athenians achieved the same result by going to war against the Thebans (Isoc. 4.54–9). Isocrates may have been particularly well versed in Greek mythology, but most Athenians would similarly have been familiar with both versions from drama.[84] Plutarch informs us that the peaceful version, also adopted by the Atthidographer Philochorus, featured in Aeschylus' *Eleusinians* (Plut. *Thes.* 29.4–5). The bellicose version is instead found in Euripides' *Suppliant Women*. It is possible that fourth-century Athenians knew both plays thanks to the re-performance of old tragedies at the dramatic festivals, but the popularity of the bellicose version may have been enhanced thanks to the orators. This variant features in all the funeral speeches that mention the myth of Adrastus (Lys. 2.7–10; Pl. *Menex.* 239b; Dem. 60.8), and appears to have been the standard version at the state funeral for the war dead. The bellicose version also appears in the speech delivered by Procles of Phlius in front of the Athenian Assembly (Xen. *Hell.* 6.5.46–8) and may have been the natural choice for envoys when asking for Athenian military intervention.[85] A third version of the myth existed, according to which the Seven received burials in Thebes. This variant appears twice in Pindar's victory odes (Pind. *Ol.* 6.12–17; *Nem.* 9.23–5), and it cannot be ruled out that it made its way into Athens thanks to the re-performance of epinician poetry during symposia.[86]

---

[84] Isocrates himself suggests that his readers will probably be familiar with the story of Adrastus, having heard it from the tragedians at the Dionysia (Isoc. 12.168–9).
[85] The bellicose version features also in Isocrates' *Plataicus*, where the Plataeans ask Athens' help in restoring their city, which had been destroyed by the Thebans (Isoc. 14.53–5). On the nature and destination of Isocrates' *Plataicus*, which was probably not composed for actual delivery by the Plataeans in front of the Athenian Assembly, see p. 205 with references.
[86] On the myth of Adrastus and its variants, see pp. 183–5; see also Gotteland 2001: 198–213; Steinbock 2013a: 155–210; Hanink 2013: 302–8.

The myth of Adrastus is a particularly fitting example, but it is by no means the only myth for which multiple variants are attested in classical Athens. In Plato's *Symposium*, for example, Phaedrus praises Achilles for having died to avenge the death of his lover (*erastēs*) Patroclus. As Phaedrus himself states, however, Aeschylus in the *Myrmidons* portrayed Patroclus not as Achilles' *erastēs*, but as his beloved (*eromenos*) (Pl. *Symp*. 179e–80a). To defend his own version, Phaedrus recalls how Homer stated that Achilles was the younger of the two (Hom. *Il*. 11.785–7), which would implicitly make him the *eromenos*. Aeschines seems to follow Aeschylus in making Achilles the *erastēs* in the speech *Against Timarchus*. There, the orator insists that Menoetius had entrusted (παρακαταθεῖτο) Patroclus to Achilles, and that Achilles had accepted to take care of him out of love (Aeschin. 1.143).[87] Phaedrus' version is instead confirmed by an Attic red-figure cup, dated c. 500 BC (Fig. 2.1). In the interior of the cup, which an Athenian would have used in a sympotic context, a hairless Achilles mends a wound of a bearded Patroclus.[88]

Several variants about the myth of Philoctetes circulated in Athens thanks to the theatre. In Sophocles' *Philoctetes*, Odysseus goes to Lemnos together with Neoptolemus to fetch Philoctetes' bow. According to Dio Chrysostom, Aeschylus instead portrayed Odysseus as acting alone, whereas Euripides showed him accompanied by Diomedes (Dio Chrys. 52.14).[89] Euripides' version came closest to the one told in the cyclic *Little Iliad*, which the Athenians may have

Figure 2.1 Achilles and Patroclus. Red-figure cup from Vulci (c. 500 BC). Berlin, Antikensammlung F 2278. Image © Antikensammlung, Staatliche Museen zu Berlin – Preussischer Kulturbesitz (J. Laurentius).

---

[87] See Fisher 2001: 290.
[88] *LIMC* s.v. Achilleus 468.
[89] At least three more *Philoctetes* tragedies are known to have been produced by minor tragedians (*TrGF* 20 F 37; 24 post F 1; 72 F 5b), but not enough survives to determine what version of the myth they dramatised.

heard from the rhapsodes at the Panathenaea.[90] If we believe Proclus, in the poem Philoctetes was brought back to Troy by Diomedes (Procl. *Chr.* 211–13). Another version, found in Pindar, may have been known to the Athenians in the context of the symposium. The poet vaguely states that the godlike heroes brought Philoctetes back from Lemnos (Pind. *Pyth.* 1.50–3). A fragmentary Attic red-figure cup dated to c. 460 BC also exemplifies a version of the myth destined for a sympotic context, and shows Philoctetes seated together with Odysseus and another character, possibly Diomedes or Neoptolemus.[91] Finally, if we believe Pausanias, a painting which showed Diomedes bringing back Philoctetes' bow could be admired in a building on the left of the Propylaea (Paus. 1.22.6).

The myth of Oedipus, which provided the subject for the epic *Oedipodia*, was a popular theme on the tragic stage. The Athenians knew the story in several variants. For example, Oedipus famously blinds himself in Sophocles' *Oedipus the King* after he discovers Jocasta's dead body (Soph. *OT* 1265–79). The self-blinding must have also featured in Aeschylus' *Oedipus*, as one can assume based on a passage in the *Seven against Thebes*, which followed *Oedipus* in the trilogy (Aesch. *Sept.* 778–84). A different version featured in Euripides' *Oedipus*, where Laius' servants blinded Oedipus while still unaware of the hero's real identity (Eur. F 541). The Great Tragedians similarly disagreed about the fate of Jocasta. The story of her suicide goes back at least to the *Odyssey*, where she is called Epicasta and hangs herself (Hom. *Od.* 11.271–80). The Athenians probably already knew the Homeric version from the rhapsodes at the Panathenaea, but they certainly encountered it on the tragic stage in the Messenger's speech in Sophocles' *Oedipus the King* (Soph. *OT* 1237–64). Euripides, on the other hand, provided a different version. In the *Phoenician Women*, Jocasta is still alive during the war between Eteocles and Polynices, and only commits suicide after the death of her two sons (Eur. *Phoen.* 1427–59). In one of the surviving fragments of Euripides' *Oedipus*, Jocasta is similarly alive after Oedipus' blinding and the two share their guilt and sorrows (Eur. F 545a.9–12).[92]

This small selection of mythical variants has illustrated the extent of the Athenians' mythical knowledge. Not only did the Athenians interact with myth at almost every level of their daily life, but they also had the opportunity to learn multiple versions through several media and institutional settings. The performance of tragedies, satyr plays and dithyrambs at the dramatic festivals, the presence of myth at the Panathenaea, the mythical allusions of the orators in several institutional settings and the use of myth in private contexts all contributed to the mythical knowledge of the Athenians and often provided them

---

[90] But performances of cyclic epics at the Panathenaea are unattested in the sources and merely hypothetical: see Burgess 2004–5.
[91] Basel, H. A. Cahn Collection, HC 1738; *LIMC* s.v. Philoktetes 55a.
[92] Gantz 1993: 499–501.

with diverging versions of the same stories. It is therefore safe to assume that, as a result of their broad mythical knowledge, the Athenians could appreciate mythical variants and their ideological value when these were deployed. This was probably even truer for those myths that tended to assume an almost fixed form in a specific institutional context, as in the case of the catalogue of the exploits in the *epitaphios logos*.

CONCLUSIONS

This chapter has demonstrated the Athenians' extensive knowledge of the Greek mythical tradition, and has shown that, for this reason, the social memory of Athens' mythical past provides a unique tool for the investigation of Athenian ideological practice. During the classical period, the Athenians engaged with myth in virtually every aspect of their public and private lives. The popularity of the theatre allowed the dramatic festivals to reach extremely broad sections of Athens' population. Because of the vast thematical range of tragedy and satyr drama (and, to a lesser extent, dithyramb), these festivals covered the entire Greek mythical tradition and provided the bulk of the mythical knowledge of the Athenians. Compared to the dramatic festivals, the Panathenaea covered a narrower range of mythical episodes, but the centrality of myth in the dithyrambic and rhapsodic contests as well as the presence of myth in the physical setting of the festival largely contributed to the Athenians' familiarity with the Homeric poems and other myths such as the Gigantomachy. The institutional settings of Athenian oratory had a relatively minor impact on the mythical knowledge of the Athenians, but the range and influence of the myths deployed varied in each of such institutions. The state funeral covered a narrow and crystallised range of mythical themes, mostly limited to Athens' mythical past. The emotional power of the funeral oration, however, probably caused the state funeral to contribute significantly to the Athenians' familiarity with those specific episodes. The lawcourts and, to a lesser degree, the Assembly and (possibly) the Council provided further arenas for the discussion of the mythical past in Athens' public life, but had a comparatively lesser potential to influence the mythical knowledge of the Athenians. The Athenians also interacted with myth in their private sphere within the family and the symposium and through the writings of the Atthidographers, whose impact on the mythical knowledge of the Athenians cannot be properly quantified. The Athenians' familiarity with the Greek mythical tradition is even more evident if one considers that they often deployed multiple versions of the same myths. The Athenians were thus capable of appreciating variations in mythical narratives, and it is safe to conclude that choosing one mythical version over another could carry ideological value.

CHAPTER 3

The Discursive Parameters of Athenian Democratic Institutions

Myth was virtually omnipresent in the private and public life of the Athenians. Their extensive knowledge of the Greek mythical tradition meant that the Athenians were potentially able to appreciate the ideological value of different mythical variants. But how could the Athenians use myth (and public discourse in general) to construct their shared ideas and values? This chapter makes the case that this process of ideological practice was enabled and influenced by the institutions of the democracy, and shows that Athenian democratic institutions conditioned the behaviour of Athenian political actors and the construction of Athenian democratic ideology through sets of discursive parameters distinctive to each institution.

The outcome of this chapter is twofold. On the one hand, it establishes a solid framework for the analysis of the specific uses of myth in Athenian ideological practice carried out in my case studies (Chapters 4 to 7). On the other, it illustrates some of the characteristics of Athenian democratic ideology described in the Introduction (Chapter 1). It highlights the constructive function of ideology typical of the culturalist tradition as well as the normative value characteristic of the Marxist tradition. More importantly, it shows the bidirectional nature of Athenian democratic ideology due to the contribution of both the mass and the elite to the process of ideological practice taking place within Athenian democratic institutions. I shall thus investigate the nature and functions of the state funeral for the war dead, the lawcourts, the Assembly and the Council, and the dramatic festivals, and determine the discursive parameters of these institutions and the respective roles played by the mass and the elite acting within them.

THE STATE FUNERAL FOR THE WAR DEAD

The ideological relevance of the state funeral for the war dead and the funeral speech (*epitaphios logos*) has been long emphasised.[1] Nicole Loraux, in particular, interpreted the funeral oration as ideological in the sense that it concealed Athens' internal divisions and imperial vocation.[2] As I have suggested in the Introduction, the *epitaphios logos* and the state funeral should be read in the light of the notion of 'imagined community' elaborated by Benedict Anderson.[3] According to Anderson, any community larger than face-to-face is an imagined community. The act of imagining is what keeps the members together and enables them not only to die for their country but also to act as a community.[4] I argue that the state funeral was ideological in the sense that, by means of an idealised narrative performed through several media, it constructed strong civic bonds within the Athenian community. This does not mean to deny that the state funeral performed further honorific and consolatory functions – they were integrated within the main purpose of the ceremony, and were constitutive of it. The casualty lists that accompanied the graves of the war dead, for example, resembled other Athenian lists in that they honoured the fallen for their service to the city and implicitly urged other people to imitate them.[5] Moreover, funeral speeches usually included a consolation directed to the relatives of the dead.[6] However, if one analyses the extant funeral speeches within their physical and ritual setting, it is clear that the state funeral's main purpose was the creation of an imagined community, and that such a function informed the discursive parameters of this institution.

The practice of the public burial of the war dead is itself revealing of a desire to build an imagined community. Attending to the bodies of the dead was traditionally a private matter pertaining to the sphere of the family, and private grave markers for wealthy Athenians who fell in battle, including for example the famous Anavysos Kouros, are attested during the sixth century. At some point between the sixth and the fifth century, the *polis* started to bury the war dead

---

[1] See notably Loraux 1981. Major studies of the state funeral and the *epitaphios logos* include Walters 1980, Loraux 1981, Thomas 1989: 196–237, Parker 1996a: 132–5, Prinz 1997, Low 2010, Shear 2013 and Arrington 2014.

[2] Loraux 1981: 340–9.

[3] See pp. 7–8.

[4] B. Anderson [1983] 2006: 5–7. On classical Athens as an imagined community, see e.g. G. Anderson 2003 and Shear 2011: 10–11.

[5] Low 2010: 344–5; Petrovic 2016: 366. On the honorific function of Athenian lists, see Liddel 2007: 196–8.

[6] Frangeskou 1998–9: 326–8. On the typical subdivision of a funeral speech into exordium, praise, exhortation and consolation, see Frangeskou 1998–9: 319.

collectively and at public expense,[7] replacing the family and supplanting traditional burial practices.[8] Through a complex discursive strategy which involved both the mass and the elite, a painful and potentially divisive occasion such as the death of one's relatives for the sake of the community was turned into a public event and source of social cohesion.[9] An important component of this strategy was the erection of casualty lists in the public burial ground (*dēmosion sēma*), which shows a concern for the creation of a community of the dead.[10] Inscribed on tall marble slabs, casualty lists usually open with the heading 'these men died' or similar phrasings (*IG* I^3 1147; 1162; 1166; 1183; 1191; 1193 bis; II^2 5221; 5222), and they often indicate the location where the fallen lost their lives (*IG* I^3 1147; 1162; 1183; II^2 5221; 5222). The names of the dead are listed without patronymics or demotics, and organised by tribe.[11] Military functions, such as 'general' (*IG* I^3 1147.5; 1162.4) or 'trierarch' (*IG* I^3 1166.2; 1186.108), are sometimes stated, and foreigners (*IG* I^3 1144.34 and 118, 1162.96) and even slaves (*IG* I^3 1144.139) are occasionally included.[12] The inclusion of military titles on the casualty lists shows that individuality, far from being repressed, was publicly acknowledged.[13] This impression is confirmed by Pausanias, who attests the presence of separate monuments for the cavalry in the *dēmosion sēma* (Paus. 1.29.3–15).[14] The absence of demotics and patronymics from the casualty

---

[7] The date of institution of the state funeral has attracted great scholarly interest. Proposed dates range from the age of Solon to the 460s: see Jacoby 1944; Gomme 1956: 94–8; Stupperich 1977; Loraux 1981: 49–52; Clairmont 1983: 7–15; Pritchett 1985: 112–24; Hornblower 1991: 292–3; Prinz 1997: 38–48; Arrington 2014: 39–49.

[8] See Arrington 2014: 66–7. For a possible mass burial (*polyandrion*) dating from the late fifth century recently discovered in the Ceramicus, see Stoupa 1997. The archaeological record shows that lavish private burials in Athens disappeared around 500 BC and reappeared around 420 BC: see Morris 1992: 128–55 and 1994. For a comprehensive study of Attic private grave reliefs, see Bergemann 1997.

[9] See Shear 2013: 513.

[10] For the idea of a community of the dead, see Arrington 2014: 96. For a detailed analysis of the functions of casualty lists, see Arrington 2011. Outside Athens, one can mention the stele of the Marathonomachoi originally set up in Marathon and found at Eua-Loukou, whose authenticity is debated: see Proietti 2013 and Tentori Montalto 2014 for two opposing views on the subject.

[11] But cf. Paus. 1.29.4, who maintains that the casualty lists stated the demes of the fallen. Given the paucity of surviving fourth-century casualty lists, it has been suggested that these monuments may have started including demotics at some point during the fourth century: see Arrington 2011: 189–90.

[12] Low 2012: 14–15; Arrington 2011: 183–4.

[13] Liddel 2007: 288–9; Low 2012: 16–23.

[14] Clairmont 1983: 3–4, 38, 40–1, 44; Low 2012: 31–2; Arrington 2014: 86–8. See also Barringer 2014, who suggests that the *dēmosion sēma* also hosted freestanding equestrian monuments for fallen knights.

lists, however, reveals a concern for egalitarianism.[15] The differences between the citizens were levelled by their death for the democratic city.[16] At the same time, the arrangement of the names by tribe framed the individual contribution of the fallen into the institutional structure of the democracy and invited the survivors to perceive the dead as members of the Athenian community.[17]

Casualty lists were not the only medium that enabled the Athenians to channel individual losses into the construction of an imagined community. The same dynamics between individual and collective can be detected in the *epitaphios logos*. The role of individuality in the funeral oration has been traditionally considered a minor one.[18] Extant funeral speeches, however, mention several named individuals. Themistocles features in two preserved speeches (Lys. 2.42; Hyp. 6.37–8), Miltiades is mentioned in Hyperides' speech (Hyp. 6.37–8) and Myronides is recalled by Lysias (Lys. 2.52). Hyperides' entire speech is dedicated to the fallen general Leosthenes. When one considers that Thucydides and the extant fragments of Gorgias' speech do not include historical narratives and that Demosthenes compresses Athens' historical exploits into two paragraphs (Dem. 60.10–11), the instances of named individuals in funeral speeches are proportionately not as rare as has previously been suggested. Yet, if some of the speeches acknowledge the contribution of named individuals to the common cause, it remains true that the *epitaphios logos* usually provides a version of Athenian history whose protagonists are the Athenians as a whole.

By acknowledging the individual sacrifice of the fallen through a collective form of commemoration, casualty lists and funeral speeches attempted to create a sense of community among the survivors. The same purpose was also attained through the rituals performed during the ceremony. These included musical, athletic and hippic contests (Lys. 2.80; Pl. *Menex.* 249b3–6; Dem. 60.13, 36; [Arist.] *Ath. Pol.* 58.1) as well as sacrifices (Pl. *Menex.* 244a3–6; Dem. 60.36) in honour of the dead.[19] As Julia Shear has recently pointed out,

---

[15] This is particularly evident in some lists which feature duplicates of the same name within the same tribe, thus making it impossible to distinguish between different individuals, let alone their socio-economic status. *IG* I³ 1147, for example, includes three men named Glaucon, three named Philinus, two named Lysias and two named Callicles. *IG* I³ 1162 features two men named Pythodorus among the dead of Erechtheis, and two men named Aristarchus among those of Cecropis.

[16] Loraux 1981: 44. But patronymics are similarly absent from a casualty list from Thespiae (*IG* VII 1888), which shows that the use of the war dead to create an imagined community may not have been limited to Athens or the democracy: see Low 2003.

[17] If one believes Petrovic 2016, this process may have been facilitated by the oral performance of the casualty lists during the state funeral.

[18] See notably Loraux 1981. Hesk 2013 has rightly argued for a revaluation of individuality in the *epitaphios logos*.

[19] Clairmont 1983: 22–8; Parker 1996a: 133–7.

these rituals cooperated with the funeral speech and the physical environment of the *dēmosion sēma* in preserving the memory of the dead and generating unity among the mourners.[20] Together with the collective decision to erect casualty lists, participation in these rituals allowed the mass to exercise a direct agency in the process of ideological practice taking place at the state funeral for the war dead.

Despite the image of cohesion conveyed by the casualty lists, the *epitaphios logos* and the rituals at the state funeral, death for the city remained a potentially problematic issue. The painful reality of war and its dangers appear, for example, in the epigrams and reliefs that were sometimes attached to the casualty lists. Funerary epigrams commemorated the fallen by lamenting their death in battle and celebrating their *aretē* and the glory they conferred upon the city (*IG* I^3 503/504; 1162.45–8; 1163.34–41; 1179.10–13; II^2 5225). Such epigrams are usually vague about the outcome of the battle, whether a victory or a defeat,[21] but focus on the struggle and death of the warriors and sometimes state the location where the battle took place.[22] The few figural reliefs securely attributed to casualty lists similarly depict battles whose outcome is undecided. These scenes focus on the ongoing struggle and its violence, and highlight the dangers the fallen warriors undertook for the safety of the city.[23] Such sacrifices on behalf of the *polis* needed to be justified to the relatives of the dead. To do so, it was necessary to create an image of the city with which most citizens would identify and for which they would be willing (and proud) to fight and even die.

To create such an image was the task of the orator chosen to perform the funeral oration. The speech illustrates the role of (mostly) elite political actors in the ideological practice that took place at the state funeral. The orators cooperated with the physical and ritual setting of the funeral in building an imagined community, and thus exemplified the constructive value of ideology. An important aspect of this process was the idealisation of Athenian democracy. By providing an ideal picture of the Athenian constitution and its advantages, orators of funeral speeches gave the Athenians a reason to fight for the city. Pericles, for example, praises the democracy for attributing deliberative power to the many instead of the few, establishing equality before the laws and granting access to the magistracies according to merit (Thuc. 2.37.1). Pericles then lists other advantages of Athenian democracy, such as the citizens' respect for

---

[20] Shear 2013.
[21] The only exception is the inscribed base for the Marathon cenotaph (*IG* I^3 503/504), which alludes to the dead having 'kept all Greece from seeing the day of slavery' (trans. E. L. Bowie).
[22] Low 2010: 346–7; Arrington 2014: 99, 105–7.
[23] Cf. Oxford, Ashmolean Museum, Michaelis no. 85; Athens, Third Ephoreia M 4551; Athens, National Archaeological Museum 2744. See Arrington 2011: 196–202.

the magistrates and the laws, and the celebration of several games and sacrifices throughout the year (Thuc. 2.37.3–38.1). Lysias explains that the ancestors established the democracy because they thought that the freedom of all was the greatest form of concord (Lys. 2.18). Demosthenes states that democracy has many noble features, and focuses in particular on freedom of speech (Dem. 60.26). Socrates ironically praises the democracy as a form of aristocracy because the magistracies are assigned to those who appear to be the best, and he commends the Athenians' equality of birth (Pl. *Menex.* 238b–39a).

The construction of an idealised picture of the democracy was coupled with the production of shared memories about Athens' past. This process served to build an imagined community because it exemplified what it meant to be an Athenian and what were the values that informed Athenian actions. Most funeral speeches include a narrative of Athenian mythical and historical exploits. These mostly consist of catalogues of Athenian victories. Defeats, when acknowledged, are addressed in a justificatory tone. Lysias thus attributes the defeat at Aegospotami to the incompetence of a general or the design of the gods and portrays it as further evidence of the valour of the ancestors (Lys. 2.58–60). Plato justifies the defeat in the Sicilian expedition, which he imputes to the lack of reinforcements due to the long distance from Athens (Pl. *Menex.* 242e6–243a7),[24] and goes as far as to claim the Peloponnesian War as an Athenian victory (Pl. *Menex.* 243c–d).[25] Funeral speeches often invite the Athenians to imitate the great deeds of their ancestors or the sacrifice of the dead of the day.[26] Pericles exhorts the survivors to have an attitude as brave as that of their relatives against the enemy (Thuc. 2.43.1). Lysias states that everyone should remember the actions of the ancestors and educate the living in the deeds of the dead (Lys. 2.3). The orator then praises the men of the Piraeus (Lys. 2.61) and the present dead (Lys. 2.69) for having imitated the virtue of the ancestors. Demosthenes praises each Athenian tribe for having emulated their respective eponymous heroes (Dem. 60.27–31). Socrates highlights the paradigmatic value of the Marathonomachoi (Pl. *Menex.* 240d–e) and invites the Athenians to remember and imitate the actions of their fathers and ancestors (Pl. *Menex.* 246b–c; 248e). Hyperides praises Leosthenes and his companions because they did not dishonour the acts of valour of their ancestors (Hyp. 6.32), and he then states that the general even surpassed those who fought alongside Miltiades and Themistocles (Hyp. 6.37–8).

---

[24] See Nouhaud 1982: 272–3.
[25] Demosthenes adopts a similar justificatory tone towards the present dead, as he blames their defeat at Chaeronea on the Theban commanders (Dem. 60.22).
[26] The educational function of the *epitaphios logos* has been highlighted by Grethlein 2010: 119–21, Shear 2013: 518–21 and Steinbock 2013b: 77.

The ancestral exploits symbolised the values that an Athenian was expected to possess. In this lies the normative value of ideology. As shown by the frequent exhortations to imitate the ancestors, the speech was not simply meant to describe, but rather to mould the typical Athenian *ethos*. Orators of funeral speeches thus constructed an idealised image of Athens, which was presented as supremely just and devoted to the cause of *philanthrōpia* and Greek freedom. These features are summarised at the beginning of Hyperides' speech. The orator states that Athens 'continuously punishes the wicked, [gives aid] to the just (τοῖς δὲ δικαίοις βοηθοῦσα), [dispenses] equality instead of injustice (τὸ δὲ ἴσον ἀντί τῆς ἀδικίας) to all, and provides [universal safety] (κοινὴν ἄδειαν) to the Greeks at its own [risk] and expense (τοῖς δὲ ἰδίοις κινδύνοις καὶ δαπάναις)' (Hyp. 6.5, trans. Herrman). Gorgias states that the Athenians are helpers of those who unjustly suffer misfortunes and punishers of those who are unjustly fortunate (θεράποντες μὲν τῶν ἀδίκως δυστυχούντων, κολασταὶ δὲ τῶν ἀδίκως εὐτυχούντων) (DK Gorg. B 6). Demosthenes, when introducing his brief section on the Athenian exploits, maintains that the ancestors never wronged anyone (ἠδίκησαν μὲν οὐδένα) and were extremely just (δικαιοτάτοις εἶναι) (Dem. 60.7). Lysias similarly insists on justice as the driving force of Athenian actions. This is especially evident in the case of the mythical exploits, but it also appears in relation to the historical exploits. When during the Persian Wars the Peloponnesians built a wall on the Isthmus of Corinth, the Athenians admonished them for abandoning the rest of the Greeks. The Peloponnesians therefore went to their aid in Plataea, because they realised that their own actions were unjust (ἄδικά τε ποιεῖν) and what the Athenians were saying was right (δίκαιά τε λέγειν) (Lys. 2.45–6). Lysias similarly praises those Athenians who in 403, fighting for what was right (περὶ τοῦ δικαίου μαχόμενοι), returned to the Piraeus and restored the democracy (Lys. 2.61).

The Athenians' devotion to justice is a component of their traditional *philanthrōpia*, which leads them to act as selfless champions of the weak and injured. Lysias, for instance, explains that the Persians attacked Athens before any other city because they knew that the Athenians would have gone to the rescue of anyone who suffered injustice (τοῖς ἀδικουμένοις ἥξουσι βοηθήσοντες) (Lys. 2.22). By the same token, Lysias praises the dead of the day for having helped their previous enemies, the Corinthians, when they had been injured (βοηθήσαντες Κορινθίοις ἀδικουμένοις) by the Spartans (Lys. 2.67–8). Plato makes the paradoxical statement that Athens, being 'compassionate to excess and the handmaid of the weak (τοῦ ἥττονος θεραπίς)' (Pl. *Menex*. 244e–45a; trans. Lamb), even went to the rescue of her worst enemy, the King of Persia. Connected with Athenian *philanthrōpia* is Athens' role as bulwark of Greek freedom. This image is central to epitaphic narratives about the Persian Wars. Lysias, for example, praises the Athenian ancestors because they 'were the only ones to undergo dangers (μόνοι διεκινδύνευσαν) against countless myriads of barbarians, on behalf of the whole of Greece (ὑπὲρ ἁπάσης τῆς Ἑλλάδος)' (Lys. 2.20; trans. Todd).[27] Plato praises the Marathonomachoi as the fathers of the freedom of all the inhabitants of the continent (τοὺς ἄνδρας φημὶ οὐ μόνον τῶν σωμάτων τῶν ἡμετέρων πατέρας εἶναι, ἀλλὰ καὶ τῆς ἐλευθερίας τῆς τε ἡμετέρας καὶ συμπάντων τῶν ἐν τῇδε τῇ ἠπείρῳ) (Pl. *Menex.* 240e). Demosthenes similarly glorifies the Athenians who fought against the Persians because they achieved the common safety of the Greeks (κοινῆς σωτηρίας πᾶσι τοῖς Ἕλλησιν) through their own individual dangers (διὰ τῶν ἰδίων κινδύνων) (Dem. 60.10).

The idealised image of Athens' *philanthrōpia* and commitment to Greek freedom is reflected also in the treatment of Athenian imperialism in the *epitaphios logos*. Funeral speeches either ignore the Athenian Empire,[28] or highlight the positive rather than exploitative nature of Athenian imperialism.[29] The latter option is best represented by Lysias, who conceptualises imperialism in terms compatible with *philanthrōpia*.[30] While the Amazon and Persian Empires

---

[27] Cf. also Lys. 2.33, 42, 44, 55–7, 60.
[28] Cf. DK Gorg. B 5a–6; Dem. 60; Pl. *Menex.*; Hyp. 6.
[29] Pericles' funeral oration is a notable exception. Not only does Pericles praise the previous generation for acquiring the Empire (κτησάμενοι ... ὅσην ἔχομεν ἀρχήν) and the current generation for expanding it (τὰ δὲ πλείω αὐτῆς αὐτοὶ ἡμεῖς ... ἐπηυξήσαμεν) (Thuc. 2.36.2–3), but he also refers to the allies as subjects under Athenian rule (μόνη οὔτε ... ἔχει ... τῷ ὑπηκόῳ κατάμεμψιν ὡς οὐχ ὑπ' ἀξίων ἄρχεται) (Thuc. 2.41.3). Pericles' crude view of the Empire, however, may be influenced by Thucydides' interest in imperialism and power dynamics (on which see D. Cohen 1984) and is paralled in the theme and tone of many other Athenian speeches reported by the historian: cf. e.g. Thuc. 1.75–7; 2.62–4; 3.37–40, 44–8; 5.89–99; 6.10–11, 17–18. One may also argue that the different approach to Athenian imperialism in fourth-century funeral speeches as opposed to Pericles' attitude was due to the loss of the Empire at the end of the Peloponnesian War. But see Badian 1995, who showed that the recovery of the Empire was a persisting feature of Athenian policies throughout the fourth century.
[30] *Pace* Loraux 1981: 101–20, this does not imply that Athenian democratic ideology, by means of the *epitaphios logos*, masked the reality of the Empire with the image of a benevolent hegemony. As noted by Low 2007: 199–210, Greek attitudes towards imperialism were ambivalent, and the distinction between the negative 'empire' (*archē*) and the positive 'hegemony' (*hegemonia*) was not always as clear-cut as it is often assumed: see n. 33 below. For positive references to imperialism in Athenian deliberative oratory, cf. e.g. Dem. 3.24; 8.60; Xen. *Hell.* 3.5.10–15; for negative references, cf. e.g. Dem. 8.41–2; 9.24–5. Athenian imperialism is harshly criticised in Isocrates' *On the Peace*, which, however, was not meant for public discourse: cf. Isoc. 8.42–4, 64–6, 85–8. If one considers that Athenian imperialism was openly acknowledged in other *loci* of ideological practice, such as the Assembly (cf. references above) and public inscriptions (e.g. the use of *hegemonia* or *hegemonē* as trireme names: cf. *IG* II² 1612.111, 122; 1618.110; 1629.771, 845; 1631.133, 202), it is clear that Athenian democratic ideology did not conceal imperialism as much as it adapted it to the discursive parameters of different institutions.

are portrayed as prone to the enslavement and domination of their subjects,³¹ the Athenian hegemony of Greece is described as acquired upon universal consent (ὑπὸ πάντων ἠξιώθησαν ... ἡγεμόνες γενέσθαι τῆς Ἑλλάδος) after the Battle of Plataea (Lys. 2.47). Lysias then states that the Athenians liberated Greece (ἐλευθέραν μὲν ἐποίησαν τὴν Ἑλλάδα) and ruled the sea (τῆς θαλάττης ἄρξαντες) for seventy years. During this period, they enabled their allies to be free from civil strife (ἀστασιάστους), enforced equality (τὸ ἴσον) in place of the slavery (δουλεύειν) of the many by the few,³² and made their allies stronger instead of weakening them (οὐδὲ τοὺς συμμάχους ἀσθενεῖς ποιοῦντες, ἀλλὰ κἀκείνους ἰσχυροὺς καθιστάντες) (Lys. 2.55–6).³³ Lysias' example is followed by Hyperides. Despite not mentioning the fifth-century Empire, he too envisions Athens' hegemonic position (τὴν δ᾽ Ἑλλάδα πᾶσαν [scil. δεομένην] πόλεως, ἥτις προστῆναι δυνήσεται τῆς ἡγεμονίας) under Leosthenes' leadership as instrumental to Greek freedom (ἐπέδωκεν ... τὴν δὲ πόλιν τοῖς Ἕλλησιν εἰς τὴν ἐλευθερίαν) (Hyp. 6.10).

The narrative of the exploits in the *epitaphios logos* thus constructed an idealised image of Athens and her past. This image was expected to console the survivors for the loss of their relatives, persuading them that they had given their lives for a good cause. The catalogue of the exploits underscored the achievements of the ancestors as the supreme example of Athenian virtue and civic values, and the orators explicitly exhorted the living to remember and imitate the deeds of the fallen. In accordance with the discursive parameters of the state funeral, the orators produced an image of the city that was functional to the construction of Athens' imagined community. The criterion for the selection of mythical and historical materials was the creation of a model community with which the citizens could identify. By exalting the qualities of the democracy and providing an idealised image of Athenian history, funeral speeches gave the Athenians a city worth dying for. In the emotionally charged context of the state funeral, the orators actively shaped the memory

---

[31] According to Lysias, the Amazons ruled (ἄρχουσαι) over many nations and enslaved (καταδεδουλωμέναι) their neighbours (Lys. 2.5), while Darius invaded Greece with the hope of enslaving (δουλώσεσθαι) Europe (Lys. 2.21).

[32] But see Todd 2007: 255, who notes Lysias' aggressive language (cf. Lys. 2.56: τὸ ἴσον ἔχειν ἅπαντας ἀναγκάσαντες) and suggests that Athens' imposition of democracy on her allies may be implied.

[33] It is worth noting that Lysias uses *archē* and *hegemonia* almost interchangeably when referring to the fifth-century Empire (Lys. 2.47: ἡγεμόνες; 55: τῆς θαλάττης ἄρξαντες) and the hegemony he envisions for present-day Athenians as a consequence of their ancestral exploits (Lys. 2.57: δεῖ μόνους καὶ προστάτας τῶν Ἑλλήνων καὶ ἡγεμόνας τῶν πόλεων γίγνεσθαι). Cf. Xen. *Hell*. 3.5.10–14, where the Thebans exhort the Athenians to recover the Empire (τὴν ἀρχὴν ἣν πρότερον ἐκέκτησθε) by helping those wronged by the Spartans, just as they used to rule when they held the hegemony of those who lived on the sea (ὅτε μὲν γὰρ ἤρχετε, τῶν κατὰ θάλατταν μόνων δήπου ἡγεῖσθε): see Low 2007: 201–3 with n. 67.

of past events in order to construct and validate the identity and beliefs of the community.[34] In its etymological sense of speech upon the grave, the *epitaphios logos* fulfilled its function towards the dead by constructing an image of Athens that justified the sacrifice of the fallen and inspired their relatives to follow their example. Thanks to the catalogue of the exploits, the dead of the day ceased to be simply names inscribed on a casualty list and were assimilated into the larger Athenian tradition of death for the city commemorated by the monuments of the previous years. By means of the *epitaphios logos*, the physical environment of the *dēmosion sēma* and the ritual setting of the ceremony, the Athenian mass and elite cooperated to produce the shared memories and beliefs that they needed in order to create an imagined community and secure its unity and cohesion.

THE LAWCOURTS

The discursive parameters of the lawcourts are delineated in Aristotle's *Rhetoric*. According to the philosopher, the aim (τέλος) of the forensic orator was the just (τὸ δίκαιον) and the unjust (τὸ ἄδικον), while all other considerations could be added as accessory (Arist. *Rh.* 1358b21–8). Aristotle's definition can be further qualified. Athenian judges were bound by the Heliastic Oath to vote in accordance with the laws and decrees of the Athenian people (Aeschin. 3.6; And. 1.2; Dem. 18.121; Lys. 15.9).[35] The Heliastic Oath also compelled the judges to vote only about issues included in the written plaint that the plaintiff had to produce to initiate a lawsuit (Aeschin. 1.154; Dem. 45.50).[36] At the court hearing, the litigants similarly swore an oath which bound them to keep to the point and not to speak outside the subject ([Arist.] *Ath. Pol.* 67.1).[37] These oaths indicate that both the mass (mostly as judges) and the elite (mostly as litigants) played a significant role in the process of ideological practice taking place at the lawcourts, and that this process was influenced by distinctive discursive parameters. Forensic orators were expected to deal not simply with issues of justice but more specifically with whether the defendant had broken a specific law, and recent studies have

---

[34] See the notion of 'intentional history' elaborated by Gehrke 2001 and 2010.

[35] The Heliastic Oath also prescribed that judges should vote according to their fairest judgement in cases where there are no laws or the laws are not clear, but such cases were very rare: see Harris 2013b: 104–14.

[36] On the jurisdiction of magistrates, see A. R. W. Harrison 1971: 7–36. On the plaint, see Harris 2013c. On the procedure to initiate a lawsuit and on the structure of court hearings, see A. R. W. Harrison 1971: 85–199; Boegehold 1995: 21–42; Hansen [1991] 1999: 196–203; Thür 2008.

[37] A similar oath was sworn by the litigants in the Council of the Areopagus (Arist. *Rh.* 1354a22–3): see Rhodes 2004: 137.

demonstrated that extant forensic speeches accordingly show a very high degree of relevance to the legal issues at stake.[38]

The available evidence shows that litigants and judges were expected to abide by their oaths. Forensic orators often mention the Heliastic Oath and the necessity of putting it into practice.[39] Demosthenes, for example, opens his speech *On the False Embassy* with an exhortation to the judges to 'hold no obligation nor any man to be of greater importance than justice and the oath' (Dem. 19.1, trans. Yunis). The speaker of Lysias' *Against the Corn Dealers* states that his accusation should be sufficient to condemn the defendants because they broke the laws and the judges swore to vote in accordance with the laws (Lys. 22.7). The speaker of Isaeus' *On the Estate of Menecles* closes his speech with an appeal to the judges to remember the law and their oath and give their verdict accordingly (Isae. 2.47). It was also common for forensic orators to accuse their opponents of speaking outside the subject. In *Against Timarchus*, for example, Aeschines anticipates Demosthenes' irrelevant arguments and invites the judges not to accept them in view of the oath they have sworn (Aeschin. 1.166–70). The speaker of Lysias' *For the Soldier* complains that his opponents have disregarded the plaint and made accusations on his character instead (Lys. 9.1). In *Against Eratosthenes*, Lysias refers to the bad habit of many speakers who pay no attention to the terms of the accusation and deceive the judges by boasting about their public service (Lys. 12.38).[40]

In accordance with the oaths sworn by litigants and judges, the discursive parameters of the lawcourts compelled forensic orators to deal with matters of justice and specific legal charges.[41] Arguments which relied on character evidence or public service, for example, were usually couched in terms of justice and lawfulness. In the speech *Against Meidias*, Demosthenes recalls the defendant's insignificant amount of public service as well as his private luxury and display in order to prove his charge of *hybris* (Dem. 21.154–9). The speaker of Isocrates' *Against Callimachus* invites the judges not to trust the defendant, whose dishonesty is proved by the fact that he once provided false testimony in court (Isoc. 18.52–7). This claim is relevant to the legal issue of the speech, since Callimachus is accused of violating the Amnesty by bringing false charges against the speaker (Isoc. 18.4). The speaker then rebuts the accusation that

---

[38] Rhodes 2004; Harris 2013b: 101–37 and 2013c. *Pace* Lanni 2006, who argues that Athenian lawcourts adopted a broader notion of relevance which encompassed both legal and extra-legal arguments; see more recently Lanni 2016: 1–14.

[39] See Harris 2013b: 101–2, 353–6.

[40] On these and other passages where the orators accuse their opponents of speaking outside the subject, see Harris 2013b: 126–8.

[41] See Harris 2013a, who has shown that the Athenians were aware of what kind of arguments were appropriate to the lawcourts as opposed to the Assembly.

he had confiscated Callimachus' money by recalling how generously he spent his wealth for the city in times of crisis and therefore was unlikely to strive for other people's money, and asks to be treated justly in view of his public service (Isoc. 18.58–67).[42]

The use of history in forensic speeches was similarly conditioned by the focus on justice and legal charges expected in the lawcourts.[43] In his speech *Against Leocrates*, Lycurgus reinforces his accusation of treason against Leocrates by comparing the attitude of the defendant to a series of mythical and historical *exempla* which illustrate the importance of the attachment to one's homeland (Lycurg. 1.83–130). The speaker of Dinarchus' *Against Demosthenes* recalls how the Athenians had punished Timotheus for taking bribes from the Chians and Rhodians despite his public service, and invites the judges to do the same against Demosthenes, who is guilty of accepting money from Harpalus (Din. 1.14–15). In his *graphē paranomon* against Ctesiphon's decree which crowned Demosthenes for his service to the city, Aeschines criticises Athens' current generosity in granting honours and compares it with the ancestors' honorary policy. The latter is shown to have been sensible, as even greater benefactors than Demosthenes, such as Themistocles, Miltiades and Aristides, were never honoured with a crown (Aeschin. 3.177–82).[44] In *Against Neaera*, Apollodorus recalls how the Athenians rightfully granted citizenship to the Plataean exiles because of their service to Athens and Greece during the Persian Wars, and contrasts their situation with that of Neaera, who is illegally behaving as a citizen ([Dem.] 59.94–107).

This brief analysis shows that the discursive parameters of the lawcourts largely influenced the ideological practice taking place within this institutional setting. While imposing strict rules of appropriateness, the oaths sworn by the judges and the litigants respectively empowered the mass and the elite to influence the construction of shared ideas about justice and lawfulness. As a result, the arguments deployed by forensic orators needed to focus on justice and the legal issues under discussion. The discursive parameters of the lawcourts also had an impact on how forensic orators referred to the past of the city. While at the state funeral orators created an idealised image of the city's past in order to build an imagined community, this process was only coincidental in the lawcourts, which rather contributed to the production of ideas about what was just and lawful. The Athenians' reverence for the glorious deeds of their ancestors, fuelled by the idealised narrative of the *epitaphios logos*, was

---

[42] On the allusions to liturgies in the orators, see Harris 2013b: 129–36, *pace* Millett 1998 and Lanni 2006: 59–64. See also Johnstone 1999: 93–100.

[43] On the functions of history in the orators, see Nouhaud 1982: 55–72.

[44] Cf. Dem. 23.196–203 for a similar argument in another *graphē paranomon*.

often exploited in court to reinforce specific arguments within the context of litigation. Forensic orators therefore recalled the past in order to convince the judges on legal matters, and couched their historical allusions in terms of justice and lawfulness.

THE ASSEMBLY AND THE COUNCIL

The Assembly was the fundamental deliberative body of Athenian democracy. During the fifth century, the Assembly had jurisdiction over foreign and domestic affairs. It enacted both general and short-term provisions, which at the time were not formally differentiated, and was in charge of running procedures for the prosecution of public officials (*eisangeliai*) and electing those magistrates and officials (such as generals and envoys) who were not selected by lot.[45] After the restoration of the democracy in 403 BC, the Athenians introduced some major reforms to their legislative procedure. A clear-cut distinction between laws (*nomoi*) and decrees (*psēphismata*) was established. Laws were general and universally valid regulations; decrees were temporary provisions applying to individual cases and included honorific decrees, citizenship grants, and decisions in matters of foreign policy, cult and, to some extent, finances. The Assembly remained directly responsible for the enactment of decrees. Laws were now enacted through a complex procedure of *nomothesia*, but this was initiated by and (to an extent which is not entirely clear) under the control of the Assembly.[46] In the course of the fourth century, the Assembly lost its power to judge cases of *eisangelia*, which became the exclusive prerogative of the lawcourts,[47] whereas its elective function came to include the appointment of new financial magistracies such as the treasurer of the military fund and the theoric board.

In accordance with its functions and powers, the Assembly had its own specific discursive parameters. No formal rules comparable to the oaths sworn by judges and litigants in the lawcourts existed for the Assembly.[48] However, Aristotle's formulations on deliberative rhetoric and an analysis of Athenian deliberative practice show that an analogous criterion of appropriateness was in place. Aristotle's *Rhetoric* states that the aim of the deliberative orator was

---

[45] Hansen 1987: 94–124; Hansen [1991] 1999: 150–60; Canevaro 2013b: 139 and forthcoming a.
[46] Hansen 1987: 98. On *nomothesia*, see Canevaro 2013b and forthcoming a.
[47] But see Harris 2016b, who rightly challenges the idea of a constitutional change which limited the powers of the Assembly from the fifth to the fourth century.
[48] But a prayer and a curse were proclaimed at the beginning of each session (Din. 2.14, 16; Dem. 19.70) and focused, among other things, on the interests of the city (Ar. *Thesm.* 295–372): see Rhodes 1972: 36–7; Hansen [1991] 1999: 142; Mack 2018: 388–9.

the expedient (τὸ συμφέρον) and the harmful (βλαβερόν), whereas all other aspects, such as the just and the unjust, or the noble and the shameful, could provide additional arguments (Arist. *Rh.* 1358b21–8). Aristotle's theorisation appears to have been firmly grounded on Athenian deliberative practice. The Athenians were well aware of the arguments which were appropriate to deliberative rhetoric, as opposed to the other genres of rhetoric. This is shown by Thucydides' Mytilenean debate (Thuc. 3.36–49).[49] The Athenians had decreed to punish the Mytilenean revolt with the execution of all male adults and the enslavement of all women and children in Mytilene. On the next day, however, they called another Assembly to re-discuss their decision. Thucydides reports Cleon's and Diodotus' opposing speeches. Cleon starts by criticising his opponents for behaving as sophists speaking in contests of epideictic rhetoric. Cleon himself, however, delivers a speech which closely resembles a forensic speech. He focuses on issues of corrective justice and obedience to the laws, and exhorts the Athenians to punish the Mytileneans as they deserve.[50] These arguments are denounced by Diodotus as irrelevant and inappropriate to the deliberative process of the Assembly (Thuc. 3.44.4). Diodotus does not deny that the Mytileneans are guilty, but focuses instead on what policy would be advantageous for Athens. He proposes to spare those Mytileneans who had not rebelled, and his motion is eventually carried out by the Athenians.

As Aristotle's theorisation and Thucydides' Mytilenean debate show, the discursive parameters of the Assembly compelled deliberative orators to focus mainly on issues of advantage. This is clearly stated in the opening of several deliberative speeches. In the *Second Philippic*, for example, Demosthenes wishes for the Athenians to choose the best and safest policy (τὰ βέλτιστα καὶ τὰ σώσοντα) instead of the easiest and most pleasant (Dem. 6.5). In the speech *On the Chersonese*, Demosthenes opens with an exhortation for the Athenians to vote what they think would be advantageous for the city (ἃ τῇ πόλει νομίζετε συμφέρειν, ταῦτα καὶ ψηφίζεσθαι καὶ πράττειν) (Dem. 8.1). At the beginning of his speech *For the Megalopolitans*, Demosthenes similarly declares that the task of the speakers in the Assembly is to consider what is best for the community (τὸ δὲ κοινῶς ὑπὲρ τῶν πραγμάτων λέγειν καὶ τὰ βέλτισθ' ὑπὲρ ὑμῶν σκοπεῖν), without siding either with Megalopolis or Sparta (Dem. 16.1–3). Public interest was therefore a recurrent argument in the rhetorical arsenal of deliberative orators. The Corcyrean envoys who address the Athenian Assembly in

---

[49] See Harris 2013a. On the passage, see also Macleod 1978.
[50] On the difference between corrective justice, which was appropriate to the lawcourts, and distributive justice, which was appropriate to the Assembly, see Arist. *Eth. Nic.* 1130b–31a with Harris 2013a: 106–8.

Book 1 of Thucydides close their speech with a pragmatic analysis of the advantages which an alliance with Corcyra would grant to Athens (Thuc. 1.35.5–36.3). In the *First Olynthiac*, Demosthenes urges the Athenians to help Olynthus against Philip in order to keep the war far away from Attica and avoid risking their own land (Dem. 1.14–15). In the speech *For the Megalopolitans*, Demosthenes argues that it is in the Athenians' interest to maintain a balance of power between Sparta and Thebes (Dem. 16.4–5).[51]

The discursive parameters of the Assembly conditioned the orators to focus on matters of advantage also when they recalled the past. Deliberative orators often exploited the idealised image of the past created at the state funeral in order to persuade the Athenians of the expediency of a policy and urge them to act on their advice. In an Assembly reported by Thucydides, Pericles encourages the Athenians not to be inferior to their fathers and face war against Sparta in order to hand down their possessions to their descendants without any losses (Thuc. 1.144.4). In Book 6, Alcibiades similarly reminds the Assembly that their fathers acquired the Empire despite the opposition of domestic and foreign enemies. He therefore persuades the Athenians to invade Sicily without fearing their enemies back in Greece (Thuc. 6.17.7), on the grounds that the Athenians' interventionist policy is what gained them their Empire and will keep their possessions safe (Thuc. 6.18.2). In the *Second Olynthiac*, Demosthenes is astonished to see that the Athenians, who opposed the Spartans for the sake of all Greeks and ran great risks for the rights of others, are now refraining from fighting Philip for their own good (Dem. 2.24). In other instances, deliberative orators provide the Assembly with negative examples from the past.[52] In the *First Olynthiac*, Demosthenes urges the Athenians to help Olynthus against Philip and recalls several instances when they had missed precious opportunities to oppose the Macedonian king (Dem. 1.8–9). In his speech *On the Embassy*, Aeschines recalls an address he had delivered in front of the Assembly three years earlier. On that occasion, he had urged the Athenians not to repeat the mistakes that led them to disaster during the Peloponnesian War, and invited them to choose peace over war for the safety of the state (Aeschin. 2.74–8).

These examples show that in the Assembly the memory of the past was part of a pragmatic discourse aiming to support policies that were presented as advantageous for Athens. But who was responsible for maintaining the discursive parameters of the Assembly? I argue that this was achieved through the respective roles of the mass and the elite, who both exerted a significant

---

[51] On the references to public interest in deliberative oratory, see Harris 2017: 56–7, who also reviews other types of arguments employed by speakers in the Assembly.

[52] See Grethlein 2010: 126–45. Grethlein's argument, however, is mostly based on Andocides' *On the Peace*, which has been shown to be a forgery by Harris 2000.

influence on the process of ideological practice taking place in this institutional setting. While members of the elite were enabled by their rhetorical education to influence deliberation and the construction of shared ideas about what was best for the city by addressing the Assembly and making proposals,[53] the mass could determine public policy through their vote and influence individual speakers through heckling and shouting (*thorybos*). The *thorybos*, in particular, is widely recognised to have been an integral part of the decision-making process in the Assembly,[54] and the power of the audience to direct the debate by cheering or shouting off speakers is a clear sign of the joint agency of mass and elite in Athenian deliberative procedure.[55]

The Assembly thus participated in Athenian ideological practice in accordance with its own discursive parameters, which allowed both the mass and elite to contribute to the production of ideas about what was advantageous for the community. The discursive parameters of the Council, on the other hand, are not as easy to determine. One problem is represented by the composition of the Council. As Hansen has calculated, over one third of the Athenian citizens over eighteen years old and about two thirds of the citizen population over forty served in the Council at least once in their lives.[56] This means that a large portion of Athens' citizen body participated in the Council at some point during their lives. On the other hand, since every Athenian could be elected as a councillor twice ([Arist.] *Ath. Pol.* 62.3), but few of them actually served in the Council more than once, it appears that each year the Athenians had to find about 375 to 400 new councillors.[57] The membership of the Council was therefore substantially different from one year to the next, and one may wonder whether the discursive parameters of the institution could be preserved through time. The frequency of the sessions, however, allowed current

---

[53] But it should be noted that, despite the existence of a relatively small category of 'professional' or 'semi-professional' politicians, addressing the Assembly and proposing decrees were not the exclusive prerogative of the elite. The epigraphical record shows that the number of citizens actively involved in politics as proposers of decrees was rather large, and suggests that hundreds of 'ordinary' Athenians must have made proposals to the Assembly once or a few times in their lives: see Hansen 1989b: 93–127; Rhodes 2016; Lambert 2018: 171–226.

[54] Hansen 1987: 70–2; Tacon 2001; Thomas 2016. For the phenomenon of the *thorybos* in the lawcourts, see Bers 1985.

[55] On the effect of *thorybos* on speakers at the Assembly, cf. e.g. Thuc. 4.28.1; Dem. 19.17–23, 112–13; Aeschin. 1.80–4; Pl. *Prt.* 319 b 5–c 8; *Resp.* 492b–c. See also Canevaro 2018a, who argues that the Athenian Assembly reached decisions through consensus rather than majority rule, and suggests that the *thorybos* was essential for expressing and solidifying such consensus and enabling the presiding officers (*proedroi*) of the Assembly to put proposals to the vote once consensus had been reached.

[56] Hansen [1991] 1999: 249.

[57] Hansen 1985: 51–5 and [1991] 1999: 249.

councillors to grow familiar with the discursive parameters of the Council. Furthermore, as Ober has pointed out, the demotic and tribal structure of the Council, together with the almost face-to-face reality of Athenian demes,[58] probably facilitated the distribution of knowledge among councillors belonging to the same deme and tribe. The fact that each councillor was part of a broader network of contacts further spread his knowledge to larger sections of the Athenian population.[59] Finally, the fact that each year around 100–125 councillors had served before helped to preserve and reproduce the discursive parameters of the Council.

It can be inferred that the dynamics of knowledge distribution highlighted by Ober made it possible for former, current and prospective councillors to be familiar with and preserve the discursive parameters of the Council. This is shown very clearly in Lysias' *For the Invalid*, a *dokimasia* speech for a subsidy holder.[60] The speaker, an old man who belonged to the poorest echelons of Athenian society, seems very familiar with arguments commonly employed in the Council. He opens with an ironic vote of thanks to his opponent for giving him the opportunity to give an account of his own life (Lys. 24.1). The speaker then mockingly defends himself from the accusation of having been a supporter of the Thirty and boasts his own participation in the democratic restoration (Lys. 24.25). The speech has of course been composed by Lysias, but it needed to be credible when delivered by the speaker. It appears therefore that a common Athenian of advanced age – and possibly a former councillor himself, if we believe Hansen's estimates – was expected to be familiar with the discursive parameters of the Council.[61]

The data on citizen participation as well as Lysias' aforementioned speech also illuminate the respective roles of the mass and the elite in the ideological practice of the Council. It has been calculated that in the Council the rich were overrepresented compared to their overall proportion within the citizen population.[62] Moreover, non-members could be authorised to address the Council upon presenting a written request to the *prytaneis* (Dem. 24.48),[63] and the allegations that the *prytaneis* often granted such permission after taking bribes make it likely that external speakers mostly belonged to the elite

---

[58] On the possibility that the deme was close to a face-to-face society, see p. 8 n. 32; Ober 2008: 134–42.

[59] Ober 2008: 142–51, esp. 150.

[60] Lysias' paternity of the speech has sometimes been doubted, but most scholars are now in favour of authenticity: see Canevaro 2016b: 44–5 with references.

[61] Account of one's life: cf. Lys. 16.1. Behaviour under the Thirty: cf. Lys. 16.3–5; 26.5, 9–10, 16–18. See Canevaro 2016b: 46–8.

[62] Rhodes 1972: 4–6; Hansen [1991] 1999: 249.

[63] Rhodes 1972: 42–3, 63; Hansen [1991] 1999: 252–3.

(schol. *ad* Ar. *Pax* 905–7; [Lys.] 6.29, 33). If these data show the importance of the elite within the Council, several indicators suggest that average Athenians also played a significant role. As I have already mentioned, a large portion of Athens' adult population must have served in the Council at some point during their lives. The great number of new councillors required every year even made it necessary to ignore a rule that forbade the *thētes*, the lowest census class in Athens, from holding any offices, including serving in the Council ([Arist.] *Ath. Pol.* 7.4).[64] The contribution of many average or even poor Athenians therefore must have been vital to ensure the smooth running of the Council,[65] to which we should add the fact that destitute Athenians could address the Council in cases of *dokimasia* for subsidy holders such as the one in Lysias' *For the Invalid*.

If it can be assumed that the Athenians succeeded in maintaining the discursive parameters of the Council through the joint contribution of the mass and the elite, it is not easy to delineate the nature of such parameters. This is partly due to the wide range of tasks performed by the Council, which held significant legislative, administrative and judicial powers. The Council's legislative power mainly consisted of the ability to propose preliminary decrees (*probouleumata*) to the Assembly. To these must be added a number of decrees enacted by the Council alone, mostly on honorific matters.[66] The Council's administrative tasks were manifold. Notable ones included control of all sanctuaries in Attica, equipping of the navy, supervision of public works, management of many aspects of the public finances and dealing with foreign envoys.[67] The Council's judicial functions included the faculty to impose fines up to 500 drachmae, the jurisdiction over its own members and the power to try magistrates through the procedure of *eisangelia* and to hold several types of scrutiny (*dokimasia*).[68]

The fact that the Council performed both deliberative and judicial functions seems to suggest that issues of justice and advantage coexisted in the discursive parameters of this institution. This impression is confirmed by the Bouleutic Oath which the councillors swore before taking office. The Bouleutic Oath required councillors to deliberate in accordance with the laws (Xen. *Mem.* 1.1.18) and decide what was best for the city and people of Athens (Lys. 31.1; [Dem.] 59.4).[69]

---

[64] Rhodes 1972: 2.
[65] Canevaro 2016b: 48. See Rhodes 1972: 5–6, who notes that the names of at least thirteen councillors among the 248 listed on an inscription probably dating to 336/5 BC (*SEG* 19.149) are otherwise unattested in Attica. The active role of ordinary Athenians in the Council has been convincingly shown by Lambert 2018.
[66] Rhodes 1972: 49–87; Hansen [1991] 1999: 255–7.
[67] Rhodes 1972: 88–143; Hansen [1991] 1999: 259–65.
[68] Rhodes 1972: 144–78; Hansen [1991] 1999: 257–9.
[69] Rhodes 1972: 194–9; Hansen [1991] 1999: 227.

The few surviving bouleutic speeches tend to conform to these criteria.[70] The deliberative element is particularly evident in Lysias' *Against Philon*, the *dokimasia* of a prospective councillor. The speech opens with an appeal to the Bouleutic Oath, which bound councillors to advise the best decisions for the city (τὰ βέλτιστα βουλεύσειν τῇ πόλει) (Lys. 31.1–2), and closes with the hope that the Council will take advantageous decisions for the city (τὰ συμφέροντα τῇ πόλει γνώσεσθαι) (Lys. 31.34). In between these sections, the speaker insists that councillors should strive for the good of the city and not, like Philon, put their private gain before the communal good (Lys. 31.5–7). The speaker, however, also appeals to corrective justice, a feature typical of the lawcourts, as an alternative to distributive justice, which was typical of the Assembly.[71] Against Philon's expectation to be honoured by the Athenians, the speaker protests that the defendant should justly (δικαίως) suffer the greatest punishment (τῆς μεγίστης τιμωρίας) for his betrayal of the city (Lys. 31.26). Deliberative features coexist with forensic features even more clearly in another *dokimasia* speech: Lysias' *On the Scrutiny of Evandrus*. The speaker points out that the men who have been wronged (τῶν ἠδικημένων) by Evandrus are the same who are going to vote about him (Lys. 26.1) and insists on Evandrus' unlawful way of conducting his political life (εἵλετο παρανόμως πολιτευθῆναι) (Lys. 26.5). The speech also raises the issue of advantage several times. The speaker reminds the councillors of the importance of the *dokimasia* for the safety of the state (Lys. 26.9), evokes the many evils Evandrus had caused to the city (Lys. 26.13) and explains that it is in the Athenians' interests (συμφέρει) to reject the defendant (Lys. 26.15).

This brief analysis has shown that the discursive parameters of the Council were constructed around notions of justice and lawfulness as well as advantage. The impact of the discursive parameters of the Council can also be observed in the historical allusions in the surviving bouleutic speeches. In Lysias' *For Mantitheus*, yet another case of *dokimasia*, recent military campaigns provide the context of the defendant's service to the city in time of war. Mantitheus reminds the Athenians that they have all derived advantage (ὠφελεῖσθε) from the dangers he had personally faced in fighting the Spartans (Lys. 16.13–18). The speaker of Lysias' *For the Invalid* reminds the councillors of his participation in the restoration of the democracy and asks them not to mete out the

---

[70] Most extant bouleutic speeches relate to cases of *dokimasia*. It is therefore possible that their characteristics are to be ascribed to this specific procedure (on which see Feyel 2009) rather than to the institutional setting of the Council. Given the poor amount of available evidence, the rest of this section will only provide a tentative reconstruction of the discursive parameters of the Council. A significant part of this section originated from fruitful discussion with Alberto Esu, to whom I am very grateful. For a detailed discussion of the influence of the Bouleutic Oath on speakers at the Council, see Esu forthcoming.
[71] See pp. 69–70 n. 50.

same treatment as for those who have committed many injustices (τοῖς πολλὰ ἠδικηκόσιν), despite him having done no wrong (μηδὲν ἡμαρτηκώς) (Lys. 24.25–6). The speaker of Lysias' *Against Philon* compares the dangers faced by the men of Phyle against the Thirty with Philon's choice of abandoning the city to prove the defendant's negligence for the safety of the state (Lys. 31.7–9). Demosthenes' *On the Trierarchic Crown*, the only surviving bouleutic speech which does not deal with a *dokimasia*, also includes a historical allusion. Demosthenes reminds the Athenians that when they had been defeated by Alexander of Pherae in a naval battle, they punished the trierarchs who had let out their trierarchies. He therefore invites them to punish his opponents for the same behaviour in view of what is just (σκοπεῖν τὸ δίκαιον) (Dem. 51.7–10).

It can therefore be concluded that the discursive parameters of the Council, in conformity with the Bouleutic Oath, conditioned the behaviour of the orators acting within this institution to focus on issues of justice and advantage. Through a process that involved both the mass and the elite, the Council therefore contributed to Athenian ideological practice by fostering ideas about what was just and advantageous. The same discursive parameters also applied when orators recalled the past in bouleutic speeches. As in the case of the lawcourts and the Assembly, in the Council the past was not used to construct an imagined community. Allusions to the past needed to be couched in terms of justice and advantage. They had to fit the orator's arguments, helping him to make his case and guide the decisions of the Council.

THE DRAMATIC FESTIVALS

Defining the discursive parameters of the dramatic festivals is not simple.[72] This task requires an analysis of the debated issue of the political significance of Attic tragedy. The present section does not aim to provide a full and comprehensive study of such a complex matter, but it briefly reviews the main scholarly trends and highlights the issues that are relevant to my enquiry. While some scholars prefer to emphasise the aesthetic and poetic aspect of Greek tragedy over its political element,[73] another popular trend sees this genre as inherently political.[74] Simon Goldhill, in particular, has argued in an influential essay that tragedy and the Great Dionysia had a deep connection with the

---

[72] The discussion will focus solely on tragedy. I do not analyse dithyrambs and satyr plays, because of the paucity of the evidence, or comedy, because of the paucity of the evidence for mythological comedy.

[73] See e.g. Schwinge 1992; Griffin 1998 and 1999; Rhodes 2003; Garvie 2009: xvi–xxii.

[74] See e.g. Seaford 1994; Griffith 1995; P. J. Wilson 2000 and 2007; Csapo 2007.

democracy. According to Goldhill, the pre-play ceremonies performed at the Great Dionysia, such as the announcement of public benefactors or the parade of the ephebes, were an expression of Athenian civic ideology. Tragedy, on the other hand, was a transgressive genre which subverted and questioned that same ideology.[75] Goldhill's approach has received much criticism. Griffin, for example, has pointed out that there is no evidence that the Athenians regularly questioned their own values or believed that engaging in such an activity was something desirable in the first place. According to Griffin, the Dionysia was not a specifically democratic event, because it was first celebrated under the tyrants during the sixth century and continued to be celebrated after the Macedonian conquest.[76] Rhodes has analysed the institutional framework of Attic theatre and has come to the similar conclusion that Attic drama was not an expression of Athenian democracy but of the Greek *polis* more broadly.[77]

William Allan and Adrian Kelly have recently put these scholarly trends under scrutiny and proposed a more sophisticated take on tragedy and its political function. Allan and Kelly point out that the idea that tragedy questioned mainstream values is anachronistic and based on a modern conception of art. They argue that there is no evidence that the Athenians perceived tragedy as a subversive genre. Tragedy did sometimes pose questions about Athenian society, but it also tried to provide reassuring answers. In Euripides' *Suppliant Women*, for example, the democracy is strongly contested by the unsympathetic Theban Herald (Eur. *Supp.* 409–25), but his criticism is finally put to rest by the Athenian victory over Thebes.[78] Allan and Kelly also stress the competitive nature of the dramatic festivals and the status of drama as a form of mass entertainment. To win first prize, playwrights had to gratify a large and socially diverse audience and ten randomly selected judges.[79] Tragedians were therefore unlikely to attack the shared values of the community. Not only did playwrights need to appeal to the core values and beliefs of the Athenians, but they also had to offer something to every social group in their audience. According to Allan and Kelly, tragedy was therefore a polyphonic genre. On the one hand, tragedians respected the values of the *dēmos*. This is shown, for example, by the sympathetic depiction of proto-democratic kings such as Pelasgus in Aeschylus' *Suppliant Women* or Theseus in Sophocles' *Oedipus at Colonus*, or the positive representation of lower-class figures such

---

[75] Goldhill 1987 and 1990.
[76] Griffin 1998: 46–50. But it is far from certain that the Great Dionysia were instituted under Pisistratus: see Connor 1989; West 1989; Scullion 2002.
[77] Rhodes 2003.
[78] Allan and Kelly 2013: 83–7.
[79] On the estimates of theatre attendance in fifth- and fourth-century Athens, see p. 28. On the mechanism of selection of the judges at the dramatic festivals, see Pickard-Cambridge [1953] 1968: 95–9; Pope 1986; Csapo and Slater 1995: 157–65; P. J. Wilson 2000: 98–102.

as Electra's farmer husband in Euripides' *Electra*.[80] On the other hand, tragedy acknowledged the greatness of the aristocratic heroes of the mythical tradition, and in doing so gratified the elite portion of the audience and the wealthy *chorēgoi* who funded the plays.[81]

The multivocality of Attic tragedy is revealing of the discursive parameters of the dramatic festivals. This institutional setting led playwrights to endorse values potentially shared by both mass and elite.[82] Tragedies, for example, often provide a negative picture of one-man rule in accordance with democrats' and aristocrats' aversion for this form of government. The most obvious case is Sophocles' depiction of Creon in *Antigone*. Despite his initial profession of devotion to the good of the city (Soph. *Ant.* 175–91), Creon eventually reveals a tyrannical personality (Soph. *Ant.* 567–81, 640–80, 734–9) that brings doom upon him and his family.[83] If the institutional setting of the dramatic festivals did not invite playwrights to directly challenge Athens' democratic ideology, it did enable them to stimulate constructive reflection about the *polis*. In doing so, tragedians could engage with the audience's experience with the institutions of the democracy and their discourse. In Euripides' *Children of Heracles*, for example, Iolaus asks the Athenian king, Demophon, to reciprocate the benefits his father Theseus received from Heracles and help the Heraclidae against Eurystheus (Eur. *Heracl.* 215–22). Iolaus' appeal is consistent with the discourse of reciprocity typically employed in Athenian honorific and deliberative practice, which many members of the audience would have known thanks to their service in the Council and their participation in the Assembly.[84] Orestes similarly employs legal language in Aeschylus' *Libation Bearers*. After killing his mother Clytemnestra, he wishes for Zeus to be his witness in court (μάρτυς ἐν δίκῃ) and defends the legitimacy of his murder of Aegisthus, who has been punished as an adulterer, as the law prescribes (ἔχει γὰρ αἰσχυντῆρος, ὡς νόμος, δίκην) (Aesch. *Cho.* 984–90).[85]

The mass participation of the Athenians in theatre events ensured that the audience was familiar with the discursive parameters of the dramatic festivals. This is even more evident if one considers that many theatre-goers may have even had direct experience of dramatic performances as members of a

---

[80] Allan and Kelly 2013: 91–2.
[81] Allan and Kelly 2013: 93–5. On the institution of the *chorēgia*, see Pickard-Cambridge [1953] 1968: 86–91; Csapo and Slater 1995: 139–57; P. J. Wilson 2000.
[82] See also Griffith 1998 for a thought-provoking discussion of the interconnection between elite and democratic ideologies in Greek tragedy.
[83] Allan and Kelly 2013: 92, 99. Specifically on Sophocles' unsympathetic characterisation of Creon as a tyrant, see Harris 2006: 41–80 and Cairns 2016a: 42–56.
[84] See Chapter 5.
[85] For this and other examples of legal language in Attic drama, see Harris 2010; more in general on the relationship between Attic drama and Athenian law, see Harris et al. 2010.

chorus. At the time of Aeschylus, tragic choruses were composed of twelve choreuts, but the number was raised to fifteen choreuts by Sophocles (*Suda* s.v. Σοφοκλῆς). If one considers only the Great Dionysia and the Lenaea, whose programmes included a total of five tragic choruses (without counting the reperformance of old plays), between sixty and seventy-five individuals would thus be involved as choreuts in tragic performances each year. To these, one could add the even larger participation in comic and dithyrambic choruses. Since each of the ten comic choruses performing at the Great Dionysia and the Lenaea each year was composed of twenty-four choreuts, a total of 240 choreuts were employed every year, while fifty choreuts manned each of the twenty dithyrambic choruses at the Great Dionysia for a total of 1,000 individuals involved every year.[86] The total number of choreuts required for tragic, comic and dithyrambic choruses at the Great Dionysia and the Lenaea thus amounted to at least 1,300 each year, to which one should also add the choreuts required for the Rural Dionysia. Moreover, choreuts were recruited mostly among Athenian citizens. With the exception of the Lenaea, where participation of metics was admitted, foreigners were not allowed to perform in any civic choruses (schol. *ad* Ar. *Plut.* 953), and legal procedures were in place that allowed the interrogation or even expulsion from a chorus of any choreut suspected to be a foreigner (Dem. 21.56–60).[87]

The Athenians' direct involvement in theatre events as choreuts is also significant to the discussion of the issue of agency in the ideological practice taking place at the dramatic festivals. While members of the elite obviously influenced this process mainly by acting as *chorēgoi* or playwrights, the mass could actively participate by contributing to man tragic, comic and dithyrambic choruses. The large number of choreuts necessary for manning the choruses at the dramatic festivals (to which one should add the dithyrambic choruses at the Panathenaea, the Thargelia and possibly other festivals) does suggest that participation in the choruses extended also to non-elite citizens,[88] and the choruses' metatheatrical references to their own dancing have even been taken as means to solicit the audience's engagement with the action on the stage.[89] Moreover, the audience in the theatre could be very vocal in expressing their feelings towards the performances of actors and choruses by clamouring, hissing or applauding (Ar. *Ran.* 757–8; Dem. 21.226; 18.265; 19.337; Pl. *Leg.* 876b; *Resp.* 492b–c). Even though Plato may overestimate their impact on the evolution of the dramatic genre

---

[86] See Pickard-Cambridge [1953] 1968: 234–6; Csapo and Slater 1995: 353.
[87] Csapo and Slater 1995: 351; P. J. Wilson 2000: 80–1.
[88] See Csapo and Miller 2007: 5 and Fisher 2011, *pace* Pritchard 2004.
[89] See Henrichs 1994–5: esp. 59.

(Pl. *Leg.* 659b–c, 700a–01b; cf. Arist. *Pol.* 1281b), these reactions plausibly allowed the mass to exert some influence on the vote of the randomly selected judges (Ael. *VH* 2.13).[90]

In conclusion, the discursive parameters of the dramatic festivals caused playwrights to endorse values that could be shared by the majority of their audience. In order to win first prize, tragedians tried to offer something to both the elite and the mass attending the dramatic contests. Tragedy was in some sense a meta-ideological genre. The dramatic festivals enabled tragedians to play with the discourse developed in other Athenian institutions. Playwrights could therefore pose questions about the core ideas of the democratic *polis* and reaffirm the validity of those values through mechanisms of heroic distance and heroic difference or through the decisive intervention of a *deus ex machina*.[91] This mechanism was facilitated by the Athenians' mass participation in theatre events and by the choreutic experience of many theatre-goers, which ensured that the audience was familiar with the discursive parameters of the dramatic festivals and allowed the masses to contribute (together with elite *chorēgoi* and playwrights) to the ideological practice taking place in this institutional setting.

CONCLUSIONS

Athenian democratic institutions were not simply an arena for the recollection and performance of Athens' mythical past. They were also a central element in Athenian ideological practice. I have shown that, in accordance with the New Institutionalism, Athenian democratic institutions were characterised by specific discursive parameters that exerted a significant influence on the behaviour of individual political actors and the development of shared ideas and values. At the state funeral for the war dead, the Athenians produced an image of the city that was functional to the construction of an imagined community. The *epitaphios logos*, in particular, provided an image of Athens that justified the sacrifice of the fallen and inspired their relatives to follow their example. In the lawcourts, orators were bound by oath to deal with issues of justice and specific legal charges. No such formal rules existed in the Assembly, but the evidence shows that speakers in this setting were expected to address issues of advantage and discuss the best policy for the city. In the Council, the focus on justice and advantage seemed to coexist in accordance with the Bouleutic

---

[90] Wallace 1997; P. J. Wilson 2000: 98–9, 101–2. It is significant that comic poets sometimes pleaded for the sympathy not only of the judges but also of the audience at large: cf. e.g. Ar. *Eccl.* 1140–3.

[91] On the concepts of heroic distance and heroic difference, see Allan and Kelly 2013: 99–101.

Oath. Finally, at the dramatic festivals, the values and beliefs of the Athenian community could be put to question and reaffirmed by tragedians.

The study of the discursive parameters of Athenian democratic institutions has also illustrated some of the characteristics of Athenian democratic ideology highlighted in the Introduction. I have shown that Athenian democratic ideology was not a fixed and monolithic set of ideas, but the product of a dynamic process through which the Athenians constructed multiple and compatible ideas about their community in accordance with the discursive parameters of each institution. This definition of Athenian ideological practice retains both the constructive value typical of the culturalist tradition on ideology and the normative element characteristic of the Marxist tradition. The constructive value appears most clearly from the integrative role of the state funeral for the war dead in building an imagined community. The normative element is evident in the fact that discourse (depending on each institution) was not merely used to describe, for example, how the Athenians typically behaved or what justice was to them, but rather to foster ideas about how the Athenians *were expected* to behave or how they *were expected* to apply justice and the law. Finally, I have established the bidirectional nature of Athenian democratic ideology. The discourse of Athenian institutions relied on the active contribution of both the elite (as orators, playwrights, or *chorēgoi*) and the mass (through participation in ritual, voting in the lawcourts and Assembly, clamouring, providing councillors or manning choruses). As a result, Athenian democratic ideology cannot be taken either as a top-down or a bottom-up process, but the product of a mutual influence between mass and elite facilitated by the institutions of the democracy.

This picture of Athenian democratic ideology is put to the test and expanded in four case studies. These apply the discursive parameters established in this chapter to a selected range of mythical variants in order to place Athenian ideological practice directly within the institutions of the democracy and illustrate the dynamic and multifaceted nature of Athenian democratic ideology. Chapter 4 analyses the versions of the myth of autochthony at the state funeral, the dramatic festivals and the lawcourts, and reads them in connection to the value of *eugeneia*. Chapter 5 explores the notions of *charis* and *philanthrōpia* in the versions of the myth of the Heraclidae produced for the state funeral, the dramatic festivals and private oratory. Chapter 6 is devoted to the Attic Amazonomachy, and analyses how the story and the notion of *hybris* were deployed at the state funeral and the dramatic festivals as opposed to private contexts. Chapter 7 discusses the accounts of the myth of Adrastus produced for the state funeral, the dramatic festivals and the Assembly as well as those in Isocrates' private rhetoric, and uses them to explore the dynamic relationship between *philanthrōpia* and *hybris*.

CHAPTER 4

Exclusiveness and *Eugeneia* in the Myth of Autochthony

Among all Athenian civic myths, autochthony was probably the most representative of Athenian identity, and held a special place in Athenian ideological practice. By claiming to be indigenous inhabitants of Attica, born from the very soil of their own land, the Athenians could reinforce their identity and civic cohesion, and at the same time mark their difference from and superiority over the rest of the Greeks.[1] It has been traditionally assumed that the Athenians developed this view at an early stage, when they pictured themselves collectively as indigenous and born from the earth. A fruitful scholarly trend inaugurated by Vincent Rosivach has convincingly shown that this was not in fact the case. The complete notion of autochthony only came about around the middle of the fifth century from the combination of two separate traditions: the early myth of Erechtheus/Erichthonius' birth from the earth, and the Athenians' belief that they had inhabited Attica from time immemorial.[2]

The earliest mention of the earthborn Erechtheus is in the 'Catalogue of Ships' in the *Iliad*. The poet defines Athens as 'the land of great-hearted

---

[1] According to Gotteland 2001: 319, autochthony has two distinct functions: it legitimises Athens' power and affirms her supremacy over other cities.

[2] See Rosivach 1987; Bearzot 2007: 9; Blok 2009; Leão 2012. Among the proponents of the traditional view, see e.g. Loraux 1979; Parker 1987: 194–5. I am not fully convinced by Shapiro 1998, who accepts most of Rosivach's argument but dates the full notion of autochthony to the period of the Persian Wars. The question of whether Erechtheus and Erichthonius were regarded as two distinct individuals does not affect my argument: on the topic see Kron 1976: 37–9, Parker 1987: 200–1, Shear 2001: 55–60 and Fowler 2013: 449. I will use the name 'Erechtheus' to refer to the adult earthborn king of Athens and 'Erichthonius' to refer to the earthborn baby.

Erechtheus' (δῆμον Ἐρεχθῆος μεγαλήτορος), and recalls how Erechtheus had been engendered by the earth (τέκε δὲ ζείδωρος ἄρουρα) and entrusted to the care of Athena. The goddess then placed him in her sanctuary, where the Athenians honoured him with yearly sacrifices (Hom. Il. 2.546–51).[3] A further Homeric reference to Erechtheus can be found in Book 7 of the Odyssey, where Athena leaves Scheria for Marathon and Athens and enters the palace of Erechtheus (Hom. Od. 7.77–81). The Homeric epics therefore clearly establish a special connection between the earthborn Erechtheus and the goddess Athena. The designation of Athens as the land of Erechtheus, however, does not necessarily imply the Athenians' direct descent from the hero or their participation in his earthborn quality, as much as the importance of Erechtheus in Athenian cult from an early date.[4]

Scenes depicting Erichthonius' birth start to appear on Attic vase painting in the early fifth century. The theme soon becomes very popular and tends to follow a fixed pattern, with Ge arising from the earth and handing the baby Erichthonius to Athena, usually in the presence of significant characters such as the other famous earthborn king, Cecrops, or Erichthonius' putative father, Hephaestus.[5] Fifth-century vases usually characterise the birth of Erichthonius as an Olympian event by depicting Zeus and other deities attending the handing over of the child (Fig. 4.1),[6] or highlight the myth's cultic implication by showing the Cecropids taking part in the action.[7] The only case where the myth seems to have a political meaning is a red-figure cup by the Codros Painter now in Berlin (c. 440/30 BC). There, the 'handing over'

---

[3] Cf. also Hdt. 8.55.1, which mentions the shrine of Erechtheus, called the earthborn (τοῦ γηγενέος λεγομένου), on the Acropolis.

[4] Rosivach 1987: 294–5. The iliadic reference to Erechtheus belongs to a problematic section of the Homeric text. Lines 553–5 were athetised by Zenodotus (schol. A ad Hom. Il. 2.553–5): see Kirk 1985: 207. Suspicions of inauthenticity were also raised in antiquity on the Salaminian entry (Hom. Il. 2.557–8), which follows the Athenian entry in the 'Catalogue of Ships' and places the Salaminian contingent right next to the Athenian one. In the sixth century, the lines were at the centre of a controversy between the Athenians and the Megarians over the possession of Salamis. The Megarians accused the Athenians of having interpolated the passage, and proposed an alternative reading that connected the Salaminian contingent with Megara (Arist. Rh. 1375b30; Strabo 9.1.10): see Kirk 1985: 207–9. No ancient authority expressed doubts about the lines dealing with Erechtheus (Hom. Il. 2.546–51), but their authenticity has been questioned in modern times: see Kron 1976: 32–7 for a review of the issue. However, even if one takes the Athenian entry in the 'Catalogue of Ships' to be a later Athenian interpolation, the passage suggests that the Athenian cult of Erechtheus went back at least to the sixth century.

[5] See Kron in LIMC s.v. Erechtheus, p. 943; Shapiro 1998: 133–9.

[6] Cf. e.g. a red-figure hydria by the Oinanthe Painter dating from c. 470/60 BC (London, British Museum, E 182), or a red-figure stamnos from Vulci dating from c. 460/50 BC (München, Antikensammlungen, 2413). See Kron in LIMC s.v. Erechtheus, p. 943; Shapiro 1998: 138–9.

[7] Cf. e.g. a fragmentary red-figure pelike dating from c. 470/60 BC (Leipzig, Antikenmuseum, T 654). See Kron in LIMC s.v. Erechtheus, pp. 943–4.

Figure 4.1 Birth of Erichthonius. Red-figure hydria by the Oinanthe Painter (c. 470–460 BC). London, British Museum E 182. Image © Trustees of the British Museum.

scene takes place in the presence not only of the Cecropids, but also of the Athenian kings Cecrops, Erechtheus – apparently distinct from Erichthonius in this depiction – and Aegeus, some of whom appear on the reverse (Figs 4.2 and 4.3).[8] This chronologically odd parade of Athenian kings might be a sign of the growing importance of the earthborn Erichthonius for the Athenian community during the second half of the fifth century.[9]

Pindar is the first to refer to the Athenians as 'Erechtheidae'. In the *Seventh Pythian*, the poet refers to the Alcmaeonidae as citizens of Erechtheus (Ἐρεχθέος ἀστῶν), and praises them for building the temple of Apollo in Delphi (Pind. *Pyth.* 7.9–12). In the *Second Isthmian*, Pindar recalls Xenocrates' victory at the Panathenaea, 'when he gained the glorious favor of Erechtheus' descendants (Ἐρεχθειδᾶν) in shining Athens' (Pind. *Isthm.* 2.19–20; trans. Race). The patronymic implies a descent that is symbolic rather than literal;[10] yet it probably

---

[8] Berlin, Antikensammlung, F 2537.
[9] See Kron in *LIMC* s.v. Erechtheus, p. 943.
[10] See Blok 2009: 260. Compare the use of the patronymic 'Theseidae', which only implies descent when it refers to Theseus' own sons (*Iliou Persis* fr. 6; Eur. *Tro.* 31; *Hec.* 122; Ion fr. 29 W). The only instance where the Athenians are referred to as 'Theseidae' is in Sophocles' *Oedipus at Colonus*, but the expression implies that the Athenians are followers, rather than descendants of Theseus, as the hero is their current king (Soph. *OC* 1066). I am grateful to Roger Brock for this suggestion.

Figure 4.2 Birth of Erichthonius. Red-figure cup by the Codros Painter (c. 440–430 BC), Side A. Berlin, Antikensammlung F 2537. Image © Antikensammlung, Staatliche Museen zu Berlin – Preussischer Kulturbesitz (J. Laurentius).

Figure 4.3 Athenian kings and the Cecropids. Red-figure cup by the Codros Painter (c. 440–430 BC), Side B. Berlin, Antikensammlung F 2537. Image © Antikensammlung, Staatliche Museen zu Berlin – Preussischer Kulturbesitz (J. Laurentius).

contributed to extending the chthonic origin of Erechtheus to the Athenians as a whole.[11] The Athenians are explicitly called earthborn for the first time in Sophocles' *Ajax*. In the play, Tecmessa addresses the Chorus of Salaminian sailors as 'members of the race descended from the earthborn Erechtheidae (γενεᾶς χθονίων ἀπ' Ἐρεχθειδῶν)' (Soph. *Aj*. 202, trans. Finglass). As Rosivach rightly noted, however, the phrasing is probably the result of a hypallage, and the patronymic 'Erechtheidae' is to be taken as a poetic usage, rather than a common way to address the Athenians.[12]

As for the word αὐτόχθων, Rosivach has pointed out that its etymological structure has nothing to do with the idea of birth from the earth. Rosivach suggested that its original meaning was rather 'always living in the same land, indigenous', as opposed to 'immigrant' (ἔπηλυς).[13] In this sense, autochthony was not a uniquely Athenian attribute but a common claim made by several Greek communities.[14] The word αὐτόχθων is first attested with the meaning of 'indigenous' in Herodotus.[15] The historian uses the term when discussing the indigenous nature of the Carians and the Caunians (Hdt. 1.171–2), or when pointing to Arcadians and Cynurians as the only indigenous nations of the Peloponnese (Hdt. 8.73.1).[16] Similarly, Thucydides only uses the word αὐτόχθων once and with the meaning of 'indigenous', when he rejects the Sicani's claim that they had been the first settlers of Sicily (Thuc. 6.2.2).[17]

The tradition of the Athenians' long-standing habitation of Attica probably emerged in the late 470s in connection with Athens' growing rivalry with the Dorian Spartans, and can be seen as a reaction to the latter's immigrant origins and their claims of descending from the Heraclidae.[18] The earliest occurrences of this belief are in Herodotus. The historian does not use the word αὐτόχθων explicitly,[19] but recalls the Athenians' Pelasgian origins

---

[11] Rosivach 1987: 295.
[12] Rosivach 1987: 295–6.
[13] See Rosivach 1987: 297–301.
[14] Bearzot 2007: 13–19; Blok 2009: 251–2.
[15] The word is first attested (in the unusual form αὐτόχθονος) in Aeschylus' *Agamemnon*, where, however, it has a different meaning. The passage refers to Paris, who as a punishment for abducting Helen 'has both lost his booty and caused his father's house to be mown down to the very ground in utter destruction (πανώλεθρον αὐτόχθονον πατρῷον ἔθρισεν δόμον)' (Aesch. *Ag.* 535–6; trans. Sommerstein): see Blok 2009: 253; Pelling 2009: 473–4.
[16] Pelling 2009: 479–80. The Arcadians, together with the Aeginetans and the Thebans, figured as autochthonous also in Hellanicus. It is not clear, however, in what sense Hellanicus interpreted the word αὐτόχθονες (*FGrHist* 4 F 161).
[17] Pelling 2009: 478–9.
[18] Rosivach 1987: 296–7.
[19] But cf. Hdt. 9.73.2, where the historian recalls how, when Helen was abducted by Theseus and the Dioscuri invaded Attica to recover her, the autochthonous Titacus (Τιτακὸς ἐὼν αὐτόχθων) betrayed the deme of Aphidnae to them.

as opposed to the Hellenic and immigrant nature of the Dorians, and stresses that the Pelasgians had never migrated (ἐξεχώρησε) anywhere (Hdt. 1.56.2).[20] In Book 7, an Athenian envoy replies to Gelon's demand of commanding the united Greek fleet by stressing that the Athenians were the most ancient nation (ἀρχαιότατον μὲν ἔθνος) and the only Greeks who had never migrated (μοῦνοι δὲ ἐόντες οὐ μετανάσται Ἑλλήνων) (Hdt. 7.161.3).[21] Thucydides also touches on the indigenous nature of the Athenians without using the word αὐτόχθων. In Pericles' funeral oration, the ancestors are praised because they have always inhabited Attica (τὴν γὰρ χώραν οἱ αὐτοὶ αἰεὶ οἰκοῦντες) and transmitted it free until the present day (Thuc. 2.36.1). When dealing with the primitive conditions of Greek cities in his 'Archaeology', Thucydides attributes the relative growth of Athens to autochthony. According to the historian, because of the poverty of its soil, Attica had always been inhabited by the same people (ἄνθρωποι ᾤκουν οἱ αὐτοὶ αἰεί). As a result, Athens became a safe haven for powerful men escaping from other Greek cities, which were subjected to civil strife and invasions because of the fertility of their lands (Thuc. 1.2.5–6).[22]

The fact that Thucydides offers a politico-economic explanation for the indigenous nature of the Athenians may be a sign that autochthony was already a well-established component of Athenian identity at his time. It was probably in connection with Pericles' citizenship law in 451/0 BC that the Athenians blended the tradition of their continuous habitation of Attica with the myth of the earthborn Erechtheus/Erichthonius and adopted the complete notion of autochthony.[23] The mutual implications of autochthony and Pericles' citizenship law are central, for example, in Euripides' *Ion*. The play constantly recalls the autochthony of the Athenians (Eur. *Ion* 15–20, 267–74, 542, 999–1000, 1465–7) and the earthborn nature of their royal line (Eur. *Ion* 29–30, 589–90, 673–5), which act as a foil to Ion's difficult integration.[24] In Euripides' *Erechtheus*, the autochthonous origins of the Athenians (αὐτόχθονες δ' ἔφυμεν) are recalled by Praxithea, wife of Erechtheus, as a reason for her willingness to sacrifice her own daughter for her land (Eur. F. 360). The manner of Erechtheus' death, buried beneath the earth by Poseidon (κατὰ

---

[20] Pelling 2009: 480–1.
[21] Cf. Isoc. 4.23–4.
[22] See Pelling 2009: 476; also Hornblower 1991: 12–13. The passage expresses the Athenian claim of autochthony and at the same time acknowledges the naturalisation (πολῖται γιγνόμενοι) of the refugees, anticipating the somewhat contradictory tendency of funeral speeches to praise the Athenians for both their autochthony and their welcoming attitude towards suppliants (e.g. the Heraclidae).
[23] See Rosivach 1987: 303 n. 34; Bearzot 2007: 12–13; Blok 2009: 261–3; Leão 2012: 137–41.
[24] These mutual implications are analysed at length by Leão 2012.

χθονὸς κρύψας), is also a possible allusion to the king's chthonic connotations (Eur. F. 370).[25] Praxithea's speech is quoted in Lycurgus' *Against Leocrates*. The quotation reinforces the charge of treason against Leocrates, depicted as lacking the devotion to his country and the spirit of sacrifice expected from an autochthonous Athenian (Lycurg. 1.98–101). The orator also laments the city's condition after Chaeronea, when the Athenians, once proud of their autochthony, proposed to extend citizen rights to foreigners (Lycurg. 1.41).[26] Autochthony features prominently in funeral speeches, where it is central to the construction of an idealised image of the city (Lys. 2.17; Dem. 60.4; Pl. *Menex.* 237b1–c6, 237e, 238e5–239a7, 245c6–d6; Hyp. 6.7). The discourse of autochthony in this context is based on nobility of birth and the metaphor of the Athenian community as a family born from the motherland. Such images could be adapted to different uses outside the formal institutions of the state. Isocrates' *Panegyricus*, for example, exploits autochthony to claim Athenian leadership for a Panhellenic campaign against Persia. The orator recalls the noble origins (καλῶς καὶ γνησίως γεγόναμεν) of the Athenians, who are autochthonous (αὐτόχθονες ὄντες) and have always lived in the land from which they were born (ἐξ ἧσπερ ἔφυμεν) (Isoc. 4.23–5). Isocrates' *Panathenaicus* also praises the Athenians by alluding to their autochthony. The motif is deployed in a similar fashion to the *Panegyricus*, but the orator adds the detail of the Athenians' descent from Hephaestus through Erichthonius. The earthborn is even mentioned explicitly and extolled for inheriting Cecrops' possessions and handing them over to his descendants down to Theseus (Isoc. 12.124–6).

AUTOCHTHONY, EXCLUSIVENESS AND *EUGENEIA*

The myth of autochthony provides a clear illustration of the dynamic nature of Athenian ideological practice. The conflation of the double tradition of the earthborn kings and the indigenous Athenians into the complete notion of autochthony implied a potential disruption of the unity of Athens' citizen body. Were the mythical kings of Attica more autochthonous than the rest of the Athenians? Did the inclusion of immigrants into the citizen body in ancient times, acknowledged for example by Thucydides,[27] imply the existence

---

[25] See Blok 2009: 261–2; Calame 2011.
[26] See Azoulay 2009: 171–3.
[27] Cf. Thuc. 1.2.6: the most powerful people from the rest of Greece arrived in Athens to escape from war and *stasis* and, becoming citizens (πολῖται γιγνόμενοι), made the population of the city even larger. See Hornblower 1991: 14–15.

of different degrees of autochthony among the Athenian citizenry?[28] This chapter shows that the complex history and extreme malleability of the notion of autochthony enabled political actors to emphasise different aspects of this myth, as they crafted their narratives in accordance with the discursive parameters of Athenian democratic institutions. By attributing the exclusiveness and nobility of birth (*eugeneia*) characteristic of autochthony to larger or smaller sections of the citizen body, the Athenians produced multiple and compatible ideas about the community and could even incorporate new values that reflected contemporary debates within the city.

After a review of the notion of *eugeneia* in Greek thought and Athenian democratic ideology, I first look at the treatment of the myth of autochthony at the state funeral for the war dead. In this institutional setting, the orators avoided any contradictions by devoting themselves entirely to the complete notion of autochthony and ignoring the earthborn kings.[29] Demosthenes and Hyperides (Dem. 60.4; Hyp. 6.7),[30] as well as Socrates in Plato's *Menexenus* (Pl. *Menex.* 237b1–c6, 238e5–239a7),[31] conceptualise autochthony as the collective *eugeneia* of all Athenian citizens. In Lysias' *Funeral Oration*, collective *eugeneia* coexists with and is subordinated to concord (*homonoia*) (Lys. 2.17). This was a topical value in the aftermath of the democratic restoration, when the speech is set. Lysias uses autochthony as aetiology of the *homonoia* that characterises the Athenians throughout the whole speech and makes them always ready to fight for justice.[32] I show that, despite Lysias' variation, all funeral speeches express autochthony

---

[28] Similar issues are raised by Blok 2009: 263–4 and Azoulay 2009: 171–2.

[29] As Gotteland 2001: 325–6 observes, orators generally prefer the collective autochthony of the Athenians over the myth of Erichthonius. Gotteland rightly points out that Isoc. 12.126 is the only passage in the orators evoking Erichthonius (320–1), but she does not note that the *Panathenaicus*, despite some similarities, does not belong to the same institutional setting as the *epitaphios logos* and does not respond to its same discursive parameters. See also Loraux [1981] 1993: 49. An allusion to Erechtheus can be found in Demosthenes' *Funeral Speech*, but it does not belong to the section about Athenian autochthony. Demosthenes recalls Erechtheus' divine origins (τὸν μὲν ἀπ' ἀθανάτων πεφυκότα) when praising the tribe of the Erechtheidae (Dem. 60.27). The orator does not mention Erechtheus' earthborn nature, but focuses on the king's sacrifice of his daughters for the salvation of Athens. Given the context of the allusion, Demosthenes points not so much to Erechtheus the king of the autochthonous Athenians, as to Erechtheus the tribal hero: on the cult of Erechtheus as a tribal hero see Kron 1976: 52–5.

[30] Cf. Dem. 60.5, which recalls how the fruits of the earth had first appeared in Attica as a proof for the belief that the ancestors were born from their very land (μητέρα τὴν χώραν εἶναι τῶν ἡμετέρων προγόνων).

[31] Cf. Pl. *Menex.* 237e, where Socrates envisions the ancestors as literally born from the earth, as proven by the fact that the Attic land was the first to produce food for humans. Cf. also Pl. *Menex.* 245c6–d6: the Athenians, being pure Greeks, are naturally haters of barbarians.

[32] Cf. Lys. 2.18, 20, 24, 43, 63; see Todd 2007: 229, who connects Lysias' insistence on *homonoia* throughout this speech with the Amnesty that followed the restoration of democracy in 403 BC.

through the same set of motifs (the opposition of individual versus collective; the metaphor of the community as a family; the language of legitimate birth), and that these reflect the discursive parameters of the state funeral for the war dead. These speeches provide an ideal picture of the Athenians as politically cohesive and equal in their communal claim for nobility of birth. Autochthony thus functioned as the glue that held the entire Athenian community together and made it unique, superior to the rest of humanity and worth dying for,[33] and in doing so it contributed to the construction of an imagined community.

I then analyse Euripides' *Ion*, which programmatically reversed the typical epitaphic motifs about autochthony. I show that the discursive parameters of the dramatic festivals enabled the tragedian to put the ideal image of the city under discussion. In the play, the potential ambiguities inherent in the myth of autochthony are acknowledged and enacted on the stage, only to be resolved by the intervention of Athena. The earthborn nature of the kings of Attica and the collective autochthony of the Athenians coexist,[34] and allow the poet to highlight the potential contradictions within the ideology of autochthony. Euripides treats *eugeneia* as an individual feature, which he constantly attributes to Creusa and her family but never to the Athenians as a whole. The image of the Athenian community as a family disappears, absorbed in and almost endangered by the private drama of the Erechtheid house. Legitimacy of birth, used only metaphorically in the extant funeral speeches, becomes a concrete problem for Ion, the alleged bastard and foreigner who is about to become the heir to the Athenian throne. All these elements of tension are finally resolved at the end of the play, which restates the ideology of autochthony.

Finally, I offer a reading of Apollodorus' allusion to autochthony in the pseudo-Demosthenic *Against Neaera*. I show that Apollodorus restricts the status of autochthonous to a limited portion of Athens' citizen population in order to reflect and produce Athenian ideas about justice and lawfulness in accordance with the discursive parameters of the lawcourts. The orator states that, in ancient times, when Athens was still a monarchy, the kingship belonged to those who were each time superior because of their autochthony (ἡ βασιλεία τῶν ἀεὶ ὑπερεχόντων διὰ τὸ αὐτόχθονας εἶναι) ([Dem.] 59.74). Apollodorus resolves the potential contradiction in the complete notion of autochthony by

---

[33] On autochthony and unity, see Bearzot 2007: 9–10 and Forsdyke 2012: 136–7. The only exception is Pericles, who does not elaborate on the theme of autochthony and simply points out that the ancestors 'dwelt in the country without break in the succession from generation to generation, and handed it down free to the present time by their valor' (Thuc. 2.36.1, trans. Crawley).

[34] For the earthborn nature of the Athenian royal house, cf. Eur. *Ion* 267–74, 999–1000, 1463–7; the concept of birth from the earth is challenged by Xuthus at Eur. *Ion* 542. For the autochthony of the Athenians as a whole, cf. Eur. *Ion* 589–90, 673–5, 735–7.

attributing the prestigious status of autochthonous exclusively to the Athenian royal line. Free from the task of creating an 'imagined community', the orator develops an aspect of autochthony that would be completely inappropriate in a funeral speech but fits his case perfectly. Apollodorus wants to prove that the non-Athenian Neaera has broken the laws by passing her daughter Phano as an Athenian citizen and marrying her to the King Archon. To further his accusations, he suggests that Phano was not worthy of performing the ritual tasks of the wife of the King Archon, as they were once the prerogative of Athens' autochthonous kings, and he crafts his mythical allusion accordingly so as to make autochthony appear even more exclusive.

EUGENEIA: FROM HOMERIC SOCIETY TO DEMOCRATIC ATHENS

Good birth was highly valued by the Greeks. The earliest examples come from Homeric society. As already noted by Calhoun, the semantic range of *eugeneia*, including synonyms such as γενναῖος, εὐπατρίδης or γεννητής, is mostly absent from the Homeric poems.[35] This does not mean that the poems did not place importance on ancestry and descent, which were among the qualities that heroes were expected to possess. The term διογενής ('sprung from Zeus, divine'), for example, occurs twenty-three times in the *Iliad* and twenty-three in the *Odyssey*, and it is used to praise some of the greatest heroes of the epics, including Achilles, Odysseus and Ajax.[36] Homeric heroes often enquire about each other's ancestry, which sometimes stems from a divine figure.[37] Glaucus proudly traces his lineage (γενεήν) back to Sisyphus and ultimately Aeolus, and recalls the deeds of his grandfather, the hero Bellerophon, noble offspring of a god (θεοῦ γόνον ἠΰν) (Hom. *Il.* 6.145–211).[38] Nestor recalls how Peleus once rejoiced in asking him about the ancestry and offspring (γενεήν τε τόκον τε) of all the Argives (Hom. *Il.* 7.123–8).[39] Diomedes balances his young age with his descent from a valiant father (Hom. *Il.* 14.112–14).

A richer vocabulary of *eugeneia* developed during the archaic period. The term εὐγενής appears for the first time in the *Homeric Hymn to Aphrodite* to describe the

---

[35] Calhoun 1934. A notable exception is the noun εὐπατέρεια, which appears three times (Hom. *Il.* 6.292; *Od.* 11.235; 22.227).
[36] Duplouy 2006: 40–1.
[37] On the vocabulary of good birth in the Homeric poems, see Duplouy 2006: 38–43.
[38] See Donlan [1980] 1999: 15; Mann 2007: 124. According to Kirk 1990: 185, there is no need to interpret Hom. *Il.* 6.191 as a reference to the variant that made Poseidon the father of Bellerophon.
[39] See Fowler 1998: 1.

goddess Themis (Hom. Hymn Ven. 94). The synonym γενναῖος is first attested with the meaning of 'highborn' in a one-line fragment of Archilochus (Archil. fr. 225 West).[40] The adjective εὐπατρίδης occurs for the first time in a late archaic Attic drinking song where the exiles who died in Leipsydrion fighting against Pisistratus are celebrated as brave in battle and born from noble fathers (μάχεσθαι ἀγαθούς τε καὶ εὐπατρίδας) (PMG 907).[41] The wealth of synonyms to express good birth goes alongside the importance of *eugeneia* in the political struggle, where appealing to the poor origins of one's opponents constituted a powerful argument.[42] Alcaeus, for example, complains that Mytilene is now ruled by the baseborn (κακοπατρίδαν) Pittacus (Alc. fr. 348 Voigt). Herodotus recalls the opposition faced by Maeandrius when he succeeded to Polycrates as tyrant of Samos. Instead of ruling over his equals, Maeandrius decided to grant them freedom and equality of rights, but one of the Samians protested that, because of his low birth (γεγονώς τε κακῶς), Maeandrius was not worthy to rule in the first place (Hdt. 3.142).[43] Theognis, troubled by the social mobility in Megara due to acquisition of wealth, complains that wealth has corrupted race (πλοῦτος ἔμειξε γένος). According to the poet, people seek for purebred (εὐγενέας) horses but do not follow the same criterion when they seek marriage. The noble man (ἐσθλὸς ἀνήρ) now wants the daughter of the lowborn man (κακοῦ) in exchange for a rich dowry, and women choose the wealthy over the noble (ἀγαθοῦ) man (Thgn. 183–92).[44]

The concept of noble birth, however, was not uncontroversial, and in the archaic period one can already observe tendencies later attested in democratic Athens. In Theognis, for example, the notions of good birth and nobility start to assume a moral value alongside their class value. The poet expresses doubt about the possibility of acquiring nobility through education. He states that 'if good sense could be made and placed in a man, there would never be a base son of a noble father (ἐξ ἀγαθοῦ πατρὸς ἔγεντο κακός), since he would heed words of wisdom. But you will never make the base man noble (οὔποτε ποιήσει τὸν κακὸν ἄνδρ' ἀγαθόν) through teaching' (Thgn. 429–38, trans. Gerber).[45] Moreover, the ideal of good birth was sometimes contested. Callinus, inviting

---

[40] That Archilochus used γενναῖος as a synonym of εὐγενής is attested by Athenaeus, who preserves the fragment (Ath. 14.653d). The adjective γενναῖος first appears in Hom. *Il.* 5.253, but not with the meaning of 'high-born'. In the passage, Diomedes claims that it is not true to his birth (γενναῖον) to run away in battle or cower down.

[41] The context of the song is provided at [Arist.] *Ath. Pol.* 19.3. Whether an aristocratic class known as Eupatrids existed and monopolised political and religious offices in pre-Solonian Athens is a matter of contention: for an outline of the issue see Pierrot 2015.

[42] See van Wees 2000; Duplouy 2006: 43–8; Mann 2007: 125.

[43] See Donlan [1980] 1999: 132–3.

[44] See van Wees 2000: 61–3; Mann 2007: 125–6.

[45] Donlan [1980] 1999: 77–80; van Wees 2000: 64–6.

the young to fight for their land, wives and children, remarks that nobody can escape death, not even if he descends from immortal ancestors (προγόνων ἦ γένος ἀθανάτων) (Callinus fr. 1.12–13 West). Phocylides similarly asks, 'what advantage is noble birth (γένος εὐγενές) to those who have nothing attractive in what they say or plan?' (Phocylides fr. 3 West, trans. Gerber).[46]

If nobility of birth was already at least partly problematic in the archaic period, the situation was more complex in classical Athens, where democracy had the potential to threaten the notion of *eugeneia*. Aristocratic families still traced their origins back to heroic or divine ancestors. Pherecydes, for example, reports the full genealogy of the Philaid family, which stemmed from Ajax's son Philaeus (*FGrHist* 3 F 2).[47] The importance of ancestry was also evident in court, where litigants sometimes mentioned the liturgies performed by their ancestors as well as their military achievements at the service of democracy.[48] In this context, speakers could highlight their loyalty to the democracy in connection to and despite their *eugeneia*. In Isocrates' *On the Team of Horses*, the speaker, Alcibiades the Younger, states that his father belonged to the Eupatrids on the male side, which testifies to his nobility of birth (εὐγένειαν), and on the female side to the Alcmeonids, who proved their devotion to democracy when they refused to share into the tyranny of Pisistratus (Isoc. 16.25). The speaker of Lysias' *Against the Subversion of the Ancestral Constitution of Athens* mentions his good birth when arguing against Phormisius' proposal to restrict citizenship only to landowners. Even though his wealth and birth (γένει) would prevent him being disenfranchised and would even make him superior (πρότερος ὤν) to his opponents, the speaker believes that the safety of the city is only possible if all Athenians participate in their citizenship rights (Lys. 34.3).[49]

The examples mentioned show that nobility of birth was not necessarily incompatible with democracy, and members of the elite could claim to be both nobly born and good citizens. Drama, however, shows that some ideological tension did exist. As in the archaic period, the ideal of good birth was open to debate, and moral and class connotations often remained intertwined in the notion of *eugeneia*. In Sophocles' *Ajax*, Menelaus tells Teucer that it

---

[46] Duplouy 2006: 44–6.
[47] See Thomas 1989: 159; Duplouy 2006: 56–64. Members of the *genē*, i.e. groups of Athenian families who had exclusive access to priesthood, were particularly eager to trace their genealogies and emphasise their pure Athenian descent: see Blok 2017: 217–25.
[48] See Thomas 1989: 108–23; Mann 2007: 138. Such appeals have sometimes been interpreted as implying a request to reciprocate public service with a positive verdict (see e.g. Millett 1998), but Harris 2013b: 129–36 has shown that Athenian litigants tended to refer to public service only if it was directly relevant to the charge and mostly during the *timēsis* part of the trial.
[49] Ober 1989a: 254 mentions these passages as examples of positive allusions to *eugeneia* but does not fully appreciate their rhetorical context and purpose.

is typical of a base man (κακοῦ ἀνδρός) to disobey those in power (Soph. *Aj.* 1069–72). Teucer replies that it is not surprising that people of insignificant birth commit some wrongs, when those who are considered wellborn (οἱ δοκοῦντες εὐγενεῖς πεφυκέναι) speak as wrongly as Menelaus (Soph. *Aj.* 1093–6).⁵⁰ In a fragment of Euripides' *Alexander*, the Chorus states that it is superfluous to praise human nobility of birth (εὐγένειαν . . . βρότειον), as the wellborn and the lowborn are one single offspring (μία δὲ γονὰ τό τ' εὐγενὲς καὶ δυσγενές) generated by the earth (Eur. fr. 61b).⁵¹ In Sophocles' *Antigone*, the heroine challenges the nobility of Ismene, who will have to prove whether she is noble (εὐγενής) or the base daughter of noble parents (ἐσθλῶν κακή) (Soph. *Ant.* 37–8). Euripides sometimes attributes *eugeneia* to characters of low status. In a fragment of *Melanippe*, for example, a messenger states that 'those who are brave and just by nature, though they are born from slaves (κἂν ὦσι δούλων), are more nobly-born (εὐγενεστέρους) than those who are mere empty appearances' (Eur. fr. 495.40–3, trans. Collard and Cropp, adapted). The characters of Euripides' *Electra* similarly discuss the nobility of Electra's peasant husband. The peasant recalls his Mycenaean ancestors, eminent by birth (λαμπροὶ γὰρ ἐς γένος) but poor, which he considers the ruin of nobility of birth (ηὑγένει' ἀπόλλυται) (Eur. *El.* 35–8).⁵² He later declares his intention not to show a lowborn character (τό γ' ἦθος δυσγενές) despite his poverty (Eur. *El.* 362–3). Electra defines her husband as a poor but noble man (πένης ἀνὴρ γενναῖος) (Eur. *El.* 253). Orestes states that worthless men are often born from a noble father (γενναίου πατρός) and good children from bad parents (ἐκ κακῶν). He concludes that Electra's husband, despite his low status, has proved to be most noble (ἄριστος), and men should be considered nobly born (εὐγενεῖς) based on their company and customs (Eur. *El.* 367–90).⁵³ Comedy, on the other hand, shows the possible counterclaims of the supporters of nobility of birth. In a fragment by Eupolis, the Chorus regrets the good old days when the generals came from the greatest families, eminent for wealth and birth (πλούτῳ γένει τε πρῶτοι) (Eup. fr. 384 K.-A.). Aristophanes shows similar concerns for Athenian politics in the parabasis of the *Frogs*. He complains that, while the citizens who are wellborn (εὐγενεῖς) and virtuous are despised, those who are brazen, foreigners and knavish are entrusted with every public affair (Ar. *Ran.* 727–33).⁵⁴

Forensic orators sometimes exploited the ideological tension associated with *eugeneia*. In *Against Meidias*, Demosthenes asserts that there is nothing,

---

⁵⁰ See Donlan [1980] 1999: 131–2.
⁵¹ See Donlan [1980] 1999: 138.
⁵² Cropp 1988: 102.
⁵³ Cf. Eur. *El.* 551: 'many who are noble (εὐγενεῖς) are no good (κακοί)' (trans. Cropp).
⁵⁴ See Mann 2007: 138–40.

even birth (γένος), wealth or power, which the Athenians should tolerate in a person if *hybris* is present (Dem. 21.143). To reinforce his accusation against Meidias, the orator recalls how even Alcibiades, who was a man of a different stamp from the plaintiff, had been punished by the Athenians for his *hybris* even though he was an Alcmeonid (Dem. 21.144–7). Nobility of birth is valued to the extent that Demosthenes can use it as the measure of the gravity of the crime of *hybris*, considered so serious that not even good birth can compensate for it.[55] By hinting at Alcibiades' excessive behaviour, the passage also testifies to the negative aspects and suspicions often associated with high birth and aristocratic lifestyle in democratic Athens. In Demosthenes' *Against Conon*, for example, Ariston anticipates that Conon will minimise his accusation of battery. The defendant will claim that the episode was simply one of the many fights over courtesans in which many sons of *kaloi kagathoi*, who playfully call themselves *ithyphalloi* or *autolēkythoi*, often get involved (Dem. 54.13–14). Ariston, who since the beginning of the speech has depicted Conon and his sons as excessive and hubristic,[56] states that the so-called *ithyphalloi* indulge in acts that respectable people would be ashamed to mention or do (Dem. 54.17).[57] What is under attack here is not so much aristocratic status as such, but the most excessive and despicable manifestations of aristocratic lifestyle.[58]

As Aristotle states in the *Politics*, *eugeneia*, together with wealth, virtue and education, was one of the marks of elite status (Arist. *Pol.* 1291b14–30).[59] As such, nobility of birth could carry some negative weight due to the excesses that the democratic *polis* sometimes associated with elite behaviour. However, even under the democracy, *eugeneia* was at the same time a desirable attribute and, somewhat paradoxically, not an exclusively aristocratic one. Aristotle in the *Rhetoric* significantly treats *eugeneia* as both an individual and a collective feature. Nobility of birth is one of the components of happiness, which according to the philosopher is always the object of discussion of speeches of exhortation and dissuasion. Aristotle states that, for nations and cities (ἔθνει μὲν καὶ πόλει), *eugeneia* consists in being autochthonous or of ancient origins (τὸ αὐτόχθονας ἢ ἀρχαίους εἶναι) and in having great ancestors. For individuals (ἰδίᾳ), on the other hand, nobility of birth is a quality acquired from either the father or the mother, and depends on one's legitimacy of birth and the renown of one's family (Arist. *Rh.* 1360b). Aristotle therefore provides a

---

[55] See Ober 1989a: 254–5, with further examples of what Ober calls 'the "convicted, though high born" topos'.
[56] Cf. Dem. 54.3–9.
[57] Ober 1989a: 255–9.
[58] On democratic suspicions towards aristocratic lifestyle, see Cairns 2003: 244–7 and Fisher 2003.
[59] Ober 1989a: 11–12.

definition of *eugeneia* that grants equal value to individual and collective claims of nobility. The philosopher's statement reflects the usage of his time, when the notion of Athenian collective *eugeneia* had been firmly established by the *epitaphios logos* thanks to the myth of autochthony.

The application of nobility of birth to the Athenian *dēmos* through the myth of autochthony has notably been interpreted as a democratisation of an aristocratic value.[60] The evidence discussed shows that this was not in fact the case. The ideal of *eugeneia* had been an object of criticism even in the pre-democratic society of the archaic period, where it provided an argument in the political struggle rather than the absolute domain of a hereditary aristocracy. The absence of a clear line dividing a class and a moral connotation of nobility, already witnessed in Theognis, similarly suggests that *eugeneia* was not necessarily connected to aristocracy. Rather than as a prerogative of aristocratic ideology that the *dēmos* communalised and claimed for itself,[61] *eugeneia* should be seen as an attribute that, although partly frowned upon in democratic Athens, was generally highly valued and could be used indifferently for praising collectives or individuals.[62] Good birth enjoyed considerable prestige since the Homeric epics, and the notion of *eugeneia* had always been employed in claims of excellence. It was therefore naturally suitable to express the exclusive status of Athenian autochthony.

AUTOCHTHONY AND COLLECTIVE *EUGENEIA* AT THE STATE FUNERAL

Autochthony was a paramount component of the rhetoric of the *epitaphios logos*. At the state funeral for the war dead, orators created a shared image of Athens and its past that contributed to building an imagined community and justifying the prospect of dying for the city. Funeral speeches therefore ignored the earthborn kings of Attica and used autochthony to claim nobility of birth (*eugeneia*) for the Athenian community. In doing so, they deployed a common set of images. These included the metaphor of the Athenian community as a family, the contrast of individual versus collective, and the language of legitimacy of birth. Through these images, orators of funeral speeches were able to paint a picture of Athens as an equal and socially cohesive society.

[60] See Ober 1989a: 259–66; Loraux [1996] 2000: 21–3; Lape 2010: 26–7; more generally, see Loraux 1981 for the idea that the Athenian democracy appropriated aristocratic values for itself.

[61] See van Wees and Fisher 2015: 33, who suggest that there is 'no reason to regard allusions to good birth and collective autochthony in Athenian political discourse as evidence that "aristocratic values" had become "democratized"'. The very existence in ancient Greece of an aristocracy in the modern sense of the term has been questioned by van Wees and Fisher 2015.

[62] See Duplouy 2006: 49–56.

Demosthenes elects *eugeneia* as a topic of praise at the beginning of his *Funeral Speech*. He states that the Athenians deserve praise not only for their courage, but also because 'it was their lot to have been nobly born (γεγενῆσθαι καλῶς) and rigorously educated to acquire wisdom, and to have dedicated their lives to the highest goals' (Dem. 60.3, trans. Worthington). The orator recalls autochthony as the proof of the Athenians' nobility of birth (ἡ γὰρ εὐγένεια τῶνδε τῶν ἀνδρῶν), which is envisioned as a collective quality levelling all social differences between citizens. The passage is constructed on the opposition between individual and collective. According to Demosthenes, not only is it possible to trace back the war dead and each of their ancestors individually (κατ' ἄνδρα) to a father, but also collectively (κοινῇ) to their entire fatherland, of which they are recognised to be autochthonous (ἧς αὐτόχθονες ὁμολογοῦνται εἶναι).[63] The coexistence of individual and collective ancestry poses no problem to the orator, and autochthony is used in order to portray the Athenian community as a family.[64] Demosthenes further exploits the connection between *eugeneia* and the image of the family as he highlights that the Athenians are the only people who have been living in the same land from which they were born (ἐξ ἧσπερ ἔφυσαν). Consequently, while those who arrive in their cities as immigrants (ἐπήλυδας) can be compared to adopted children (ὁμοίους εἶναι τοῖς εἰσποιητοῖς τῶν παίδων), the Athenians are legitimate (γνησίους) citizens of their fatherland by birth (Dem. 60.4). The orator develops the image of the family by exploiting the similarities between the language of naturalisation and that of adoption and family law:[65] the Athenians are the only ones who can be regarded as legitimate children (*gnēsioi*), as opposed to the other nations, who are made up of immigrants and can be compared to adopted children (*eispoiētoí*).[66]

In Demosthenes' *Funeral Speech*, autochthony is thus intertwined with the themes of nobility and legitimacy of birth; not only does the myth supply the foundation of Athens' harmony and social cohesion, but it also provides a prestigious claim of superiority over the rest of the nations. Hyperides adopts a

---

[63] Loraux [1996] 2000: 24–5 interpreted the passage as excluding Athenian women from the generation of citizens. Such gender issues, however, if at all present, are not raised explicitly by the orator.

[64] Loraux [1981] 1993: 51.

[65] Naturalised citizens could be referred to as ποιητοὶ πολῖται (cf. Arist. *Pol.* 1275a6; Dem. 45.78) or δημοποίητοι (cf. Plut. *Sol.* 24.2): see M. J. Osborne 1983: 139. Adopted children could be referred to as εἰσποιητοὶ υἱοί (cf. [Dem.] 44.34; Isae. 3.61) or ποιητοὶ υἱοί (cf. [Dem.] 44.39; Isae. 5.6). On adoption in classical Athens, see Rubinstein 1993.

[66] See Ogden 1996: 168. Demosthenes then reinforces the image by giving a literal twist to the metaphor of the family. For the orator, the fact that the fruits of the earth first arose in Attica is the proof that the land itself was the mother of the Athenian ancestors (μητέρα τὴν χώραν εἶναι τῶν ἡμετέρων προγόνων) (Dem. 60.5).

similar strategy in his *Funeral Speech*. Like Demosthenes, Hyperides constructs the praise of Athenian autochthony on the opposition of individual versus collective, and contrasts the pure and noble origins of the Athenians with the mixed origins of other nations. According to the orator, to trace the individual (κατ' ἄνδρα) genealogy of the war dead would be necessary in the case of other nations, who have gathered in one city from many places (πολλαχόθεν) and brought their individual lineage (γένος ἴδιον) to the common stock. To relate the ancestry of the Athenians individually (ἰδίᾳ), on the other hand, would be superfluous, because their common origin (ἡ κοινὴ γένεσις) due to their autochthony (αὐτόχθοσιν οὖσιν) grants them unsurpassed *eugeneia* (Hyp. 6.7). Hyperides therefore downplays the importance of the individual family (*genos*) and extends *eugeneia* to the entire Athenian community, adopting at the same time an oppositional strategy in defining Athenian purity against the composite nature of other nations.[67]

The theme of *eugeneia* opens the praise of the Athenians also in Plato's *Menexenus*, where Socrates elects the Athenians' nobility of birth as the first topic of his speech (Pl. *Menex.* 237a). In his parody of the *epitaphios logos*, Plato abandons the dialectic between individual and collective and gives a literal interpretation of the metaphor of the Athenian community as a family. Socrates states that their ancestors' non-immigrant origin (ἡ τῶν προγόνων γένεσις οὐκ ἔπηλυς οὖσα) is the prime cause of the nobility (εὐγενείας) of the war dead and, implicitly, of the Athenians as a whole. The Athenians are characterised as indigenous (αὐτόχθονας) inhabitants of their fatherland as opposed to foreign residents (μετοικοῦντας) (Pl. *Menex.* 237b). More importantly, they are represented literally as children of their land.[68] According to Socrates, the Athenians are the only ones who have not been raised (τρεφομένους) by a stepmother (μητρυιᾶς), but by their very mother-land (μητρὸς τῆς χώρας). Their land itself gave birth to them (τεκούσης), reared them and received them at the moment of their death (Pl. *Menex.* 237c). The status of children of the land is not limited to the first earthborn Athenian ancestors,[69] but is extended to the whole citizen body through the war dead, whose noble birth (ἡ τῶνδε εὐγένεια) is restated at the end of the passage (Pl. *Menex.* 237c). The idea of collective *eugeneia* is again exploited as a distinctive quality of the Athenians

---

[67] The concept of an oppositional strategy of self-definition, applied here to Athenian identity, is borrowed from Hall 1997: 44–51. In investigating the construction of Greek ethnic identity, Hall distinguishes between an aggregative mechanism of self-definition, typical of archaic Greece and based on the claim of common descent from Hellen, and an oppositional mechanism that came about after the Persian Wars and defined the Greeks through comparison and opposition with the barbarians.

[68] Cf. also Pl. *Menex.* 237e. See Tsitsiridis 1998: 201–2.

[69] *Pace* Tsitsiridis 1998: 198.

in comparison with non-Athenians. Through the contrast between mother and stepmother and the corresponding dichotomy between αὐτόχθονας and μετοικοῦντας,[70] Socrates therefore carries out the same oppositional strategy deployed by Demosthenes and Hyperides.

To provide the grounds for the Athenian claim to *eugeneia* is the main but not only function of autochthony in Plato's *Menexenus*. When praising the constitution of the Athenians, Socrates recalls autochthony as an aetiology of their *isonomia*. Socrates, not without a hint of irony, defines Athens' constitution as an aristocracy (ἀριστοκρατία), understood in the etymological sense of 'rule of the best'.[71] He then states that nobody is excluded from the city's political life 'by his weakness or poverty or by the obscurity of his parentage' (Pl. *Menex*. 238d; trans. Lamb).[72] Socrates in turn traces the root (αἰτία) of Athens' constitution back to the Athenians' equality of birth (ἡ ἐξ ἴσου γένεσις). He states that the other cities are inhabited by people of diverse origins; this results in their tyrannical and oligarchic regimes, where the citizens regard each other as slaves or masters. The Athenians, on the other hand, are all brothers born of the same mother (μιᾶς μητρὸς πάντες ἀδελφοὶ φύντες) and politically equal. Their equality of birth (ἡ ἰσογονία) according to nature (κατὰ φύσιν) results in their equality of rights (ἰσονομίαν) according to law (κατὰ νόμον) (Pl. *Menex*. 238e–39a). Plato thus carries on with the opposition between Athens and the other *poleis*. He insists on the superiority of the Athenian constitution, which grants all citizens equality of rights as a consequence of their equality of birth deriving from autochthony. The political cohesion of the Athenian community is once again expressed through the metaphor of the family, as the Athenians are now literally envisioned as brothers born from one mother, the Attic land.

The notion of *eugeneia* and the metaphor of the family are less prominent in Lysias, who nevertheless insists on social cohesion as the natural result of Athenian autochthony and introduces the notion of *homonoia* otherwise unattested in the surviving funeral speeches.[73] After a long narrative on the mythical exploits of the

---

[70] See Tsitsiridis 1998: 201. Cf. also Pl. *Menex*. 245c6–d6, where the Athenians are the only pure Greeks who did not mix up with barbarians (αὐτοὶ Ἕλληνες, οὐ μιξοβάρβαροι) and are by nature haters of the barbarians (φύσει μισοβάρβαρον).

[71] See Tsitsiridis 1998: 225.

[72] Cf. Thuc. 2.37.1.

[73] But see Bearzot 2015: 104–7, who notes that Pericles' funeral speech, without relying on the vocabulary of *homonoia*, conveys a picture of Athens that emphasises the peaceful coexistence of its citizens and establishes a connection between democracy and concord (Thuc. 2.37.2–3). It cannot be ruled out, as suggested by Frangeskou 1998–9: 320, that Lysias' status as a metic (and the fact that he was granted Athenian citizenship for having supported the democratic restoration, only to be later disenfranchised: see Todd 2007: 6 n. 20) had an impact on his unusual rendition of the myth of autochthony. This, however, does not affect my argument that Lysias' treatment of autochthony reflects the discursive parameters of the state funeral for the war dead.

ancestors, Lysias goes on to explain these deeds by referring to the autochthonous origins of the Athenians.[74] The orator states that the ancestors, having one single mind (μιᾷ γνώμῃ χρωμένοις), used to fight for justice, because the origin of their life was itself just. Unlike most nations (οἱ πολλοί), they did not gather from multiple places, nor did they drive other people out and inhabit a land that did not belong to them (τὴν ἀλλοτρίαν). Because of their autochthony (αὐτόχθονες ὄντες), the Athenian ancestors had the same land as their mother and fatherland (τὴν αὐτὴν ἐκέκτηντο μητέρα καὶ πατρίδα) (Lys. 2.17).

The passage is constructed on the usual oppositional strategy, which here contrasts the autochthonous and righteous Athenians with the unjust and ethnically diverse majority of nations. Lysias, however, does not fully develop the motif of *eugeneia* and legitimate birth. Nobility of birth is mentioned only in passing at the beginning of the historical narrative on the Persian Wars. There, the orator states that, because they were nobly born (φύντες καλῶς), the ancestors accomplished many admirable deeds (Lys. 2.20). The metaphor of legitimacy of birth only appears later in the speech, when Lysias comments that at Salamis the Athenians 'taught the barbarians of Asia that their own valour was of legitimate birth and native to their soil (γνησίαν δὲ καὶ αὐτόχθονα)' (Lys. 2.43, trans. Lamb, adapted). At the same time, the orator expands the traditional opposition between autochthonous and immigrants. He characterises the other nations as illegitimate inhabitants of lands that belong to others, and turns autochthony into an aetiology of the Athenians' commitment to the cause of justice and humaneness (*philanthrōpia*).[75] The metaphor of the Athenian community as a family is present, but Lysias exploits it very briefly. The orator simply states that the Athenians, because of their autochthony, had the same land (τὴν αὐτήν) as mother (μητέρα) and fatherland (πατρίδα). The structure of the passage, based on the correlation between τὴν ἀλλοτρίαν and τὴν αὐτήν, makes it clear that the metaphor is here a component of the broader oppositional strategy; rather than focusing on the motif of pure descent and nobility of birth, it furthers the argument of the Athenians' natural devotion to justice due to their autochthonous origins.

Even though he does not fully exploit the set of motifs which orators of funeral speeches traditionally use to conceptualise autochthony, Lysias shares their purpose in recalling this myth. In accordance with the discursive parameters of the state funeral for the war dead, autochthony contributes to building an ideal image of Athens as socially and politically cohesive.

---

[74] Todd 2007: 227 rightly notes that Lysias' *Funeral Oration* is distinctive in its use of autochthony as a summary to ease the transition from the mythical to the historical exploits.

[75] For a detailed discussion of Athenian *philanthrōpia*, see Chapter 5, pp. 122–6.

Set during the long aftermath of the democratic restoration,[76] Lysias' *Funeral Oration* achieves this goal by relying on the concept of concord (*homonoia*). This notion emerged during the civil unrest affecting Athens in the last decade of the fifth century and quickly became a keyword in Athenian public discourse.[77] *Homonoia* is introduced for the first time in the speech when Lysias establishes it as an ancestral quality of the Athenians, whose unity of intent (μιᾷ γνώμῃ χρωμένοις) in fighting for justice is made to derive from their autochthonous origins.[78] The centrality of *homonoia* in Lysias' account of Athenian autochthony is even more evident if one reads the passage together with the following paragraph, as the Greek itself suggests by linking them through the correlative particles μέν and δέ. The passage introduces the topic of Attica's synoecism. The orator states that the Athenians had been the first and only ones to expel the oligarchies (δυναστείας) in power among them and to establish a democracy,[79] as they believed that the freedom of all was the greatest form of concord (ὁμόνοιαν). Lysias goes on to add that the Athenians made the hopes deriving from their perils common (κοινάς) to one another and administered the state with free souls (Lys. 2.18). Not only does the passage reprise the traditional contrast between individual and communal, but it also restates the theme of *homonoia* just alluded to in the paragraph on autochthony. By making this notion one of the guiding principles of the founders of the democracy, Lysias therefore grounds Athenian democracy itself in *homonoia*.

Lysias' interest in *homonoia* does not just affect his view of autochthony. Due to the historical context of the speech, which is set about ten years after the democratic restoration and reflects the political climate of the Amnesty,[80]

---

[76] Todd 2007: 163–4, who sees the speech as a display piece written for private circulation, places the dramatic date in the late 390s. Piovan 2011: 291–4 defends the possibility that Lysias actually delivered the speech, but similarly dates it to the period between 393 and 391/0 BC.

[77] On the notion of *homonoia* and its history, see de Romilly 1972; Thériault 1996: 6–13; Cuniberti 2007; Daverio Rocchi 2007; Cobetto Ghiggia 2012; Bearzot 2015. The verb ὁμονοέω is first attested in Thuc. 8.75.2, while the noun ὁμόνοια occurs for the first time in Thuc. 8.93.3. Both passages deal with events connected to the oligarchic coup in 411 BC. For the theme of *homonoia* in the orators, cf. e.g. Lys. 25.20, 27; 18.17–19; Andoc. 1.73, 76; Dem. 20.110; 22.77; 24.185; Isoc. 12.178. Cuniberti 2007: 51–2 posits that *homonoia* originated as a philosophical concept and later passed into the political realm, thus explaining its use by both democrats and sympathisers of oligarchy.

[78] See Todd 2007: 229 for this connection.

[79] Todd 2007: 228 notes the implicit connection between autochthony and the institution of the democracy in Lysias' treatment, and argues that the link 'presumably relies on the idea that autochthony is something in which all true-born Athenians share equally'. For a survey of the values of the word δυναστεία, see Bearzot 2003: 24–35.

[80] On the date of the speech, see n. 76 above. On the democratic restoration and the Amnesty, see Loraux [1997] 2002, Wolpert 2002 and Shear 2011.

the notion occurs multiple times in the *Funeral Oration*.[81] After appearing in the account of the founding of democracy, *homonoia* is again recalled at the beginning of the narrative on Athens' historical exploits. Lysias states that the ancestors performed noble and marvellous deeds 'because of the nobility of their nature and the harmony of their thoughts' (γνόντες ὅμοια),[82] thus summarising the main themes of the sections on autochthony and the synoecism (Lys. 2.20; trans. Todd). Lysias alludes to *homonoia* again when describing the mental disposition of the Athenians in facing the Persian threat at Marathon, where they marched against the enemy all of one accord (ταῦτα μιᾷ γνώμῃ πάντες γνόντες) (Lys. 2.24). Finally, the orator praises those who fought against the Thirty and restored the democracy because they made it clear that the city was in harmony (ὁμονοοῦσαν) and not divided into factions (στασιαζούσης) (Lys. 2.63).[83] The successful return of the *dēmos* in spite of the ongoing civil strife (στασιάσαντες πρὸς ἀλλήλους) is taken as evidence that, if the Athenians had been of one mind (ὁμονοοῦντες), they would easily have won the war against the Peloponnesians (Lys. 2.65). Lysias' insistence on *homonoia* is not surprising. In the political climate in which the speech – if not actually delivered – is imagined to take place, the state funeral for the war dead offered a valuable occasion for rekindling Athens' imagined community, and appealing to *homonoia* was an appropriate way to achieve this goal.

Given the prominence of the theme throughout the speech, *homonoia* becomes the natural focus of Lysias' section on autochthony together with and even more than *eugeneia*. In attributing autochthonous origins to the ancestors as a whole, the orator establishes not only their unique propensity to fight for justice but also their social cohesion and unity of intent as innate attributes of the Athenians. Lysias adopts a sort of cyclic composition starting from the autochthonous origins of the ancestors and culminating in the democratic restoration. In doing so, he stresses the importance of *homonoia* throughout the whole of Athenian history. If concord had seemingly been lost during the dramatic events connected with the rule of the Thirty, the men of the Piraeus proved this to be contrary to the Athenian nature. Together with

---

[81] See Todd 2007: 229. The importance of *homonoia* in the aftermath of the democratic restoration (and as one of the founding values of democracy according to Lysias) is rightly highlighted by Piovan 2011: 302–4. See also B. D. Gray 2015: 37–41, who shows how reconciliation agreements within divided communities could be based on *homonoia*.

[82] See Todd 2007: 230.

[83] A further occurrence can be found in Lys. 2.43, but here the verb ὁμονοέω is used metaphorically to argue that the Athenians derived from their victory at Salamis a prosperity equal to their dangers.

the democracy, they restored that *homonoia* that (at least in Lysias' narrative) had always been a distinctive feature of their community.

Whether they focus on the Athenians' collective *eugeneia* or praise their natural *homonoia*, the extant funeral speeches all share the same rhetorical strategy and a common set of motifs when dealing with the topic of autochthony. At the state funeral, orators paid no attention to the earthborn kings of Attica. In doing so, they resolved the potential ambiguities inherent in the complete notion of autochthony by unequivocally attributing autochthony to the Athenians as a whole. This collective focus was achieved through a rhetoric based on the contrast between individual and collective, the metaphor of the Athenian community as a family, and the language of legitimacy of birth. Autochthony was also taken as a sign of Athenian uniqueness. It was part of a strategy of identity-making that opposed Athens to all other cities and contrasted the autochthonous to the immigrants. This view of Athenian autochthony, which in most surviving funeral speeches is summarised under the rubric of collective *eugeneia*, in Lysias' *Funeral Oration* is conceptualised mainly (though not exclusively) in terms of *homonoia*. Lysias' account of autochthony is instructive in two respects. First, the inclusion of the notion of *homonoia*, a relative newcomer in Athenian public discourse, attests to the dynamic nature of Athenian ideological practice. The ideas and values of the Athenian *dēmos*, in other words, were not a fixed monolith; they were constantly discussed and re-discussed inside and outside the formal institutions of the state, and the role of the orators in these dynamics was far from negligible.[84] Second, despite his variations on the epitaphic script of Athenian autochthony, Lysias shares with the other orators of funeral speeches the same image of Athens as a cohesive community where social and political inequalities are levelled by the common autochthonous origins of its inhabitants.[85] This in turn illustrates the discursive parameters which operated at the state funeral for the war dead. Such parameters required the orators to provide the mourners with an image of Athens that could console them for the sacrifice of their relatives and inspire them to follow their example. By appealing to the Athenians' collective *eugeneia* and to their natural *homonoia*, the *epitaphios logos* was not ideological in the sense that it concealed the internal divisions of the Athenian citizen body,[86] but rather in the sense that it focused on the integrative and cohesive side of autochthony in order to create an imagined community.

---

[84] *Pace* Ober 1989a: esp. 304–6.
[85] The Athenian model of autochthony as a source of social cohesion contrasted with Thebes' divisive model of autochthony: see Montanari 1981: 151–5.
[86] *Pace* Loraux 1981: esp. 206–7.

DECONSTRUCTING AUTOCHTHONY ON THE TRAGIC STAGE

The traditions of the Athenians' collective autochthony and the earthborn kings of Attica coexist on the tragic stage in Euripides' *Ion*.[87] The play tells the story of Creusa, daughter of Erechtheus and only surviving member of Athens' earthborn royal family. Creusa arrives in Delphi with her non-Athenian husband Xuthus to consult the oracle about their childlessness. Her secret purpose, however, is to enquire about the fate of the son she had begotten after being raped by Apollo and whom she had then exposed. The boy is now a servant in the temple of Apollo in Delphi, where mother and son, unaware of their respective identities, meet and engage in conversation. Xuthus is advised by the oracle that the first person he will meet outside the temple will be his son. Having run into the young servant, Xuthus mistakes him for a son he may have had from some Delphian girl. He therefore names him Ion, and persuades him to follow him to Athens to become the future king of the city. Feeling betrayed by her husband and Apollo, Creusa follows the advice of her Old Tutor and makes an attempt on Ion's life. When her plan is discovered, she flees to the altar of the god to avoid Ion's revenge. There, however, the recognition between mother and son takes place, and Ion and Creusa are finally reunited. The play ends with the arrival of Athena, who invites Creusa to set Ion on Athens' royal throne as Xuthus' son. The goddess foretells that Ion's descendants will colonise Ionia, while Xuthus and Creusa's future sons, Dorus and Achaeus, will originate the Dorians and the Achaeans.[88]

Creusa's personal tragedy runs parallel with her political tragedy. Not only is she ignorant of the fate of the son she once exposed, but she also feels the pressure of having to perpetuate the earthborn line of the Erechtheidae and grant a suitable king to the autochthonous people of Athens.[89] The theme of autochthony is thus omnipresent throughout the play, as Euripides explores the ideal picture of Athenian autochthony traditionally produced at the state

---

[87] See Loraux [1981] 1993: 200.
[88] For a survey of the themes of the play, which are not limited to autochthony, see Lee 1997: 30–8.
[89] Most scholars interpret Euripides' *Ion* not as an enthusiastic endorsement of the ideology of autochthony, but as somewhat critical of it: see e.g. Walsh 1978; Saxonhouse 1986; Loraux [1981] 1993: 184–236; Lape 2010: 95–136; Leão 2012; Kasimis 2013. But see Lee 1997: 36, who rightly notes that Euripides' treatment of autochthony is ambiguous, and states that 'if *Ion* cannot be treated simply as a vehicle for national pride, subversive readings too need to take account of the complexity of the play and of Euripides' work generally'. On the ambivalence of Euripides' *Ion* in the treatment of several themes, including autochthony, see recently G. Martin 2018: 6–12.

funeral.⁹⁰ The poet reinterprets and reverses the images that funeral speeches associate with autochthony. In doing so, he subtly highlights the ambiguities and contradictions within the Athenians' claim of autochthony.⁹¹ This operation would have been inappropriate at the state funeral for the war dead. The dramatic festivals, however, empowered Euripides to pose questions about the Athenian ideology of autochthony, which is finally reaffirmed at the end of the play thanks to the *ex machina* intervention of Athena.

While the surviving funeral speeches all ignore the earthborn kings in their discussion of autochthony, Euripides puts Creusa and the Erechtheid family right at the centre of it. This of course is partly due to the nature of the tragic genre, where the individual stories of the protagonists play the main role. Hermes therefore introduces Creusa as a direct descendant of the earthborn Erichthonius (γηγενοῦς Ἐριχθονίου) (Eur. *Ion* 20–1), and Ion is curious to know whether Erichthonius had really been born from the earth (ἐκ γῆς πατρός σου πρόγονος ἔβλαστεν πατήρ;) (Eur. *Ion* 267–74). The earthborn origin of the Erechtheid family is also evoked in a dialogue between Creusa and her Old Tutor (Eur. *Ion* 999–1000), and again by Creusa, when she rejoices for the luminous future of the earthborn house (γηγενέτας δόμος) after her recognition with Ion (Eur. *Ion* 1466–7). Yet, since the play's prologue, Creusa's earthborn legacy coexists with the broader claim of Athenian autochthony, as Hermes recalls how he once had to go to the autochthonous people of famous Athens (λαὸν εἰς αὐτόχθονα κλεινῶν Ἀθηνῶν) to save the baby of Apollo and Creusa (Eur. *Ion* 29–30).

By focusing on Creusa's individual tragedy, Euripides reverses the treatment of one of the main components of the discourse of autochthony in the *epitaphios logos*: the theme of *eugeneia*. Nobility of birth is constantly recalled throughout the play and is highly valued by the characters, but is always employed as an individual feature.⁹² During his first encounter with Creusa, Ion immediately recognises her noble status (γενναιότης) and states that it is usually possible to tell from one's appearance whether one is nobly born (εὐγενής) (Eur. *Ion* 237–40). After enquiring about Creusa's earthborn pedigree, Ion asks her about her husband and assumes that he must also be nobly born (εὐγενῆ) (Eur. *Ion* 289–92). The theme of *eugeneia* is picked up again by Xuthus. When trying to persuade Ion to follow him to Athens, he promises

---

⁹⁰ As noted by Saxonhouse 1986: 254, it is Xuthus, not Euripides, who denies the notion of autochthony as birth from the earth (Eur. *Ion* 542), but the poet nevertheless 'forces the citizens of Athens to look critically at the Athenian myth of autochthony [...] to make them reflect on the implications of such a myth'.

⁹¹ See Leão 2012: 150–1. But see Lape 2010: 135, who rightly rejects the view that 'Ion's bastardy should be read as ironic or critical of Athenian ideology'.

⁹² See Walsh 1978: 301.

him that instead of ill-born (δυσγενής) and poor he will be called well-born (εὐγενής) and rich (Eur. *Ion* 579–80). The Chorus, when praying for the success of Creusa's plot against Ion, wishes that nobody from another family would ever rule the city in place of the noble Erechtheidae (τῶν εὐγενετᾶν Ἐρεχθειδᾶν) (Eur. *Ion* 1058–60).[93] Creusa praises Apollo because he gave Ion to Xuthus as his son despite being the boy's real father and established him in a noble house (εὐγενῆ δόμον) (Eur. *Ion* 1540–1). Apollo's benefaction to Ion is later confirmed by Athena, who states that the god gave Ion to the noblest house (οἶκον εὐγενέστατον) (Eur. *Ion* 1561–2).

In contrast with the constant concern of the characters in the play with individual nobility of birth, Euripides never uses the vocabulary of *eugeneia* to refer to the Athenians as a whole.[94] This is significant, if one considers that the Athenians' collective *eugeneia* is constantly associated with autochthony in the extant funeral speeches, where it is the main marker of the cohesion of the Athenian community. Euripides focuses on nobility of birth as an individual feature, and particularly as a characteristic of Creusa and her earthborn family. In doing so, he reveals the ambiguity of appealing to autochthony – as Socrates, for example, does in Plato's *Menexenus* – as the source of the Athenians' equality of birth and *isonomia*. More importantly, the absence of the rhetoric of collective *eugeneia* shows that in Euripides' *Ion* the myth of autochthony is not recalled to build the Athenian identity and construct an imagined community. The image of social cohesion that funeral speeches convey through the notion of collective *eugeneia* is here downplayed, and the author problematises the ideology of autochthony.

The metaphor of the Athenian community as a family, cherished by the orators at the state funeral, disappears on the background of the private drama of Creusa and her household. The Athenian claim of autochthony is briefly introduced by Hermes in the prologue, and during the rest of the play is only seen through the eyes of foreign characters. These either highlight the exclusive aspects of autochthony, or challenge the very concept of birth from the

---

[93] Lee 1997 at Eur. *Ion* 1058–9 accepts Murray's emendation ἄλλος ἥκων instead of the transmitted text ἄλλος ἄλλων ἀπ' οἴκων, and renders the passage as 'never may a newcomer rule my city in place of the Erechtheidai of noble birth'. This may lead one to interpret τῶν εὐγενετᾶν Ἐρεχθειδᾶν as referring not literally to the Erechtheid family but figuratively to the Athenians as a whole. Yet, the context of the passage, where the Chorus wishes for the poison to reach 'the one making an attack on the house of the Erechtheidai (τῶν Ἐρεχθεϊδᾶν δόμων)' (Eur. *Ion* 1056–7; trans. Lee), suggests that the expression refers to the Erechtheid family.

[94] *Pace* Walsh 1978: 313, who argues that 'against the conflict of class loyalty and patriotism, the *Ion* depicts the Athenians as sharing a common εὐγένεια'. See also Loraux [1981] 1993: 203, and Lape 2010: 108, who suggests that 'aristocratic *eugeneia* was not the measure of worth in the democratic polis; it was rather the democratically revised conception of *eugeneia* as birth from two natives'.

land that was a corollary of the complete notion of autochthony. When Ion, still unaware of his mother's identity, wonders whether he may have been born from the earth (γῆς ἆρ' ἐκπέφυκα μητρός;), Xuthus, the foreigner married to the *über*-autochthonous Creusa, mockingly replies that the ground does not bear children (οὐ πέδον τίκτει τέκνα) (Eur. *Ion* 542).[95] Ion later expresses doubts over following Xuthus to Athens because he is aware that he would be treated as an outsider.[96] He states that, if he will arrive among the autochthonous (αὐτόχθονας) people of Athens, who are said not to be an immigrant race (οὐκ ἐπείσακτον γένος), he will be regarded as suffering from two plagues (δύο νόσω): having a foreign father (πατρός τ' ἐπακτοῦ) and being of bastard birth (νοθαγενής) (Eur. *Ion* 589–92).[97] The theme of legitimacy of birth, which orators of funeral speeches employ metaphorically in order to praise the superiority of the Athenians over the other Greeks as legitimate children of their land, takes a very concrete twist for Ion. The boy then worries that he who joins a pure (καθαράν) city, even if he is a citizen by name, has the mouth of a slave and does not enjoy freedom of speech (Eur. *Ion* 670–5).

In the eyes of Xuthus and Ion, Athens does not appear as a united family, but as a close community which is reluctant to welcome outsiders into its social fabric.[98] This contradiction within the image of the city comes to an extreme when Creusa, unaware of his real identity, plans to kill Ion. Her attempted murder of her own son endangers Creusa's own family, but also risks compromising the harmony of the metaphorical family of the autochthonous Athenians, given that Ion is himself an earthborn Athenian. The recognition scene and the *ex machina* appearance of Athena resolve this potential conflict, and implicitly restate the ideology of autochthony. Creusa rejoices at the thought that her newly found son will restore the earthborn house of Erechtheus (Eur. *Ion* 1463–7). The issue of Ion's bastardy is circumvented thanks to Xuthus' unaware adoption of the boy (Eur. *Ion* 1601–3). This deception, sanctioned by and perpetrated upon Athena's advice, would have probably been more acceptable to an Athenian audience than the solution planned by Xuthus, who wanted to introduce Ion, his supposed son, into the Athenian citizen body gradually and make him the next king. Ion discovers that he has

---

[95] Loraux [1981] 1993: 206–7.
[96] See Walsh 1978: 301–2; Loraux [1981] 1993: 205–6.
[97] On Ion's bastardy, see Loraux [1981] 1993: 204; Lape 2010: 128–36; Leão 2012: 148–9.
[98] Cf. Lycurg. 1.41, who in the lawcourts exploits the oppositional aspect of autochthony to further his accusation of treason against Leocrates: 'anyone would have shared their pain and would have wept to see the people who prided themselves on their freedom and racial purity (ἐπὶ τῷ αὐτόχθων εἶναι) voting to grant slaves their freedom, give citizenship to foreigners, and restore privileges to the disenfranchised' (trans. Harris).

an Athenian mother and a divine father. He is thus proven to be a member of the earthborn family of Erechtheus and a suitable citizen of Athens' autochthonous community.[99]

In the *epitaphios logos*, the oppositional strategy which highlights the uniqueness of the Athenians compared to the other Greeks is part of a wider discourse that portrays Athens as a cohesive, equal and democratic society. Euripides plays out the contradictions within this image and highlights the exclusive aspect of autochthony even within the Athenian community.[100] The coexistence of the collective notion of autochthony with the myth of the earthborn kings of Attica is functional to this process, and is revealing of the discursive parameters of the dramatic festivals. Playwrights were free from the task of constructing an imagined community, and could participate in Athenian ideological practice by inviting the audience to reflect upon the ideal image of the city and the values of the community. Euripides therefore reflects on the image of Athens produced at the state funeral, and plays with the themes that funeral speeches commonly associate with the myth of autochthony. The poet downplays the Athenians' collective *eugeneia* in favour of individual nobility, absorbs the image of the city as a family into Creusa's private household, and provides a concrete reading of the metaphor of legitimacy of birth. Through the conflict between the earthborn Creusa and her son, he even raises the spectre of discord within Athens' autochthonous community, until the intervention of Athena finally resolves the tension and restates the ideology of autochthony.

---

[99] Euripides' treatment of autochthony is also connected to Hellenic genealogy. At the end of the play, Athena foretells the origins of the Ionians, the Dorians and the Achaeans (Eur. *Ion* 1575–94). According to a version that goes back to Hesiod's *Catalogue of Women*, Ion was the legitimate son of Xuthus and Creusa (Hes. fr. 10(a).20–4; cf. Hdt. 7.94, 8.44; Eur. fr. 481.9–11; Paus. 7.1.2–5), while Dorus, Xuthus and Aeolus were all sons of Hellen (Hes. fr. 9): see G. Martin 2018: 13–15. Euripides chooses (or possibly invents: see Lee 1998: 39) a version where Ion is instead the son of Apollo and Creusa, his descendants are the colonisers of Ionia (rather than Ionians themselves), and Dorus and Achaeus are the sons of Xuthus and Creusa. Euripides therefore reconciles the myth of autochthony with the tradition of the Athenians' Ionian origins, and states the priority of the Athenians over the Dorians within Hellenic genealogy. These choices have been seen in the light of the historical context of the play (traditionally dated to the 410s), and interpreted as reflecting Athenian attitudes towards the Ionians and the Spartans in the final stage of the Peloponnesian War: see Hall 1997: 51–5. On the dating of Euripides' *Ion*, see Lee 1998: 40 and G. Martin 2018: 24–32.

[100] Walsh 1978: 313 even suggests that, by choosing a servile and unsympathetic character such as the Old Tutor as the main mouthpiece of 'an extreme doctrine of racial purity, the poet invites his audience to reject it'. But see the reasonable doubts expressed by Lee 1998: 36 about readings that interpret the play as openly critical of Athenian ideology. See also Saxonhouse 1986: 273.

AUTOCHTHONY AND EXCLUSIVENESS IN APOLLODORUS' *AGAINST NEAERA*

Autochthony is the subject of a brief account in the pseudo-Demosthenic *Against Neaera*. The passage resolves the ambiguity of the complete notion of autochthony by moving the focus onto the earthborn kings, and reinterprets autochthony so as to reflect and produce Athenian ideas on justice and lawfulness in accordance with the discursive parameters of the lawcourts. In the speech, Apollodorus prosecutes the former courtesan Neaera, non-Athenian concubine of Stephanus, an Athenian citizen.[101] Stephanus and Neaera are accused of living as a married couple in violation of a law that forbade marriages between Athenian citizens and non-Athenians.[102] In what is ultimately an attack against Stephanus, Apollodorus has to show that Neaera is an alien and has been living with Stephanus as a wife. To address the second point, Apollodorus questions the citizen status of Stephanus' children. The orator makes the case that these were in fact Neaera's own children, and not Stephanus'. Stephanus allegedly enrolled them as citizens and passed them off as his own children from a previous marriage with an Athenian woman. Apollodorus focuses in particular on Phano, allegedly Neaera's daughter and therefore a non-Athenian herself. Stephanus had given her in marriage first to Phrastor and then to Theogenes, both Athenian citizens and unaware of Phano's real identity.[103]

Apollodorus' narrative of Phano's marriage with Theogenes is especially interesting. The orator makes the case that Stephanus and Neaera, not content with having passed Phano as a citizen, gave her in marriage to Theogenes. The latter was an Athenian of noble birth (εὐγενῆ), but poor and politically inexperienced, who had just been elected King Archon ([Dem.] 59.72). The last detail is of utmost importance. Giving an alien woman in marriage to an Athenian citizen was itself a crime,[104] but the fact that the Athenian citizen in question

---

[101] Scholars agree in attributing *Against Neaera* to Apollodorus, who delivers most of it: see Trevett 1992: 50–76; Carey 1992: 17; Kapparis 1999: 48–51; MacDowell 2009: 99–100, 121–6. The first part of the speech ([Dem.] 59.1–15) is delivered by Apollodorus' brother-in-law, Theomnestus, who had formally brought the charge against Neaera. On Apollodorus' enmity with Stephanus and on the circumstances leading to Neaera's prosecution, see Carey 1992: 4–8 and Kapparis 1999: 29–31.

[102] The text of the law is quoted in [Dem.] 59.16, but its authenticity has been rightly questioned by Canevaro 2013a: 183–7.

[103] For an outline of the case, see Kapparis 1999: 31–43, who rightly argues that Apollodorus' allegations rested on very weak grounds.

[104] The law forbidding alien women to be given in marriage to Athenian men is quoted at [Dem.] 59.52–3. Apollodorus recalls how Phrastor, Neaera's first husband, had brought a public charge against Stephanus in accordance with this law, but had later dropped it when Stephanus decided to settle their dispute through an arbitration. The text of the law, however, has been shown to be a later forgery by Canevaro 2013a: 187–90.

was the King Archon made the issue appear even more serious. Apollodorus insists on the gravity of this marriage. He points out that Phano, despite being an alien and a prostitute, as wife of the King Archon had performed the rites connected to the festival of the Anthesteria. Such rituals, which included the secret sacrifices and the Marriage of Dionysus, were precluded even to the average Athenian citizen.[105] Apollodorus constantly hints at the exclusivity of these rites, which he characterises as 'many and sacred and not to be spoken of' (πολλὰ καὶ ἅγια καὶ ἀπόρρητα). He stresses that Phano had seen what was not proper for a foreigner to see, and that despite her wicked nature she had entered where only the wife of the King Archon out of all Athenians can enter ([Dem.] 59.73).[106] Even the stele preserving the law which established the criteria that the wife of the King Archon was expected to fulfil was stored in an exclusive location. This was 'the most ancient (ἀρχαιοτάτῳ) and holy (ἁγιωτάτῳ) shrine of Dionysos in the Marshes', and Apollodorus states that it was open only once a year so that only a few people would be able to read the inscription (ἵνα μὴ πολλοὶ εἰδῶσιν τὰ γεγραμμένα) ([Dem.] 59.76; trans. Carey).

To reinforce his allegations against Phano, Apollodorus introduces a digression explaining how the magistracy of the King Archon had come to be instituted. The orator states that in antiquity Athens was a monarchy (δυναστεία) and the kingship belonged to those who each time were prominent because they were autochthonous (ἡ βασιλεία τῶν ἀεὶ ὑπερεχόντων διὰ τὸ αὐτόχθονας εἶναι). At that time, the King used to make all the sacrifices, while his wife, the Basilinna, used to perform the holiest and secret ones ([Dem.] 59.74). After Theseus completed the synoecism and founded the democracy and the city became populous, the ritual functions of the King and his wife passed on to the King Archon, now a magistrate elected by the *dēmos*, and his wife. The Athenians also enacted a law establishing that the wife of the King Archon should be a citizen (ἀστήν) and a virgin at the moment of her wedding ([Dem.] 59.75).[107]

Given the insistence on the exclusivity of the rites illicitly performed by Phano and the centrality of citizenship rights to the trial under discussion, an allusion to autochthony is not surprising. What is unusual in this account is

---

[105] On the Anthesteria and the relative rites, see Parke 1977: 107–20; Kapparis 1999: 324–31; Parker 2005: 290–326.

[106] Blok 2017: 216–17.

[107] Apollodorus reinforces this argument by adding that, according to the law on seduction, Phano should have been excluded from all the rituals of the city in the first place ([Dem.] 59.85–7). The orator is here alluding to Phano's alleged affair with a man named Epaenetus: cf. [Dem.] 59.64–71. The document preserving the text of the law, quoted at [Dem.] 59.87, is likely to be a later forgery: see Canevaro 2013a: 190–6. As Kapparis 1999: 353 has rightly pointed out, Apollodorus' argument is faulty and contradictory: if Phano were a prostitute, as the orator portrays her at [Dem.] 59.64–71, then the law on seduction did not apply to her and she would have been free to participate in any rituals.

the fact that the orator implicitly presents autochthony as a factor of inequality within the citizen body. The phrasing of Apollodorus' statement implies a tradition of hereditary kingship that was transmitted by virtue of the unique autochthonous nature of the royal family. The genitive τῶν ἀεὶ ὑπερεχόντων, attached to the nominative ἡ βασιλεία in the predicative position, indicates that the orator is not simply stating that the city was then the kingdom of the autochthonous people of the Athenians, superior to the rest of humanity.[108] Apollodorus is rather stating that the ancient kings of Athens were the exclusive detainers of autochthony and were thus distinguished from the majority of the population.[109] In other words, the orator is subtly alluding to the myth of the earthborn kings of Attica, which at the time of the trial was already intertwined with the notion of Athenian autochthony.

If one reads the passage in conjunction with the following paragraph, however, an alternative interpretation might be possible. Apollodorus states that after Theseus instituted the democracy and the city became populous (πολυάνθρωπος), the Athenians nonetheless kept electing the king, whom they voted via show of hands among preselected candidates on the basis of valour (κατ' ἀνδραγαθίαν) ([Dem.] 59.75). The passage from a hereditary system based on autochthony to an elective system based on worth is made to coincide not only with the birth of democracy but also with the enlargement of Athens' citizen population following the synoecism.[110] Is thus πολυάνθρωπος to be understood not simply as indicating an increase in the amount of Athens' inhabitants but also an inflow of population of disparate origins? A passage in Aristotle's *Politics* seems to support this hypothesis. The philosopher maintains that a great state is not the same as a populous (πολυάνθρωπος) state, and correlates the adjective πολυάνθρωπος with the multitude (πλῆθος) inhabiting a city, which includes slaves, metics and aliens (Arist. *Pol.* 1326a17–25). A passage in Thucydides confirms this interpretation. The historian, when discussing the foundation of Epidamnus by Corcyra, mentions the participation of Corinthian colonists and other Dorians, and states that the city ended up becoming a great and populous (πολυάνθρωπος) power (Thuc. 1.24.3). Although Corinth was Corcyra's mother city and they were both part of the Dorian tribe, the passage nonetheless presents the foundation and demographic growth of Epidamnus as the result of the contribution of people coming from disparate places. Apollodorus may therefore imply that, while under the monarchy Athens was a community of autochthonous people and the King was an expression of such a community, after the synoecism Athens' citizen body

---

[108] Smyth p. 315, par. 1302.
[109] This is how Carey 1992: 123 interprets the passage in his commentary; both Kapparis 1999 and Bers 2003 share the same view in their translations.
[110] See Trevett 1990: 418.

became ethnically heterogeneous and the city started to elect the King Archon on the basis of valour. This hypothesis, however, does not match the logic of Apollodorus' argument, which rather highlights the continuity between the Basilinna and the wife of the King Archon as well as the seriousness of Phano's usurpation of this title.[111] Moreover, by restricting autochthony to the royal family and not to an original core of Athens' population, the orator would make the role of the wife of the King Archon even more exclusive.

Whether one interprets the passage as an allusion to the earthborn nature of the kings or to their membership of an original autochthonous core of Athens' population as opposed to the ethnically diverse population of the democratic city, the orator clearly depicts autochthony as a distinctive feature of a limited part of the citizen body. This is a significant change from the picture provided at the state funeral, where autochthony is envisaged as the unifying quality of the entire Athenian community. Having to persuade the judges of the seriousness of Stephanus and Neaera's offence, Apollodorus exploits the contradictions inherent in the myth of autochthony. He makes the case that, by illegally giving Phano in marriage to the King Archon, the defendants had caused a foreign prostitute to misappropriate a role that was originally meant for the more authentically autochthonous part of the Athenian community. His allusion to the myth of autochthony is therefore couched in terms of justice and lawfulness, and at the same time aims to influence the way the judges think about a specific matter of justice and lawfulness.

The comparison between Apollodorus' allusion to autochthony in the lawcourts and the treatment of the same myth at the state funeral illuminates the different discursive parameters of the two institutional settings. Orators of funeral speeches focused on those aspects of autochthony that claimed Athens' superiority over the rest of the Greeks and at the same time attested the social and political cohesion of the Athenian citizen body. This was consistent with the discursive parameters of the state funeral for the war dead, where the orator was expected to provide the Athenians with an idealised image of a city and create an imagined community. Already a mark of exclusivity in funeral speeches, where it isolated the Athenians from the rest of the Greeks, autochthony was made even more exclusive in the forensic speech *Against Neaera*. Apollodorus set an autochthonous subgroup apart from the rest of the Athenian community in order to further his argument against Phano and her mother. Such a claim, which would have been inappropriate at the state funeral, was instead suitable to the lawcourts. This institutional setting enabled orators to diverge from the ideal image of the city provided at the state funeral. On the other hand, it compelled them to craft their

---

[111] For the same reason, as Kapparis 1999: 334–5 points out, Apollodorus compressed the progressive transition from a hereditary to an elected *basileus* in two stages.

historical and mythical allusions according to the discursive parameters of the lawcourts. These placed importance on the relevance to issues of justice and to the legal charges under discussion, and conditioned the orators into reflecting and creating shared ideas about what was just and lawful.

CONCLUSIONS

Autochthony was a very significant myth for the Athenians, who rehearsed it on countless public occasions. In its final form, which resulted from the combination of the independent traditions of the earthborn kings of Attica and the indigenous Athenians, autochthony was though a potentially ambiguous notion on the ideological level. The mythical figures of the earthborn kings could be perceived as more autochthonous than the rest of the Athenians and imply a disruption of the ideal unity of the citizen body. Political actors resolved this ambiguity by moving the focus away from or onto the earthborn kings, or preferred to play the myth out in its contradictory aspects. In doing so, they attributed exclusiveness and *eugeneia* to larger or smaller sections of the Athenian citizen body and produced more or less inclusive ideas about autochthony. Their choices were conditioned by the discursive parameters of Athenian democratic institutions, and are evidence of the fluid and dynamic nature of Athenian ideological practice.

The myth of autochthony was a myth of exclusiveness and opposition. It always implied the existence of a restricted, superior group distinguished from outsiders by its exclusive participation in the prerogatives of autochthony. This chapter has shown that the size of the autochthonous group was not fixed but could be stretched or narrowed under the influence of different institutions of the democracy, and that autochthony as a result could produce different ideas about the Athenian community. At the state funeral for the war dead, autochthony was couched in terms of opposition and superiority to the rest of the Greeks. Funeral speeches ignored the earthborn kings and portrayed autochthony as a common trait of the whole Athenian community. They relied on a common set of motifs (the opposition between collective and individual, the metaphor of the Athenian community as a family and the language of legitimacy of birth) to convey the idea that the Athenians all shared a collective *eugeneia*. The orators thus provided an image of Athens as socially and politically cohesive which contributed to creating an imagined community.

At the dramatic festivals, the Athenians' collective autochthony could coexist with the individual earthborn nature of the Erechtheid family. Euripides' *Ion* accordingly plays with the epitaphic motifs about autochthony and does not shy away from their contradictory aspects. The poet downplays the Athenians' collective *eugeneia* in favour of Creusa's individual nobility of birth. Political and social cohesion, at least from the point of view of the outsiders Xuthus and Ion, are replaced by the exclusive side of Athenian autochthony, and the metaphor of the Athenians as legitimate children of their land becomes painfully real for Ion. The image of the Athenian community as a family seems shattered as a result of the individual drama of the Erechtheid family, until the poet finally reinstates it thanks to Athena's intervention and Ion's successful integration into Athens' citizen body.

In the lawcourts, the orators could even narrow the commonly accepted picture of Athenian autochthony. This is the case in Apollodorus' *Against Neaera*, where autochthony ceases to be a feature of the Athenian community as a whole and becomes the exclusive domain of the mythical kings of Attica. The speech is a prosecution of the foreign prostitute Neaera, accused of illicitly living with the Athenian Stephanus as a wife. To strengthen his accusation, Apollodorus argues that Neaera gave her daughter, Phano, in marriage to the King Archon. He complains that Phano, herself an alien and a prostitute, as wife of the King Archon had performed the rituals of the Anthesteria, once the exclusive prerogative of the wife of the autochthonous King. The claim of autochthony, sign of Athenian superiority over the rest of the Greeks in the *epitaphios logos*, is made even more exclusive in Apollodorus' forensic speech. The orator pushes the exclusiveness of autochthony to an extreme to make Neaera's infringement of Athens' citizenship laws plain and clear to the judges, and thus uses autochthony to reflect and promote shared ideas about justice and lawfulness.

The dynamic and evolving nature of Athenian ideological practice has been especially illustrated by the account of autochthony in Lysias' *Funeral Oration*. Set in the aftermath of the democratic restoration, the speech shows a certain degree of innovation in handling the myth of autochthony compared to the other funeral speeches. Lysias keeps nobility of birth in the background and focuses instead on the relatively new notion of *homonoia*. The latter, presented as an innate feature of the Athenians due to their autochthonous origins and finally reinstated after the defeat of the Thirty, complements the role of *eugeneia* in expressing the social and political cohesion of the Athenian community. Lysias' treatment of autochthony reinforces the conclusion that, even when introducing variations on the typical rhetorical strategy of the *epitaphios logos*, orators of funeral speeches all responded to the same discursive parameters. At the same time, it attests that Athenian democratic ideology was not a fixed set of ideas, but could come to include new ideas and values that reflected contemporary debates within the *polis*.

CHAPTER 5

Between *Charis* and *Philanthrōpia*: The Heraclidae

The story of how Athens protected the Heraclidae against Eurystheus held a special place in Athenian social memory. This is to some extent surprising, given the strong Peloponnesian connotations of Heracles and his children. The return of the Heraclidae was at the core of Sparta's foundation narrative. The belief that the Spartan kings were the descendants of the Heraclidae can be traced back at least to the seventh century, when it featured in the poems of Tyrtaeus (Tyrtaeus frr. 2.12–15; 11.1; 19.8 West).[1] Heracles, however, figured prominently in Attic pottery of the sixth century. Heracles' fight against Nereus and his introduction to Olympus were particularly popular scenes, and the hero's incidence in Athenian architectural sculpture of the same period is remarkable compared with the rest of Greece.[2] The vases depicting Heracles' introduction to Olympus, which usually show Athena riding a chariot together with the hero, are especially interesting. The scene has been linked with Pisistratus' second rise to power. On that occasion, if we believe Herodotus and the Aristotelian *Constitution of the Athenians*, the future tyrant entered Athens on a golden chariot accompanied by a woman who posed as Athena (Hdt. 1.60; [Arist.] *Ath. Pol.* 14.4). This led John Boardman to postulate that the vases reflect the political use of Heracles on the part of Pisistratus, who fostered the idea of his own identification with the hero.[3]

---

[1] For ancient accounts of the return of the Heraclidae cf. Diod. 4.57–8; Apollod. 2.8; Paus. 2.18.7–8; 3.1.5; 4.3.3–8; see Malkin 1994: 15–45; Hall 1997: 56–65; Luraghi 2008: 47–67; Fowler 2013: 334–42.

[2] Boardman 1975: 1–3. For the 'Nereus' scenes, see *LIMC* s.v. Nereus 16–20; 34–48. For the 'Introduction' scenes, see *LIMC* s.v. Herakles 2847–60; 2881–906.

[3] See Boardman 1972 and 1975. But Boardman 1989: 159 stresses that the vases were not 'the medium for any deliberate political propaganda'.

The Spartans' claim to descend from Heracles, which stems from the myth of the return of the Heraclidae, made its first appearance in Athens at the end of the sixth century in the aftermath of the fall of the Pisistratids. Herodotus recounts how the Spartan king Cleomenes, when trying to impose Isagoras as Athens' ruler, had not been allowed in the temple of Athena on the Acropolis. To the priestess of Athena who accused him of being a Dorian, Cleomenes protested his Achaean ancestry (Hdt. 5.72.3). Cleomenes therefore tried to gain access to the shrine by downplaying the Dorian ancestry of the Spartans as a whole and emphasising the Heraclid ancestry of Sparta's royal families.[4] Herodotus says nothing about the priestess' reply to Cleomenes, but the fact that she was unaware of the king's Achaean roots is in itself significant. Her ignorance of Cleomenes' pedigree may indicate that sixth-century Athenians were unfamiliar with the return of the Heraclidae, or at least with its implications for the Spartans and their control over the Peloponnese.[5] This may be connected with the fact that Athens was at the time still a minor player in the international arena, whose interests probably did not extend much outside Attica.[6] Alternatively, one might read the words of the priestess as implicitly questioning the Spartans' alleged kinship to Heracles. If one credits Boardman's theory, it may even be suggested that, in the instability following the fall of the Pisistratids, the Athenians as a whole tried to appropriate the tyrants' Heraclean imagery. Whatever its interpretation, the episode of Cleomenes and the priestess shows that, at the end of the sixth century, the myth of the return of the Heraclidae was starting to be employed in an Athenian context. This, in conjunction with Heracles' popularity in early Athenian visual arts, led the Athenians to elaborate on an episode in the myth of the Heraclidae where their city played the main role.[7]

The earliest explicit mention of Athens' involvement with the Heraclidae dates to the 470s. Pherecydes tells the story of how, after Heracles' death,

---

[4] Parker 1998: 4–5.

[5] Bremmer 1997: 13–17. The Spartans' claim of descending from the Heraclidae must have been well known in fourth-century Athens, if Procles of Phlius could invite the Athenians to help the Spartans as they once helped their ancestors, the Heraclidae (Xen. *Hell.* 6.5.47). The return of the Heraclidae must have been a familiar myth in Athens already during the fifth century, when Euripides produced four Heraclid plays: *Archelaus* (Eur. F 228–46), *Cresphontes* (Eur. F 448a–59), *Temenidae* (Eur. F 728–40) and *Temenus* (Eur. F 741a–51a). *Archelaus*, however, had been originally produced in Macedonia and may never have been performed in Athens: see Collard and Cropp 2008: 229–33. On the importance of the return of the Heraclidae for the geopolitical order of the Peloponnese, see Luraghi 2014: 139–46.

[6] See Frost 1984a and G. Anderson 2003: 147–51, who both connect Cleisthenes' reforms with the introduction of a proper citizen army and the consequent increase in Athens' military activity. But this view has been recently questioned by van Wees 2013: 63–75.

[7] See Allan 2001: 24–5, who highlights the prestige the Athenians derived from their assimilation of the Heraclid myth and their association with Heracles.

Eurystheus expelled the hero's children from their land and became king. The Heraclidae found shelter in Athens, but Eurystheus invaded the city when the Athenians refused to hand them over and was eventually killed in battle (*FGrHist* 3 F 84).[8] Herodotus' account of the dispute between the Athenians and the Tegeans before the Battle of Plataea suggests that the Athenian stage in the return of the Heraclidae may have been already well established at the time of the Persian Wars. In the passage, the Athenians use their intervention in defence of the Heraclidae as an argument to claim the command of the left wing of the Greek army (Hdt. 9.27).[9] A possible, even earlier allusion to Athens' assistance to the Heraclidae can be found in a fragment of Hecataeus. There Ceyx, king of Trachis, sends the Heraclidae away and suggests that they go to some other country (ἐς ἄλλον τινὰ δῆμον ἀποίχεσθε) (*FGrHist* 1 F 30). Ceyx's advice that the Heraclidae should find refuge somewhere else has been interpreted as a reference to their stay in Athens and may push the invention of the episode to before the end of the sixth century.[10]

The Athenian intervention on behalf of the Heraclidae was a perfect illustration of Athens' military excellence and commitment to the protection of the weak. It is then not surprising that the episode achieved popularity on the tragic stage and in oratory. Only five fragments survive of Aeschylus' *Children of Heracles* (Aesch. frr. 73b–75a, 77), which may have dealt with Athens' help to the Heraclidae or with a theme similar to Sophocles' *Women of Trachis*.[11] Another *Children of Heracles* play was produced by Pamphilus in the fourth century and certainly included a supplication scene (*TrGF* 51 T 1). The only surviving tragedy which relates the story of the Heraclidae in Attica is Euripides' *Children of Heracles*. The play has often been deemed a poetic failure, and modern interpreters have offered diverging interpretations on its meaning and possible political allusions.[12] The Athenian help to the Heraclidae

---

[8] Pindar's *Ninth Pythian* seems to transmit a version that did not feature Athenian intervention. The poet states that Iolaus was buried in Thebes after killing Eurystheus (Pind. *Pyth.* 9.79–83). However, both this detail and a scholion which mentions Eurystheus' burial in Thebes (schol. *ad* Pind. *Pyth.* 9.82) do not necessarily imply that the battle occurred in Thebes (*pace* Allan 2001: 29–30 and Fowler 2013: 343): the bodies may have been transferred to Thebes, and Pindar may have overlooked the Attic setting and Athens' involvement in order not to obscure Iolaus and Thebes. On the dating of Pherecydes' activity see p. 170 with references. The detail of Eurystheus' death in Attica will later appear in Thucydides (1.9.2).

[9] Herodotus, however, wrote many years after the Persian Wars and may have attributed these words to the Athenians under the influence of the funeral speeches.

[10] Fowler 2013: 342. An even earlier date may be suggested by an Attic inscription from c. 550 BC (*IG* I³ 972), which M. Jameson 2005: 19 has read as a dedication of an altar or precinct to the Heraclidae; but this interpretation is far from secure, given the poor state of the inscription.

[11] Wilkins 1993: xviii–xix.

[12] See, among others, Zuntz 1955: 26–54; Garzya 1956; Avery 1971; Burian 1977; Allan 2001; Tzanetou 2012: 73–104.

was a standard element in the catalogue of Athens' mythical exploits in the *epitaphios logos* (Lys. 2.11–16; Dem. 60.8–9; Pl. *Menex.* 239b). The fortune of the episode in Attic oratory was not limited to funeral speeches, and the story was employed more generally to praise Athens (Isoc. 4.54–60; 5.33–4; 10.31; 12.194) or Theseus (Isoc. 10.31).

ATHENS AND THE HERACLIDAE: *CHARIS* OR *PHILANTHRŌPIA*?

The war against Eurystheus on behalf of the Heraclidae exemplifies the role of institutions in enabling different ideas about the community to coexist in Athenian ideological practice.[13] This is particularly evident if one looks at the ideological significance of the motivations for Athens' intervention. In Euripides' *Children of Heracles*, the Athenian king, Demophon, is persuaded by Iolaus to succour the Heraclidae in order to repay the favour (ἀντιδοῦναί ... χάριν) that Heracles had once conferred on Theseus, Demophon's father, when he rescued him from the underworld (Eur. *Heracl.* 215–22). Such a private obligation is unparalleled in Lysias' *Funeral Oration*. The orator stresses that the Athenians helped the Heraclidae despite the fact that they did not personally (ἰδίᾳ) receive any benefactions from Heracles and did not know what kind of men the Heraclidae would turn out to be. Lysias implies that Athens, far from having any personal interests at stake, protected the Heraclidae entirely out of altruism and love for justice (Lys. 2.11–16). In other words, he implicitly attributes the Athenians' intervention to their traditional humaneness (*philanthrōpia*).

Strictly speaking, there is no formal contradiction between Euripides' and Lysias' versions. To deny the existence of a collective debt of the Athenians towards Heracles does not necessarily mean to deny Theseus' private obligation towards the hero. Lysias may have simply omitted an aspect of the story without openly arguing against it. There is, however, a significant difference of emphasis between the two accounts: while Euripides focuses on reciprocity (*charis*), Lysias ignores, if not even denies the same notion in favour of Athenian *philanthrōpia*. One possible explanation for such an opposite use of the value of *charis* might be the disappearance of Theseus, Athens' 'national' hero, from the narrative horizon of the *epitaphios logos*.[14] This striking absence has been interpreted by Nicole Loraux as a sign of a democratic re-elaboration of

---

[13] The term 'Heraclidae' can either refer to the children of Heracles or to Heracles' descendants in general. In the rest of the chapter, 'Heraclidae' will only be used to refer to the children of Heracles.

[14] On the adoption of Theseus as Athens' 'national' hero, see Walker 1995: 35–81; Calame [1990] 1996: 398–419; Mills 1997: 1–41; G. Anderson 2003: 134–45; Steinbock 2013a: 169–72.

Athens' mythical past, with the Athenian *dēmos* replacing Theseus as the real hero.¹⁵ Moreover, Loraux exploited this feature of funeral speeches to connect the origins of the *epitaphios logos* with the political environment of the so-called radical democracy. She therefore interpreted the disappearance of Theseus as a repudiation of Cimon, who according to several scholars used Theseus in his political propaganda.¹⁶

Loraux's interpretation of the absence of Theseus from the extant funeral speeches is problematic. Loraux uses the contingent (and hypothetical) desire of the newly born radical democracy to banish the memory of Cimon to explain a long-lasting feature of the epitaphic genre. In this respect, her theory is reminiscent of the controversial tendency to identify hidden (and often forced) allusions to contemporary political figures in Attic tragedy.¹⁷ Moreover, while it is true that Theseus does not feature in epitaphic narratives of Athenian exploits, the hero does appear in Demosthenes' catalogue of Athenian tribes, where he is praised as the founder of Athenian political equality (Dem. 60.28). Similarly, if a bias against Cimon really existed in the *epitaphios logos*, it would have been inappropriate for Hyperides to mention Cimon's father, Miltiades, among the great Athenians of the past (Hyp. 6.37). Finally, the belief that Theseus was strictly connected to Cimonian propaganda is itself the result of a modern reconstruction based on Cimon's alleged recovery of Theseus' bones in the early fifth century. Yet, a recent study has shown that the story of this recovery was a tradition invented during the fourth century or possibly later, and has raised reasonable doubts against the existence of a Cimonian propaganda based on Theseus.¹⁸ Even if one assumes that such a propaganda existed and presented Cimon as the new Theseus, Loraux's theory is based on a circular argument. It employs the absence of Theseus as proof that the *epitaphios logos* originated in the aftermath of Cimon's ostracism, but the existence of an equivalence between Theseus and Cimon in funeral speeches can only be postulated if one accepts this dating.

Not only is Loraux's explanation of the absence of Theseus from the *epitaphios logos* unsatisfactory; it is also unhelpful for explaining the ideological rationale of Euripides' and Lysias' narratives of the myth of the Heraclidae. This chapter argues that these accounts were influenced by the discursive parameters of the dramatic festivals and the state funeral for the war dead respectively. These allowed the Athenians to construct two distinct but compatible ideas

---

[15] See Loraux 1981: 65–6.
[16] See Loraux 1981: 66. On Theseus and Cimonian propaganda, see Podlecki 1971; Calame [1990] 1996: 416–17; Parker 1996a: 168–70.
[17] For a recent attempt, see Vickers 2008, who looks for allusions to Alcibiades in the works of Sophocles and Euripides.
[18] See Zaccarini 2015.

about their community: the beliefs that the Athenians always reciprocate benefactions, and that they always offer gratuitous help to the victims of injustice. In this light, it appears clear that Theseus was not removed from the story because of his alleged Cimonian connotations, but because his debt towards Heracles hindered the altruistic picture of the Athenians expected at the state funeral.

First, I establish the place of *charis* and *philanthrōpia* in Athenian democratic ideology. I then move to the analysis of Euripides' *Children of Heracles*. I show that the dramatic festivals enabled the poet to play with his audience's familiarity with Athenian deliberative and honorific practice, where *charis* played a significant part, and portray a fairly realistic exchange of benefactions between Demophon and the Heraclidae. Third, I demonstrate that Lysias' *Funeral Oration* was conditioned by the discursive parameters of the state funeral for the war dead and accordingly focused on Athenian justice and selflessness. Lysias thus provided an idealised image of the Athenians as champions of *philanthrōpia* which contributed to the construction of Athens' imagined community. Finally, I introduce a comparison with Isocrates' *Panegyricus*, which states that the Heraclidae sought the help of the Athenians alone because they considered them the only ones capable of reciprocating (ἀποδοῦναι χάριν) Heracles' benefactions to humanity (Isoc. 4.56). The speech was produced for a private setting and was not bound by the discursive parameters of Athenian democratic institutions.[19] I show that Isocrates was thus able to downplay both the Athenians' belief in the importance of reciprocating favours to benefactors and their ideas about *philanthrōpia*, and exploited the value of *charis* to make the case that, while all mankind was indebted to Heracles, only Athens was powerful enough to return the favour.

BETWEEN *CHARIS* AND *PHILANTHRŌPIA*

Before moving to the analysis of the myth of the Heraclidae in Athenian ideological practice, it is necessary to define the two values that provide the poles of my discussion: reciprocity (*charis*) and humaneness (*philanthrōpia*). These values may at first glance appear irreconcilable, but they should not be seen as completely separate and opposed to one another. I will show that the altruistic disposition of *philanthrōpia* cannot be understood outside of the reciprocal dynamics regulating Greek life and society, and that *charis* and *philanthrōpia* were two compatible and interconnected aspects of the same cultural and ideological framework.[20]

---

[19] Gotteland 2001: 176–85 rightly notes the differences between Euripides', Lysias' and Isocrates' accounts of the reasons for Athens' intervention, but does not highlight their institutional and ideological implications.

[20] The compatibility between *charis* and *philanthrōpia* is also stressed by Azoulay 2004: 318–26.

The concept of reciprocity has entered the domain of classical studies from anthropological research, where it is taken as a central factor in the economic processes of primitive societies.[21] The theories of Marshall Sahlins, in particular, have enjoyed considerable popularity among ancient historians. Sahlins identified three distinct and progressive degrees of reciprocity: generalised, balanced and negative.[22] Generalised reciprocity refers to an altruistic form of exchange, where the expectation of requital exists but is indefinite and might even be disappointed. Balanced reciprocity refers to a direct, *quid pro quo* exchange where the return is immediate and equivalent to the good received. Negative reciprocity is described as 'the attempt to get something for nothing with impunity' and can manifest itself in the economic shape of the barter or in more cunning or violent forms. Reciprocity can incline towards any of these degrees depending on kinship distance, with members of the same kinship or social group tending towards the generalised type. Moreover, Sahlins noted how generosity and thus generalised reciprocity can create rank through indebtedness, and (conversely) how a dominant position implies a certain amount of generosity as a sort of *noblesse oblige*.

Reciprocity has been found to affect many aspects of the Greek world.[23] In Homeric society, for example, reciprocity (*charis*) operated in the practice of gift-giving and hospitality, and has been used to explain the relations between individuals and those between leader and subjects.[24] In the classical period, dynamics based on reciprocity have been identified in Spartan diplomatic rhetoric and Athenian forensic language.[25] Some degree of reciprocity was also involved in Greek notions of justice. In Plato's *Republic*, Polemarchus defines justice as the art 'which renders (ἀποδιδοῦσα) benefit to friends and harm to our enemies' (Pl. *Resp.* 331d–32d, trans. Emlyn-Jones and Preddy).[26] One can see this principle in action in Thucydides' Mytilenean debate (Thuc. 3.36–50). There, Cleon exhorts the Athenians to persevere in their decision to execute the entire adult male population of Mytilene despite the fact that only the wealthy had rebelled against Athens. Cleon stresses the injustice of the Mytileneans, who turned against the same Athenians who had granted

---

[21] For a survey on anthropological research about reciprocity, see van Wees 1998.
[22] Sahlins 1972: 193–210. For an attempt to challenge the traditional views of anthropologists on reciprocity, see Graeber 2011.
[23] See Seaford 1998.
[24] See Donlan 1998; Postlethwaite 1998. Reciprocity remained an essential feature of friendship, hospitality and gift-giving also in classical Greece: see Mitchell 1997; Battezzato 2003.
[25] On reciprocity in Spartan diplomatic rhetoric, see Missiou 1998, who downplays the role of *charis* in Athenian diplomatic rhetoric. On forensic *charis* in Athens, see Harris 2013b: 129–36, *pace* Millett 1998.
[26] See Dover 1974: 180–1, who provides further passages where this notion is employed; see also Havelock 1978: 309–11.

them many honours (Thuc. 3.39.2–3). Cleon, in other words, accuses the Mytileneans of giving harm in return for benefits, and clearly conceives justice in terms of reciprocity. Punishing the Mytileneans is exactly what justice requires (Thuc. 3.40.4), and even Cleon's opponent, Diodotus, does not deny this principle. Even though he advocates a milder treatment for the sake of advantage, Diodotus agrees on the intrinsic justice of Cleon's speech (Thuc. 3.44.4; 47.5), thus acknowledging the reciprocal nature of justice itself.[27]

If the Athenians were keen to reciprocate harm to their enemies, at least in their own self-perception they were even more concerned with requiting benefits to their friends. Their zeal in reciprocating favours to public benefactors was a quality that the Athenians proudly considered as their prerogative. This is well exemplified in Demosthenes' *Against Leptines*. Demosthenes repeatedly accuses Leptines' law of being shameful because it abolishes the honours the Athenians have always granted to public benefactors as a due reward for their good actions towards the city (Dem. 20.43–4, 64, 81, 141, 156). The orator insists that the law should be repealed to protect the good reputation of the Athenians, who would otherwise appear as ungrateful (ἀχάριστοι) in the eyes of the Greeks (Dem. 20.10).[28] The epigraphic record shows that the Athenian community shared Demosthenes' concern for public *charis*. As several scholars have pointed out,[29] fourth-century honorific decrees stressed the eagerness of the Athenian *dēmos* (or sometimes both the *dēmos* and the *boulē*) to reciprocate the *charis* due to those who had benefited the city.[30] In this sense, reciprocating public *charis* was itself a matter of justice, and one in which the Athenians believed to excel.

The other pole of my discussion of the Heraclid myth is the notion of humaneness (*philanthrōpia*).[31] With this term, I refer to the righteous and altruistic attitude which the Athenians typically associated with themselves.[32] According to Isocrates' *Panegyricus*, for example, the Athenians have shown their *philanthrōpia* since their origins, when they chose to share with the rest of

---

[27] Diodotus' argument is that (corrective) justice is not the province of the Assembly, and that Cleon delivered a forensic speech instead of a deliberative speech: see Harris 2013a.

[28] See Canevaro 2016a: 89–91.

[29] See Whitehead 1983: 62–4; Liddel 2007: 167–70; Luraghi 2010: 250–2.

[30] Cf. *IG* II² 196.11–14; 391.10–12; 392.1–3; II³, 1 306.13–14; 378.17–20; 452.11–16; 475.9–14.

[31] On *philanthrōpia* see Dover 1974: 201–5; de Romilly 1979: 43–52; Christ 2013; B. D. Gray 2013. In the *Poetics*, Aristotle describes *to philanthrōpon* as the possible response to the view of a bad person who passes from good to bad fortune (Arist. *Poet.* 1453a2–6). As a sympathetic response to one's misfortune regardless of desert, *to philanthrōpon* thus differs from pity (*eleos*), which consists in a sympathetic response to one's undeserved misfortune: see Konstan 2001: 46–7 and 2006: 214–18.

[32] Christ 2013 suggests that *philanthrōpia* was transformed into a democratic virtue by Demosthenes. Even if one accepts Christ's conclusions, the combination of justice and altruism typical of *philanthrōpia* was already predicated of the Athenians prior to Demosthenes.

humanity the gifts they had received from Demeter (Isoc. 4.29). In the speech *Against Meidias*, Demosthenes asserts that the Athenians' *philanthrōpia* and mildness are well known to all mankind thanks to the Athenian law on *hybris*. This law punishes even the outrages perpetrated against slaves, even though the Athenians have suffered many wrongs from the barbarian countries where the slaves are purchased (Dem. 21.48–9).[33] The *philanthrōpia* of Athenian law is once more the object of praise in Demosthenes' *Against Timocrates*. There, the orator states that the Athenian procedures to enact new laws impose to the citizens to act humanely and kindly (φιλανθρώπως καὶ δημοτικῶς) (Dem. 24.24). Athens has such a reputation for *philanthrōpia* that some people may even take advantage of it, as the speaker of Demosthenes' *Against Aristocrates* accuses Charidemus of doing (Dem. 23.156).

But is it possible to reconcile the altruistic character of *philanthrōpia* with the importance of reciprocity in Athenian society? If one interprets altruism as an inclination to help others regardless of the possibility of receiving compensation, the concept of *philanthrōpia* can be accommodated in the discourse of reciprocity, and specifically within generalised reciprocity.[34] Their eagerness to honour public benefactors is itself an indicator of the value the Athenians attached to public acts which, even though rewarded, one can define as altruistic.[35] The compatibility between *charis* and *philanthrōpia* is particularly evident in Demosthenes' *Against Leptines*. There, Demosthenes calls the Athenians *philanthrōpoi* because they rewarded the Corinthians who had been exiled for allowing into Corinth the Athenian soldiers defeated in the Battle of Nemea in 394 BC. Demosthenes then warns his fellow citizens against cancelling these rewards and proving to be ungrateful (ἀχάριστοι) (Dem. 20.55).[36] The Athenians' generosity in granting rewards to the Corinthians is labelled an act of *philanthrōpia*, and its opposite is seen as a denial of the *charis* due to benefactors. Not only was altruism compatible with reciprocity, but it was even a significant factor in the generalised reciprocity which regulated the relationship between the *polis* and its citizens. Traces of such a complementarity can be found already in archaic thought. In the *Works and Days*, Hesiod stresses the importance of paying back one's debts in fair measure (εὖ δ' ἀποδοῦναι, αὐτῷ τῷ μέτρῳ), but invites his audience to render even more (καὶ λώιον) than what is due (Hes. *WD* 349–50). The anticipation of an eventual return (ὡς ἂν χρηΐζων καὶ ἐς ὕστερον ἄρκιον εὕρῃς) (Hes. *WD* 351) does not undermine the other-concern of the action. In

---

[33] See Canevaro 2018b: 118–19 for a discussion of the passage.
[34] Zanker 1998: 76. On the issue of applying the modern conception of altruism to the ancient world, see Christ 2012: 4–6.
[35] See Liddel 2007: 168–70, who highlights the altruism displayed by the *dēmos* in reciprocating public benefactors with honours.
[36] Christ 2013: 208–9.

fact, it confirms that forms of generosity which can be ascribed to altruism were embedded in dynamics of reciprocity.

The altruistic disposition of *philanthrōpia* held an important place in the perception of Athens' international relations in Athenian democratic ideology.[37] In the context of foreign policy, *philanthrōpia* was translated into the Athenian helping paradigm. This consisted in the idealised image of the Athenians as altruistic champions of justice and helpers of the weak, which was traditionally constructed at the state funeral for the war dead.[38] The same image could also be employed in other settings. This is exemplified in Demosthenes' *For the Megalopolitans*. The orator warns the Athenians that the Spartans, soon after capturing Megalopolis, will attack Messene. Demosthenes exhorts the Assembly to vote a pre-emptive intervention in defence of Megalopolis, which would be a nobler and more humane way (καλλίονα καὶ φιλανθρωποτέραν) to prevent Sparta from committing injustices (Dem. 16.9). This decision would be consistent with Athens' traditional policies, which always aim to save the victims of injustices (τοὺς ἀδικουμένους σῴζειν) (Dem. 16.14–15), and Demosthenes will conclude his speech accordingly by inviting his fellow citizens always to side with the weak against the powerful (Dem. 16.32). The orator insists that an alliance with Megalopolis would be both just and advantageous. A later intervention in defence of Messene, on the contrary, would damage the reputation of the Athenians, who would appear to act not out of concern for justice but out of fear of the Lacedaemonians (Dem. 16.10).

If the Athenians were keen to ascribe to themselves the role of righteous champions of the weak, they were equally eager to deny that such *philanthrōpia* might also characterise other nations. In the *Against Leptines*, for example, Demosthenes compares the Thebans' cruelty and baseness (ὠμότητι καὶ πονηρίᾳ) to the Athenians' *philanthrōpia* and desire for justice (φιλανθρωπίᾳ καὶ τῷ τὰ δίκαια βούλεσθαι) (Dem. 20.109).[39] Philip's false *philanthrōpia* (τῆς δὲ φιλανθρωπίας, ἣν ... ἐκεῖνος ... ἐπλάττετο) is

---

[37] Athenian altruism has been the subject of scholarly debate in recent years. Herman 2006: esp. 373 holds an almost utopian idea of Athenian altruism and argues that a 'strategy of generosity' regulated Athenian foreign policy. Christ 2012 argues instead that the Athenians often refrained from helping people outside their family circle and held very pragmatic foreign policies. Despite their opposite conclusions, both scholars share a similar, unsatisfactory approach. Instead of focusing on altruism as an element of Athenian ideology and self-image, they try to assess the actual participation of the Athenians in the practice of altruism. See instead Low 2007: 175–211, who argues that Greek interstate relations included a norm of intervention based on the principle of 'helping the wronged'. This norm, not necessarily limited to the Athenians, 'not only functions as an ideal, but can even sometimes be argued to involve some obligation'.

[38] For some examples, see pp. 63–4.

[39] See Canevaro 2016a: 370–1.

the object of Demosthenes' criticism in the speech *On the Crown* (Dem. 18.231). Another passage from Demosthenes' *For the Megalopolitans* deserves even more attention. The orator questions the Spartans' support for the territorial claims of the other Greeks: the Spartans have not suddenly become *philanthrōpoi* (ὀψὲ γὰρ ἂν φιλάνθρωποι γεγονότες εἶεν); they are merely obliging the Greeks to help them against Messene and avoid appearing unjust for not reciprocating the favour (μὴ τὴν ὁμοίαν αὐτοῖς χάριν ἀποδιδόντες) (Dem. 16.16–17). Demosthenes therefore contrasts the Spartans' selfish use of *charis* with Athens' traditional *philanthrōpia*, which the Spartans can only pretend to embody.

Athenian *philanthrōpia* and the helping paradigm were deeply rooted in Athenian democratic ideology. Any challenges to these ideas were doomed to meet with suspicion and disapproval in public discourse. This appears clearly in Demosthenes' *On the False Embassy*. According to Demosthenes, Aeschines once invited the Athenians in the Assembly not to remember the achievements of the ancestors. Aeschines reached such a level of shamelessness that he even advocated a law forbidding the Athenians from helping any Greeks who had not previously helped them (μηδενὶ τῶν Ἑλλήνων ὑμᾶς βοηθεῖν, ὃς ἂν μὴ πρότερος βεβοηθηκὼς ὑμῖν ᾖ) (Dem. 19.17). Demosthenes accuses Aeschines of exhorting the Athenians to reject their traditional *philanthrōpia* in favour of a form of balanced reciprocity incompatible with the idealised picture of Athenian interstate relations. Demosthenes introduces Aeschines' supposed assertions as 'words deserving many deaths' (πολλῶν ἀξίους . . . θανάτων λόγους) (Dem. 19.16), and they would have certainly sounded outrageous to his audience as well. This is especially evident from Aeschines' account of the same event in his speech *On the Embassy*. In what sounds like a reply to Demosthenes' accusations, Aeschines is keen to show that he had never directly challenged the Athenian helping paradigm. The orator makes no mention of his alleged law proposal; far from arguing against helping the weak *per se*, Aeschines states that he had simply warned the Athenians against giving aid to others while Athens herself was in greater danger. According to Aeschines, the Athenians should keep emulating the exploits performed by their ancestors during the Persian Wars, but at the same time avoid repeating the mistakes made during the Peloponnesian War (Aeschin. 2.75–6).[40] Demosthenes' eagerness to depict Aeschines as an opponent of the Athenian helping paradigm and Aeschines' defensive reply attest how dangerous it was for one's reputation to question the idealised image of Athens' *philanthrōpia*.[41]

---

[40] See MacDowell 2000: 212–13.
[41] See Canevaro 2019: 141–2. For a detailed analysis of the Aeschines passage, see Steinbock 2013b and Barbato 2017.

We can now finally turn to the last problematic point: the relationship between *philanthrōpia* and justice. The two concepts have sometimes been seen as incompatible,[42] but ancient sources do not support this view. In Demosthenes' *Against Timocrates*, for example, Diodorus mentions a law that forbade citizens convicted in court from resorting to supplication. He praises the law, whose purpose is to prevent any public losses deriving from the Athenians' *philanthrōpia*. Such *philanthrōpia* is not contrasted with justice, but with advantage (διὰ ταύτην [= τὴν φιλανθρωπίαν] ἑώρα περὶ πολλῶν ὑμᾶς ἑκόντας ἤδη ποτὲ μεγάλα ζημιωθέντας) (Dem. 24.51–2). In the same speech, Diodorus draws a distinction between laws concerning private affairs, which should be characterised by kindness and humanity (ἠπίως καὶ φιλανθρώπως), and those concerning public matters, which need to be strict and severe (Dem. 24.192–3). The fact itself that the speaker admits *philanthrōpia* in the sphere of private law underscores that *philanthrōpia* was not in principle incompatible with justice.[43] Demosthenes' *Against Meidias* does seem to include a direct attack against *philanthrōpia*. The orator states that it would not be righteous (θεμιτόν) to deem Meidias worthy of benevolence (φιλανθρωπίας). Yet, Demosthenes does not oppose *philanthrōpia* to justice as such. He merely warns the judges against showing *philanthrōpia* towards an unworthy individual such as Meidias, one who has never stood out for words, deeds or noble birth (Dem. 21.148–50). Justice and *philanthrōpia* could thus coexist in Athenian public discourse. As we will see, the Athenians saw themselves as eager to sustain massive efforts and personal risks to fight in defence of the weak and correct or prevent injustices committed between third parties. Together with altruism, devotion to justice was therefore a central component of Athenian *philanthrōpia* in international relations.

EURIPIDEAN TRAGEDY AND RECIPROCITY

Issues of reciprocity play a central role in Euripides' treatment of the Athenian war on behalf of the Heraclidae in *Children of Heracles*. The play opens with the Heraclidae sitting as suppliants at the Temple of Zeus in Marathon, where they are seeking help against the Argive king Eurystheus. The Heraclidae are young and helpless, and they are accompanied by Heracles' mother, Alcmena, and Heracles' old friend, Iolaus. An Argive Herald arrives to demand the restitution of the Heraclidae, but Demophon, son of Theseus and king of Athens, decides to accept the children's supplication and grant them help. The Athenians now have to face a war against the Argives, but learn from the oracles that Athens'

---

[42] See de Romilly 1979: 116–25, and B. D. Gray 2013: 141.
[43] See also Harris 2013b: 274–301, who analyses cases where the principle of fairness (*epieikeia*) was applied and suggests that mildness was built into the Athenian legal system.

victory will only be achieved through the sacrifice of a maiden. One of Heracles' daughters volunteers to be the victim, and the battle can finally start. The Athenians, together with a rejuvenated Iolaus and Heracles' older son, Hyllus, are able to defeat the Argives and take Eurystheus as a prisoner. At the end of the play, Alcmena obtains the execution of Eurystheus despite the opposition of the Athenians, to whom Eurystheus promises his protection after his death as a reward for their attempt to save his life.[44]

The importance of reciprocity is revealed early on in the play, when Euripides introduces a contest of speeches (*agōn logōn*) between the Herald and Iolaus, who debate over the fate of the Heraclidae.[45] The two characters each deliver a speech (*rhēsis*) in front of Demophon, who is eventually persuaded by Iolaus to grant help to the Heraclidae (Eur. *Heracl.* 134–252). As part of his argument, Iolaus recalls how Heracles once saved Theseus from the underworld and asks Demophon to repay his father's debt of *charis* towards Heracles (Eur. *Heracl.* 215–22). Euripides' choice to focus on reciprocity reflects the discursive parameters of the dramatic festivals.[46] First, it employs a value, *charis*, which was not exclusively democratic and could appeal to any Greeks in the audience. Second, the *agōn logōn* between the Herald and Iolaus plays with the audience's familiarity with Athenian deliberative practice (and specifically diplomacy) and the language of honorific decrees, which the Athenians experienced thanks to their participation in the Assembly and the Council. Seen in this light, Iolaus' reference to Theseus' debt of *charis* is reminiscent of the language of reciprocity typical of the Assembly and the Council.[47] Significantly, Iolaus' *rhēsis* contrasts with the speech of the Herald, which programmatically reverses Athenian diplomatic etiquette. By juxtaposing a positive and a

---

[44] Ancient sources disagree on the position of the burial place of Eurystheus, which Euripides locates in Pallene (Eur. *Heracl.* 849–50; 1030–1). According to Pausanias, Eurystheus was buried at the Scironian rocks, near Megara (Paus. 1.44.10), while Strabo states that he was buried at Gargettus (Strabo 8.6.19). Pindar even locates Eurystheus' burial place in Thebes (Pind. *Pyth.* 9.79–83). On the issue see Kearns 1989: 49 and Allan 2001: 30. The role of Alcmena in the death of Eurystheus may have been Euripides' innovation: see Allan 2001: 28–9 and Mendelsohn 2002: 119–26.

[45] The importance of rhetoric in Euripides' *Children of Heracles* has been noted by several commentators: see Burian 1971: 95; Collard 1975a: 62–4; Lloyd 1992: 72–6; Allan 2001: 143–55.

[46] The centrality of *charis* in Euripides' *Children of Heracles* can also be ascribed to the nature of the play, which belongs to the category of suppliant drama: see Burian 1971: 1, who includes in this category Aeschylus' *Suppliants*, Sophocles' *Oedipus at Colonus*, and Euripides' *Suppliants* and *Children of Heracles*. These plays all share a similar structure of their storyline, of which the suppliants' successful plea for help and ensuing demonstration of gratitude are some of the main staples: see Burian 1971: 16–29. On supplication, see Naiden 2006.

[47] One should also note that in Athens (at least during the fourth century), supplications by foreigners such as Iolaus were heard in the Council and the Assembly: see Hansen 1987: 27; Naiden 2006: 173–7.

negative example of deliberative language, Euripides therefore showed how to conduct a diplomatic exchange properly and guided his audience towards the natural outcome of the *agōn logōn* between Iolaus and the Herald.

The *agōn logōn* starts with the Herald's *rhēsis*, which opens with an appeal to a principle of international law: Iolaus and the Heraclidae are Argives and therefore subjected to the authority of Eurystheus (Eur. *Heracl.* 134–43).[48] Issues of international law were a common argument employed in front of the Assembly.[49] In Book 1 of Thucydides, for example, the Corcyrean envoys urge the Athenians to accept them as allies and reassure them that this would not violate their treaty with the Spartans (Thuc. 1.35). The Corinthian envoys protest that an alliance between Athens and Corcyra would indeed break the existing treaty, and appeal to their right to deal with their colony Corcyra as they please (Thuc. 1.38–40). However, the way Euripides' Herald deploys this legitimate argument is striking. While apparently insisting on the justice of his claim (δίκαι' ... δίκαιοι ... δίκας), the Herald actually threatens Demophon with the danger of Argive violence.[50] He states that every other city gave in to Eurystheus' demands because they did not dare bring any evil upon themselves (κοὐδεὶς ἐτόλμησ' ἴδια προσθέσθαι κακά) (Eur. *Heracl.* 144–6). The Herald adds that it would be foolish to take pity on the Heraclidae (Eur. *Heracl.* 147–52). This statement, coupled with the Herald's final exhortation to Demophon not to indulge in the Athenian habit of always siding with the weak (Eur. *Heracl.* 175–8), openly challenges the principle of Athenian *philanthrōpia*. Not only does it emphasise the Herald's reliance on force rather than justice, but it would have also been inappropriate in Athenian public discourse.

The Herald then draws a comparison between the benefits the Athenians would get if they sided with Eurystheus and the harm they would suffer if they refused to give up the children (Eur. *Heracl.* 153–78). This pragmatic evaluation of pros and cons is in line with the nature of deliberative oratory, which tended to focus on the advantageous (*to sympheron*) and the harmful (*to blaberon*) (Arist. *Rh.* 1358b22).[51] Once again, however, the Herald deviates from Athenian deliberative practice while developing a legitimate argument. He asks Demophon: 'what will you gain (τί κερδανεῖς) by admitting these people into your country or by allowing us to take them away?' (Eur. *Heracl.* 154, trans. Allan). The Herald's insistence on gain (*kerdos*) is controversial. The theme of *kerdos* is frequently attested in

---

[48] But see Allan 2001: 143–4, who highlights the inaccuracy of the Herald's legal argument. *Pace* Gastaldi 2007: 44–5, on this occasion the Herald does not employ the language of kinship typical of Greek diplomacy.
[49] See Harris 2017: 58.
[50] Allan 2001: 143–5.
[51] See Carey 2000: 196–203; Harris 2013a.

Athenian public discourse, but usually holds a negative value.⁵² Deliberative orators often expressed concern over *kerdos* and tended to advise their audience against pursuing it.⁵³ In Thucydides' Mytilenean debate, Cleon warns the Athenians against orators who deceive the people for profit (κέρδει) (Thuc. 3.38.2). In Xenophon's *Hellenica*, Thrasybulus addresses the men of the city in the Assembly and blames them for the crimes they committed for the sake of gain (ἕνεκα κερδέων) (Xen. *Hell*. 2.4.40). Demosthenes, in the *Third Philippic*, complains that the Greeks are eager to gain (κερδᾶναι) from each other's ruin instead of uniting against Philip for the salvation of Greece (Dem. 9.29). In *On the Navy*, he asks the Athenians who would want to sacrifice their own ancestors, graves and land for the sake of gain (εἵνεκα κέρδους) (Dem. 14.32).

Euripides intentionally attributed a cynical and inappropriate appeal to *kerdos* to the Herald, whose unsympathetic nature has been noted by several commentators.⁵⁴ The Herald's rhetoric is reminiscent of the Athenian envoys in Thucydides' Melian Dialogue. The diplomatic exchange between Melians and Athenians does not take place before the people (οὐ πρὸς τὸ πλῆθος) but before the few (ἐς τοὺς ὀλίγους), and the Athenians openly reject the arguments they would normally use in a democratic deliberative setting (Thuc. 5.85, 89). The dialogue is thus a perversion of Athenian diplomatic practice, and the similarities with the *rhēsis* of the Herald are significant. The Athenians refuse to comply with justice, and state that between non-equals there is no question of right, but only of force (Thuc. 5.89). Their rejection of justice in favour of force parallels the Herald's overconfidence in the power of Eurystheus. The Athenians also share the Herald's positive attitude towards *kerdos*. They argue that Melos' surrender would benefit both Melians and Athenians. The Athenians would gain (κερδαίνοιμεν) from not destroying the Melians, while the Melians would submit and avoid suffering worse consequences (Thuc. 5.93).⁵⁵ The Herald's speech shows Euripides' knowledge of the deliberative practice of diplomacy, which in Athens took place before the Assembly and the Council. The poet programmatically reversed such practice and shaped the Herald as an anti-orator.⁵⁶ In accordance with

---

⁵² Cozzo 1988: 37–71; Balot 2001: 1. *Kerdos* already holds a negative value in Hesiod: cf. Hes. *WD* 321–4 with Balot 2001: 33.
⁵³ Forensic orators tended to attribute love of gain to their opponents to portray them in a negative light: cf. e.g. Lys. 18.16; Dem. 24.65, 201; 52.26; Isae. 9.26. *Kerdos* holds a negative meaning also in Lysias' *Funeral Oration*, where it features among Xerxes' motivations for invading Greece (Lys. 2.29–30).
⁵⁴ See Avery 1971: 558 n. 41; Burian 1977: 5; Allan 2001: 35.
⁵⁵ See Allan 2001: 145, who draws a parallel with Thucydides' Mytilenean debate (Thuc. 3.36–50) and describes the Herald's argument as an example of *Realpolitik*.
⁵⁶ *Pace* Gastaldi 2007.

the discursive parameters of the dramatic festivals, Euripides played with the audience's familiarity with Athenian democratic institutions (and specifically the Assembly and the Council), and presented the Herald as the natural loser of the *agōn logōn*.

The Herald's speech contrasts with Iolaus' reply, which closely reflects the audience's knowledge of diplomatic practice as well as Athenian attitudes to reciprocity. Iolaus rebuts the Herald's legal argument by stating that the children and himself are exiles and thus Eurystheus holds no legal power upon them (Eur. *Heracl.* 184–90). After praising Athens and the freedom of her people (Eur. *Heracl.* 191–201), Iolaus stresses Demophon's kinship with the Heraclidae, pointing out that both Theseus and Heracles descended from Pelops (Eur. *Heracl.* 207–13). Appealing to kinship was a common strategy in Greek diplomacy and international relations.[57] Herodotus, for example, recalls how a Persian herald appealed to the kinship between the Argives and the Persians to persuade the former not to join the Greeks against Xerxes (Hdt. 7.150). In Book 1 of Thucydides, the Corinthians urge the Spartans to help Potidaea, a Corinthian colony, against Athens and invite them not to abandon their own friends and kinsmen (ἄνδρας τε φίλους καὶ ξυγγενεῖς) (Thuc. 1.71.4). In Aristophanes' *Lysistrata*, the heroine addresses the ambassadors from Athens and Sparta and blames both Athenians and Spartans for going to war against each other despite the rituals which they share as kinsmen (ὥσπερ ξυγγενεῖς) (Ar. *Lys.* 1128–32). Iolaus therefore imitates a typical diplomatic argument, which the audience would probably have recognised and found effective.

It is at this stage that Iolaus, before performing the traditional gestures of a suppliant (Eur. *Heracl.* 226–31),[58] appeals to Theseus' debt of *charis* towards Heracles. Iolaus recalls how he sailed with Theseus as part of Heracles' campaign against the Amazons, and reminds Demophon that Heracles once rescued Theseus from the underworld.[59] Demophon is then requested to return the favour (ὧν ἀντιδοῦναί σ' οἵδ' ἀπαιτοῦσιν χάριν) by not handing the Heraclidae to Eurystheus (Eur. *Heracl.* 215–20).[60] As we have seen in the previous section, reciprocity was a fundamental Greek value, which could appeal to Euripides' audience at large. It was therefore natural for the poet to include the argument of *charis* in Iolaus' plea to Demophon. The Athenian king himself later admits that

---

[57] C. P. Jones 1999: 27–35; Low 2007: 48–51.
[58] On the customary gestures of supplication see Naiden 2006: 44–62.
[59] Because of the alleged weakness of the argument and the irregular syntax of the passage, some scholars have inserted a lacuna after l. 217. It has therefore been suggested that Iolaus' appeal also included an allusion to Heracles' gift of Antiope to Theseus: see Wilkins 1993: 79–80; Kovacs 1995: 4–5 and 31; Allan 2001: 149–50.
[60] As noticed by Allan 2001: 150, obligations of *charis* could be inherited from previous generations: cf. Eur. *Orest.* 244 and 453.

his father's debt (τὸ προυφείλειν) to Heracles is one of the reasons compelling him to take the Heraclidae under his protection (Eur. *Heracl.* 240–1). But the value of *charis* was also institutionalised in Athenian deliberative and honorific practice.[61] Iolaus' argument reflected the inescapable sense of obligation towards benefactors that the Athenian community had elevated to the status of a fundamental civic value.[62] His appeal to *charis* was designed to strike a chord with Euripides' audience and their institutional expertise. Accordingly, Iolaus' wording resembles the vocabulary of reciprocity attested in the rhetorical practice and honorific decrees of the fourth century, and aims to create in Demophon the same feeling of obligation.

Let us start with the verb ἀπαιτέω, employed by Iolaus to request Demophon's protection on behalf of the Heraclidae. The word implies that the speaker is demanding back something that rightfully belongs to him.[63] Orators often use the verb in connection with the *charis* due to benefactors. In the speech *Against Leptines*, Demosthenes uses ἀπαιτέω three times to refer to the benefactors whom Leptines' law would unjustly punish if they claimed the reward they rightfully earned (Dem. 20.156–8).[64] The speaker of Isocrates' *Against Callimachus*, accused of confiscating a sum of money belonging to Callimachus, recalls the honours he received from the city in return for his services and asks back the *charis* which the community owes him (ἡμῖν τε παρὰ τῷ πλήθει τῶν πολιτῶν χάρις ὀφείλοιτο· ἣν ὑμᾶς νῦν ἀπαιτοῦμεν). The speaker reinforces the verb ἀπαιτέω with the verb ὀφείλω, which relates to the idea of debt.[65] Far from requesting to be accorded more than is just, he states that such *charis* will serve as proof of his innocence (Isoc. 18.67).[66] The verb ἀπαιτέω was also a technical term of Greek diplomacy. Thucydides, for example, recalls how a herald from Ambracia found out that the reinforcements sent by his city had been annihilated and gave up demanding the return of the dead (οὐκέτι ἀπῄτει τοὺς νεκρούς) out of despair (Thuc. 3.113.5). In Book 5 of Thucydides, the Spartans send an embassy to Athens to ask back (ἀπαιτήσοντες) Pylos in exchange for Panactum (Thuc. 5.44.3). The author of the speech *On Halonnesus* reminds the Athenians of an embassy they had sent to Philip to demand back (ἀπαιτοῦντες) a prisoner ([Dem.] 7.38).

---

[61] On reciprocity as an argument in deliberative rhetoric, see Harris 2017: 57.
[62] See Monoson 1994: 267–8, who identifies in Pericles' funeral speech a celebration of the reciprocal relationship between *polis* and citizens. In particular, she points out that 'citizens understand that if they act to cultivate the city's virtue they can expect to receive, in turn, the gratitude or favor (charis) of the city'.
[63] LSJ s.v. ἀπαιτέω, I. 1.
[64] See Canevaro 2016a: 417–22 on the rationale of the passage.
[65] Cf. Hdt. 6.59; Ar. *Clouds* 1135; Dem. 45.33; 36.41.
[66] On 'forensic *charis*' see Harris 2013b: 129–36, *pace* Millett 1998.

Iolaus' phrasing ἀντιδοῦναι ... χάριν also requires discussion. The wording resembles the expression χάριν ἀποδίδωμι, which orators typically employ when they rely on the language of reciprocity. A striking parallel is found in Isocrates' account of the Heraclidae episode in his *Panegyricus*, where the orator describes Athens as the only city powerful enough to return the favour owed (ἀποδοῦναι χάριν) to Heracles for his benefactions to mankind (Isoc. 4.56). The same expression features in deliberative oratory and diplomacy. In Xenophon's *Hellenica*, for example, a Theban ambassador reminds the Athenians of Thebes' refusal to join the Spartans against the Athenian democrats during the civil war, and requests Athens' assistance against Sparta. In his reply, Thrasybulus acknowledges Thebes' benefaction and promises to return the favour in greater measure (χάριτα ... ἀποδοῦναι μείζονα) (Xen. *Hell.* 3.5.16). Demosthenes' *For the Megalopolitans* warns the Athenians against Sparta's benefactions, which are only meant to oblige the Greeks to make an equal return to the Spartans (τὴν ὁμοίαν αὐτοῖς χάριν ἀποδιδόντες) (Dem. 16.17). The verb ἀποδίδωμι is also usually matched with *charis* in Athenian honorific decrees. An inscription dating from 344/3 BC, for instance, states that the stele stands as a memorial of the fact that the Athenian *dēmos* rewards his benefactors with great favours (ἀποδίδωσιν χάριτας μ[εγ]άλας) (*IG* II³, 1 451). Similar formulae appear in several other honorific decrees,[67] and the Athenians would have been familiar with them thanks to their service in the Council and the Assembly.

Instead of ἀποδίδωμι, Iolaus uses the verb ἀντιδίδωμι. Compared to the more compelling ἀποδίδωμι, which means 'to render what is due',[68] ἀντιδίδωμι has the more neutral meaning of 'to give something in return'.[69] Despite the different nuances, the two verbs were practically synonymous. This appears from a passage in Book 3 of Thucydides. There, the Thebans criticise the behaviour of the Plataeans, who reciprocated the benefactions they had received from the Athenians by helping them to enslave the Greeks. The Thebans add that the real shame lies in not returning favours in equal measure (τὰς ὁμοίας χάριτας μὴ ἀντιδιδόναι), rather than refusing to return favours which are justly due but lead to injustice when paid back (ἐς ἀδικίαν δὲ ἀποδιδομένας) (Thuc. 3.63.4). Euripides' audience would have thus recognised the language of reciprocity typical of Athenian rhetorical and honorific practice. Moreover, the presence of the verb ἀπαιτέω compensates for the absence of ἀποδίδωμι and gives a compelling sense of obligation to Iolaus' plea. This is especially evident if one compares Iolaus' wording with a parallel passage from Euripides' *Heracles*. In that play, Theseus promises Heracles shelter and heroic honours in Athens as a return for having been rescued from the underworld (χάριν σοι τῆς ἐμῆς σωτηρίας τήνδ'

---

[67] See p. 122 and n. 30.
[68] See LSJ s.v. ἀποδίδωμι, I. 1.
[69] LSJ s.v. ἀντιδίδωμι, I.

ἀντιδώσω) (Eur. *HF* 1336–7). The verb ἀντιδίδωμι confers a gentle tone on Theseus' friendly plea, which is meant kindly to lead Heracles to accept help. Iolaus, on the other hand, employs ἀντιδίδωμι together with ἀπαιτέω in order to stress Demophon's debt towards Heracles. Iolaus' purpose is to put pressure on the Athenian king and oblige him to protect the Heraclidae. His rhetorical strategy proves to be successful. Not only does Demophon accept Iolaus' request, but he also employs the verb προὐφείλω ('to owe') to emphasise his debt towards the Heraclidae as a reason for his intervention in their defence (Eur. *Heracl.* 240–1).

As this analysis has shown, Iolaus' language is reminiscent of the vocabulary of reciprocity typical of Athenian deliberative and honorific practice. It shares with such contexts the same compelling sense of obligation to return benefits received. It is also worth noting that *charis* is a major theme in Euripides' *Children of Heracles*, and is evoked by several characters throughout the play.[70] Demophon, for example, is ready to repay his debt towards the Heraclidae, but is also equally keen to rebound this *charis* back at them and assert the credit he has now acquired (Eur. *Heracl.* 333–4).[71] In this sense, Euripides provides us with a fairly realistic description of how a relationship based on *charis* worked. In accordance with the discursive parameters of the dramatic festivals, the poet played with his audience's familiarity with Athenian deliberative oratory (and specifically diplomacy) and honorific practice. The rhetoric of Iolaus and the Herald was meant respectively to reflect and reverse the language typical of such contexts and guide the audience towards Iolaus' victory in the *agōn logōn*. Iolaus appealed to a value, *charis*, which could be shared by the entirety of Euripides' diverse audience, while Demophon's acceptance of Iolaus' plea reflected specifically Athenian ideas about reciprocity: just like Demophon in the play, the historical Athenians believed to be always eager to reciprocate benefactions, and this belief was grounded in the discourse of the Assembly and the Council.

LYSIAS AND ATHENIAN *PHILANTHRŌPIA*

Lysias includes the story of the Heraclidae in the narrative of Athens' mythical exploits at the beginning of his *Funeral Oration*. According to the orator, after Heracles' death, the children of the hero arrived in Athens as suppliants to escape the persecution of Eurystheus. Unlike the rest of the Greeks, the

---

[70] See Scully 1973: 331–42.
[71] On these and other grounds, Garzya 1956: 22–3 rejected the traditionally positive interpretation of the character of Demophon, whom he described as 'tortuoso calcolatore e sostanzialmente meschino'.

Athenians refused to hand the Heraclidae to Eurystheus. Out of respect for Heracles, and indifferent to the upcoming dangers, the Athenians chose not to gratify (χαριζόμενοι) the powerful and went to war for the weaker on the side of justice (ὑπὲρ τῶν ἀσθενεστέρων μετὰ τοῦ δικαίου διαμάχεσθαι). They faced Eurystheus in battle despite the fact that they had not personally received any benefits from Heracles (ἀγαθὸν μὲν οὐδὲν ἰδίᾳ ὑπὸ τοῦ πατρὸς αὐτῶν πεπονθότες) and did not know what sort of men the Heraclidae would have become. Lysias stresses that the Athenians had no previous quarrel with Eurystheus, nor any prospect of gain (κέρδους) except for good reputation. They thus fought alone against all Peloponnesian forces and freed the Heraclidae from fear (Lys. 2.11–16).

Lysias never mentions Theseus and his debt of *charis* towards Heracles. As I have shown, this striking absence cannot be ascribed to a politically motivated desire to banish Cimon through the omission of Theseus, his alleged mythical counterfigure. The exclusion of the Athenian hero from Lysias' narrative is better explained if we read the passage from an institutionalist perspective. The discursive parameters of the state funeral for the war dead compelled Lysias to provide an idealised image of Athens aimed at the construction of an imagined community. Through the myth of the Athenian help for the Heraclidae, Lysias therefore painted a picture of Athenian international relations as guided by principles of *philanthrōpia*. Focusing on Theseus' debt of *charis* towards Heracles risked endangering this picture, because it implied that the Athenians may have supported the Heraclidae for reasons other than pure altruism. This detail of the story was inappropriate to the state funeral, and Lysias needed to downplay it in favour of more suitable motivations.

In accordance with the discursive parameters of the state funeral, Lysias downplayed Athens' personal obligations towards the Heraclidae. This is consistent with the treatment of the episode in the other extant funeral speeches. In Plato's *Menexenus*, Socrates simply lists the Athenian war on behalf of the Heraclidae among Athens' noble deeds for the freedom of the Greeks (Pl. *Menex.* 239b). Demosthenes states that the Athenians saved the children of Heracles, who himself had saved the other Greeks (ὃς τοὺς ἄλλους ἔσῳζεν).[72] Demosthenes therefore acknowledges a reciprocal relation between Heracles' actions and Athens' help for his children, but implies that the Athenian intervention was meant to reciprocate benefactions conferred on other cities and not on Athens specifically (Dem. 60.8). Lysias raises this point more explicitly and shifts the focus from *charis* onto Athenian *philanthrōpia*. He states that the

---

[72] That the expression refers to the other Greeks can be inferred from the previous sentence, where Demosthenes states that the Athenians drove the army of Eumolpus not only out of their own land but also those of the other Greeks (ἐκ τῆς τῶν ἄλλων Ἑλλήνων χώρας).

Athenians remained determined in the face of the imminent danger, even though they had not personally received any benefit from Heracles (ἀγαθὸν μὲν οὐδὲν ἰδίᾳ ὑπὸ τοῦ πατρὸς αὐτῶν πεπονθότες) and did not know what kind of men the Heraclidae would turn out to be (Lys. 2.13).

Lysias denies that the Athenians expected anything in return from the Heraclidae. These were still young and the Athenians could not know whether they would grow up as base or valiant men.[73] The Heraclidae, in other words, may have never been able or willing to reciprocate Athens' benefaction. At the same time, the expression ἀγαθὸν μὲν οὐδὲν ἰδίᾳ ὑπὸ τοῦ πατρὸς αὐτῶν πεπονθότες stresses that the Athenians had no obligation towards Heracles to fulfil. The adjective ἴδιος has the main meaning of 'private, personal',[74] and here is employed in its adverbial function (ἰδίᾳ). In this form, it is usually paired with δημοσίᾳ or κοινῇ to create an opposition between the private and the public sphere, between the individual and the collective dimension.[75] A parallel independent use of ἰδίᾳ in the Lysianic corpus can be found in the first speech *Against Alcibiades*. There, the speaker maintains that Alcibiades has to be considered an enemy even if nobody has personally suffered any injustices from him (εἰ μή τις ἰδίᾳ ἀδικούμενος ὑπ' αὐτοῦ τυγχάνει) (Lys. 14.1). In Lysias' *Funeral Oration*, the adjective ἴδιος is sometimes used to qualify something that sets the Athenians apart from the other Greeks. Thus the Athenians, trusting only on their own forces, fought against the army which Eurystheus gathered from the whole Peloponnese (παραταξάμενοι δ' ἰδίᾳ δυνάμει τὴν ἐξ ἁπάσης Πελοποννήσου στρατιάν) (Lys. 2.15). In the Battle of Salamis, they similarly won freedom for the whole of Greece by relying on their own valour alone (τῇ ἰδίᾳ ἀρετῇ κοινὴν τὴν ἐλευθερίαν καὶ τοῖς ἄλλοις ἐκτήσαντο) (Lys. 2.44).

Through the adverbial form ἰδίᾳ, Lysias isolates the Athenians from the rest of the Greek world benefited by Heracles. Far from denying Heracles' merits towards humanity, Lysias stressed that the hero did not benefit Athens in particular.[76] Heracles' benefactions towards mankind are openly acknowledged. Lysias recalls how the hero had been responsible for many benefactions to all humanity (ἀγαθῶν πολλῶν αἴτιος ἅπασιν ἀνθρώποις), but could not punish his own enemy, Eurystheus (Lys. 2.16). The orator also stresses that the Athenians respected (ᾐδοῦντο) Heracles' virtue more than they feared for their own dangers (μᾶλλον ... ἢ τὸν κίνδυνον τὸν ἑαυτῶν ἐφοβοῦντο) (Lys. 2.12). Yet, this reference to the Athenians' *aidōs* for Heracles does not imply any obligation on their part. When intended as respect, *aidōs* entails an acknowledgement of someone's

---

[73] Todd 2007: 224–5.
[74] LSJ s.v. ἴδιος, I. 1.
[75] Cf. e.g. Lys. 2.61; 6.47; 13.2, 69.
[76] Todd 2007: 224.

honour.⁷⁷ The notion can express obligation to other people,⁷⁸ but this is not the case in Lysias' passage, where the vocabulary of reciprocity is completely absent. Lysias does not focus on *aidōs* as such. He merely mentions the Athenians' respect for Heracles to mirror their altruistic disregard for their own danger.⁷⁹ Reciprocity is explicitly denied, sacrificed on the altar of Athenian *philanthrōpia*, when Lysias states that the Athenians choose to fight on behalf of the weak for the sake of justice instead of gratifying the powerful (τοῖς δυναμένοις χαριζόμενοι) by giving up those who had been wronged (Lys. 2.12).

Lysias' attitude towards *charis* in the Heraclidae episode is consistent with his treatment of the notion throughout the speech. The clearest parallel is his narrative of the myth of Adrastus. There, Lysias states that the Athenians fought against Thebes over the bodies of the Seven despite the fact that they had no previous enmity with the Thebans or intention to gratify the Argives who were still alive (οὐδὲ τοῖς ζῶσιν Ἀργείων χαριζόμενοι) (Lys. 2.8).⁸⁰ When it is not openly denied, *charis* is at least ignored as a motivation for Athenian action. The word χάρις only occurs three times in Lysias' *Funeral Oration*. In one such occurrence, the term is used in a prepositional function to describe the Amazons' invasion of Attica as motivated by excessive glory and high ambition (πολλῆς δόξης καὶ μεγάλης ἐλπίδος χάριν) (Lys. 2.5). The word χάρις appears again in Lysias' account of the Battle of Marathon. On that occasion, the Athenians chose to fight alone at Marathon because they did not want to owe their own safety to anyone else (οὐδ' ᾠήθησαν δεῖν ἑτέροις τῆς σωτηρίας χάριν εἰδέναι) (Lys. 2.23). Only on one instance does Lysias' *Funeral Oration* employ and endorse the traditional vocabulary of reciprocity. There, the orator invites the Athenians to repay their war dead with the gratitude owed to them (μόνην δ' ἄν μοι δοκοῦμεν ταύτην τοῖς ἐνθάδε κειμένοις ἀποδοῦναι χάριν) (Lys. 2.75).⁸¹

The fact that this is the only instance in the entire speech where Lysias acknowledges a debt of *charis* on the part of the Athenians is significant. The orator implies that the Athenians can only be indebted and grateful to the Athenians themselves.⁸² Such a notion would have been inconceivable in

---

⁷⁷ Cairns 1993: 13–14.
⁷⁸ Cairns 1993: 183–8 and 2011: 30.
⁷⁹ See Todd 2007: 223, who notes how Lysias takes particular care 'not to use the language of personal benefit'.
⁸⁰ See Todd 2007: 220, who stresses that this sentence was meant to 'make the Athenian action more the disinterested product of a desire for justice'. Cf. Eur. *Supp.* 1167–79, where Theseus and Adrastus stipulate a bond of *charis* which obligates the Argives to remember and honour the help they received from the Athenians.
⁸¹ See Todd 2007: 271.
⁸² See Battezzato 2003: 23, 26, who notes that the *charis* due to the war dead was meant to foster social cohesion and motivate the living to be brave in battle.

the Assembly and the Council. As we have seen, Athenian honorific decrees emphasised the Athenian eagerness to reciprocate benefactions, and reciprocal obligations were often acknowledged in the deliberative practice of diplomacy. At the state funeral, on the other hand, orators were reluctant to admit any sort of obligations on Athens' part. In Pericles' funeral speech, the Athenians are described as unique because they make friends not by receiving favours but by granting them. As a result, they avoid being in the inconvenient position of having to reciprocate benefactions not as simple favours but as proper debts (οὐκ ἐς χάριν, ἀλλ' ἐς ὀφείλημα τὴν ἀρετὴν ἀποδώσων) (Thuc. 2.40.4).[83] The Athenians appear as the natural recipients of *charis* from the other Greeks, a role which Socrates (not without irony) emphasises several times in Plato's *Menexenus*. Socrates states that the Athenians who fought at the Eurymedon, in Cyprus and in Egypt should be remembered and rendered thanks (ὧν χρὴ μεμνῆσθαι καὶ χάριν αὐτοῖς εἰδέναι) because they put an end to the Persian threat to Greece (Pl. *Menex.* 241e). The Athenians' entitlement to *charis* is even more evident when Socrates alludes to the ungrateful behaviour of the other Greeks. These invaded Attica and thus repaid the Athenians with an unworthy *charis* (ἀναξίαν χάριν ἐκτινόντων) (Pl. *Menex.* 242c). Socrates insists that the Greeks, despite the benefactions received from the Athenians, paid them back with such a *charis* (εὖ παθόντες ὑπ' αὐτῆς οἵαν χάριν ἀπέδοσαν) that they deprived Athens of her ships and walls (Pl. *Menex.* 244b–c).[84] According to Hyperides' *Funeral Oration*, Leosthenes deserves eternal gratitude (δίκαιον δ' ἐστὶν ... Λεωσθένην ἀεὶ χάριν ἔχειν) not only for his deeds but also for the Greek victory against the Macedonians which followed his death and for the benefits deriving from his campaign (Hyp. 6.14).[85]

---

[83] According to Loraux 1981: 81–2, Pericles' words are an expression of aristocratic spirit and relegate Athens' friends to the subordinate rank of debtors who cannot participate in the city's glory. But see Missiou 1998: 190–1, who rightly reads the passage in connection with the following paragraph. There, Thucydides emphasises the generosity of the Athenians, who confer favours without considering their own advantage (τοῦ ξυμφέροντος) (Thuc. 2.40.5). Yet, Missiou wrongly suggests that the Athenians rejected reciprocity not only in the idealised image of their foreign policy, but also in the practice of diplomatic rhetoric. Cf. Arist. *Eth. Nic.* 1167b17–1168a27, according to which benefactors seem to love their beneficiaries more than their beneficiaries love them. Aristotle rejects the creditor-debtor analogy because it involves personal interest, and emphasises the nobility of the act.

[84] *Pace* Walters 1980: 6–8, such accusations need not be attributed to an Athenian 'deep anxiety over their isolation from the rest of Greece'.

[85] Among the passages mentioned, only Plato's may tend towards the balanced pole of reciprocity, but this can be ascribed to the parodic nature of *Menexenus*. Funeral speeches generally avoid the idea of *quid pro quo* exchanges in Athenian interstate relations. Although such speeches sometimes stress that Athenian actions deserve gratitude, they do not fall outside the altruistic pattern of generalised reciprocity. To acknowledge the *charis* that the Athenians deserve for their benefactions does not mean to imply that they performed such benefactions to win credit and favours from the Greeks.

If *charis* is clearly not a keyword of Lysias' *Funeral Oration*, the speech constantly emphasises Athenian *philanthrōpia*. In his narrative about the Heraclidae, Lysias makes every effort to stress Athens' altruism and devotion to justice. The orator states that the Athenians' respect for the virtue of Heracles was stronger than their fear of danger. He adds that the Athenians were more concerned with fighting in defence of the weak on the side of justice (ὑπὲρ τῶν ἀσθενεστέρων μετὰ τοῦ δικαίου διαμάχεσθαι) than with gratifying the powerful (Lys. 2.12). Lysias insists that the Athenians went to war on behalf of the Heraclidae because they thought this was the right thing to do (δίκαιον δὲ νομίζοντες εἶναι) (Lys. 2.13). He then delineates Athens' other noble reasons for fighting Eurystheus. The Athenians had no previous quarrel with the Argive king, nor were they pursuing any gain other than good reputation (οὐδὲ κέρδους προκειμένου πλὴν δόξης ἀγαθῆς). They were acting out of pity for the victims of injustice (τοὺς μὲν ἀδικουμένους ἐλεοῦντες) and hatred for those guilty of *hybris*. Finally, they obeyed the principles of freedom, justice (δικαιοσύνης) and courage (Lys. 2.14). Many of these themes are reminiscent of the *agōn logōn* of Euripides' *Children of Heracles*. Both the Herald (Eur. *Heracl.* 137–8; 142–3; 253) and Iolaus (Eur. *Heracl.* 187–90; 194–5) maintain that they have justice on their side. Demophon himself defends against the Herald his rightful decision to protect the suppliants (Eur. *Heracl.* 253–4). The *kerdos* that the Herald offers to Athens in vain (Eur. *Heracl.* 153–7) is the same which Lysias' Athenians refuse to pursue. Just as Demophon wants to avoid dishonour (Eur. *Heracl.* 242), Lysias' Athenians have good reputation as their only goal. Finally, Iolaus (Eur. *Heracl.* 197–8) and Demophon (Eur. *Heracl.* 243–6; 286–7) stress Athenian freedom, a sentiment that is echoed in Lysias.

The intense net of similarities between Lysias' account about the Heraclidae and the *agōn logōn* in Euripides' *Children of Heracles* makes the absence of *charis* from Lysias' narrative all the more striking. The orator's focus on Athenian *philanthrōpia*, on the other hand, is particularly evident if one concentrates on Lysias' treatment of the theme of justice. There are twenty-four instances of words relating to justice throughout the *Funeral Oration*, and seven of them are in the section about the Heraclidae.[86] In many of the occurrences, the Athenians are portrayed as fighting for what is right in defence of the victims of injustice.[87] It is no coincidence that the orator, immediately after the Heraclidae episode, devotes a paragraph to describing the autochthonous origins of the Athenians as the root of their commitment to justice. According to Lysias, to fight for what was right was typical of the Athenian ancestors (πολλὰ μὲν ὑπῆρχε τοῖς ἡμετέροις προγόνοις . . . περὶ τοῦ δικαίου διαμάχεσθαι). Because they were born from the soil and did not inhabit a land stolen from another nation, the

---

[86] Lys. 2.12 (twice), 14 (four times), 16.
[87] Lys. 2.10, 12, 14, 22, 61, 67.

Athenians had been righteous since the origins of their life (ἥ τε γὰρ ἀρχὴ τοῦ βίου δικαία) (Lys. 2.17).

Lysias' stress on the value of *philanthrōpia* is not unique. It reflects the discursive parameters of the state funeral and creates an idealised image of Athens with which the Athenians could identify.[88] The same focus on *philanthrōpia* can be detected in the other extant funeral speeches. Pericles stresses how the Athenians in their public life are respectful of the laws concerning help to the victims of injustices (Thuc. 2.37.3); he then praises the Athenians for their eagerness to help other people without pursuing any personal interest (Thuc. 2.40.5). Demosthenes recalls the ancestors' justice as one of their many virtues, and states that they never wronged any man (Dem. 60.7). Demosthenes also stresses Athenian altruism. According to the orator, the Athenians privately undertook great risks for the common good of the Greeks in order to punish the injustices committed by the Persians, and they were always ready to fight on the side of justice (Dem. 60.10–11). Hyperides summarises all these ideas in one paragraph, where he states that Athens punishes the evil and helps the just, and grants the Greeks common safety at her individual risk (Hyp. 6.5). In Plato's *Menexenus*, the idealisation of Athenian *philanthrōpia* at the state funeral emerges very clearly through the distorting filter of parody. According to Socrates, the Athenians are so compassionate and eager to help the weak that they went to the rescue not only of the same Greeks who had previously wronged them, but even of their own historical enemy, the king of Persia (Pl. *Menex.* 244e–45a).

Now that we have analysed Lysias' narrative about the Heraclidae from an institutionalist perspective, we can safely conclude that Theseus' absence was not motivated by a desire to obliterate Cimon's alleged mythical counterfigure. Theseus' debt of *charis* towards Heracles was a central part of Iolaus' rhetorical strategy in Euripides' *Children of Heracles*. This was partly due to the nature of the tragic genre, which was based on individual interactions between mythical characters on the stage. More importantly, Euripides was conditioned by the discursive parameters of the dramatic festivals. He therefore relied on *charis* as a value universally recognised by the entire Athenian community. At the same time, the institutional setting enabled him to manipulate his audience's familiarity with Athenian deliberative and honorific practice, which reflected their ideas about reciprocity. For the same reasons, Theseus' debt of *charis* was not appropriate to the state funeral for the war dead. In accordance with the discursive parameters of this institution, Lysias omitted Theseus' debt to Heracles to emphasise *philanthrōpia* and reflect Athenian attitudes towards this

---

[88] The idealised image of Athens' *philanthrōpia* constructed at the state funeral was often reproduced in other settings: cf. e.g. Eur. *Heracl.* 329–32 and Eur. *Supp.* 377–80, where the Chorus praise the Athenians as the champions of the weak.

value.[89] Only the Athenians were so righteous and selfless as to face the power of Eurystheus for the sake of the Heraclidae despite having no personal enmity towards the former or obligations towards the latter. To place emphasis on their debt of *charis* with Heracles would have prevented the Athenians from performing their traditional role as *philanthrōpoi* and Lysias from constructing an imagined community.

CHARIS AND PHILANTHRŌPIA IN ISOCRATES' PANEGYRICUS

The relationship of reciprocity between Athens and the Heraclidae resurfaces along with an incomplete picture of Athenian *philanthrōpia* in Isocrates' *Panegyricus*. The speech, purportedly composed for a panegyric festival, was most probably a literary exercise circulated in writing.[90] It therefore exemplifies how the myth of the Heraclidae could be deployed in a private context, independently of the discursive parameters of Athenian democratic institutions. The *Panegyricus* accordingly mixes epideictic and deliberative features,[91] and does not reflect Athenian ideas about *charis* or *philanthrōpia* to the same extent as Euripides' *Children of Heracles* or Lysias' *Funeral Oration*. According to Isocrates, the Heraclidae sought Athens' help because they deemed it the only city capable of returning Heracles' benefits towards mankind (τὴν δ' ἡμετέραν ἱκανὴν νομίζοντες εἶναι μόνην ἀποδοῦναι χάριν ὑπὲρ ὧν ὁ πατὴρ αὐτῶν ἅπαντας ἀνθρώπους εὐεργέτησεν) (Isoc. 4.56). Isocrates constructs an incomplete picture of *philanthrōpia*. While he does not imply that the Athenians received any personal benefit from Heracles and alludes to their altruism, the orator does not mention Athenian justice. At the same time, Isocrates restores the argument based on *charis* – but merely to prove that Athens was the only city worthy of Heracles, and thus emphasise her power.

Not bound by the discursive parameters of the state funeral, Isocrates was able to describe the relationship between the Athenians and the Heraclidae through the typical vocabulary of reciprocity. The orator acknowledges that the Athenians paid back the *charis* (ἀποδοῦναι χάριν) due to Heracles by helping his children. At the same time, Isocrates does not mention Theseus and stresses that Athens merely repaid a debt owed to Heracles on behalf

---

[89] The Athenian intervention in defence of the Heraclidae is explicitly called an act of *philanthrōpia* in a decree quoted in Demosthenes' *On the Crown* (Dem. 18.187). The text of the decree, however, is probably a forgery: see Yunis 2001: 29–31 and Canevaro 2013a: 310–18.
[90] Usher 1990: 19–21; Too 1995: 79–80; Papillon 2004: 23–5, 27.
[91] Buchner 1958: 7–15; Papillon 2004: 25–6.

of the whole humanity (ὁ πατὴρ αὐτῶν ἅπαντας ἀνθρώπους εὐεργέτησεν). Isocrates' concern with reciprocity is restated shortly afterwards, when the orator describes Athens' help for the Heraclidae as one of the city's many benefactions (εὐεργεσιῶν) to the Spartans. Mindful of Athens' rescue of their ancestors, the Spartans should have avoided invading Attica and endangering their own saviours. Isocrates concludes that, even if one leaves issues of gratitude (τὰς χάριτας) aside, it is not natural for the benefited to lead the benefactors (ἡγεῖσθαι ... τοὺς εὖ παθόντας τῶν εὖ ποιησάντων) (Isoc. 4.61–3). Isocrates' insistence on reciprocity would have been inappropriate at the state funeral. In that institutional setting, acknowledging that Athens helped the Heraclidae because of a debt of *charis* towards Heracles would have compromised the idealised image of the Athenians as *philanthrōpoi*. Isocrates, however, had no interest in emphasising such image. Justice does not feature in his account of the myth of the Heraclidae. Isocrates does mention Athenian altruism, but only as a mirror of the ingratitude of the Spartans, who have endangered the city which once ran risks (προκινδυνεύσασαν) to defend Sparta's ancestors, the Heraclidae (Isoc. 4.62).

Isocrates did not aim to construct an imagined community, nor to reproduce Athenian approaches to reciprocity in deliberative contexts. His purpose was to prove that Athens was the most powerful city in Greece and naturally disposed to a role of leadership. This is openly declared at the beginning of the speech, where Isocrates addresses Sparta's alleged ancestral right to lead the Greeks and ascribes this honour to the Athenians instead (Isoc. 4.18). The argument is consistent with the overall purpose of the *Panegyricus*, which invokes a Panhellenic campaign against Persia under the joint leadership of Athens and Sparta.[92] Isocrates' insistence on reciprocity is functional to this rhetorical strategy. The orator avoids mentioning Theseus' private debt of *charis* with Heracles, and stresses Heracles' benefactions to all Greeks. This allows him to show that the Heraclidae did not deem the other Greeks able to offer them any help (τὰς μὲν ἄλλας πόλεις ὑπερορῶντες ὡς οὐκ ἂν δυναμένας βοηθῆσαι ταῖς ἑαυτῶν συμφοραῖς), despite the fact that they all owed favours to Heracles. The Heraclidae asked the help of the Athenians alone, because they considered them the only ones capable of reciprocating Heracles' benefactions (Isoc. 4.56).

Isocrates uses the war against Eurystheus to prove that Athens already held a hegemonic position in mythical times (κατ' ἐκεῖνον τὸν χρόνον ἡ πόλις ἡμῶν ἡγεμονικῶς εἶχε) (Isoc. 4.57). He then recalls how the Athenians subdued

---

[92] Isocrates alternates a claim for Athenian leadership with a call for joint leadership of Athens and Sparta. The second option was more realistic in the historical context of c. 380 BC, when the speech was completed, because Greece was at the time under Spartan hegemony; see Papillon 2004: 26–7.

Eurystheus, who had been able to impose his yoke upon the mighty and semi-divine Heracles, and implies that they thus proved to be even stronger than Heracles himself (Isoc. 4.60). Isocrates concludes that their victories over Argos, Thebes and Sparta in mythical times earned the Athenians the right to be considered the prime power in Greece (Isoc. 4.64–5). Isocrates' praise of Athens, therefore, differed from those commonly produced for the state funeral for the war dead. Lysias' *Funeral Oration* suppressed Theseus' private debt of *charis* towards Heracles in order to emphasise the *philanthrōpia* of the Athenians, who rescued the Heraclidae out of altruism and devotion to justice. Isocrates, writing in a private context, also downplayed Theseus' involvement, but did not fully develop the value of *philanthrōpia* and acknowledged Athens' relationship of reciprocity with Heracles. At the same time, unlike Euripides, Isocrates did not stress the Athenian belief that all benefactions should be reciprocated as such, but exploited it to pursue the aim of the speech. By stating that the Heraclidae sought the help of the Athenians alone because they were the only ones able to reciprocate Heracles' favours to humanity, Isocrates could thus highlight Athens' power and recommend the city as the leader of the Greeks.

CONCLUSIONS

The Heraclidae entered Athenian social memory by the beginning of the fifth century, when the Athenians started to take pride in their own intervention in defence of the young and helpless children of Heracles against Eurystheus. This myth could be informed by and foster either of two distinct and only apparently contrasting ideas: the Athenians' solicitude in reciprocating the *charis* due to benefactors, and their altruistic disposition to *philanthrōpia*. This chapter has compared the accounts of the myth of the Heraclidae in Euripides' *Children of Heracles* and Lysias' *Funeral Oration*, produced respectively for the dramatic festivals and the state funeral for the war dead, as well as in Isocrates' *Panegyricus*, which was written for a private setting. It has shown that the Athenians' seemingly incompatible attitudes towards *charis* and *philanthrōpia* coexisted within Athenian democratic ideology thanks to the discursive parameters of the institutions of the democracy.

The Athenians portrayed themselves both as eager to repay their debts of *charis* and as ready to grant gratuitous help to the victims of injustice. Both images were of course idealised to some extent – the Athenians always repaid their benefactors, and they always helped the wronged – but were suitable to different institutional settings. Considerations of reciprocity were appropriate to the Assembly and the Council. They featured in the language of deliberative (and diplomatic) rhetoric and honorific practice. Athenian honorific decrees, in particular, emphasised Athens' eagerness to reciprocate the *charis* due to benefactors and thus fostered the continuous flow of benefactions towards the city.[93] The dramatic festivals enabled Euripides to play with his audience's familiarity with these contexts. In *Children of Heracles*, Iolaus thus emphasises Theseus' debt of *charis* towards Heracles and appeals to the Athenians' eagerness to reciprocate benefactions in order to win the *agōn logōn* against the Argive Herald. Lysias' *Funeral Oration* has instead shown that Athenian *philanthrōpia* was the trademark of the state funeral of the war dead. In accordance with the discursive parameters of this institution, Lysias denied the existence of any reciprocal ties between Athens and the Heraclidae, and emphasised Athenian *philanthrōpia* by depicting the Athenians as the altruistic champions of justice. He thus produced an idealised image of Athens that would stir the Athenians' pride in their national character and contribute to the construction of an imagined community.

The role of institutions in Athenian ideological practice has been further illustrated through a comparison with Isocrates' account of the myth of the Heraclidae in his *Panegyricus*. Writing Athens' praise in a private setting, Isocrates was not bound by the discursive parameters of Athenian democratic institutions. The orator provided an incomplete picture of *philanthrōpia* which overlooked the Athenians' justice and hinted to their altruism, while he emphasised the bond of *charis* between Athens and the Heraclidae. Yet, he replaced Theseus' private obligation with mankind's collective debt towards Heracles, and stressed that Athens was the only city powerful enough to reciprocate Heracles' favours. Isocrates' version was informed neither by the Athenians' belief in the importance of reciprocating favours to benefactors nor by their ideas about *philanthrōpia*, but merely exploited *charis* to praise Athens' power and advocate a Panhellenic expedition against Persia under shared Athenian and Spartan leadership.

[93] Liddel 2007: 163–4; Lambert 2011: 193–5, 198 and 2012: 96; Canevaro 2016a: 77–97.

CHAPTER 6

Fading Shades of *Hybris*: The Attic Amazonomachy

The Amazons have always fascinated both the ancient and the modern imagination.[1] Greek myths about Amazons, with particular attention for their gender implications, have been investigated by several generations of scholars.[2] Archaeological and osteological findings in the Eurasian steppes have revealed that women in those areas commonly practised horse-riding and warfare.[3] Contact with this very different civilisation probably prompted the Greeks to elaborate stories about a nation of Amazon warriors. In Athens, in particular, the Amazon myth held a significant place in the remote and idealised history of the city, which credited the Athenians with the successful repulsion of an Amazon invasion. Yet, stories about the Amazons were not the exclusive domain of the Athenians, but were popular and widespread in Greek mythology more widely.

The Amazons made their earliest literary appearance in Homeric and cyclic epics. In the *Iliad*, Priam recalls his military encounter with the Amazons on the river Sangarius (Hom. *Il.* 3.182–90), and Glaucus mentions Bellerophon's victory against the Amazons in Lycia (Hom. *Il.* 6.171–86). The epithet ἀντιάνειραι – whether it is to be interpreted as 'opposite to men' or 'equal to men' – qualifies the Amazons in both passages and implicitly emphasises their atypical gender status compared to Greek standards.[4] The Amazons played a significant part in the cyclic *Aethiopis*, where they joined the Trojan War as

---

[1] On traditions about Amazons outside the Greek world, see Mayor 2014: 357–429.
[2] See A. Stewart 1995: 572–6 and Blok 1995: 21–143 for an outline of the scholarly debate on the topic.
[3] Davis-Kimball et al. 1995; Mayor 2014: 63–83.
[4] On the expression Ἀμαζόνες ἀντιάνειραι, see Blok 1995: 145–93.

allies of the Trojans. In the poem, Achilles slayed Penthesilea, queen of the Amazons, and then killed the Greek Thersites, who had accused him of being in love with the woman (Procl. *Chr.* 175–81; schol. T *ad* Hom. *Il.* 24.804).[5] The poetic tradition also attributed Amazonomachies to Heracles and Theseus. Heracles went to the Amazons' capital Themiscyra to fetch the girdle of their queen, Hippolyta (Pind. fr. 172 Maehler; Eur. *HF* 408–18; *Ion* 1144–45; cf. Apollodoros 2.5.9; Diodoros 4.16).[6] The motif appears on Attic vase painting starting from c. 575 BC.[7] Theseus was also given an expedition to Themiscyra, probably for him to compete with Heracles' Amazonomachy. Whether he participated in Heracles' campaign (Hegias *ap.* Paus. 1.2.1; Plut. *Thes.* 26.1 = *FGrHist* 328 F 110; Eur. *Heracl.* 215–17) or went on his own expedition (Plut. *Thes.* 26.1 = *FGrHist* 3 F 151, *FGrHist* 4 F 166, *FGrHist* 31 F 25a), it is on this occasion that Theseus acquired his Amazon wife, whom the tradition calls either Antiope or Hippolyta (Pind. fr. 175 Maehler; Isoc. 12.193; Plut. *Thes.* 26).[8] Theseus and Heracles were even represented fighting Amazons on two metopes of the Athenian Treasury in Delphi, while the entire east side of the building was dedicated to an unidentified Amazonomachy.[9]

The Amazons acquired particular importance in Athenian social memory. Probably in connection with the Greek victories against the Persians, the successful repulsion of the Amazon invasion of Attica achieved great popularity in Athenian literary and artistic production. The story, already attested outside Athens in Pindar (Pind. fr. 174 Maehler), might have featured in the

---

[5] A. Stewart 1995: 576–7; Blok 1995: 195–288; Dowden 1997: 98–9. For the motif of Achilles and Penthesilea in Attic vase painting, see Bothmer 1957: 4, 70–3, 143, 148; *LIMC* s.v. Amazones 175–80.

[6] In addition to Themiscyra, the tradition knew of another place associated with the Amazons: Dowden 1997: 103–16 distinguishes the epic site of Themiscyra from an ethnographic site in the Caucasus. Both sites feature in Hdt. 4.110–16: the Amazons, defeated and captured by the Greeks at Themiscyra, killed their captors and ended up on the shores of Lake Maeotis; there, they eventually married Scythian youths, thus giving origin to the untraditional customs of Sauromatian women.

[7] Bothmer 1957: 6–29; Boardman 1982: 7; Tyrrell 1984: 2–3; A. Stewart 1995: 577; Dowden 1997: 100–1.

[8] Bothmer 1957: 124–30; Boardman 1982: 8–10; Tyrrell 1984: 3–5; A. Stewart 1995: 577; Dowden 1997: 101–2; Fowler 2013: 485–6.

[9] Bothmer 1957: 125–6; Culasso Gastaldi 1977: 291–2; Boardman 1982. On the dating of the Athenian Treasury in Delphi, see Gensheimer 2017: 1–3 and Neer 2004: 67, with references. The identification of the Amazonomachy on the east side of the Treasury is debated. Bothmer 1957: 118, Boardman 1982: 14 and Barringer 2008: 118–21 prefer Heracles and Theseus' joint expedition to Themiscyra, while Devambez 1976: 273–4 favours the Attic Amazonomachy. Gensheimer 2017: 9–14 recently suggested that both the east and west sides of the Treasury featured Amazonomachies: each side would have been devoted to Heracles' and Theseus' Amazonomachies respectively.

epic *Theseis*, whose content, however, is a matter of speculation.[10] In Book 9 of Herodotus, the Athenians recall the episode in a speech before the Battle of Plataea (Hdt. 9.27.4). The allusion may well be a retrospection of a later rhetorical *topos*, and thus one cannot take it as proof that the Attic Amazonomachy was already current in Athens in 479 BC.[11] Aeschylus alludes to the myth in the *Eumenides*, where the Amazon invasion provides the aetiology of the name of the Areopagus (Aesch. *Eum.* 685–90). Hellanicus adds that the Amazons reached Athens after crossing the frozen Cimmerian Bosporus (Plut. *Thes.* 27.2 = *FGrHist* 4 F 167). A painting of the Amazonomachy by Micon featured in the Cimonian iconographic programme of the Theseion (Paus. 1.17.2).[12] The motif appeared also in the Painted Stoa. In this building, which was also connected to Cimon, an Amazonomachy painted by Micon appeared alongside paintings depicting the fall of Troy, the Battle of Oenoe and the Battle of Marathon (Paus. 1.15.2).[13] The Amazonomachy was part of the Periclean building programme as well. The theme featured on the west metopes of the Parthenon and on the shield of Athena Parthenos.[14]

The presence of the Amazonomachy on public buildings attests the ideological potential of this episode, which was exploited at its best at the state funeral for the war dead. The successful repulsion of the invasion was a recurring element of the historical narrative of the *epitaphios logos*. The story usually opened the account of Athens' mythical exploits and provided a precedent for Athens' victories against Persian imperialism (Lys. 2.4–6; Dem. 60.8; Pl. *Menex.* 239b).[15] While Athens' official rhetoric usually presented a skeletal account of the story, a particularly detailed description of the campaign was offered by the fourth-century Atthidographer Cleidemus, who even recalled the extension of the wings of the Amazon army (Plut. *Thes.* 27.3–4 = *FGrHist* 323 F 18). The role of Antiope/Hippolyta in the war varied according to the

---

[10] Tyrrell 1984: 3–4; Dowden 1997: 102.
[11] Boardman 1982: 6.
[12] Tyrrell 1984: 10–11; Castriota 1992: 43–57. The exact location of the Theseion is still uncertain: see Thompson and Wycherley 1972: 125. The temple should not be confused with the building on Kolonos Agoraios, formerly known as Theseion and now generally identified with the Hephaisteion: see Thompson and Wycherley 1972: 140–2.
[13] Tyrrell 1984: 11–12; Castriota 1992: 76–89. Culasso Gastaldi 1977: 294–5 highlighted how the simultaneous presence of the Amazonomachy and the Battle of Marathon contributes to the parallel between Amazons and Persians; see also Castriota 1992: 82–5 and 2005. The identification of the Oenoe painting is debated: see Stansbury-O'Donnell 2005: 78–81 for an outline of the issue.
[14] Bothmer 1957: 208–14; Tyrrell 1984: 19–21; Castriota 1992: 143–51. The identification of the west metopes of the Parthenon with the Amazonomachy has been doubted by Brommer 1967: 192–5.
[15] Tyrrell 1984: 13–19.

sources.[16] A version preserved by Diodorus and found in Attic vase painting presented Antiope fighting on Theseus' side against the invading Amazons (Diod. 4.28).[17] Another version, if we believe Plutarch, was told by the poet of the *Theseid* in a lost *Insurrection of the Amazons*. In this poem, Antiope attacked Athens together with her fellow Amazons after Theseus had replaced her with Phaedra, and was eventually killed by Heracles. Plutarch does not give the story much credit (Plut. *Thes.* 28.1), but scenes where Antiope fights alongside the Amazons against Theseus do appear in Attic vase painting.[18] Connected to Theseus and Antiope was a myth concerning their son, Hippolytus. The story of Phaedra's tragic love for him was brought on the stage by Euripides in the extant *Hippolytus Wearing a Crown* and in its previous version, the lost *Hippolytus Veiled*.

HYBRIS AND THE CAUSES OF THE ATTIC AMAZONOMACHY

The Attic Amazonomachy provides an excellent case to test the influence of institutions on the production of multiple and compatible ideas within Athenian democratic ideology. Theseus' role in the events posed a potential problem to those who recalled the episode in Athenian public discourse. Was Theseus' abduction of Antiope the reason behind the Amazons' invasion of Athens? Acknowledging Athenian responsibility for the outbreak of the conflict could have a significant impact on the image of the city. The Athenians accordingly used different strategies to address the potential embarrassment deriving from Theseus' involvement. They could either omit the abduction and construct an idealised image of the Athenians as righteous punishers of *hybris*, or acknowledge the role of Theseus to different extents and ignore or even challenge the Athenians' attitude towards *hybris* or justice. This chapter therefore compares accounts of the Attic Amazonomachy destined for public settings with those produced for private contexts, and shows that Athenian democratic institutions conditioned the degree of ambiguity about Athens' responsibility for the Amazon invasion and the ideas and values conveyed by this myth.

---

[16] Mayor 2014: 275–6. As a rule, I will refer to Theseus' Amazon wife as Antiope, except when discussing the sources where she is explicitly called Hippolyta.

[17] For Antiope fighting on Theseus' side in Attic vase painting see *LIMC* s.v. Antiope II 16–19; Bothmer 1957: 165–7, 169–70.

[18] For Antiope fighting on the Amazon side in Attic vase painting see *LIMC* s.v. Amazones 232, 236; Bothmer 1957: 170, 183; Mayor 2014: 275.

After reconstructing the meaning of the Greek notion of *hybris*, I first illustrate the impact of the state funeral on Lysias' narrative of the Attic Amazonomachy in the *Funeral Oration*, which ignores Theseus' role in the events (Lys. 2.4–6). I show that Lysias constantly hints at the Amazons' hubristic nature,[19] and creates by contrast an idealised image of the Athenians as the champions of justice against *hybris* that is functional to the construction of an imagined community. I then analyse two versions that include possible, ambiguous allusions to Theseus' abduction of Antiope. First, I look at a brief passage in Aeschylus' *Eumenides*, where the invasion is motivated by the Amazons' *phthonos* against Theseus (Aesch. *Eum.* 685–90).[20] Because of Aeschylus' vague phrasing and the multivalence of the Greek concept of *phthonos*,[21] the Amazons' *phthonos* can either be understood in its negative value of envy,[22] as from the point of view of the Athenians, or seen from the point of view of the Amazons as a justified resentment for a wrong suffered,[23] and thus as a subtle allusion to the abduction. I argue that, in accordance with the discursive parameters of the dramatic festivals, Aeschylus' ambiguous version produced two contrasting images to appeal to different sections of his audience: it either hinted at or challenged the epitaphic idea that the Athenians always fight just wars against imperialistic invaders. Then, I analyse Isocrates' *Panegyricus*, where the Attic Amazonomachy is recalled as an example of Athens' achievements against imperialistic powers. Neither Theseus, Antiope, nor the abduction are mentioned explicitly, but Isocrates' reference to the accusations (ἐγκλήματα) raised by the Amazons against the Athenians to justify the invasion may well be an allusion to the abduction of Antiope (Isoc. 4.66–70). I thus show that the speech mixes deliberative and epideictic features, but does not abide by the discursive parameters of either the Assembly or the state funeral. As a result, Isocrates does not use the Amazonomachy to produce ideas about the advantage of the community nor about the Athenians' attitudes towards *hybris*.

Finally, after determining what the Athenians knew about Theseus' abduction of Antiope through the evidence of the figurative arts, I look at three versions produced for private settings where the episode is mentioned explicitly. I thus analyse the accounts of the Atthidographer Philochorus and the mythographer Pherecydes. According to Philochorus, Theseus participated in Heracles' expedition against the Amazons and received Antiope as a prize (γέρας). Pherecydes, on the other hand, stated that Theseus took Antiope

---

[19] Castriota 1992: 51.
[20] Pindar too, according to Paus. 7.2.7, knew of an attack brought by the Amazons against Athens and Theseus.
[21] Sanders 2014: 33–46 identifies twelve different values of the Greek word *phthonos*.
[22] See Fisher 2003: 185–8; Cairns 2003: 242–4; Sanders 2014: 38–9. See also Ober 1989a: 205–14.
[23] See Sanders 2014: 43–4; Cairns 2003: 246–8; Fisher 2003: 185 n. 16, 198–202.

captive (αἰχμάλωτον) during an independent expedition (Plut. *Thes.* 26.1 = *FGrHist* 328 F 110 = *FGrHist* 3 F 151), or that he abducted (ἁρπάζει) her with the help of Phorbas (schol. *ad* Pind. *Nem.* 5.89 = *FGrHist* 3 F 152).[24] These versions attribute some role to Theseus in causing the attack of the Amazons,[25] and produce ideas inappropriate to Athenian public settings. While the military versions imply that the Athenians conduct aggressive foreign policies, the abduction version may even suggest that the Athenians support those guilty of *hybris*.[26] I then examine Isocrates' allusion to the Amazonomachy in the *Panathenaicus*, where Theseus' Amazon wife, here called Hippolyta, falls in love (ἐρασθεῖσαν) with the hero and willingly follows him to Athens (Isoc. 12.193).[27] I argue that, despite blaming the war on Hippolyta and even mentioning the Amazons' *hybris* (Isoc. 12.196),[28] Isocrates' narrative is problematic because it implicitly characterises Theseus as guilty of seduction (*moicheia*) and potentially challenges the epitaphic image of the Athenians as champions of justice.[29]

HYBRIS: AN INTRODUCTION

Hybris is one of the most widely studied values in Greek morality and thought, and one that enjoys great popularity even in the common modern language. Yet, its meaning has long been misunderstood. It took decades of scholarly debate to clarify how exactly the Greeks understood *hybris*. The word is commonly translated as 'pride' and (especially in everyday language) interpreted in religious terms.[30] *Hybris* accordingly would be a religious offence consisting in one's overstepping of one's own mortal limits and resulting in the outraged

---

[24] In the same passage, Plutarch ascribes Pherecydes' version also to Hellanicus of Lesbos (*FGrHist* 4 F 166) and Herodorus of Pontus (*FGrHist* 31 F 25a).

[25] Cf. Pind. fr. 175 Maehler *apud* Paus. 1.2.1 for a (non-Athenian) less generous attitude towards Theseus.

[26] Acts of sexual violence such as Theseus' abduction of Antiope could be taken as acts of *hybris*: see p. 173.

[27] Isocrates' account is very similar to that of Hegias of Troezen found in Paus. 1.2.1: here Antiope falls in love (ἐρασθεῖσαν) with Theseus, who is aiding Heracles in his campaign against Themiscyra, and betrays her country.

[28] Isocrates' treatment of Hippolyta is reminiscent of Hecuba's accusations to Helen in Eur. *Tro.* 987–1001: see discussion at p. 177.

[29] On the relevance of legal concepts (such as *moicheia*) in Greek tragedy, and consequently in extra-legal contexts, see Harris et al. 2010, and in particular Harris 2010 on the familiarity of the Athenian audience with legal terminology and practice.

[30] For the notion of *hybris* in everyday language, see *OED* s.v. hybris: 'Presumption, orig. towards the gods; pride, excessive self-confidence'.

reaction of the gods.³¹ In the past few decades, however, much effort has been made to reassess the traditional view, and we now possess a clearer understanding of the Greek notion of *hybris*.³² The connection with the divine as an intrinsic feature of *hybris* has been questioned and rejected by most scholars, who are now more interested in the moral and legal aspects of the notion.³³

MacDowell, after examining the evidence from fifth- and fourth-century Athens, defined *hybris* as the act of 'having energy or power and misusing it self-indulgently', and argued against the idea that *hybris* was an inherently religious offence.³⁴ MacDowell also discussed the Athenian law about *hybris*, which he dated to the sixth century,³⁵ and noted that it covered offences which were regulated by other laws as long as they were committed with a hubristic state of mind.³⁶ Dickie, on the other hand, provided a fairly traditional definition of *hybris* as 'unchecked arrogance, engendered by good fortune, and manifesting itself in transgressing the boundaries that divide men from the gods', and pointed out that *hybris* is often opposed to quietness (*hēsychia*) in archaic poetry.³⁷ Despite their different standpoints, both MacDowell and Dickie rightly stressed the importance of the hubristic agent's disposition in the definition of *hybris*, but failed to appreciate the intimate connection between *hybris* and honour (*timē*).³⁸

Nick Fisher, in a series of articles and in his groundbreaking book *Hybris: A Study in the Values of Honour and Shame in Ancient Greece*, has convincingly shown that *hybris* was not intrinsically related to religion but was indeed associated with the notion of honour. Fisher builds his thesis on Aristotle's discussion of *hybris* in the *Rhetoric*. According to Aristotle, the man who commits *hybris* slights (ὁ ὑβρίζων δὲ ὀλιγωρεῖ), and *hybris* consists in doing and saying things that cause shame (αἰσχύνη) to the victim for the mere purpose of obtaining pleasure (Arist. *Rh.* 1378b23–35). On these grounds, Fisher defines *hybris* as 'the committing of acts of intentional insult, of acts which deliberately inflict shame and dishonour on others';³⁹ he stresses the intentional nature (*prohairesis*) of hubristic acts, and points to the pleasure of insulting

---

[31] See e.g. Dodds 1951: 31, 48 and Bowra 1964: 81.
[32] The history of the scholarly debate on *hybris* is summarised by Fisher 1992: 2–5.
[33] The main studies on the subject are MacDowell 1976, Dickie 1984, Fisher 1992 and Cairns 1996. See also Dover 1974: 54, who briefly touched upon the theme of *hybris* and defined it as a 'behaviour in which a citizen treats a fellow-citizen as if he were dealing with a slave or a foreigner'.
[34] MacDowell 1976: 21–2.
[35] But MacDowell based his argument on the text of the *graphē hybreōs* preserved in Dem. 21.94, which is very likely to be a forgery: see Harris in Canevaro 2013a: 224–31.
[36] MacDowell 1976: 24–9.
[37] Dickie 1984: esp. 85.
[38] Canevaro 2018b: 103, 107.
[39] Fisher 1992: 148.

as the cause for committing such acts.[40] Accordingly, *hybris* as such does not constitute a religious offence, but only when the act of intentional insult is directed towards a god's *timē*.[41]

Particularly interesting for the case of the Amazons is Fisher's analysis of Herodotus' account of the Persian debate concerning the invasion of Greece (Hdt. 7.5–16). Xerxes is persuaded by Mardonius to start an expedition against Greece and declares his plans to the Persian Council. Xerxes brings several arguments to his cause: the Persian custom which imposes every king to extend the Empire's territories; the glory and fertile lands the Persians would acquire if they conquered Greece; and the opportunity to take vengeance on the Athenians for their past offences (Hdt. 7.8a–8b). Xerxes then wishes to extend the borders of the Persian Empire up to the sky of Zeus and submit both the guilty and the innocent under the yoke of slavery (Hdt. 7.8c). The view of the king is supported by Mardonius. The latter shows no respect for the strength of the Greeks and acknowledges that the Persians' drive for conquest led them to attack nations who did them no wrong (Hdt. 7.9–9c). Xerxes' uncle Artabanus, on the other hand, speaks against the expedition. He highlights the risks deriving from Xerxes' plan to bridge the Hellespont, and recalls Darius' failed invasion of Scythia. He then warns the king that the god strikes with his thunderbolt those who make a display, because he does not allow anyone but himself to think big (φρονέειν μέγα) (Hdt. 7.10e).

Xerxes is angered by Artabanus' words at first, but he then changes his mind and decides to cancel the expedition. The king, however, is led by a dream to reconsider his position again, and consults his uncle on the matter. Artabanus will finally be persuaded by the same dream to approve the invasion. Before this happens, he explains the reason for his previous disappointment towards the behaviour of the king. 'When there were two motions for action placed before the Persians,' he says, 'one of which was tending to increase *hybris*, the other to diminish it, by saying that it is a bad thing to teach the soul always to seek to have more than what is in front of one, when these two motions were placed before us you chose the one that would be worse both for you and for the Persians' (Hdt. 7.16a.2, trans. Fisher). In Fisher's opinion, the *hybris* against which Artabanus warns Xerxes is not simply an individual characteristic of the king, but an expression of the traditional imperialistic policy of the Persians and their acquisitiveness (*pleonexia*).[42] Fisher also argues that the concept of 'thinking big' (*mega phronein*) can be one of the factors inducing *hybris*, with which it is often associated, but the two notions need not be equated. Fisher suggests that this distinction applies to the Herodotus passage as well, and that

---

[40] Fisher 1992: 11.
[41] Fisher 1992: 142–8.
[42] Fisher 1992: 371.

Artabanus is here using the milder language of *mega phronein* in order not to attack the king openly with an accusation of *hybris*.[43]

Douglas Cairns has reconciled Fisher's ideas on *hybris* with those of his critics and provided a more advanced synthesis of their respective positions. Cairns has further developed Fisher's conclusion that *hybris* is intimately connected with honour, but he questioned Fisher's fundamentally (although not completely) behaviourist approach and advocated a revaluation of the dispositional aspect of *hybris*.[44] Cairns considers Arist. *Rh.* 1378b23–35 within the broader context of Aristotle's ethical theory. In particular, he notes that in Aristotle *prohairesis* does not simply denote intentionality, but more specifically a deliberate choice deriving from one's developed and settled state of character (*hexis*). He therefore comes to the conclusion that *hybris* is not limited to the act of insulting others with the specific intention of dishonouring them. *Hybris* is rather a disposition to overvalue one's own worth and honour, which can (but need not) result in specific attacks on the honour of others.[45] Moreover, Cairns argues against Fisher that the concept of pride, or 'thinking big' (*mega phronein*), coincides with the dispositional aspect of *hybris*, of which it is a 'regular feature'.[46] This is well exemplified by the Herodotean passage just discussed, which is an expression not so much of Persian national imperialistic character, but of the individual personalities of the kings who are responsible for Persia's imperialistic policy.[47] Acknowledging the dispositional aspect of *hybris* is very important for appreciating the presence or lack of a hubristic characterisation of the Amazons in our evidence. As we shall see, this characterisation is only evident in Lysias' *Funeral Oration*, where the Amazons display a disposition to *mega phronein* and to overvaluing their own honour which leads them to commit injustices and disrespect the honour of other nations.

LYSIAS: THE STATE FUNERAL AND THE DISCOURSE OF *HYBRIS*

Lysias' account of the Attic Amazonomachy in his *Funeral Oration* (Lys. 2.4–6) was informed by the discursive parameters of the state funeral for the war dead and accordingly aimed to construct an imagined community. The episode is commonly recalled in funeral speeches. Demosthenes lists the repulsion of the Amazons among the noble deeds performed by the Athenians in self-defence

---

[43] Fisher 1992: 372–4.
[44] See also Canevaro 2018b, who investigates the Athenian *graphē hubreōs* based on the framework proposed by Cairns.
[45] Cairns 1996: 2–8.
[46] Cairns 1996: 10–17.
[47] Cairns 1996: 13–15.

(Dem. 60.7–8). Socrates, in Plato's *Menexenus*, mentions the victory over the Amazons as an example of Athenian battles for the freedom of the Greeks (Pl. *Menex.* 239a–b). While Demosthenes and Plato discussed the Attic Amazonomachy very briefly, Lysias devoted a detailed narrative to the episode. The orator ignored Theseus' role in the events and characterised the Amazons as hubristic. As I demonstrate, the latter are portrayed as overstepping the limits of the traditional role of women, excessive in their pursuit of glory (*doxa*) and completely uninterested in justice. In other words, the Amazons overvalue their own honour (*timē*) and are disrespectful of the honour of other nations. The moral contrast with the Amazons produced an idealised image of the Athenians as the righteous punishers of *hybris*.[48] This picture illustrated the ideas about and attitude towards *hybris* that the Athenians were expected to embody, and thus fostered their pride, sense of belonging to the community, and motivation for giving their lives for the city.

Lysias never uses the word ὕβρις or its derivatives to describe the Amazons. Yet, his narrative clearly portrays the Amazons as guilty of *hybris*. The first element of this characterisation lies in the Amazons' unusual gender status compared to Greek standards. Lysias notes that the Amazons were the daughters of Ares, and locates them in the area of the river Thermodon.[49] He then describes the Amazons' innovative fighting style, based on the use of iron weapons and horse-riding, which gave them a considerable advantage over their enemies.[50] Lysias also highlights the contrast between the Amazons' female nature and their courage, which made them appear similar, if not superior, to men (Lys. 2.4).[51] Because of their unnatural inclination for warfare, the Amazons represent a distortion of traditional gender roles, and this idea does come out in Lysias' text.[52] However, the role of women in society was not central in the discursive parameters of the state funeral.[53] At no point does Lysias suggest

---

[48] The image of Athens as the punisher of *hybris* is a common feature of funeral speeches: cf. Dem. 60.8, 28; Lys. 2.14; Hyp. 6.20.

[49] For the Amazons' descent from Ares, cf. *FGrHist* 3 F 15; Todd 2007: 215 links this detail to Amazon militarism. For the location of the Amazons' homeland, see Tyrrell 1984: 55–9; Dowden 1997: 100–1, 103–16.

[50] See Todd 2007: 215–16, who follows Tyrrell 1984: 17 in considering these details as 'designed to represent the Amazons as the moral inferiors of Greek hoplites'. On Amazons and horse-riding, see Mayor 2014: 170–90.

[51] Tyrrell 1984: 18.

[52] See Tyrrell 1984: 18, whose analysis, however, overestimates the importance of gender roles in Lysias' account.

[53] Only Pericles' funeral speech in Thucydides devotes a brief section to the role of women in Athenian society. Pericles exhorts Athenian women to pursue female excellence, which consists in being 'least talked of among men' (Thuc. 2.45.2). No other funeral speech stresses the Amazons' unusual gender status: *pace* Loraux 1981: 170–1, the *epitaphios logos* did not portray the Amazonomachy mainly in terms of a struggle between sexes.

that the Amazons were trying to impose a different, female-centric order, which the Athenians were able to prevent. The orator does not focus on the Amazons' reversal of gender roles as such.[54] Instead, he makes clear that the Amazons, despite their female nature, were a very powerful enemy and posed a real threat to Athens, which made their defeat all the more impressive. More importantly, by describing the Amazons as overstepping the limits of the legitimate role of women, Lysias implicitly depicts them as guilty of *hybris*.

In classical Athens, respectable women were expected to live indoors and avoid contact with non-related men. Non-elite women, it is true, were often forced by economic circumstances to work outside the household,[55] and activities such as wet-nursing and midwifery could even be sources of female social capital.[56] Ritual and priesthood also allowed women some scope for participating in civic life and acquiring honour.[57] Yet, female seclusion was a commonly held Athenian ideal (Thuc. 2.45.2; Lys. 1.6–8; 3.6; Dem. 57.35; Xen. *Oec.* 7.22–3). According to this view, a woman's role in society was to run her household and give her husband legitimate heirs, and her main occupations included weaving and taking care of her children (Lys. 1.6–7; [Dem.] 59.122; Xen. *Oec.* 3.10–12; 7.24–5, 35–6).[58] The Amazons' practice of horsemanship and warfare is therefore an appropriation of features alien to the female domain. One can take a famous line in Euripides' *Medea* as evidence of the traditional Athenian view on women and warfare. Medea opposes the condition of women inside the household to that of men fighting on the battlefield, and declares that she would rather 'stand three times with a shield in battle than give birth once' (Eur. *Med.* 248–51, trans. Kovacs). The Amazons themselves, in Herodotus' account of their encounter with the Scythians (Hdt. 4.110–16), stress their unconventional lifestyle in comparison to the customs of Scythian women. The Amazons point out how their own habits, which include archery, throwing the javelin and riding horses, are incompatible with traditional female occupations (ἔργα δὲ γυναικήϊα), which Scythian women regularly perform (Hdt. 4.114.3).[59]

That women who exceeded the limits of their traditional role and *timē* could be perceived as guilty of *hybris* appears from some passages in Aristophanes' *Lysistrata*.

---

[54] See Barringer 2008: 59–108 for a reading of the Amazonomachy (specifically on the west metopes of the Parthenon) which emphasises male anxieties about the role of women in Athenian society.
[55] Brock 1994; Kosmopoulou 2001.
[56] See recently Taylor 2017: 133–47.
[57] See Connelly 2007; Blok 2017.
[58] Fantham et al. 1994: 101–6; Pritchard 2014: 182–3. The gulf between reality and the ideology of female seclusion is emphasised by Brock 1994.
[59] Hardwick 1990: 17; Fantham et al. 1994: 133–4; Dowden 1997: 107.

As scholars have pointed out,[60] on several occasions the attitude of the women in the play, with their rebellious intrusion into the male domain of war and foreign policy (Ar. *Lys.* 507–20),[61] is labelled as *hybris* by male characters (Ar. *Lys.* 399–401, 425, 658–9). In a passage that bears clear sexual overtones, the leader of the men's Chorus even worries about the possibility that the women will follow the example of the Amazons depicted in the Painted Stoa and turn to horse-riding (Ar. *Lys.* 676–9). It can therefore be concluded that the Amazons' anomalous gender status is only a component – albeit an important one – of a broader discourse of *hybris* that characterises the entire passage in Lysias' *Funeral Oration*.

Another indication of the Amazons' *hybris* is their characterisation as excessive in their desire for conquest and glory. Lysias' Amazons embody the image of the imperialistic power, who submits weaker nations and rules over a vast empire.[62] The orator describes them as 'ruling over many nations' (ἄρχουσαι δὲ πολλῶν ἐθνῶν) and states that they had enslaved (καταδεδουλωμέναι) the peoples around them. The Amazons' greed and desire for conquest seem to have no limits. They became attracted to Athens' great fame (κλέος μέγα) and decided to make war against the city. The motivations which Lysias attributes to the Amazons are particularly interesting. The orator states that the Amazons mustered a powerful army against Athens for the sake of much glory (πολλῆς δόξης) and great ambition (μεγάλης ἐλπίδος) (Lys. 2.5).

The orator's insistence on glory (*doxa*) and ambition (*elpis*) as the reasons leading the Amazons to start their campaign conveys the idea of their hubristic disposition to *mega phronein*. The notion of *doxa* could of course hold a positive value and be achieved through honourable means. In Demosthenes' *Against Leptines*, for example, the Athenians are encouraged to pursue a good reputation (δόξαν χρηστήν). This derives from reciprocating favours to benefactors and following in the footsteps of the ancestors (Dem. 20.10, 25). Lysias himself, in the *Funeral Oration*, speaks of the Athenian ancestors as pursuing good reputation (δόξης ἀγαθῆς), which they attained by saving the Heraclidae from Eurystheus (Lys. 2.14). The Amazons, however, are described as excessive in their pursuit of glory. They were not motivated by good *doxa* or even simply by *doxa*, but acted for the sake of excessive glory (πολλῆς δόξης χάριν). Unlike the Athenians, the Amazons did not achieve their *doxa* through acts of *philanthrōpia*, but by conquering the lands of other nations and imposing slavery on their own enemies.

The Amazons' great *elpis*, which can be translated as 'hope' or 'ambition', can also be taken as an indication of their hubristic disposition. In Greek thought, *elpis*, especially if further qualified, can have a negative meaning,

---

[60] Castriota 1992: 51–3; A. Stewart 1995: 591–4; see also Pritchard 2014: 177.
[61] Cf. Hom. *Il.* 6.490–3.
[62] On the Athenians' ambivalent attitude towards imperialism, see p. 64 n. 30.

because it often presupposes a gap between excessive expectations and negative or even disastrous outcomes.⁶³ Pindar, for example, points out that men perform bold acts (μεγαλανορίαις) because they are driven by shameless hope (ἀναιδεῖ ἐλπίδι). The poet then advocates a measured life in order to avoid the acts of madness (μανίαι) which derive from unattainable desires (Pind. *Nem.* 11.44–8).⁶⁴ Similarly, the Chorus in Sophocles' *Antigone* notes that *elpis* can be a source of profit, but can also lead to deception, especially when the god drives one's mind towards *atē* (Soph. *Ant.* 615–24).⁶⁵ *Elpis* is explicitly associated with *hybris* in an oracle reported by Herodotus before the account of the Battle of Salamis. There, it is foreseen that, after the Persians have sacked Athens in mad hope (ἐλπίδι μαινομένῃ), 'divine Justice will extinguish mighty Greed (*Koros*) the son of *Hybris*' (Hdt. 8.77, trans. Godley, adapted).⁶⁶

The bad consequences of excessive hope and imperialism are emphasised in Isocrates' *To Philip*. In a passage that bears many resemblances to Lysias' Amazon narrative, Isocrates recalls how the Thebans made bad use of their hegemony. They engaged in an expansionistic policy, undertaking the enslavement (καταδουλοῦσθαι) of the Thessalians, and brought war against the Phocians. However, instead of conquering the cities of the Phocians, the Thebans have lost (ἀπολωλέκασιν) their own. Isocrates significantly concludes that the Thebans 'have reached the point where, although they once hoped (ἐλπίσαντες) to have all Greece in their control, now their hopes (τὰς ἐλπίδας) for their own safety lie with [Philip]' (Isoc. 5.53–5, trans. Papillon). One can observe the same ideas in Lysias' characterisation of the Amazons. There, the combination of excessive desire for *doxa* and great *elpis* conveys the idea of the Amazons' *hybris* and tendency to *mega phronein*. The actions of the Amazons will be later labelled as acts of folly (*anoia*), and their hopes will result in the complete annihilation of their nation and reputation.

The general impression of *hybris* attached to the Amazons is reinforced by Lysias' description of the disastrous outcome of the invasion. When they had to fight against brave men, the Amazons proved to be women and their *doxa* became the opposite of the one they had previously achieved (ἐναντίαν τὴν δόξαν τῆς προτέρας λαβοῦσαι μᾶλλον ἐκ τῶν κινδύνων ἢ ἐκ τῶν σωμάτων ἔδοξαν εἶναι γυναῖκες) (Lys. 2.5). They all died in Athens, and their massive

---

⁶³ See Cairns 2016b, who has recently shown that the meaning of the Greek word ἐλπίς ranges from the neutral 'expectation' to the desiderative 'hope', and that the notion could be employed in both a positive and a negative sense. On the negative aspect of *elpis*, due to the uncertainty and unpredictability of the future, see also Cornford 1907: 167–72.
⁶⁴ See Cairns 2016b: 35–7. On the theme of *elpis* in Pindar, see Theunissen 2000.
⁶⁵ See Cairns 2016b: 39–42.
⁶⁶ Fisher 1992: 375–6.

defeat was the punishment for their folly (δοῦσαι δίκην τῆς ἀνοίας). The orator concludes that, because they had desired unjustly (ἀδίκως ἐπιθυμήσασαι) the land of another people, the Amazons justly (δικαίως) lost their own (Lys. 2.6). Lysias states that the Amazons' defeat occurred when they had to face brave men (ἀγαθῶν ἀνδρῶν), but does not stress the clash between genders. Instead, he points to the superiority of the Athenians over the nations which the Amazons had been able to submit. The orator's insistence on *doxa* (πολλῆς δόξης . . . ἐναντίαν τὴν δόξαν . . . ἔδοξαν εἶναι γυναῖκες) confirms the impression that the gender issue is a component of a broader discourse of *hybris*. The Amazons overvalued their own *timē* and were excessive in their pursuit of *doxa*. This led them not only to fail in achieving a greater reputation, but also to lose the one they already enjoyed. When they had to fight against stronger enemies, they experienced a reversal of their former *doxa*. Moreover, the Amazons' course of action is labelled a case of *anoia*, reminiscent of both the deception deriving from *elpis* and the failing of rationality sometimes associated with *hybris*.[67]

Finally, the conclusion of Lysias' narrative describes the Amazons' fate in terms of justice and punishment of *hybris*. The Amazons' greed and desire for a land that did not belong to them are labelled as unjust.[68] As a result, the Amazons rightfully lost their own land. The orator implicitly opposes the Amazons' unjust imperialistic recourse to war not only to the Athenians' traditional role as champions of justice, but also to their status as an autochthonous people who have never deprived other nations of their lands (Lys. 2.17).[69] Moreover, the opposition between justice and excessive behaviour reflects Solonian views of justice. In one of the surviving fragments of his poetry, Solon warns the Athenians that their city will perish because of the greed of its citizens, and anticipates the doom which awaits the leaders of the people. These leaders have an unjust mind (ἄδικος νόος), and will suffer great pains because of their great *hybris* (ὕβριος ἐκ μεγάλης). The poet adds *koros* to the picture, and describes the excesses in the conduct of the leaders as well as their acquisitive behaviour (Solon fr. 4.5–16 West).[70] Solon therefore establishes a link between *hybris*, excessive behaviour and injustice, and foresees the inevitable punishment which derives from this combination. Lysias' Amazons, with their excessive ambition and pursuit of glory as well as their unjust desire for the lands of others, fit perfectly into Solon's pattern: their invasion of Attica and its disastrous outcome are a clear case of rightly punished *hybris*.

---

[67] Cf. Aesch. *Pers.* 749–50.

[68] See MacDowell 1976: 19, who notes how one of the possible manifestations of *hybris* is the 'act of taking from someone else a thing which belongs to him, or preventing him from receiving what should be his'.

[69] On this opposition see Tyrrell 1984: 114–16; on autochthony see Chapter 4.

[70] Fisher 1992: 70–3. Canevaro forthcoming b stresses how the connection between *hybris*, *koros*, injustice and retribution was typical of archaic Greek thought.

Lysias' description of the Amazons' defeat as the just punishment of their *hybris* is coherent with the absence of justice among the reasons for the invasion. Other versions of the Attic Amazonomachy created grounds for possible complaints on the part of the Amazons. Theseus' abduction of Antiope, in particular, risked shedding a negative light on the Athenians and making them appear as the aggressors. One reason to pass over this detail was the necessity of presenting the Athenians as the wronged party and blaming the conflict on the Amazons. At the same time, by obliterating any Athenian responsibility for the outbreak of the war, Lysias managed to exclude justice from the moral horizon of the Amazons. Not only is justice replaced by excessive *doxa* and *elpis* in the account of the reasons for the invasion; it is also explicitly denied at the end of the narrative, when Lysias describes the Amazons' desire for the lands of other nations as contrary to justice (Lys. 2.6). This description contributes to the creation of a moral opposition between Amazons and Athenians. The Amazons ignored the norms of intervention that regulated Athens' foreign policy and made the Athenians champions of justice and defenders of the weak.[71] Focusing on the *hybris* of the Amazons therefore highlights by contrast the justice and good character of the Athenians.

Lysias' depiction of the Amazons as guilty of *hybris* is also confirmed by their significant similarities with the other great hubristic invaders of Attica in Athenian social memory: the Persians. In the aftermath of the Greek victory in the Persian Wars, the Attic Amazonomachy became a popular subject of monumental art. This episode was placed side by side with the Battle of Marathon in the Painted Stoa and was included in the iconographic programme of the Parthenon, the quintessential victory monument for the Persian Wars. It also featured in the Theseion and on the Shield of Athena Parthenos.[72] These depictions, probably reflected in Attic vase painting,[73] have led many scholars to assume that the Amazons symbolised (and feminised) the Persians in Athenian official art.[74] Recent scholarship has raised doubts over this view,[75] and suggested that the

---

[71] See Low 2007: 175–211 on the norm of intervention based on the principle of 'helping the wronged'. For further discussion of the helping paradigm and the image of the Athenians as altruistic champions of justice, see pp. 124–5.

[72] For Attic red-figure vase painting which possibly reflects monumental Cimonian Amazonomachies, see Bothmer 1957: 161–92; for the Amazonomachies on the west metopes of the Parthenon and the Shield of Athena Parthenos, see Bothmer 1957: 208–14 and E. B. Harrison 1966.

[73] Bothmer 1957: 161–92.

[74] See e.g. Devambez 1976: 273–4; Culasso Gastaldi 1977: 294–6; Boardman 1982: 13–15; Castriota 1992: *passim* and 2005. Athenian art started to portray Amazons in oriental (specifically Scythian and Thracian) outfit in the middle of the sixth century, while Amazons dressed as Persians started to appear at the beginning of the fifth century: see Shapiro 1983; Veness 2002: 98–9; B. Cohen 2012: 462–3.

[75] Veness 2002: 99–104; Mayor 2014: 280–3.

Athenian victory against the Amazons simply provided a mythical precedent for their glorious victory over the Persian invaders.[76] Lysias' narrative participates in this trend. His account of the Amazonomachy closely resembles the description of Darius' and Xerxes' campaigns against Greece in fifth- and fourth-century Athenian sources, which portray the Persian invasions as motivated by *hybris* and imperialism.

The very fact that Lysias claims that the Amazons dominated a multi-ethnic empire mirrors the reality of the Persian Empire.[77] The Amazons' propensity to the enslavement of other nations resembles Persian hubristic and imperialistic attitudes. Later in the speech, Lysias states that Darius, not content with his Asian dominions, invaded Greece in the hope of enslaving Europe (ἐλπίζων καὶ τὴν Εὐρώπην δουλώσεσθαι). Darius' frustrated *elpis* in the passage shows a further parallel with the Amazons (Lys. 2.21).[78] Similarly, in Herodotus' account of Xerxes' decision to attack Greece, the Persian king immediately abandons his rightful complaints against the unprovoked injustices that his father Darius had suffered at the hands of the Greeks (Hdt. 7.8b), and expresses his hubristic desire to enslave both the guilty and the innocent (οὕτω οἵ τε ἡμῖν αἴτιοι ἕξουσι δούλιον ζυγὸν οἵ τε ἀναίτιοι) (Hdt. 7.8c.3).[79]

The Amazons' motivations for going to war against Athens (πολλῆς δόξης καὶ μεγάλης ἐλπίδος χάριν) also recall those of the Persians. Darius' *elpis* in Lysias' account has already been stressed; as for Xerxes, Lysias mentions his frustrated hope (ἐψευσμένος δὲ τῆς ἐλπίδος) as one of the reasons which led him to war (Lys. 2.27). In Book 7 of Herodotus, Xerxes plans to use the campaign against Greece to defeat his predecessors in a competition for gaining more power for the Empire and winning the most *timē*. From his victory against the Greeks, the Persian king expects to obtain both glory (*kydos*) and fertile land (Hdt. 7.8a.2). Not only does Xerxes fail to recognise the Greeks' honour, but he also proves to be excessive in his pursuit of *timē* and *kydos*, as he plans to yoke the Hellespont (Hdt. 7.8b.1) and make the Persian Empire border on the dominions of Zeus (Hdt. 7.8c.1–2).[80] The ghost of Darius in Aeschylus' *Persians* condemns Xerxes' expedition against Greece. In particular, Darius disapproves of his son's impious *elpis* of holding the sacred Hellespont as a slave (Ἑλλήσποντον ἱρὸν δοῦλον ὣς δεσμώμασιν ἤλπισε σχήσειν) (Aesch. *Pers.* 745–6). If this only amounts to an

---

[76] As Mayor 2014: 280–3 suggests, in the fifth century the Amazons did not symbolise or stand for Persians but were merely ancient precursors of the Persians as first eastern invaders of Greece.

[77] See Todd 2007: 216, who stresses that the extent of the Amazon Empire was a new detail, 'serving primarily to highlight their fall from power and the scale of the Athenians' victory'.

[78] See Todd 2007: 231, who rightly stresses that the motif of enslavement portrays the Persian invasion as an act of 'gratuitous expansionism rather than revenge for Athens' activities at Sardis'.

[79] Fisher 1992: 367–8.

[80] Cairns 1996: 13.

implicit accusation of *hybris*,[81] Darius labels the expedition explicitly as an act of *hybris* shortly afterwards (Aesch. *Pers.* 803–8). On this occasion, the former king insists again on the vain hopes (κεναῖσιν ἐλπίσιν) that persuaded Xerxes to leave chosen troops in Greece awaiting disaster. Darius then defines *hybris* as having excessive thoughts (ὑπέρφευ . . . φρονεῖν) and portrays *atē* as its natural consequence (Aesch. *Pers.* 820–2).[82] Xerxes' excessive behaviour is thus very similar to that of Lysias' Amazons.[83]

Another important similarity between the hubristic portrayal of Amazons and Persians lies in the absence of justice from the motivations of the Persian invasion. If the Amazons are not concerned with justice and Lysias explicitly describes their expansionistic policy as a form of injustice, Herodotus at first includes justice among the reasons for Xerxes' campaign. The Persian king declares his desire to punish the Athenians for the wrongs (ἄδικα) they inflicted on his father (Hdt. 7.8b.2). Xerxes, however, fallen victim to his hubristic desires, immediately forgets his initial motivations and declares his plan to enslave both the guilty and the innocent (Hdt. 7.8c.3). Similarly, the Athenian help for the Milesian Revolt, which could be seen as their original wrong against the Persians, is omitted in the narrative of the Persian Wars in Lysias' *Funeral Oration* (Lys. 2.21). Just as with the Amazons, Lysias removes any possible Athenian responsibility for the war, and presents the Persians as driven only by expansionistic desires and uninterested in justice.[84]

Persian expansionism eventually clashed against Athens' opposition. Just as he highlighted how the fortunes of the Amazons came to an end when they encountered *agathoi andres* in the persons of the Athenians, Lysias later describes Xerxes as inexperienced with brave men (ἄπειρος ἀνδρῶν ἀγαθῶν) prior to his invasion of Greece (Lys. 2.27). The orator points to the Athenians' superiority over the nations that Amazons and Persians had been able to subdue. In both cases, he implies that the hubristic ambitions of imperialistic powers, although successful against other nations, were doomed to fail against the Athenians, *agathoi andres* and enemies of the powerful *par excellence*.

Finally, in Aeschylus' *Persians*, Darius describes Xerxes as lacking good judgement (οὐκ εὐβουλίᾳ) because of his hubristic yoking of the Hellespont, and he ascribes his son's dreadful choices to a disease of the mind (νόσος φρενῶν)

---

[81] *Pace* Garvie 2009: 295, who argues that in this particular passage Aeschylus portrays the bridging of the Hellespont as a foolish but not hubristic act.

[82] Garvie 2009: 314–15; Cairns 1996: 16 n. 68. But Garvie 2009: xxii–xxxii downplays the importance of *hybris* in the general economy of Aeschylus' *Persians*.

[83] A significant difference is Aeschylus' portrayal of Xerxes as impious and sacrilegious (Aesch. *Pers.* 809–12), which is unparalleled in Lysias' characterisation of the Amazons, but both passages represent clear cases of *hybris*.

[84] Todd 2007: 230–2.

(Aesch. *Pers.* 749–50).[85] The Amazons, even though their *hybris* was not directed towards the gods, were similarly affected by *anoia* according to Lysias' *Funeral Oration*. Both Amazons and Persians experienced a failing of their intellective faculties (and therefore of their abilities to determine their appropriate *timē* and that of others) which derived from their hubristic attitude and drive for conquest. In both cases, the result is disaster (*atē*): Lysias' Amazons are completely annihilated, while Aeschylus' Chorus of Persian elders lament Persia's tragic defeat together with a prostrate Xerxes (Aesch. *Pers.* 908–1076).

Lysias therefore used the Amazons to reflect and produce ideas about *hybris* and illustrate how the Athenians were expected to behave towards hubristic opponents. His account of the Attic Amazonomachy was conditioned by the discursive parameters of the state funeral for the war dead. In this context, the orators provided a positive image of Athens which justified her military actions as motivated by altruism or self-defence.[86] Lysias accordingly put all the blame for the war on the Amazons. His narrative never mentions Theseus' abduction of Antiope, and there is no hint at any possible Athenian fault. More importantly, Lysias painted a picture of the Amazons as guilty of *hybris*, clearing Athens of any responsibility for the conflict or embarrassment for the role played by Theseus. The *hybris* of the Amazons is not a fixed element of this myth, and is a sign of the influence of the state funeral on Lysias' account. Just as other orators of funeral speeches, Lysias presented the Athenians as the righteous punishers of *hybris*. To achieve this goal, he portrayed the Amazons as unjust, excessive in their desire for conquest and glory, and disrespectful of other peoples' *timē*. Even the Amazons' reversal of traditional gender roles contributes to their overall characterisation as hubristic, which is reinforced by the parallel with the Persian invasion of Greece. From a moral point of view, the Amazons are characterised as the anti-Athenians. This contrast contributed to the idealised image of the Athenians as the righteous punishers of *hybris*, and to the construction of an imagined community.

THESEUS AND THE AMAZONS IN AESCHYLUS' *EUMENIDES*

Lysias' insistence on portraying the Amazons' *hybris* as the only cause of the war is itself a sign that the Athenians were familiar with alternative versions where the invasion resulted from Theseus' abduction of Antiope. At the state funeral for the war dead, any mentions of the abduction would have endangered the

---

[85] Garvie 2009: 297.
[86] Cf. Dem. 60.7, where the orator states that the Athenian ancestors were noble and just, and in defending themselves (ἀμυνόμενοι) they performed great deeds.

image of the Athenians as the righteous punishers of *hybris*. In other institutional settings, however, alluding (even if vaguely) to this episode was not as problematic, and could provide a picture not as unilateral and straightforward as the one painted by Lysias. This is the case of a brief allusion to the Attic Amazonomachy featured in Aeschylus' *Eumenides*. Aeschylus was free from the task of constructing an imagined community and was not compelled to adopt an idealised version of Athenian history. The poet was conditioned by the discursive parameters of the dramatic festivals, which led playwrights to appeal to the whole socio-political span of their audience in order to win first prize. Aeschylus hinted at the Amazons' *phthonos* against Theseus and relied on the multivalence of this notion to construct an ambiguous version of the invasion. This allowed him to produce two contrasting images that could appeal to different sections of his audience: on the one hand, the epitaphic picture of the righteous Athenians always fighting against imperialistic invaders reinforced the ideas of the majority of the *dēmos*; on the other, the possibility that the Athenians were themselves responsible for the invasion was attractive to those who questioned those ideas.

Aeschylus' allusion to the Amazonomachy appears halfway through the play. To solve the dispute between Orestes and the Erinyes over the murder of Clytemnestra, Athena institutes the Council of the Areopagus and grants it jurisdiction over homicide cases. The goddess alludes to the Attic Amazonomachy as an aetiology of the name of the location. Athena recalls how the Amazons had once invaded Athens because of their *phthonos* towards Theseus (Θησέως κατὰ φθόνον), and how the hill where they established their camp and performed sacrifices to Ares had been hence known as the Areopagus (Aesch. *Eum.* 685–90). Unlike Lysias, Aeschylus mentions Theseus in connection with the Amazonomachy, but does not clarify the hero's involvement in the events. Even though the playwright does not describe the grounds of the invasion clearly, one needs to consider the possibility that the ambiguous *phthonos* of the Amazons may have concealed an allusion to Theseus' abduction of Antiope.

The Greek word φθόνος does not have a precise and univocal equivalent in English. The notion encompassed many different values, both negative and positive.[87] One of its possible meanings was the negative value of 'envy'.[88] Aristotle, for example, includes *phthonos* among those emotions which are regarded as intrinsically evil (Arist. *Eth. Nic.* 1107a8–12). He defines the envious man (ὁ φθονερός) as he who suffers at any good fortune of others. To this he opposes the rightly resentful man (ὁ νεμεσητικός), who suffers only at the

---

[87] See Sanders 2014: 33–46, who identifies twelve different 'scripts' of the notion of *phthonos*.
[88] LSJ s.v. φθόνος, I. 1.

undeserved good fortune of others (Arist. *Eth. Nic.* 1108a35–b6).[89] *Phthonos* was something that one rarely claimed for oneself,[90] but it was often predicated on others. Pindar's *Seventh Pythian*, for example, accuses the Athenians of feeling *phthonos* towards Megacles because of his athletic victories and good fortune (Pind. *Pyth.* 7.17–18). In the *Antidosis*, Isocrates on several occasions accuses his own enemies of acting against him out of *phthonos* (Isoc. 15.4, 13, 142–3).[91] The *phthonos* Aeschylus attributes to the Amazons as the reason for their invasion of Attica may therefore be simply a sign of their negative character. The poet may be presenting them as envious of Theseus' good fortune, power and wealth. If one credits this interpretation, Aeschylus' Amazons, though not characterised by *hybris*, would not be particularly different from Lysias' Amazons, who decided to invade Attica when they heard of Athens' fame (Lys. 2.5).

The meaning of envy was not the only value that the Greeks attached to the word φθόνος. On several instances, *phthonos* was felt as justified and even invoked as a rightful reaction to injustices. In this sense, the word can be considered equivalent to the English 'indignation'. A classic case is the resentment of the gods towards successful mortals (*phthonos theōn*).[92] Pindar, for example, prays that the gods' favour for Xenarces, father of the addressee of the *Eight Pythian*, may be without *phthonos* (θεῶν δ' ὄπιν ἄφθονον) (Pind. *Pyth.* 8.71–2). The Messenger in Aeschylus' *Persians* states that Xerxes did not perceive the *phthonos* of the gods towards him (Aesch. *Pers.* 362). In Book 7 of Thucydides, Nicias encourages the Athenian troops in Sicily and says that, if their expedition caused the *phthonos* of a god (εἴ τῳ θεῶν ἐπίφθονοι ἐστρατεύσαμεν), the Athenians have already been punished for it (Thuc. 7.77.3). The idea of a rightful form of *phthonos* was not limited to the gods and can be observed in Athenian oratory in several instances.[93] Isocrates invokes justified *phthonos* against the Persians, who have undeservedly acquired a power too great for men (Isoc. 4.184).[94] In *Against Meidias*, Demosthenes claims that *phthonos*, and not pity, is the appropriate reaction to Meidias' wealth and hubristic behaviour (Dem. 21.196). In his second speech *Against Aphobus*, Demosthenes

---

[89] Cf. Arist. *Rh.* 1386b11–12, where Aristotle opposes *phthonos* to *nemesis*. The former is the pain felt at the good fortune of those who are equal and alike, while the latter is the pain felt at the good fortune of those who do not deserve it. See Fisher 2003: 183; Cairns 2003: 247 n. 42.

[90] See Sanders 2014: 36, who points out that in only three instances in the classical corpus (Eur. *Bacch.* 820; Eur. fr. 334.1–2; Xen. *Cyr.* 3.1.39.8) does someone explicitly attribute *phthonos* to himself.

[91] Fisher 2003: 185–8; Cairns 2003: 242–4; see also Sanders 2014: 38–9 for other examples.

[92] Walcot 1978: 22–51; Cairns 2003: 249–50; Sanders 2014: 42.

[93] Sanders 2014: 43–4.

[94] In this usage, *phthonos* is reminiscent of *nemesis* (cf. Arist. *Rh.* 1386b11–12), as noted by Cairns 2003: 247.

similarly invites the judges to be justly indignant (φθονήσειε δικαίως) towards the defendant, his former guardian Aphobus, because he robbed him of his inheritance and tried to prevent him from reacquiring it (Dem. 28.18).[95] The *phthonos* of the Amazons in Aeschylus' *Eumenides* may therefore be their (more or less) justified resentment for Theseus' abduction of Antiope.[96]

Because of the multivalence of the notion of *phthonos* and the ambiguity of Aeschylus' phrasing, it is hard to determine the version of the myth which is alluded to in the play. Aeschylus may have chosen the Amazonomachy over other possible aetiologies of the name of the Areopagus because the Amazons provided a significant parallel with Clytemnestra's monstrous, non-feminine behaviour.[97] The dual interpretation of the Amazons' motivations may even reflect the ambivalent portrayal of Clytemnestra's motivations in the first play of the trilogy, *Agamemnon*. There, the queen shows both a rightful indignation for the sacrifice of Iphigeneia (Aesch. *Ag.* 1377–8; 1432–3) and an envy of (and tendency to misappropriate) Agamemnon's male status and power (Aesch. *Ag.* 10–11; 1069–71).[98] Aeschylus may have thus been deliberately ambiguous, leaving the audience free to choose either version of the Amazonomachy. This was in line with the discursive parameters of the dramatic festivals, which invited playwrights to appeal to all sections of their audience. Aeschylus' vague mention of Theseus may have triggered in part of the audience the memory of the abduction of Antiope, whose currency is testified by the popularity of the motif in Attic vase painting.[99] This version blamed the war on the Athenians. Because they were presented as the recipients of the Amazons' rightful *phthonos*, the

---

[95] Cairns 2003: 246–8; Fisher 2003: 185 n. 16, 198–202; Sanders 2014: 43–4.

[96] Whether or not this resentment should be considered justified depends on the different versions of the myth, as in some accounts Antiope is portrayed as Theseus' legitimate acquisition: see Chapter 6, pp. 171–3.

[97] *Suda* s.v. Ἄρειος πάγος gives two possible explanations for the name of the Areopagus. This either depends from the Areopagus' jurisdiction in matters of homicides, which were the domain of the god Ares, or it derives from the myth of Halirrhothius, son of Poseidon, whose death at the hands of Ares had been the first case of homicide judged by the Areopagus (cf. Eur. *El.* 1258–62; Dem. 23.66; Apollod. 3.14.2; Paus. 1.21.4): see Wallace 1989: 9–10 and Fowler 2013: 454–5. Wallace 1989: 88 rightly notes that Aeschylus' aetiology conveyed the idea that Orestes, not Ares, was the first defendant tried by the Council of the Areopagus. Modern scholarship has often seen Aeschylus' *Eumenides* as a reaction to Ephialtes' reform of the Areopagus (see e.g. Podlecki 1966: 74–100; Sommerstein 2010: 281–8; Leão 2010: 42), but the historicity of the reform as we know it has been convincingly questioned by Zaccarini 2018 and Harris 2019. On the parallels between Clytemnestra and the Amazons cf. Aesch. *Eum.* 625–30, with Zeitlin 1978: 155 and Tyrrell 1984: 93–122.

[98] See Winnington-Ingram 1948: 130–7.

[99] Cf. Apollod. *Epit.* 1.16–17 for a late account of the Amazonomachy as the direct consequence of the abduction of Antiope. On the abduction of Antiope in vase painting, see Chapter 6, pp. 167–70.

Athenians may even have appeared to some as guilty of *hybris*. Such an image contrasted with the idealised picture produced at the state funeral, and was probably appealing for those members of the audience who did not identify with the official rhetoric and ideology of the democracy. Part of the audience, on the other hand, would have interpreted Aeschylus' vague phrasing as an allusion to the self-congratulatory Amazonomachies of funeral speeches. This interpretation certainly resonated with the majority of the *dēmos*, who could perceive their ideas about the righteous character of their city being restated on the tragic stage.

AN ALLUSION TO THE ABDUCTION IN A PRIVATE SETTING?

Another possible allusion to Theseus' abduction of Antiope in connection with the Attic Amazonomachy can be found in Isocrates' *Panegyricus*. The speech was composed for private circulation and exemplifies a case where an orator was not conditioned by the institutions of Athenian democracy. The *Panegyricus* mixes epideictic and deliberative features,[100] but does not reflect clearly the discursive parameters of the state funeral nor those of the Assembly. As a result, Isocrates' version of the Amazonomachy does not construct an imagined community through the production of ideas about the Athenians' attitude towards *hybris*, nor does it express ideas about the advantage of the community.

The object of the speech is the proposal of a Panhellenic campaign against Persia under joint Athenian and Spartan leadership. To support Athens' claim to leadership, Isocrates recalls a series of Athenian exploits against barbaric imperialistic nations that tried to extend their dominions at the expense of the Greeks. Among such exploits was the Amazonomachy (Isoc. 4.66–7). According to the orator, the Amazons and their Scythian allies raised accusations (ἐγκλήματα) against Athens and invaded Attica (Isoc. 4.68).[101] Isocrates' vague reference to the accusations put forward by the Amazons may well be an allusion to the events regarding Antiope. As in Aeschylus' *Eumenides*, the phrasing is ambiguous, but could have been enough to make an Athenian think of Theseus' abduction of Antiope.

Isocrates seems to admit (though vaguely) the existence of possible grounds for complaint on the part of the Amazons, but does not speak of

---

[100] On the nature, destination and themes of Isocrates' *Panegyricus*, see Usher 1990: 19–21; Too 1995: 79–80; Papillon 2004: 24–7.

[101] Cf. Diod. 4.28, where the Amazons led an army together with the Scythians in order to punish the Athenians for Theseus' enslavement of Antiope (διὰ τὸ τὸν Θησέα καταδεδουλῶσθαι τὴν ἡγεμόνα τῶν Ἀμαζόνων Ἀντιόπην).

Athenian responsibility explicitly and does not even mention Theseus or Antiope. Rather than well-founded accusations, the ἐγκλήματα sound like pretexts fabricated by the Amazons and their Scythian allies to initiate a war against Athens. Not unlike Lysias, Isocrates is keen to describe the Amazons as an imperialistic power and their military campaign as moved by their desire for conquest. From their first mention in the *Panegyricus*, the Amazons are associated with imperialism. Their invasion of Attica is introduced as one of the wars moved against Greece by the nations who were the most suited for command (ἀρχικώτατα μὲν τῶν γενῶν) and possessed the greatest dominions (μεγίστας δυναστείας ἔχοντα). These were the Scythians, the Thracians and the Persians (Isoc. 4.67). Isocrates stresses their imperialism further when he states that Scythians and Amazons were trying to rule (ἐπῆρχον) over Europe. The orator adds that, although they hated the whole race of the Greeks (μισοῦντες μὲν ἅπαν τὸ τῶν Ἑλλήνων γένος), the Amazons raised accusations against the Athenians in particular (ἰδίᾳ) because they knew that if they attacked Athens they would have conquered the entirety of Greece (Isoc. 4.68).[102] It is clear, then, that the ἐγκλήματα and the possible allusion to Theseus' abduction of Antiope are only the alleged reason for the Amazons' invasion, and their importance is notably diminished by the description of the war as an expansionistic campaign.

The passage has to be read in the light of the rhetorical purpose of the speech. Isocrates stresses Athens' power in order to endorse the city's leadership in the prospective campaign against Persia. Unlike Lysias, Isocrates is not influenced by the discursive parameters of the state funeral. Accordingly, he does not focus on the image of the Athenians as the righteous punishers of *hybris*. Isocrates' possible allusion to Theseus' abduction of Antiope as one of the causes of the war does not challenge explicitly the idealised image of Athens constructed at the state funeral, but could hardly have figured in a funeral speech. While indirectly triggering the memory of a well-known version of the myth, Isocrates shows not only that the Amazons' real aim was the complete conquest of Greece, but also that to achieve this aim they needed a pretext for attacking the Athenians, and the Athenians alone. Athens therefore emerges as the prime power of Greece, the only city powerful enough to lead the Greeks against the Persians. At the same time, the instrumental use of the past in support of a policy is reminiscent of deliberative rhetoric. Isocrates twice states that recalling Athens' wars against the barbarians is appropriate when discussing the leadership of a campaign against Persia (Isoc. 4.66, 71). Yet, the speech explicitly questions the principle of advantage (*to sympheron*) which was central to the discursive parameters of the Assembly. Before relating the myths of Athens' help for Adrastus and the Heraclidae, Isocrates defends the Athenian custom of protecting the weak against the powerful. The orator claims that the

---

[102] Cf. Aesch. *Pers.* 234; Lys. 2.22.

Athenians deserve praise because they willingly side with the weak against their own advantage (παρὰ τὸ συμφέρον) instead of favouring the powerful for their own profit (τοῦ λυσιτελοῦντος ἕνεκα) (Isoc. 4.53). As a private speech, Isocrates' *Panegyricus* therefore did not reflect the discursive parameters of any of the institutions of Athenian democracy where it could have belonged.

THESEUS' ABDUCTION OF ANTIOPE IN THE FIGURATIVE ARTS

Theseus' acquisition of Antiope was mentioned explicitly as the cause of the Attic Amazonomachy by Philochorus and Pherecydes, as well as by Isocrates in the *Panathenaicus*. These sources all belonged to private contexts, not conditioned by the discursive parameters of the formal institutions of Athenian democracy. Their accounts of the causes of the Amazonomachy show small but significant differences, to the extent that it is even questionable whether they all portray the episode of Antiope as an abduction. At the same time, they all agree in attributing to Theseus some kind of responsibility for the outbreak of the war. Before turning to the analysis of the versions of the story produced by Philochorus, Pherecydes and Isocrates, it is necessary to consider how Theseus' acquisition of Antiope was depicted in the figurative arts. This can help clarify what fifth- and fourth-century Athenians knew about the episode.

The abduction of Antiope appeared in Athenian art between the end of the sixth and the beginning of the fifth century. The motif first occurs on the west pediment of the temple of Apollo Daphnephoros in Eretria, which was built during the last decades of the sixth century and then destroyed by the Persians in 490 BC. Similarities in style, as well as the subject of the sculptures, have suggested a connection with Athens, if not even a form of patronage.[103] For these reasons, the pediment probably reflects mythical traditions which were current in Athens at the time. The pediment shows Theseus holding Antiope with his left arm while placing her on his chariot in the act of carrying her off. Athena features in the centre of the scene, which might have also included Theseus' companions fighting against Amazons.[104]

The abduction scene was relatively popular in Attic vase painting of roughly the same period. Ten such depictions survive, dating from the end of the sixth century to around 450 BC.[105] This suggests that Athenians in the classical period

---

[103] Bothmer 1957: 126; Boardman 1991: 156.
[104] See Bothmer 1957: 125–6; Boardman 1991: 156; *LIMC* s.v. Antiope II 2.
[105] See *LIMC* s.v. Antiope II 4–13. According to Bothmer 1957: 126–7, the vases depicting the episode were not later than 490 BC, and the vase painters might have been partly influenced by the abduction scene on the temple of Apollo in Eretria.

Figure 6.1 Theseus abducts Antiope. Black-figure amphora from Cumae (c. 510–500 BC). Napoli, Museo Archeologico Nazionale 128333. Image © Museo Archeologico Nazionale di Napoli.

had long been familiar with the motif, although nothing is implied about a possible retaliation by the Amazons. Most vases show Antiope gesturing to her companions or looking back in search of help, which suggests that she is being carried off by force.[106] An Attic black-figure amphora from Cumae stored in Naples (Fig. 6.1), for example, portrays Theseus running towards his chariot with Antiope in his arms. The woman, in hoplitic dress, looks back helplessly.[107] In an Attic red-figure cup in London found in Vulci, Theseus, accompanied by Pirithous and Phorbas, carries off Antiope and steps onto his chariot. The Amazon is dressed in oriental attire and extends her left arm in the opposite direction while still carrying her bow.[108] An Attic red-figure amphora from Vulci displayed in the Louvre shows Theseus and Pirithous running away. Theseus carries Antiope in his arms; the woman, who wears a richly decorated oriental dress, stretches her right arm towards her pursuing companions (who are not represented).[109] A similar scene is depicted on a red-figure cup in Oxford (Fig. 6.2). Theseus is stepping onto his chariot with Antiope in his arms; the Amazon, dressed as an oriental archer, looks back and extends both hands.[110] An interesting exception to the established pattern can be found on an Attic black-figure amphora from Vulci, now in Munich (Fig. 6.3). Theseus is

---

[106] See Bothmer 1957: 127–30, who analyses these vases, together with several other instances of the abduction in Attic vase painting.
[107] Napoli, Museo Archeologico Nazionale, 128333; *LIMC* s.v. Antiope II 5.
[108] London, British Museum, E 41; *LIMC* s.v. Antiope II 8.
[109] Paris, Musée du Louvre, G 197; *LIMC* s.v. Antiope II 10.
[110] Oxford, Ashmolean Museum, 1927.4065; *LIMC* s.v. Antiope II 9.

Figure 6.2 Theseus abducts Antiope. Red-figure cup (c. 510 BC). Oxford, Ashmolean Museum AN1927.4065 Oltos, 'Attic red-figure stemmed pottery cup depicting a mythological scene'. Image © Ashmolean Museum, University of Oxford.

Figure 6.3 Theseus and Antiope step together onto a chariot. Black-figure amphora from Vulci (c. 510–500 BC). München, Staatliche Antikensammlungen und Glyptothek 1414. Image © Staatliche Antikensammlungen und Glyptothek München (R. Kühling).

again stepping onto his chariot with Antiope in his arms. The Amazon, however, does not look back in search for help but keeps hold of the chariot rail with her right hand, a detail which has been interpreted as a sign of her willingness to follow Theseus.[111]

---

[111] München, Staatliche Antikensammlungen und Glyptothek, 1414; *LIMC* s.v. Antiope II 4. See Bothmer 1957: 127.

The artistic evidence shows that, at least at the dawn of the fifth century, the Athenians knew that Theseus seized Antiope with the help of his Athenian companions. Heracles, who according to Philochorus was involved in the episode, never appears in the iconography of the abduction. In the west pediment of the temple of Apollo in Eretria, as well as in most of the vase depictions, Theseus carries off Antiope by force. The scene never features an actual battle, which suggests an abduction rather than a legitimate acquisition as a result of a military enterprise.[112] On the Munich amphora, on the other hand, Antiope does not show signs of resistance, and the direction of her gaze suggests that she may be following Theseus willingly. If that were the case, the vase would provide a precedent for Isocrates' account in the *Panathenaicus*.[113]

THE ABDUCTION OF ANTIOPE IN MYTHOGRAPHERS AND ATTHIDOGRAPHERS

Theseus' encounter with Antiope, portrayed as an abduction (or an elopement) in the visual arts, gave origins to slightly diverging versions in the writings of mythographers and Atthidographers. Their accounts are unfortunately lost, but Plutarch summarises them in his *Life of Theseus*, where he uses the work of Philochorus and Pherecydes to illustrate the causes of the Attic Amazonomachy (Plut. *Thes.* 26–8).[114] Pherecydes of Athens, author of a reference work on Greek mythology, was active during the 470s,[115] while Philochorus wrote his *Atthis* during the late fourth or early third century.[116] Both authors illustrate how the episode of Theseus and Antiope could be discussed explicitly in an Athenian private context, not influenced by the discursive parameters of democratic institutions. Philochorus described Antiope as Theseus' legitimate acquisition through military endeavour, whereas Pherecydes may

---

[112] See Culasso Gastaldi 1977: 290–1; Fowler 2013: 485–6. Some Attic vases depicting Theseus' abduction of Helen similarly show the armed hero lifting the girl up without implying a military context: see *LIMC* s.v. Helene 31–4.

[113] Antiope's consent would not have made Theseus any less guilty from a legal point of view: on the Athenians' perception of sexual offence, see Harris 2006; against the traditional view that the Athenians regarded seduction as a worse crime than rape see Harris 1990, *pace* Carey 1995.

[114] On Plutarch's use of sources in the *Life of Theseus* see Frost 1984b: esp. 68–9; Pelling 2002: 177–8; Cooper 2007: esp. 228–31.

[115] Dolcetti 2004: 12–15; Pàmias i Massana 2008: 19; Fowler 2013: 708–9. On the issue of the identity of Pherecydes of Athens and his possible identification with Pherecydes of Syrus, see Fowler 1999 with references.

[116] Harding 2008: 8–9; Jones' Biographical Essay in *BNJ* 328.

have either followed a similar version or presented the episode as an abduction. A comparison with Lysias' and Aeschylus' versions shows that, in both cases, Philochorus and Pherecydes conveyed ideas that were not appropriate to the state funeral and the dramatic festivals: they either acknowledged Athens' aggressive military policy, or even implied the Athenians' support for Theseus' hubristic behaviour.

Because of the nature of Plutarch's *Lives*, my analysis approaches this evidence with due caution. Plutarch provides us with information on otherwise lost sources. His testimony is highly valuable, if not indispensable, but Plutarch was not a historian. Plutarch's biographies had a moral and paradigmatic purpose, and this could influence the way he handled his sources. In other words, Plutarch may have filtered the information according to his moral and narrative aims. Moreover, Plutarch introduces Philochorus' and Pherecydes' accounts about Theseus' acquisition of Antiope to explain the causes of the Attic Amazonomachy, but we cannot safely assume based on his testimony that those authors considered the two episodes connected, or that they discussed the Amazon invasion of Attica in the first place. Finally, as we shall see, Plutarch's testimony is partly contradicted by a scholion to Pindar (schol. *ad* Pind. *Nem*. 5.89) that provides slightly different information about Pherecydes' version of the story.

Plutarch mentions Philochorus' account first. According to the Atthidographer and other authors, Theseus joined Heracles' expedition to the Euxine Sea to fight the Amazons and received Antiope as a war prize (γέρας Ἀντιόπην ἔλαβεν) (Plut. *Thes*. 26.1).[117] Unlike the iconographic evidence, Philochorus does not envisage Theseus' encounter with Antiope as an abduction, but portrays Antiope as Theseus' legitimate acquisition through military endeavour. Plutarch, however, immediately rejects Philochorus' version and recalls another variant. According to the Athenian mythographer Pherecydes and the majority of writers (including Hellanicus and Herodorus of Pontus), Theseus went on his own expedition to the Euxine Sea, independently and after Heracles, and on this occasion took Antiope as a spear-captive (τὴν Ἀμαζόνα λαβεῖν αἰχμάλωτον).[118] Plutarch explicitly declares his preference for this version, on the grounds that none of those sharing in Heracles' expedition took an Amazon captive (Plut. *Thes*. 26.1).

The adjective αἰχμάλωτος and its derivatives are used in tragedy and historiography specifically to indicate war prisoners or spoils. Aeschylus uses

---

[117] Theseus' participation in Heracles' campaign against the Amazons is mentioned by Iolaus in Eur. *Heracl*. 215–17; cf. also Diod. 4.16.4: [Ἡρακλῆς] τῶν δ' αἰχμαλωτίδων Ἀντιόπην μὲν ἐδωρήσατο Θησεῖ.

[118] This was, according to Fowler 2013: 485–6, the original version of this myth, while the Heracles version was first attested around 430 BC.

αἰχμάλωτος for Cassandra in *Agamemnon* (Aesch. *Ag.* 1440) and Sophocles employs it for Iole in *Women of Trachis* (Soph. *Trach.* 417), while Euripides uses the noun αἰχμαλωτίς for the captive women of Troy in *Trojan Women* (Eur. *Tro.* 28–9). Spear-won terminology is similarly frequent in Thucydides. At the end of Book 2, for example, the Athenians sail home with the free men among the prisoners they had captured in the sea battles (τούς τε ἐλευθέρους τῶν αἰχμαλώτων ἐκ τῶν ναυμαχιῶν ἄγοντες) (Thuc. 2.103.1). In Book 4, an ally of the Athenians teases one of the Spartans who had been taken captive in Sphacteria (ἕνα τῶν ἐκ τῆς νήσου αἰχμαλώτων) (Thuc. 4.40.2). In Book 9 of Herodotus, a woman from Cos, concubine of the Persian Pharandates and taken prisoner by the Greeks at Plataea, supplicates Pausanias to spare her from captive slavery (αἰχμαλώτου δουλοσύνης). She then explains that Pharandates had taken her by force (βίῃ λαβών) in Cos (Hdt. 9.76.1–2). The use of the adjective αἰχμάλωτος to refer to her future captivity clearly distinguishes the woman's prospective status as a war prisoner from her former status as a concubine acquired by force and sexual violence.[119]

As in the case of γέρας in Philochorus' version, αἰχμάλωτος in Pherecydes' account characterises Antiope not as a victim of abduction, but as a war prisoner and therefore Theseus' legitimate possession.[120] When recalling his sources on the episode, Plutarch seems to make an effort not to use expressions that would clearly indicate sexual violence.[121] This is particularly evident from a comparison with Plutarch's treatment of Theseus' other abductions. In those cases, the biographer regularly uses the verb ἁρπάζω or the noun ἁρπαγή. Plutarch states that one of the features that Theseus shared with Romulus, his Roman counterpart in the *Lives*, was the fact that they both abducted women (ἁρπαγὴ δὲ γυναικῶν ἑκατέρῳ πρόσεστιν) (Plut. *Thes.* 2.1). Theseus is said to have abducted (ἁρπάσαι) the Troezenian Anaxo and committed sexual violence (συγγενέσθαι βίᾳ) on the daughters of Sinis and Cercyon (Plut. *Thes.* 29.1). Plutarch repeatedly refers to Theseus' encounter with the young Helen as an abduction (Plut. *Thes.* 29.2: τὴν Ἑλένης ἁρπαγήν; 31.1: ἁρπάσαι; 31.2: ἁρπάσαντες). Aedoneus, king of the Molossians, is said to have seized Theseus and Pirithous, who intended to abduct (ἁρπασομένους) his daughter Cora (Plut. *Thes.* 31.4). Whether any distinction of this sort existed in his sources, Plutarch seems to separate Antiope from Theseus' other love interests. While the cases of Anaxo, Helen and Cora are clearly

---

[119] Cf. Plut. *Thes.* 34.1, where Theseus' mother Aethra is taken captive (αἰχμάλωτον) by the Dioscuri when they made war against Aphidnae to recover Helen.

[120] As Harris 2016b: 84 has recently observed, 'the universal rule among the Greeks was that persons captured in battle belonged to the victors by right of conquest': cf. e.g. Pl. *Resp.* 468a–b; Arist. *Pol.* 1255a6–7; Xen. *Cyr.* 7.5.73.

[121] Cf. Pind. fr. 175 Maehler *apud* Paus. 1.2.1, where Antiope is carried off (ἁρπασθῆναι) by Theseus and Pirithous.

treated as abductions, and those of the daughters of Sinis and Cercyon seem to be described as cases of rape, Antiope on the other hand is acquired by Theseus as the result of military victory and treated as a war prisoner.[122]

Portraying Antiope as the victim of an abduction or as a war prisoner had different implications for Theseus' image and for the legitimacy of the Amazons' reaction. Scholars usually think that seduction and sexual violence were not punished as offences against women *per se*, or as violations of their right to choose their sexual partners, but rather as offences against the woman's guardian (*kyrios*).[123] Whether or not that was the case, these acts were liable to heavy punishment. In Athens, men caught in the act of having (consensual or non-consensual) sexual intercourse with another's wife, daughter, mother, sister or concubine could be subjected to justifiable homicide.[124] Men guilty of sexual violence could also be prosecuted under a public charge for *hybris* (*graphē hybreōs*). This procedure seems to have been rarely used, but it could result in the death penalty.[125] Moreover, Herodotus' account of the origins of the enmity between Greeks and barbarians shows that war, at least in a mythical context, could be a reasonable reaction to an abduction.[126] The historian recalls how Io, daughter of the king of Argos, had been carried off (ἁρπασθῆναι) by the Phoenicians. The Greeks replied by abducting (ἁρπάσαι) Europa, daughter of the king of Tyre, and later abducted (ἁρπάσαι) Medea, daughter of the king of Colchis. Two generations later, Paris carried off (ἁρπάσαντος) Helen. When the Greeks sent messengers to Troy and were refused Helen's return, they reacted with war (Hdt. 1.1–4).[127] Plutarch similarly recalls how the Dioscuri, when Theseus abducted their sister Helen, went to Athens to ask for her restitution. The Athenians replied that they ignored Helen's location, and the Dioscuri went to war against them (Plut. *Thes*. 32.2).

---

[122] Plutarch does mention a version where Theseus' encounter with Antiope was treated as an abduction. According to this story, attributed to Bion, Theseus abducted Antiope through deceit (ταύτην παρακρουσάμενον οἴχεσθαι λαβόντα) (Plut. *Thes*. 26.2). Plutarch gives no clear indication about Bion's identity. Jacoby ascribed the fragment to Bion of Proconnesus (*FGrHist* 332 F 2), who was the author of two books in Ionic dialect (*FGrHist* 332 T 1) and lived before the Peloponnesian War (*FGrHist* 332 T 2). It is hard to tell if Bion operated in Athens, or if his work was directed to an Athenian audience (see Jones in *BNJ* 332 F 2): it is therefore sensible to exclude his account from the scope of this chapter.

[123] See T. Harrison 1997: 190, 193; Harris 2006: 307–20.

[124] Harris 1990: 371–2; Carey 1995: 409–10. The text of the law on lawful homicide is preserved in Dem. 23.53, but see Canevaro 2013a: 64–70 on the issue of its authenticity.

[125] Harris 1990: 373–4 and 2006: 316–20; Carey 1995: 410.

[126] In historical contexts, on the other hand, the idea that a war could be caused by an abduction could be perceived as rather absurd: cf. Ar. *Ach*. 524–9, where Dicaeopolis attributes the outbreak of the Peloponnesian War to mutual abductions of prostitutes perpetrated by the Athenians and the Megarians: see Olson 2002: 209.

[127] Harris 2006: 309–11.

War prisoners, on the other hand, were more commonly released by means of diplomacy.[128] In Book 1 of the *Iliad*, Chryses, priest of Apollo, offers ransom to Agamemnon to obtain the restitution of his daughter Chryseis (Hom. *Il.* 1.12–21). Apollo punishes the Achaeans with the plague only after Chryses' offer had been rejected and because of Agamemnon's disrespectful behaviour towards the priest (Hom. *Il.* 1.92–100). Thucydides tells how the Corinthians released Corcyraean prisoners of war (αἰχμάλωτοι) in exchange for 800 talents (Thuc. 3.70.1). In Book 5, the Boeotians return some war prisoners to the Athenians (Thuc. 5.42.1) as a result of previous negotiations between Athenians, Spartans and Boeotians (Thuc. 5.39.2–3). Philochorus and Pherecydes, therefore, by portraying Antiope as a war prisoner and Theseus' legitimate acquisition, preserved Theseus' good name and made the Amazons' reaction appear unjustified.

The malleability of the myth of Theseus' acquisition of Antiope is even more striking if we consider that our sources do not even agree in recounting Pherecydes' version of the myth. According to a scholion to Pindar's *Fifth Nemean*, Pherecydes stated that Phorbas was Theseus' charioteer when the hero abducted (ἁρπάζει) Antiope (schol. *ad* Pind. *Nem.* 5.89 = *FGrHist* 3 F 152). Unlike Plutarch, the scholiast uses the verb ἁρπάζω and attributes the abduction version to Pherecydes. The scholiast probably transmits valuable information, as the Pindaric scholia are thought to derive from the works of the Alexandrian scholars.[129] Moreover, his testimony is not influenced by rhetorical or narrative purposes, while Plutarch may have had his own agenda when presenting the evidence.[130] Plutarch himself, as if forgetful of his own treatment of the story in the *Life of Theseus*, seems to agree with Pindar's scholiast in the *Comparison of Theseus and Romulus*. There, he enumerates Antiope among the women who had been abducted by Theseus (ἥρπασε γὰρ Ἀριάδνην καὶ Ἀντιόπην καὶ Ἀναξὼ τὴν Τροιζηνίαν, ἐπὶ πάσαις δὲ τὴν Ἑλένην) (Plut. *Comp. Thes. Rom.* 6.1). On these grounds, we should be inclined to prefer the scholiast's opinion over Plutarch's, or at least to cast some doubt on the trustworthiness of Plutarch's testimony.

Whether we want to trust Plutarch or Pindar's scholiast, in both cases Pherecydes, just like Philochorus, implies some sort of responsibility on Theseus' part. If Antiope had been the victim of an abduction, as Pindar's scholiast implies,

---

[128] See Bielman 1994: 277–309; see also Canevaro and Rutter 2015: 14–18 on the Athenian prisoners in the Sicilian expedition.

[129] See Dickey 2007: 39.

[130] The repulsion of the (illegitimate) invasion of the Amazons may be taken as part of a narrative progression leading from Theseus' glorious achievements to his decadence and death. Plutarch may have tried to portray Theseus' involvement in the Attic Amazonomachy in a good light, as opposed to the expedition of the Dioscuri for the recollection of Helen, which increased the internal opposition against Theseus (Plut. *Thes.* 32.2) and contributed to his downfall: see Leão and do Céu Fialho 2008: 13 and 28–9.

the Amazons' reaction would have been justifiable. This version could even implicitly transfer the accusations of *hybris* from the Amazons to Theseus.¹³¹ If, on the other hand, Theseus had acquired Antiope as a spear-captive or received her as a war prize from Heracles, the Amazons' retaliation would have been illegitimate and unjustified. Yet, even in this version, Theseus was portrayed as leading or participating in a military expedition against the Amazons in the first place. Both versions fostered ideas incompatible with the discursive parameters of the state funeral. The abduction version made the Athenians not the punishers, but the supporters of those guilty of *hybris*. The γέρας/αἰχμάλωτος version, on the other hand, portrayed Theseus as the original aggressor, which contradicted the idealised image of Athenian foreign policy produced in funeral speeches. Philochorus' and Pherecydes' accounts would have been inappropriate also at the dramatic festivals. Aeschylus' vague reference to the Amazons' *phthonos* towards Theseus could have been interpreted either as a tribute or a challenge to the idealised image of Athens constructed at the state funeral. An explicit allusion to Theseus' abduction of Antiope or to his legitimate acquisition of the woman through military endeavour would probably have been unappealing to a significant part of the audience, thus limiting the playwright's chances of winning the contest.¹³²

THE ABDUCTION OF ANTIOPE IN ISOCRATES' PRIVATE RHETORIC

Isocrates had already touched upon the causes of the Amazonomachy in the *Panegyricus*. There, the orator did not mention Theseus or Antiope directly, but referred to unspecified accusations that the Amazons had moved against the Athenians, possibly alluding to the episode of the abduction. In his *Panathenaicus*, Isocrates includes a more detailed discussion of the origins of the invasion. Theseus' acquisition of Hippolyta (as Isocrates calls Theseus' Amazon wife) is explicitly mentioned as the cause of the war (Isoc. 12.193). Yet, despite adopting the elopement version and blaming the war on Hippolyta herself, Isocrates' praise of Athens implies a potential accusation of seduction (*moicheia*)

---

¹³¹ Cf. Isoc. 10.19, where Theseus' abduction of Helen is described in hubristic terms. According to the orator, Theseus was unable to obtain Helen from her guardians. Despising (ὑπεριδών) the power of Tyndareus and disdaining (καταφρονήσας) the strength of Castor and Pollux, Theseus therefore took Helen by force (βίᾳ λαβών). Isocrates then feels the need to justify Theseus and reaffirm his virtue in spite of this dishonourable episode (Isoc. 10.21).

¹³² An allusion to Heracles' gift of Antiope to Theseus has been included in the text of Euripides' *Children of Heracles* by some modern editors (Eur. *Heracl.* 218–19), but the conjecture is far from certain: see p. 130 n. 59.

against Theseus and potentially endangers the epitaphic idea that the Athenians are always the champions of justice.

Isocrates declares the purpose of the *Panathenaicus* at the beginning of the speech. He explains that his aim is to extol Athens by discussing the city's benefactions towards Greece (Isoc. 12.35). Isocrates then states his intention to achieve this goal through a comparison between Athens and Sparta (Isoc. 12.39–41). The orator recalls the Amazonomachy later in the speech when dealing with a specific aspect of this comparison: the different nature of Athens' and Sparta's respective military achievements. While the Spartans only care about acquiring the possessions of other peoples, the Athenians' only interest has always been to be highly esteemed (εὐδοκιμεῖν) by the whole Greek world (Isoc. 12.188). This is exemplified by Athens' prominent role in all the wars that the Greeks fought against the barbarians (Isoc. 12.189). These include the Attic Amazonomachy, which is listed together with the wars against the Thracian Eumolpus, the Persians led by Darius and – oddly – the Peloponnesians led by Eurystheus (Isoc. 12.193–5).

When relating the causes of the Amazonomachy, Isocrates explicitly mentions the episode of Theseus and Hippolyta. To preserve the Athenians' reputation in accordance with the purpose of the passage, however, the orator needs to present the episode in a fashion favourable to the Athenians. Isocrates states that the Amazons, together with the Scythians, organised the expedition against Hippolyta (τὴν στρατείαν ἐφ᾽ Ἱππολύτην ἐποιήσαντο). The woman had transgressed the laws of her country (τὴν τούς τε νόμους παραβᾶσαν τοὺς παρ᾽ αὐταῖς κειμένους) when out of love (ἐρασθεῖσαν) she had followed Theseus to Athens (Isoc. 12.193). The detail of Hippolyta's willingness to follow Theseus may have featured in Attic vase painting, as shown by the Munich amphora.[133] The elopement was thus an already attested, though probably minor variant of the abduction. This version allowed Isocrates to shift the focus from Theseus' actions to Hippolyta's own choice. Hippolyta is always the subject of the action, while Theseus passively participates in her initiative. It is Hippolyta who falls in love (ἐρασθεῖσαν) with the Athenian hero; it is she who follows

---

[133] A similar version, if we believe Pausanias, was told by Hegias of Troezen. Hegias stated that Antiope fell in love (ἐρασθεῖσαν) with Theseus, who was besieging Themiscyra together with Heracles, and betrayed her own country (Paus. 1.2.1). The identity of Hegias is far from certain. If he was the same person as the Agias of Troezen mentioned by Proclus as the author of the cyclic *Nostoi* (Procl. Chr. 277–303), he could have influenced Isocrates. The identification, however, is rejected by most scholars: see Fowler 2013: 486. Fowler's objection that the Attic Amazonomachy could not feature in the *Nostoi* for geographical and chronological reasons is inconclusive, as the episode could have been quoted as a historical example: see Willcock 1964 on the use of historical examples in the Homeric epics. Stronk's Biographical Essay in *BNJ* 606 suggests that Hegias was not a poet, but the Hellenistic author of a local history of Troezen.

him (συνακολουθήσασαν) out of her land and lives with him (συνοικήσασαν) in Athens; it is she who transgresses the laws of her country (τοὺς νόμους παραβᾶσαν). The Amazon invasion itself is not described as a campaign against Theseus, but as an expedition against Hippolyta (ἐφ' Ἱππολύτην).[134] The orator therefore managed to put the blame for the war on Hippolyta and preserve Athens' good reputation, as opposed to Sparta's acquisitiveness.

Isocrates probably relied on the fact that Athenian laws recognised a difference between women who had been victims of rape and those who were guilty of adultery – for only the latter were subjected to punishment.[135] Moreover, it was not unusual to insist on the woman's consent in order to downplay the man's responsibility. In Herodotus, the Persians blame the Greeks for having reacted with war to Helen's abduction, and point out that, if a woman does not want to be carried off, she would not be carried off (Hdt. 1.4.1–2). The Phoenicians similarly object to the Persians' account of the abduction of Io, and claim that she left willingly because of the shame of being pregnant out of wedlock (Hdt. 1.5.2). In Euripides' *Trojan Women*, Hecuba and the Trojan captives blame Helen for the destruction of their city (Eur. *Tro.* 130–7; 766–73). Hecuba also accuses Helen in front of Menelaus. She claims that Paris had not taken Helen by force and that she had followed him willingly (Eur. *Tro.* 987–1001). Even Menelaus acknowledges Helen's guilt in leaving with Paris voluntarily, as well as her agency in dishonouring him, and announces his decision to stone her to death as a requital for the sufferings she caused to the Achaeans (Eur. *Tro.* 1036–41). Menelaus, however, also protests that he had not come to Troy for the sake of a woman but to punish Paris, who had betrayed his hospitality and carried off (ἐλῄσατο) his wife (Eur. *Tro.* 864–8). Menelaus might be downplaying the importance of Helen in order not to lose face, but he also makes clear that Helen's consent did not make Paris any less guilty. Not only did Paris disrespect the customs of hospitality, but he also seduced and appropriated a woman who was under the authority of another *kyrios*, her husband Menelaus. In other words, Paris could be considered guilty of seduction.[136]

---

[134] The passage is usually translated as '[the Amazons] made the expedition to recover Hippolyte' (trans. Norlin); '[the Amazons] made the campaign to recover Hippolyta' (trans. Papillon). The combination στρατεία ἐπί with accusative, however, never occurs in Isocrates with the meaning of 'expedition to recover someone, expedition on account of someone', but is regularly used with the meaning of 'expedition against someone': cf. Isoc. 4.15, 34, 55, 99, 118; 5.16, 56, 111, 128, 135; 9.17; 10.67; 12.13, 71.

[135] The laws prescribed that women caught in adultery should not be allowed to adorn themselves nor be admitted to public sacrifices; if anybody caught them not abiding by these prescriptions, he was allowed to inflict upon them any punishment he wanted with the exception of death and mutilation: cf. Dem. 59.86; Aeschin. 1.183; see Fisher 2001: 336–7; also Carey 1995: 414.

[136] Cf. Hdt. 2.113–15 with Harris 2006: 310–11. A common scholarly trend assumes that the Athenians considered seduction a worse crime than rape: this view, partly defended by Carey 1995, has been convincingly refuted by Harris 1990 and 2006: 293–4.

Isocrates' account of the Attic Amazonomachy in the *Panathenaicus* is highly malleable and shows how an orator writing in a private context could manipulate the ideas about the Athenian community.[137] On the one hand, Isocrates can shift the focus onto Hippolyta's transgression of the laws of her country. The phrasing of the episode serves the rhetorical purpose of the passage, namely that the wars fought against the barbarians demonstrate the Athenians' exclusive interest in their good reputation. Isocrates preserves Athens' innocence, to the extent that he can even include the Amazons among the enemies who were punished by the Athenians for their *hybris* (Isoc. 12.196). From this point of view, Isocrates' account is not very distant from the discursive parameters of the state funeral for the war dead. Yet, Isocrates' version does not acquit Theseus completely. The hero's responsibility has only been moved onto the background. An Athenian would probably have perceived the episode as a case of *moicheia*. This would have not been conceivable at the state funeral. In that institutional setting, the Athenians' support for Theseus despite his status as a seducer would have endangered their image as the champions of justice and the construction of an imagined community.

CONCLUSIONS

The Attic Amazonomachy was an important episode in Athens' remote history. In public rhetoric and art, the Athenians proudly claimed to have defeated the invading horde of the Amazons. Theseus' role in the events, however, was potentially problematic. Attic vase painting shows that the Athenians had been familiar with Theseus' abduction of Antiope at least since the end of the sixth century.[138] The abduction version and its variants implied some sort of Athenian responsibility for the outbreak of the war, an issue that needed to be tackled when using the Amazonomachy in Athenian public discourse. This chapter has shown that the discursive parameters of Athenian democratic institutions had a strong impact on how the Athenians conceptualised the causes of the Amazon invasion and used them to foster different ideas about the Athenian community (most notably the Athenians' attitude towards *hybris*). Accounts of

---

[137] It is significant that the internal audience of the speech detects a degree of ambiguity in Isocrates' arguments. The orator recalls how one of his pupils argued that the *Panathenaicus*, while overtly criticising the Spartans, covertly praised them instead (Isoc. 12.239–40). Isocrates then states that he neither confirmed nor denied his pupil's interpretation (Isoc. 12.265), and it has been suggested that Isocrates wanted the interpretation of the *Panathenaicus* to be open: see V. J. Gray 1994b for an outline of the issue. See also Blank 2013 and 2014, who has recently argued that Isocrates' speeches were concerned with moral education and deliberately included ambiguities and inconsistencies in order to encourage readers to use critical thinking.

[138] Cf. Pind. fr. 175 Maehler *apud* Paus. 1.2.1.

the episode produced for private contexts, which were not subjected to the same institutional constraints, have provided a useful tool for highlighting the ideological specificity of the accounts produced for public settings.

At the state funeral for the war dead, the orators could not admit Theseus' involvement in the Attic Amazonomachy. Whether he forcibly abducted Antiope, seduced her, or legitimately acquired her through military endeavour, Theseus made the Athenians at least partly responsible for the Amazon invasion. This would have contradicted the idealised image of the city which funeral speeches were expected to produce.[139] Lysias' *Funeral Oration* accordingly makes no mention of Theseus, Antiope or the abduction. The orator provides a monochromatic account of the Amazons as an imperialistic power moved by excessive *elpis* and desire for *doxa*. Lysias' narrative of the causes of the Amazonomachy participates in his general characterisation of the Amazons as guilty of *hybris*. This depiction opposes the Athenians to their moral counterpart. The Amazons are the embodiment of *hybris* as much as the Athenians are the embodiment of justice: the Amazons, in other words, are depicted as the anti-Athenians. The Amazons' excessive desire for *doxa* fulfilled through military conquest contrasts with the Athenians' pursuit of *doxa* through *philanthrōpia*; their indifference to justice with the Athenians' mission as champions of justice; their unjust desire for the lands of other nations with Athenian autochthony. This moral contrast was functional to the construction of an imagined community, because it fostered the Athenians' aversion to *hybris* and their pride in their traditional role as the righteous punishers of hubristic invaders.[140]

The Amazons' *hybris* was central to Lysias' narrative of the Amazonomachy, but was by no means a fixed element of the myth. Aeschylus alluded to the Amazon invasion in the *Eumenides* but did not characterise the invaders as hubristic. At the dramatic festivals, the playwright offered a brief and ambiguous account of the causes of the war. Athena's reference to the Amazons' *phthonos* against Theseus as the reason for their attack could be interpreted as an allusion to their rightful indignation for the abduction of Antiope. The goddess's vague phrasing, however, may as well have referred to the Amazons' envy of Theseus' power and good fortune, a reading compatible with the ideal image of Athens produced at the state funeral. Aeschylus may have been deliberately vague, allowing the audience to choose either version. In doing

---

[139] The surviving funeral speeches, when dealing with the Amazonomachy, never mention Theseus and do not usually provide many details on the war: cf. Dem. 60.8; Pl. *Menex.* 239b. The same is also true, however, of the other mythical exploits, which are usually recalled in a very vague and generic manner. On Theseus' absence from the *epitaphios logos*, see Chapter 5, pp. 118–19, *pace* Loraux 1981: 65–6.

[140] Funeral speeches employ a similar oppositional strategy to the same effect when praising the Athenians for their autochthony vis-à-vis the other Greeks: see Chapter 4, pp. 97–100.

so, he produced two contrasting ideas: he either questioned Athenian justice or paid homage to the epitaphic idea that the Athenians always fight just wars against imperialistic invaders. In accordance with the discursive parameters of the dramatic festivals, the playwright thus appealed to those Athenians who were not enthusiastic about the city's official rhetoric, and at the same time reaffirmed that same rhetoric and the beliefs of the majority of the audience.

Isocrates' vague mention of the Amazons' accusations (ἐγκλήματα) against the Athenians in the *Panegyricus* may have triggered the memory of the abduction in his readers. At the same time, the orator's insistence on the Amazons' imperialism as the true reason for the invasion assimilates these accusations to mere pretexts. Thematically, the speech resembles both epideictic and deliberative rhetoric, but does not obey the discursive parameters of the state funeral nor those of the Assembly. Isocrates does not challenge explicitly the epitaphic image of the Athenians as punishers of *hybris*, but does not emphasise it either. He uses the past to support his proposal of a Panhellenic campaign against Persia, but does not insist on (and at times even questions) the deliberative principle of advantage. In other words, the private setting of the speech allows the orator to ignore ideas about the interests of the community as well as the Athenians' attitude towards *hybris*. Isocrates' presentation of the Attic Amazonomachy is functional to his rhetorical needs. According to the orator, the Amazons had to fabricate accusations against the Athenians in order to attack Athens and conquer the whole of Greece. Isocrates therefore emphasises Athens' power and primacy among the Greeks, and reinforces his claim for Athenian leadership in the expedition against the Persians.

Theseus' abduction of Antiope (and its variants) could be mentioned explicitly among the causes of the Attic Amazonomachy in private contexts. Philochorus made Antiope a war prize (γέρας) whom Theseus won during Heracles' expedition against the Amazons. According to Pherecydes, if we believe Plutarch, Theseus obtained Antiope as a spear-captive (αἰχμάλωτος) during his independent expedition to the Euxine Sea. Both versions portray Antiope as Theseus' legitimate acquisition. In doing so, they implicitly question the legitimacy of the Amazons' invasion of Attica, but also make Theseus the original aggressor. If we believe Pindar's scholiast, Pherecydes had Theseus and his charioteer Phorbas abduct (ἁρπάζει) Antiope. This version, as the one commonly depicted in Attic vase painting, implicitly justifies the Amazons' reaction and acknowledges the responsibility, if not of the Athenians, at least of their mythical king. Isocrates' *Panathenaicus* states that Hippolyta fell in love (ἐρασθεῖσαν) with Theseus and followed him to Athens willingly. Hippolyta transgressed the laws of her country, and the Amazons reacted with a military expedition against her (ἐφ' Ἱππολύτην). By focusing on Hippolyta's misconduct, the orator preserves Athens' good reputation, but at the same time keeps Theseus' act of *moicheia* in the background. All these versions produce ideas inappropriate to Athenian public settings and can act as a foil to the discursive parameters of the state funeral for the war dead. The γέρας/αἰχμάλωτος version portrayed Theseus as the original aggressor of the Amazons and contrasted with the idealised image of Athenian foreign policy produced in funeral speeches. The abduction version risked portraying the Athenians as participating in their king's *hybris*, rather than fighting against hubristic enemies. Finally, Isocrates' elopement version explicitly accused the Amazons of *hybris*, but the Athenians' support of Theseus' *moicheia* would have endangered their epitaphic image as the champions of justice.

CHAPTER 7

Combining *Hybris* and *Philanthrōpia*: The Myth of Adrastus

The Athenians prided themselves on having helped the Argive king Adrastus to recover the bodies of his seven chieftains and their soldiers who had died in war against Thebes. The story was the sequel of the myth of the Seven against Thebes, which told of Adrastus' failed campaign to settle the enmity between Oedipus' sons, Eteocles and Polynices, and restore Polynices to the Theban throne. The war between the brothers was attested as early as in the *Iliad*, which recalls Tydeus' participation in the Argive expedition (Hom. *Il*. 4.376–98; 5.801–8; 10.285–90). The myth of the Seven was the subject of the lost epic *Thebaid*. The poem attributed the enmity between Eteocles and Polynices to Oedipus' curse upon them (*Thebaid* frr. 2–3 Bernabé), but the surviving fragments do not tell us anything about the quarrel and ensuing campaign.[1] Some authors seem implicitly to attribute the responsibility of the conflict to Polynices. According to Stesichorus, Jocasta proposed a lot to determine which of her sons should keep the throne and which take the flocks and gold and leave the city to avoid bloodshed (*PMGF* 222b). Hellanicus similarly wrote that Polynices forfeited the throne in exchange for the tunic and necklace of Harmonia and went to Argos (*FGrHist* 4 F 98). Other authors straightforwardly make Eteocles responsible for the conflict. Pherecydes maintained that Eteocles expelled Polynices by force (*FGrHist* 3 F 96; cf. Soph. *OC* 1292–8). In Euripides' *Phoenician Women*, Eteocles and Polynices agreed to rule in alternate years, but Eteocles broke the pact and exiled his brother (Eur. *Phoen*. 55–80).[2] Adrastus' unsuccessful expedition against Thebes and

---

[1] Gantz 1993: 502–3; Edmunds 2006: 22–4; Fowler 2013: 408–9.
[2] Gantz 1993: 502–6; Fowler 2013: 409.

the mutual killing of the two brothers became a popular subject on the tragic stage.³ The story was most famously performed in Aeschylus' *Seven against Thebes* and Euripides' *Phoenician Women*, whereas the impending war between Eteocles and Polynices was central in Sophocles' *Oedipus at Colonus*.

Two traditions existed about the burial of the Seven. According to one tradition, the Seven received burial in Thebes. Already in the *Iliad* we read that Tydeus had been buried in Thebes (Hom. *Il.* 14.114).⁴ The burial of the Seven in Thebes is mentioned twice by Pindar. In the *Sixth Olympian*, the poet recalls Adrastus' eulogy of Amphiaraus in Thebes after the pyres of the Seven had been consumed (ἑπτὰ δ' ἔπειτα πυρᾶν νεκρῶν τελεσθεισᾶν Ταλαϊονίδας εἶπεν ἐν Θήβαισι τοιοῦτόν τι ἔπος) (Pind. *Ol.* 6.12–17). In the *Ninth Nemean*, Pindar describes how the Argives had lit the pyres of the Seven on the banks of the Ismenus (Pind. *Nem.* 9.23–5).⁵ The tradition of the Theban burial of the Seven is confirmed by a fragment of the fifth-century historian Armenidas, which mentions a place in Thebes called Seven Pyres either after the Seven against Thebes or after the children of Niobe (*FGrHist* 378 F 6). The site has been identified with the Castellia Hills. These hosted Bronze Age burials, and their location coincides with Pindar's description.⁶ A sixth-century heroon discovered in Argos and including a pillar with an inscription dedicated to 'the heroes [who are buried? who died?] in Thebes' (ερōον τōν εν Θεβαις) has been interpreted as a cenotaph of the Seven and as a further indication of the belief that the Seven were buried in Thebes.⁷

According to another tradition, the Thebans refused to hand over the dead for burial, but Adrastus fled to Athens and recovered the corpses with the help of the Athenians. Already in the *Thebaid* Adrastus was the only survivor of the expedition against Thebes (*Thebaid* frr. 7–8 Bernabé), and his survival was also attested in the aforementioned passage from Pindar's *Sixth Olympian*.⁸ Some locations in Boeotia and Attica were associated with Adrastus' flight to Athens. A fragment by Philochorus states that Adrastus was saved by the inhabitants of Harma, a village in the territory of Tanagra,

---

³ For the plays dealing with the myth of the Seven against Thebes, see Table 2.1.
⁴ Cf. also Paus. 9.18.1–3.
⁵ The story of the burial in Thebes was either a longstanding Theban tradition or Pindar's own invention in response to the Athenian tradition of Thebes' refusal to grant burial to the Seven: see Steinbock 2013a: 165–9, with references.
⁶ Steinbock 2013a: 167–8; A. S. Anderson 2015: 302–3. Cf. Eur. *Phoen.* 159–60, which plausibly alludes to this location and identifies it with the tomb of Niobe's daughters; Steinbock 2013a: 168–9 interprets Euripides' statement as a strike against the tradition of the Theban burial of the Seven.
⁷ Pariente 1992; Steinbock 2013a: 166–7; A. S. Anderson 2015: 304.
⁸ Steinbock 2013a: 161.

near the Attic border (*FGrHist* 328 F 113).⁹ A heroon to Adrastus was located in Colonus Hippius (Paus. 1.30.4), a hill to the northwest of Athens where Adrastus was believed to have stopped his flight (*Etym. Magn.* s.v. Ἱππία; schol. *ad* Soph. *OC* 712).¹⁰ Two locations in Attica were associated with the burial of the Seven and their soldiers. Several authors placed the tombs of the Seven in Eleusis (Hdt. 9.27.3; Lys. 2.10; Plut. *Thes.* 29.4–5; Paus. 1.39.2),¹¹ and Mylonas has identified the landmark with a group of Middle Helladic tombs enclosed by a *peribolos* wall and containing evidence of Late Geometric offerings.¹² The graves of the common soldiers were instead believed to be in Eleutherae, near the Boeotian border (Eur. *Supp.* 754–9; Plut. *Thes.* 29.4), and it has been suggested that at an earlier stage they might have been thought of as the tombs of the Seven themselves.¹³

The Athenian recovery of the corpses of the Seven acquired great significance in Athenian social memory.¹⁴ The story was first dramatised in Aeschylus' *Eleusinians*, of which only two very short fragments survive (Aesch. F 53a–54). According to Plutarch, in the play the Athenians recovered the bodies through diplomacy and allowed Adrastus to bury the Seven in Eleusis and their soldiers in Eleutherae (Plut. *Thes.* 29.4–5).¹⁵ Plutarch states that this version was adopted by most authors, including Philochorus, who argued that this was the first ever truce for the recovery of the war dead (Plut. *Thes.* 29.4 = *FGrHist* 328 F 112). Most extant sources, however, adopt a different version, in which the Athenians recovered the dead through military intervention against Thebes. In Book 9 of

---

⁹ Some scholars incorrectly infer from Philochorus that the inhabitants of an area in Attica also called Harma held a rival claim to have saved Adrastus: see Harding 2008: 71; Steinbock 2013a: 162–3. Philochorus' fragment is quoted by Strabo, who does distinguish between the Boeotian and Attic Harmai but mentions the story of Adrastus as an aetiology of the name of the Boeotian Harma. This derived either from Amphiaraus' or Adrastus' chariot. Strabo quotes Philochorus concerning the second aetiology: while some say that Adrastus was saved by his horse, Arion (διὰ τοῦ Ἀρείονος σωθῆναι), Philochorus writes that he was saved by the inhabitants of the village (ὑπὸ τῶν κωμητῶν σωθῆναί) (Strabo 9.2.11). Since both aetiologies regard the Boeotian Harma, Philochorus' version must also have referred to the Boeotian rather than the Attic Harma.
¹⁰ Steinbock 2013a: 162.
¹¹ But cf. Eur. *Supp.* 1165–75, where the Seven are cremated in Eleusis but their bones are transported to Argos.
¹² Mylonas 1975: 153–4, 262–3; Kearns 1989: 130–1. While Steinbock 2013a: 160–1 believes that the cult of the Seven at the tombs in Eleusis predated Aeschylus' *Eleusinians*, A. S. Anderson 2015: 305–11 argues that the burial in Eleusis was invented by Aeschylus, who was responsible for the identification of the tombs in Eleusis with the resting place of the Seven.
¹³ See Steinbock 2013a: 163–4, with references.
¹⁴ A related myth dealt with Antigone's opposition to Creon's prohibition to bury Polynices and was famously dramatised in Sophocles' *Antigone*. See Bennett and Tyrrell 1990, who note the similarities between Antigone in Sophocles' play and the Athenians in the funeral speeches.
¹⁵ Sommerstein 2008: 56–7; Steinbock 2013a: 177–80.

Herodotus, the Athenians deploy the bellicose version in their debate with the Tegeans over the leadership of the left wing of the Greek army in Plataea (Hdt. 9.27.3).[16] The same version was performed in Euripides' *Suppliant Women*. The myth of Adrastus was particularly popular in oratory. Isocrates deployed the bellicose version on several occasions (Isoc. 4.54–9; 10.31; 14.53–4), while he adopted the peaceful version and even stressed the Thebans' moderation in the *Panathenaicus* (Isoc. 12.168–74). The myth of Adrastus features alongside the defence of the Heraclidae in Procles' address to the Athenian Assembly in Xenophon's *Hellenica* (Xen. *Hell.* 6.5.45–6). Finally, the bellicose version of the myth was commonly deployed by the orators at the state funeral for the war dead, where the Athenian intervention on behalf of Adrastus featured among Athens' mythical exploits (Lys. 2.7–10; Dem. 60.8; Pl. *Menex.* 239b).

PHILANTHRŌPIA AND *HYBRIS*: VALUES IN INTERACTION

The myth of Adrastus is a perfect illustration of the dynamic interaction between values in Athenian ideological practice. The Athenians' efforts to allow the Argives to bury their dead provided a prominent example of the justice and altruism that constituted the Athenian value of humaneness (*philanthrōpia*). The conflict with the Thebans illustrated the Athenians' ancestral hatred for *hybris*, which in turn reinforced Athenian *philanthrōpia*. Yet, the malleability of the causes of Adrastus' expedition had serious implications for the character of Athens' intervention and was a potential source of contradictions within Athenian democratic ideology. Did Adrastus unjustly lead a campaign on behalf of Polynices despite the latter's voluntary resignation from the Theban throne? Or did he legitimately make war against Thebes to rectify the wrongs suffered by Polynices? While the first version could imply a rupture between the components of justice and altruism within *philanthrōpia* and affect the Athenians' attitude towards *hybris*, the second risked ascribing to the Argives the exclusively Athenian value of *philanthrōpia*. The choice between the bellicose and peaceful versions of the myth was also a possible cause of ambiguity on the ideological level. The peaceful version risked minimising Athenian altruism, but the bellicose version potentially conflicted with Athens' self-interest.

This chapter shows how Athenian democratic institutions enabled a dynamic interaction between Athenian *philanthrōpia* and Theban *hybris* which allowed the Athenians to emphasise, downplay, deconstruct or recompose these values to different ends, from deliberating on public policy to fostering political cohesion through the creation of an imagined community. The different configurations

---

[16] See Steinbock 2013a: 196–8.

of these values are analysed in connection with each author's version of the myth of Adrastus and compared with allusions to the same story in private contexts in order to highlight their implications for Athenian ideological practice. I thus show not only that Athenian values were themselves flexible, but also that their mutual interplay resulted in a fluid ideology that accommodated and resolved potential contradictions within and between values.

I first examine Lysias' veiled allusion to Adrastus' injustice in his *Funeral Oration* and show how the orator manipulated *philanthrōpia* and *hybris* to construct an imagined community in accordance with the discursive parameters of the state funeral for the war dead. Lysias defends the legitimacy of Athens' intervention and emphasises *philanthrōpia* as a harmonious and uniquely Athenian combination of justice and altruism, while using Theban *hybris* as the counterpart of Athenian *philanthrōpia* (Lys. 2.7–10). Second, I analyse Euripides' discussion of Adrastus' faults in *Suppliant Women*, which portrays the Argives as guilty of *hybris* as much as the Thebans. I argue that the dramatic festivals enabled the playwright to enact and recompose a fracture between justice and altruism within Athenian *philanthrōpia*, and in turn reconcile the selfless nature of *philanthrōpia* with the interests of Athens. I then investigate the influence of the Assembly on Procles' speech in Xenophon's *Hellenica*. Not only does the orator ignore the issue of Adrastus' culpability and disregard Theban *hybris*, but he also downplays justice and altruism and incorporates Athenian *philanthrōpia* into an advantageous chain of acts of reciprocity (Xen. *Hell.* 6.5.45–6). The last two sections discuss the accounts of the myth of Adrastus in two speeches meant for private circulation. I show that the private nature of Isocrates' *Plataicus* enabled the speaker to conceptualise Athenian *philanthrōpia* mainly in terms of justice despite the fictional deliberative setting of the speech, and allowed him to ignore Theban *hybris* and question the legitimacy of Adrastus' campaign (Isoc. 14.52–5). For the same reason, Isocrates was able to provide an underdeveloped image of Athenian *philanthrōpia* and question Theban *hybris* in the *Panathenaicus*, where he ignores the issue of Adrastus' culpability and adopts the peaceful version of the myth (Isoc. 12.168–74).

ATHENIAN *PHILANTHRŌPIA*, THEBAN *HYBRIS*: LYSIAS' *FUNERAL ORATION*

The values of *philanthrōpia* and *hybris* are emphasised and closely intertwined in Lysias' account of the myth of Adrastus in the *Funeral Oration*. Lysias recalls how, after Adrastus and Polynices' defeat at Thebes and the Thebans' refusal to grant burial to the Seven, the Athenians sent heralds to request the return of the dead. The Athenians believed that, if the Argives had committed any wrongs, they had already been punished with death (εἴ τι ἠδίκουν, ἀποθανόντας δίκην ἔχειν τὴν μεγίστην), and that the Thebans were preventing the gods below from receiving their dues and were causing the gods above to be treated with impiety (τοὺς δὲ κάτω τὰ αὑτῶν οὐ κομίζεσθαι, ἱερῶν δὲ μιαινομένων τοὺς ἄνω θεοὺς ἀσεβεῖσθαι). Upon the Thebans' refusal to hand over the corpses, the Athenians successfully made war against Thebes for the sake of both the Thebans and the Argives (ὑπὲρ ἀμφοτέρων ἐκινδύνευσαν). The Thebans were thus prevented from continuing to commit *hybris* against the gods (πλείω περὶ τοὺς θεοὺς ἐξυβρίσωσιν), while the Argives were not denied an ancestral honour (πατρίου τιμῆς), Greek *nomos* (Ἑλληνικοῦ νόμου) and common expectation (κοινῆς ἐλπίδος) (Lys. 2.7–10).

In accordance with the discursive parameters of the state funeral for the war dead, Lysias provides an idealised image of Athens aimed at the construction of an imagined community. On the one hand, Lysias uses the myth of Adrastus to emphasise Athenian *philanthrōpia* as a harmonious combination of justice and altruism. He prevents any accusations of injustice against Athens for supporting Adrastus despite his possible faults, and praises the Athenians' selfless defence of Panhellenic *nomos*. On the other hand, Lysias stresses Athens' struggle against Theban *hybris*. The Thebans are characterised as guilty of *hybris* both against the gods and the Argives, and their hubristic nature acts as a foil to the Athenians' *philanthrōpia*.

Let us first analyse Lysias' depiction of the two constitutive elements of *philanthrōpia*: justice and altruism. The orator immediately tackles the issue of Argive injustice and its implications for Athens' intervention. He states that, if the Argives had committed any wrongs, they had already been punished with death (εἴ τι ἠδίκουν, ἀποθανόντας δίκην ἔχειν τὴν μεγίστην) (Lys 2.7). The impression that Adrastus' expedition may have been unjust is also implicitly raised in the following paragraph. Lysias condemns the Thebans' cowardly display of courage over the corpses of the Seven, but concedes that they may have been brave in exacting *timōria* from the Argives while they were alive (ἀνδρῶν μὲν ἀγαθῶν εἶναι ζῶντας τοὺς ἐχθροὺς τιμωρήσασθαι) (Lys. 2.8). This expression is significant because *timōria* was often sought by victims of injustice.[17] The speaker of Antiphon's *Against the Stepmother for Poisoning*, for example, aims to prove that his stepmother intentionally murdered his father. He urges the judges to exact *timōria* from her on behalf of both the laws and the victim (τιμωρῆσαι πρῶτον μὲν τοῖς νόμοις τοῖς ὑμετέροις ... δεύτερον δ' ἐκείνῳ τῷ τεθνηκότι), and asks where else he could find refuge if not with the judges

---

[17] The Greek notion of *timōria* is commonly translated as 'revenge' or 'punishment' but cannot be univocally identified with either concept. The term belongs to the semantic sphere of honour (*timē*) and denotes a demand for the restoration of one's honour and rights: see Cairns 2015. For some attempts to identify the concepts of revenge and punishment in Greek thought, see Mackenzie 1981: 5–17; Saunders 1991: 21–2; Allen 2000: 18–25.

and justice (ποῖ τὴν καταφυγὴν ποιήσεται ἄλλοθι ἢ πρὸς ὑμᾶς καὶ τὸ δίκαιον;) (Antiph. 1.3–4). In Apollodorus' *Against Neaera*, Theomnestus similarly recalls the wrongs his family has suffered from Stephanus (ἠδικήμεθα ὑπὸ Στεφάνου μεγάλα) and declares his intention to obtain *timōria* (τιμωρούμενος) through the present trial ([Dem.] 59.1).[18] By acknowledging that the Thebans demonstrated valour in exacting *timōria* from the Argives, Lysias may therefore imply that they had indeed sought redress for an injustice.

As we have seen, some versions of the myth of the Seven claimed that Polynices had forfeited Thebes' throne voluntarily or as a result of a lot, and thus implicitly acknowledged Adrastus' responsibility for the outbreak of the war with Eteocles. Lysias might have one of these versions in mind when he raises the issue of Argive injustice, and his justificatory tone implies that the legitimacy of Athens' help for Adrastus may have been open to criticism. Lysias does not explicitly deny Adrastus' culpability, but presents the Argives' wrongs merely as hypothetical.[19] More importantly, he stresses that the Argives had already been punished with their deaths and thus unambiguously asserts the devotion to justice that was a fundamental component of the Athenians' traditional *philanthrōpia*.[20]

But why does Lysias avoid openly claiming the justice of Adrastus' campaign against Thebes? The orator could have followed Euripides' *Phoenician Women* or Pherecydes in adopting a version where the Argive expedition was justified by Eteocles' unlawful appropriation of the Theban throne. This choice would have preserved both the Argives' and the Athenians' justice. Yet, it would also have implicitly characterised Adrastus' expedition as an altruistic and rightful act in defence of the injured Polynices; in other words, as an act of *philanthrōpia*. Instead, Lysias subtly alludes to a version where the Argives had waged an unjust war against Thebes, but stresses that they had been punished with their death in battle and thus cleared of their wrongs. This allows him not only to defend the legitimacy of Athens' intervention, which he openly declares when he states that the Athenians had justice as their ally (τὸ δὲ δίκαιον ἔχοντες σύμμαχον) (Lys. 2.10), but also to claim *philanthrōpia* as the Athenians' exclusive prerogative.[21]

Lysias completes his picture of Athenian *philanthrōpia* by stressing the altruism of the Athenians. He points out that they had no previous quarrel with the Thebans (οὐδεμιᾶς διαφορᾶς πρότερον πρὸς Καδμείους ὑπαρχούσης) and were not gratifying the Argives who were still alive (οὐδὲ τοῖς ζῶσιν Ἀργείων χαριζόμενοι) (Lys. 2.8). The verb χαρίζομαι in combination with

---

[18] On the relation between *timōria* and justice, see Cairns 2015: 658–61.
[19] Todd 2007: 219.
[20] See Gotteland 2001: 200–1.
[21] On *philanthrōpia* as the Athenians' exclusive prerogative, see pp. 124–5.

the negative οὐδέ suggest that the Athenians were not fulfilling an obligation towards Adrastus or aiming to oblige the Argives through a bond of reciprocity (*charis*). Just as in his account of the myth of the Heraclidae, Lysias stresses that the Athenians had no personal interests at stake and excludes *charis* from the realm of Athenian international relations.[22] Unlike the Heraclidae, however, Adrastus is never described as a suppliant.[23] This is probably due to the controversial causes of his campaign against Thebes, which could provide the Athenians with reasonable grounds for rejecting his plea.[24] Rather than as a response to Adrastus' supplication, Lysias characterises Athens' intervention as a spontaneous act of altruism in defence of Panhellenic *nomos*.[25] The orator states that the Athenians aimed to preserve the Greek customs that granted burial to the war dead (τοὺς τεθνεῶτας ἐν τῷ πολέμῳ ἀξιοῦντες τῶν νομιζομένων τυγχάνειν) and even makes the paradoxical claim that, by fighting the Thebans, the Athenians underwent dangers for the sake of both the Argives *and* the Thebans (ὑπὲρ ἀμφοτέρων ἐκινδύνευσαν).

Altruism on a Panhellenic level was commonly ascribed to the Athenians at the state funeral for the war dead. Socrates' allusion to the myth of Adrastus in Plato's *Menexenus* provides a particularly appropriate parallel. Socrates lists the episode among the wars fought by the Athenians for the freedom of the Greeks both against barbarians and other Greeks (ὑπὲρ τῆς ἐλευθερίας καὶ Ἕλλησιν ὑπὲρ Ἑλλήνων μάχεσθαι καὶ βαρβάροις ὑπὲρ ἁπάντων τῶν Ἑλλήνων) (Pl. *Menex.* 239a–b). Lysias goes one step further and portrays Athens' intervention on behalf of Adrastus as a selfless and righteous crusade in defence of Panhellenic *nomos*. This is evident not only from his characterisation of the Athenian expedition as beneficial to both Argives and Thebans, but also from his conclusion that the Athenians prevented the Argives from being excluded from Greek *nomos* (Ἑλληνικοῦ νόμου) and failing to achieve a communal expectation (κοινῆς ἐλπίδος) (Lys. 2.9).

Lysias' emphasis on both components of Athenian *philanthrōpia* goes hand in hand with his insistence on Theban *hybris*. The orator hints at the Thebans' hubristic disposition when he describes their reaction to their victory against the Argives. Excessive responses to one's own success or good fortune were typical traits of hubristic agents. This is stated clearly in Aristotle's *Nicomachean*

---

[22] For a discussion of reciprocity and its relation to *philanthrōpia*, see Chapter 5, pp. 123–4; specifically on Lysias' treatment of reciprocity in his narrative about the Heraclidae, see Chapter 5, pp. 134–6.
[23] Cf. Lys. 2.11, which emphasises the suppliant status of the Heraclidae.
[24] As shown by Naiden 2006: 105–69, esp. 144–5, acceptance of a supplication was not automatic, and valid reasons to reject a supplication included the belief that the suppliant had started an unjust war.
[25] Todd 2007: 220.

Ethics. The philosopher contrasts the great-souled man, who behaves moderately in regards to wealth, power, and good and bad fortune (περὶ πλοῦτον καὶ δυναστείαν καὶ πᾶσαν εὐτυχίαν καὶ ἀτυχίαν μετρίως ἕξει), with haughty and hubristic men (ὑπερόπται δὲ καὶ ὑβρισταί), who cannot deal appropriately with success because of their lack of virtue (ἄνευ γὰρ ἀρετῆς οὐ ῥᾴδιον φέρειν ἐμμελῶς τὰ εὐτυχήματα) (Arist. *Eth. Nic.* 1124a26–b6). Lysias' aforementioned criticism of the Thebans for exacting *timōria* from the Argives after their death (Lys. 2.8) suggests their inappropriate attitude towards success and can thus be taken as an indication of their hubristic nature.

The Thebans' behaviour is equally characterised as hubristic, as their actions are represented as offensive against the honour (*timē*) of the gods. *Hybris* was not an inherently religious notion and only assumed a religious value when it infringed the honour and prerogatives of a god.[26] Such an infringement is evident in Lysias' impious portrayal of the Thebans. The orator stresses that the Thebans were preventing the gods below from receiving their dues (τοὺς δὲ κάτω τὰ αὑτῶν οὐ κομίζεσθαι) and were causing the gods above to be treated with impiety because of the pollution of the shrines (ἱερῶν δὲ μιαινομένων τοὺς ἄνω θεοὺς ἀσεβεῖσθαι) (Lys. 2.7).[27]

Granting burial to the dead was a custom (*nomos*) recognised by all the Greeks.[28] Those who violated this *nomos* could be perceived as defying the honour and prerogatives of the gods. In Sophocles' *Antigone*, the protagonist reproaches her sister, Ismene, for accepting Creon's edict against the burial of Polynices and thus dishonouring what is honoured by the gods (σοὶ δ', εἰ δοκεῖ, τὰ τῶν θεῶν ἔντιμ' ἀτιμάσασ' ἔχε) (Soph. *Ant.* 76–7). In Sophocles' *Ajax*, Teucer similarly demands that Menelaus does not dishonour the gods (μή νυν ἀτίμα θεούς) by preventing Ajax's burial (Soph. *Aj.* 1129–31).[29] Moreover, as offences against the honour of the gods and if committed with a hubristic mindset, acts of impiety (*asebeia*) could be conceived of as acts of *hybris*.[30] In Aeschylus' *Persians*, Darius' ghost predicts that Xerxes and the Persians will be punished for their *hybris* and impious thoughts (ὕβρεως ἄποινα κἀθέων φρονημάτων), because they showed disrespect for the altars

---

[26] Fisher 1992: 142–8 and Cairns 1996: 17–22. For a full discussion of the notion of *hybris*, see Chapter 6, pp. 149–52.
[27] On the distinction between chthonian gods and Olympian gods, see Parker 1996b.
[28] Specifically on the importance of allowing the burial of the war dead, see Pritchett 1985: 94–102 and 235–41; Parker [1983] 1996c: 43–8; Harris 2006: 65–7.
[29] On Athenian attitudes to funeral honours, specifically with regard to Sophocles' *Antigone*, see Cairns 2016a: 37–42.
[30] On *asebeia*, see Dover 1974: 247–8; Parker [1983] 1996c: 144–90; Filonik 2013: 13–14; Naiden 2016: esp. 59–60. Gotteland 2001: 205 stresses the connection between Theban *hybris* and impiety in the passage.

and statues of the gods (οὐ θεῶν βρέτη ᾑδοῦντο συλᾶν οὐδὲ πιμπράναι νεώς). Darius then reaffirms the hubristic nature of the Persians' sacrilegious acts with an agricultural metaphor stating that *hybris* crops disaster and tears (ὕβρις γὰρ ἐξανθοῦσ᾽ ἐκάρπωσεν στάχυν ἄτης, ὅθεν πάγκλαυτον ἐξαμᾷ θέρος) (Aesch. *Pers.* 805–22).[31] In Book 8 of Herodotus, Themistocles describes Xerxes' defeat as the result of divine resentment (*phthonos theōn*), which was a common response to human *hybris*.[32] He then links Xerxes' desire to be the sole ruler of Asia and Europe, which Xerxes himself had previously expressed in hubristic tones (Hdt. 7.8c), with his impious and wicked personality (ἐόντα ἀνόσιόν τε καὶ ἀτάσθαλον) (Hdt. 8.109.3).[33]

The Theban refusal to grant burial to the Seven, described by Lysias as an infringement of the prerogatives of the gods and as an act of *asebeia*, implicitly amounts to an act of *hybris*. This is evident in Demosthenes' *Funeral Speech*, where the Athenians intervene on behalf of Adrastus in order to prevent funerary rights from suffering *hybris* (τὰ τῶν κατοιχομένων νόμιμ᾽ οὐ περιεῖδον ὑβριζόμενα) (Dem. 60.8). Lysias himself makes his hubristic characterisation of the Thebans explicit by adopting the vocabulary of *hybris* later in his narrative. He states that the Athenians believed that the war dead should receive their customary rites (τοὺς τεθνεῶτας ἐν τῷ πολέμῳ ἀξιοῦντες τῶν νομιζομένων τυγχάνειν), and claims that they stopped the Thebans from committing *hybris* against the gods by wronging the dead (ἵνα μηκέτι εἰς τοὺς τεθνεῶτας ἐξαμαρτάνοντες πλείω περὶ τοὺς θεοὺς ἐξυβρίσωσιν) (Lys. 2.9).

Not only does Lysias portray the Thebans as hubristic against the gods, but he also suggests that they committed *hybris* against the Argives. Violating the Greek *nomos* about the burial of the dead was an offense against the honour of the deceased as much as against that of the gods. This is most evident in the prologue of Sophocles' *Antigone*, where the heroine denounces Creon's edict for granting Eteocles his honour among the dead (τοῖς ἔνερθεν ἔντιμον νεκροῖς) whilst dishonouring the body of Polynices (τὸν δ᾽ ἀτιμάσας) (Soph. *Ant.* 21–5). As an infringement of the honour of the dead, the prohibition of burial could be perceived as an act of *hybris* against them. In Sophocles' *Ajax*, for example, the Chorus admonishes Menelaus, who has just forbidden the burial of Ajax, not to be hubristic against the dead (μή ... ἐν θανοῦσιν ὑβριστὴς γένῃ) (Soph. *Aj.* 1091–2). Lysias' account of the myth of Adrastus similarly stresses the Argives' potential loss of honour in such a way as to

---

[31] Fisher 1992: 258–61; Garvie 2009: 310–11, 314–15. *Pace* Garvie 2009: 311, there is no distinction between the Persians' hubristic behaviour and their impious state of mind, but both are aspects of the Persians' *hybris*; on the dispositional aspect of *hybris*, see Cairns 1996.

[32] Cairns 1996: 14–15. On *phthonos*, see pp. 162–4. On divine *phthonos* and *hybris*, see Cairns 1996: 17–22.

[33] On the hubristic character of Xerxes' sacrilegious acts, see Fisher 1992: 376–82; Cairns 1996: 15.

imply *hybris* on the part of the Thebans. The orator claims that the Athenians prevented the Thebans from committing *hybris* against the gods, and the Argives from going home deprived of an ancestral honour (πατρίου τιμῆς ἀτυχήσαντες) (Lys. 2.9). Lysias juxtaposes the Thebans' religious *hybris* with the dishonour the Argives risked suffering as a result, and thus implicitly characterises the Argives as victims of Theban *hybris*.

A dual focus on Athenian *philanthrōpia* and Theban *hybris* is therefore evident throughout Lysias' narrative. But how do the two values interact with one another? I suggest that Athenian *philanthrōpia* and Theban *hybris* are mutually reinforcing each other. Lysias exploits Theban *hybris* in order to depict the Thebans as the moral opposites of the Athenians; in other words, as the anti-Athenians.[34] This is especially evident in the conclusion of the narrative, where Lysias' characterisation of the Athenians programmatically reverses his portrayal of the Thebans (Lys. 2.10). As much as the Thebans are guilty of *hybris* against the gods and infringe the Greek *nomos* on the burial of the dead, the Athenians can claim to have justice on their side (τὸ δὲ δίκαιον ἔχοντες σύμμαχον). The legitimacy of Athens' intervention, which Lysias defended in connection with the issue of Argive injustice, is thus positively declared. The Athenians' moderation in dealing with success is the opposite of the Thebans' immoderate behaviour after their victory over the Argives. While the hubristic Thebans were led by their success to exact an inappropriate *timōria* from the corpses of the Seven (Lys. 2.8), the Athenians are not roused by their own good fortune to seek a greater *timōria* from the Thebans (οὐχ ὑπὸ τῆς τύχης ἐπαρθέντες μείζονος παρὰ Καδμείων τιμωρίας ἐπεθύμησαν). Instead, they content themselves with taking the bodies of the Argives for which they had come (αὐτοὶ δὲ λαβόντες τὰ ἆθλα ὧνπερ ἕνεκα ἀφίκοντο).[35] Finally, Lysias juxtaposes the Thebans' *asebeia*, which he has already described as a sign of their *hybris*, with the Athenians' virtue (ἀντὶ τῆς ἀσεβείας τὴν ἑαυτῶν ἀρετὴν ἐπεδείξαντο) and altruism, which are epitomised in their choice of taking the bodies of the Argives as their only trophy.

Depicting the Thebans as guilty of *hybris* allowed Lysias to make the Athenians' moral excellence stand out. The Athenians are shown to be supremely selfless and determined in defending the victims of injustice (and specifically *hybris*). In other words, Lysias' characterisation of Thebes as Athens' hubristic counterpart contributes to emphasising the typically Athenian value of *philanthrōpia*. At the state funeral for the war dead, Athenian *philanthrōpia* and Theban *hybris* thus mutually reinforce each other to create Athens' imagined

---

[34] Thebes' depiction as the anti-Athens was common in tragedy: see Zeitlin 1990; for a discussion of the perception of Thebes in Athenian public discourse, see Steinbock 2013a. Lysias also characterises the Amazons as the anti-Athenians: see p. 179.
[35] Todd 2007: 221.

community. As demonstrated by Lysias' *Funeral Oration*, orators of funeral speeches use the myth of Adrastus and its background to construct an idealised image of Athens. The Athenians can take pride in their traditional devotion to justice and altruism and find a source of political cohesion in their shared aversion for *hybris*.

PHILANTHRŌPIA, *HYBRIS* AND ADVANTAGE IN EURIPIDES' *SUPPLIANT WOMEN*

The interaction between *philanthrōpia* and *hybris* is more complex in Euripides' *Suppliant Women*. Due to the influence of the dramatic festivals, the poet is able to use Theban *and* Argive *hybris* as a tool to dissect Athenian *philanthrōpia*.[36] The play opens at the temple of Demeter and Kore in Eleusis, where Adrastus and the Chorus of Argive mothers sit as suppliants after the defeat of the Seven. The Thebans have been refusing to hand over the bodies of the Argive dead, and Adrastus pleads Theseus to help him recover and bury the fallen. The Athenian king censures Adrastus' expedition against Thebes and initially rejects his supplication, but is then persuaded by his own mother, Aethra, to change his mind. The Thebans, however, restate their refusal to hand over the corpses, and Theseus engages in a debate about democracy with an arrogant Theban Herald. The Athenians have no choice but to go to war against Thebes, and a Messenger soon reports the news of their victory. After burying the common soldiers in Eleutherae, Theseus brings back the corpses of the Seven and invites Adrastus to deliver a funeral oration in their honour. The Seven are finally cremated in Eleusis, and Evadne, wife of Capaneus, commits suicide by jumping into her husband's pyre. The sons of the Seven bring their fathers' ashes and vow to one day avenge their deaths. To them, as well as to Adrastus and the Argive mothers, Theseus asks to remember the favour they were granted by Athens. The play ends with the departure of the Argives, who, following Athena's advice, are requested to swear that they will never attack Athens and will defend her against any invaders.[37]

---

[36] Before Euripides, the myth of Adrastus had been dramatised in Aeschylus' *Eleusinians* (Aesch. F 53a–54). Because of the paucity of the evidence, however, not much can be said about Aeschylus' lost play except that it deployed the peaceful version of the myth (Plut. *Thes.* 29.4–5).

[37] Euripides' *Suppliant Women* belongs to the category of suppliant drama, on which see Burian 1971: 1–29. The play has given rise to contrasting interpretations, focusing especially on whether it should be seen as unambiguously patriotic or somewhat ironic and critical of Athens: see Collard 1975b: 23–5; Mendelsohn 2002: 1–12.

Euripides' reflection on *philanthrōpia* and *hybris* is set on the background of the decision-making process within the political community.[38] Theseus is called to deliberate on Adrastus' request for help, and only comes to a decision after listening to his mother's advice and receiving the endorsement of the Athenian people (Eur. *Supp.* 286–364). The Theban Herald criticises the ability of democracies to achieve good decision-making and is then proved wrong by the Athenian victory over Thebes (Eur. *Supp.* 399–462). The sorrow of the Argive mothers over the corpses of their sons illustrates the dreadful consequences of poor deliberation upon the community (Eur. *Supp.* 955–89). The theme of decision-making acquires even greater significance if one accepts the standard dating of the play to 423 BC.[39] *Suppliant Women* has accordingly been interpreted as a reaction to the Theban refusal to return the Athenian dead after the Athenian defeat in the Battle of Delium in 424 (Thuc. 4.90–100).[40] The Thebans' impious decision had in turn been prompted by the Athenians' impious occupation of the temple of Apollo at Delium and may have inspired Euripides to address the delicate topic of the relationship between decision-making and religious piety.[41]

Placing Athenian *philanthrōpia* within the context of political deliberation allowed Euripides to problematise Theseus' decision to help Adrastus and thus deconstruct the idealised image of Athens as protector of the weak and injured typically produced at the state funeral.[42] The playwright dissects the causes of Adrastus' expedition against Thebes. He highlights the injustice and *hybris* of both the Thebans and the Argives, and reveals their implications for Athenian *philanthrōpia* and decision-making. Are justice and altruism compatible components of *philanthrōpia*? How can *philanthrōpia* in turn be accommodated into

---

[38] The importance of decision-making in the economy of the play has been noted by several scholars: see Konstan 2005; Hesk 2011; also Shaw 1982, who stresses Euripides' focus on *ethos* and good leadership. Deliberation was by no means the only theme of the play; other themes included the tending of the dead, Panhellenism, religious piety, and the education of the young: see Collard 1975b: 23–31; Morwood 2007: 1–3; Storey 2008: 90–104.

[39] On the date of Euripides' *Suppliant Women*, see Collard 1975b: 8–14, who also discusses other hypotheses ranging from 424 to 416 BC.

[40] See Mills 1997: 91–7; Gotteland 2001: 209–10; Steinbock 2013a: 192–3.

[41] As rightly suggested by Collard 1975b: 13, we should not look for references to Athenian politicians behind the characters, but merely appreciate that the play may have reflected contemporary debates within the Athenian community.

[42] Euripides' manipulation of the discourse of other Athenian democratic institutions is particularly evident if one considers that the poet has Adrastus deliver a public funeral speech in honour of the Seven (Eur. *Supp.* 857–917). Adrastus' eulogy of the Seven was already part of the myth in Pindar's *Sixth Olympian* (Pind. *Ol.* 6.12–17), but for an Athenian audience it must have been suggestive of the *epitaphios logos*. On the relationship between the *epitaphios logos* and Adrastus' funeral speech see Collard 1972; Prinz 1997: 164–76.

the discourse of advantage typical of deliberative settings?[43] In accordance with the discursive parameters of the dramatic festivals, Euripides brings these issues onto the stage. He provides the audience with reassuring answers, while leaving enough room for interpretation to appeal to any critics of the democracy who could have been present in the audience.

Euripides at first seems to challenge Athenian *philanthrōpia*. Despite the pitiful sight of the Argive mothers and children, Theseus initially rejects Adrastus' supplication (Eur. *Supp.* 219–49).[44] As we shall see, Euripides portrays the Argives as unjust and guilty of *hybris* and provides Theseus with sensible reasons for denying help to Adrastus. By questioning the justice of the prospective recipients of Athenian altruism, the playwright opens a fracture between the two constitutive elements of Athenian *philanthrōpia*. The anomaly is ultimately fixed when Aethra persuades Theseus to help the Argives (Eur. *Supp.* 297–364).[45] The Thebans are shown to be equally guilty of injustice and *hybris*, and Thebes' infringement of divine and Panhellenic *nomos* allows Euripides to recompose the conflict within Athenian *philanthrōpia*.

The issue of Argive injustice is the focus of an exchange between Theseus and Adrastus in the first episode of the play. Approached by Adrastus with the request to recover the bodies of the Seven, Theseus enquires about the causes of the Argive expedition against Thebes. Adrastus explains that he undertook the campaign as a favour to his sons-in-law (δισσοῖσι γαμβροῖς τήνδε πορσύνων χάριν), Tydeus and Polynices. To Theseus' surprised reaction at his choice of marrying his daughters to foreigners, Adrastus replies that he had done so under the influence of Apollo's oracles. The two kings then discuss the enmity between Eteocles and Polynices. Adrastus explains that Polynices left Thebes to avoid killing his brother in fulfilment of Oedipus' curse (ἀραῖς πατρῴαις, μὴ κασίγνητον κτάνοι), and Theseus praises the wisdom of his voluntary exile (σοφήν γ' ἔλεξας τήνδ' ἑκούσιον φυγήν).[46] Adrastus recalls how Eteocles had then wronged the absent Polynices (ἀλλ' οἱ μένοντες τοὺς ἀπόντας ἠδίκουν), and Theseus infers that Eteocles had robbed his brother of his inheritance (οὔ πού σφ' ἀδελφὸς χρημάτων νοσφίζεται;). The Argive king finally claims that he made war on Thebes to avenge these wrongs (ταύτ'ἐκδικάζων ἦλθον) (Eur. *Supp.* 131–54).[47]

---

[43] See Konstan 2005, who similarly investigates the compatibility of pity with political deliberation.
[44] See Konstan 2005: 54–6; also Mills 1997: 107.
[45] For a detailed analysis of the scene between Aethra and Theseus, see Mendelsohn 2002: 161–70; see also Morwood 2007: 6–7 on Aethra's educational role.
[46] Theseus recalls this voluntary exile (φυγῇ ... αὐθαίρετος) again in his brief praise of Polynices after Adrastus' funeral oration (Eur. *Supp.* 928–31).
[47] Following Collard 1975b: 148, I here accept Hermann's conjecture ταύτ'ἐκδικάζων in place of the manuscript's ταυτὶ δικάζων, but I find Murray's correction ταύτῃ δικάζων also plausible.

Adrastus' decision to attack Thebes is described as motivated by bonds of kinship and *charis*, both appropriate arguments in deliberative contexts.[48] Moreover, Polynices is said to have left Thebes voluntarily, only to be later robbed of his χρήματα by Eteocles. Euripides uses the rather generic χρήματα to refer to the object of the quarrel between the two brothers. The word may merely refer to Polynices' share in his father's wealth, but it may also allude to the throne that was the source of such wealth.[49] This is the case in Euripides' *Phoenician Women*, where Jocasta explains that Polynices demanded his father's sceptre and his share of the land (πατρῷ' ἀπαιτεῖ σκῆπτρα καὶ μέρη χθονός) (Eur. *Phoen.* 79–80), but Polynices himself claims to be after his wealth (τὰ χρήματ' ἀνθρώποισι τιμιώτατα . . . ἀγὼ μεθήκω δεῦρο μυρίαν ἄγων λόγχην) (Eur. *Phoen.* 439–42). One can reasonably infer that, just as *Phoenician Women*, Euripides' *Suppliant Women* adopts a version where Polynices and Eteocles agreed to rule in alternate years.[50] The playwright makes it clear that Polynices did suffer wrongs from his brother, and this is demonstrated by Theseus' acquiescence towards Adrastus' explanation of the quarrel with Eteocles.

Up to this point, Adrastus' campaign appears reasonable and even supported by justice.[51] Adrastus' faults, however, are revealed in the final lines of the dialogue, where Adrastus confesses that he went to war against the advice of the seer Amphiaraus (ἦλθον Ἀμφιάρεώ γε πρὸς βίαν). By his own admission, the Argive king was driven out of his senses by the clamour of young men (νέων γὰρ ἀνδρῶν θόρυβος ἐξέπλησσέ με), and Theseus reproaches him for trusting courage instead of good judgement (εὐψυχίαν ἔσπευσας ἀντ' εὐβουλίας) (Eur. *Supp.* 155–61).[52]

Theseus expands on Adrastus' mistakes in a speech that represents his actions in terms of injustice and *hybris*. After illustrating the gifts of the gods towards humanity with a list that significantly culminates with divination, the Athenian king condemns those men who are led by pride and presumption

---

[48] On the use of *charis* in deliberative settings, see Harris 2017: 57. On kinship in Greek interstate relations, see C. P. Jones 1999: 27–35; Low 2007: 48–51.

[49] See Collard 1975b: 148.

[50] Collard 1975b: 147–8; Gotteland 2001: 201. If one takes χρήματα to refer only to Eteocles' misappropriation of Polynices' wealth, then Euripides may have adopted the same version as in Stesichorus and Hellanicus, where Polynices forfeited the throne in exchange for his father's properties. Even this version, however, would present Polynices as the wronged party and Eteocles as not fulfilling his part of the bargain.

[51] Gotteland 2001: 201.

[52] As rightly noted by Hesk 2011: 128–9, Adrastus' reference to the clamour (θόρυβος) of young men as the cause of his poor deliberation echoes the *thorybos* of the crowd in the Athenian Assembly. This is yet another sign of the play's concern with political deliberation and tendency to play with the audience's familiarity with the discourse of democratic institutions. On the *thorybos* and its influence on the decision-making process in the Assembly see p. 72.

to believe themselves to be stronger and wiser than the gods (ἡ φρόνησις τοῦ θεοῦ μεῖζον σθένειν ζητεῖ, τὸ γαῦρον δ' ἐν φρεσὶν κεκτημένοι δοκοῦμεν εἶναι δαιμόνων σοφώτεροι). Theseus explicitly accuses Adrastus of belonging to this category (Eur. Supp. 195–219). He explains that Adrastus gave his daughters to foreigners in obedience to the oracles of Apollo (κόρας μὲν θεσφάτοις Φοίβου ζυγεὶς ξένοισιν ὧδ' ἔδωκας), as if the gods gave them in marriage (ὡς δόντων θεῶν) (Eur. Supp. 220–1),[53] but then brought ruin upon Argos by going to war in spite of the will of the gods proclaimed by the seers (ἐς δὲ στρατείαν πάντας Ἀργείους ἄγων, μάντεων λεγόντων θέσφατ[α] . . . ἀπώλεσας πόλιν) (Eur. Supp. 229–31).[54] Adrastus, in other words, thought he could abide by or dispose of the oracles at his own convenience, behaving as someone who believes himself to be smarter than the gods. Moreover, by betrothing his daughters to Tydeus and Polynices, Adrastus damaged the purity of his family and unwisely mixed just and unjust people (χρῆν γὰρ οὐδὲ σώματα ἄδικα δικαίοις τὸν σοφὸν συμμιγνύναι) (Eur. Supp. 222–5).[55] Finally, with his decision to attack Thebes, he dishonoured and violently disregarded the gods (ἀτιμάσας βίᾳ παρελθὼν θεούς) (Eur. Supp. 230–1).

The symptoms of *hybris* are clearly at work in Adrastus. His tendency to 'think big' (*mega phronein*) is evident in his attitude towards oracles, which Theseus links to the presumption and arrogance (ἡ φρόνησις . . . τὸ γαῦρον) of men who believe themselves superior to the gods. As a result of his actions, Adrastus has brought dishonour upon the gods (ἀτιμάσας βίᾳ παρελθὼν θεούς). Both the dispositional and the behavioural aspects of *hybris* are thus present, because Adrastus is characterised as someone who tends to overvalue his own honour and consequently infringes the honour of others. Adrastus' propensity to *hybris* is even more explicit when Theseus points out that his decisions have been influenced by young men who pursue war for their own interests, which include committing *hybris* by seizing power (ὡς ὑβρίζῃ δύναμιν ἐς χεῖρας λαβών) (Eur. Supp. 235).

---

[53] I here follow Collard 1975b: 168–9 in adopting the conjecture δόντων in place of the manuscript's ζώντων. As noted by Morwood 2007: 161, the passage does not imply that Adrastus misinterpreted the oracle.

[54] Collard 1975b: 168 makes a convincing case for correlating μέν at l. 220 with δέ at l. 229 rather than with the closer δέ at l. 222.

[55] Morwood 2012, who reads *Suppliant Women* in connection with Pericles' citizenship law of 451/0 BC, may be right in interpreting the passage as Theseus' 'condemnation of the exogamy of Adrastos' daughters', but might go too far when he takes the whole play as a critique of Athenian nationalism. Collard 1975b: 169–70 rightly notes the use of medical language in the passage and argues that the adjectives δίκαιος and ἄδικος here mean 'healthy' and 'unhealthy'; yet, out of metaphor the expression still alludes to the injustice of Adrastus' sons-in-law (or at least to that of Tydeus, who is said to have left his homeland after killing a relative: cf. Eur. Supp. 148).

The hubristic nature of Adrastus and the Argives is confirmed by other characters in the play. The Theban Herald states that the Seven have been destroyed by their *hybris* (ὕβρις οὕς ἀπώλεσεν), as proved by the divine punishments suffered by Capaneus, who was hit by Zeus' thunderbolt, and Amphiaraus, who was swallowed by the earth (Eur. *Supp.* 494–505).[56] It is of course not surprising that a Theban would move such accusations against the Argives. The reaction of the Chorus, however, corroborates the Herald's view. The Argive mothers do not counter the Herald's allegations, but state that the punishment they received from Zeus was sufficient (ἐξαρκέσας ἦν Ζεὺς ὁ τιμωρούμενος). The Chorus thus implicitly acknowledge the *hybris* of the Seven, but balance it by accusing the Thebans of committing *hybris* in turn (ὑμᾶς δ' ὑβρίζειν οὐκ ἐχρῆν τοιάνδ' ὕβριν) (Eur. *Supp.* 511–12).

If Theseus, the Theban Herald and the Chorus portray the Argives as hubristic, a combined reading of the statement of Aethra and the Argive characters depicts the Thebans as equally guilty of *hybris*. Moved by pity for the Argive mothers after Theseus' initial rejection of Adrastus' supplication, Aethra asks her son to change his mind and help the Argives. She advises Theseus against dishonouring the will of the gods (τὰ τῶν θεῶν σκοπεῖν κελεύω μὴ σφαλῇς ἀτιμάσας) (Eur. *Supp.* 301–2).[57] The expression is reminiscent of Antigone's censure of Ismene for obeying Creon in Sophocles' *Antigone* (σοὶ δ', εἰ δοκεῖ, τὰ τῶν θεῶν ἔντιμ' ἀτιμάσασ' ἔχε) (Soph. *Ant.* 66–7).[58] Given the similarity of the context, Aethra's advice should be taken as a warning against tolerating the Thebans' refusal to bury the Seven and participating in their offence against the honour of the gods.[59] After declaring her duty to be brave for the victims of injustice (εἰ μὲν μὴ ἀδικουμένοις ἐχρῆν τολμηρὸν εἶναι, κάρτ' ἂν εἶχον ἡσύχως), Aethra shows Theseus the appropriate path to honour (νῦν δ' ἴσθι σοί τε τοῦθ' ὅσην τιμὴν φέρει). This passes through the defence of divine and Panhellenic *nomos*. Aethra claims that the Thebans are preventing the dead from receiving their dues (ἄνδρας βιαίους καὶ κατείργοντας νεκροὺς τάφου τε μοίρας καὶ κτερισμάτων λαχεῖν), and exhorts Theseus to force them to do what they must (ἐς τήνδ' ἀνάγκην σῇ καταστῆσαι χερί) and stop them from confounding the laws of the whole of Greece (νόμιμά τε πάσης συγχέοντας Ἑλλάδος παῦσαι) (Eur. *Supp.* 304–12). Aethra implicitly characterises the Thebans as hubristic. Unlike Theseus, who is urged to claim his honour by

---

[56] As noted by Collard 1975b: 243, Amphiaraus' negative characterisation may be due to Theban bias, as the Argive seer is elsewhere portrayed in a positive light (cf. e.g. Aesch. *Sept.* 609–14). In his eulogy of Amphiaraus, Theseus recalls the manner of his death as a sign of divine blessing (Eur. *Supp.* 825–7).

[57] Gotteland 2001: 205–7.

[58] See Collard 1975b: 188.

[59] Cf. Eur. *Supp.* 16–19, where Aethra explains that the Thebans' refusal to grant burial to the Argive dead insults the laws of the gods (νόμιμ' ἀτίζοντες θεῶν).

upholding divine and Panhellenic *nomos*, the Thebans are unjustly asserting their honour by infringing that same *nomos*.

The hubristic characterisation of the Thebans, which is only implied by Aethra, is made explicit by the Argive characters in the play. After Theseus' reply to the Theban Herald's attack against democracy,[60] the Chorus comments that wicked men, when they are favoured by fate, commit *hybris* as if their fortune were to last forever (ὑβρίζουσ' ὡς ἀεὶ πράξοντες εὖ) (Eur. *Supp.* 464–5). A similar judgement on the Thebans is uttered by the Messenger, a former servant of Capaneus who brings the news of Athens' victory (Eur. *Supp.* 634–40). The Messenger praises Theseus' hatred for hubristic people (μισεῖ θ' ὑβριστὴν λαόν), who are led by their good fortune to climb the utmost rungs in the ladder of success and end up destroying their current happiness (ὃς πράσσων καλῶς ἐς ἄκρα βῆναι κλιμάκων ἐνήλατα ζητῶν ἀπώλεσ' ὄλβον ᾧ χρῆσθαι παρῆν) (Eur. *Supp.* 723–30).[61]

Euripides therefore portrays both Argives and Thebans as guilty of *hybris*.[62] Why then does Theseus decide to support the Argives? How does he choose between two hubristic parties? The answer lies in the Thebans' breach of divine and Panhellenic *nomos*, which reinforces the Argives' claim to justice and allows Euripides to reconcile the Athenians' justice and altruism and reaffirm their *philanthrōpia*. This can be inferred from Theseus' replies to Aethra and the Theban Herald. Theseus is particularly responsive to his mother's warning about not appearing a coward, which motivates him to defend his reputation as the punisher of the wicked (ἀεὶ κολαστὴς τῶν κακῶν καθεστάναι) (Eur. *Supp.* 337–41). The expression κολαστὴς τῶν κακῶν clearly hints at Athenian *philanthrōpia*. Hyperides' *Funeral Speech*, for example, praises Athens for punishing the wicked and helping the just (τοὺς μὲν κακοὺς κολάζουσα, τοῖς δὲ δικαίοις βοηθοῦσα) (Hyp. 6.5). Athenian *philanthrōpia* is explicitly connected with the defence of *nomos* in Lysias' *Funeral Oration*. There, the Athenians are said to honour the virtuous and punish the wicked in accordance with *nomos* (νόμῳ τοὺς ἀγαθοὺς τιμῶντες καὶ τοὺς κακοὺς κολάζοντες) because they

---

[60] The unsympathetic nature of the Theban Herald is striking from his very first line, where he looks for the tyrant (τύραννος) of the land (Eur. *Supp.* 399).

[61] As noted by Collard 1975b: 296, the metaphor of the ladder is reminiscent of the image of the hubristic Capaneus raising his ladder against the gates of Thebes (Eur. *Supp.* 496–9). Morwood 2007: 200 interestingly suggests that the Messenger's comment on Theban *hybris* is also 'a sideswipe at Argive hubris' specifically directed against Adrastus.

[62] This picture is summarised in Adrastus' response to the Messenger's report. Adrastus regrets the Argives' belief that they were invincible (ἡμῖν γὰρ ἦν τό τ' Ἄργος οὐχ ὑποστατόν), which led them to reject Eteocles' offer of a fair agreement and be destroyed. He then states that the Thebans, because of their recent fortune, behaved with extreme *hybris* (ὕβριζ', ὑβρίζων) and perished in turn (Eur. *Supp.* 737–44). Adrastus' allusion to Eteocles' appeasing offer is probably Euripides' *ad hoc* invention to emphasise Argive folly: see Collard 1975b: 298–9.

believe that men should determine what is just through *nomos* (ἀνθρώποις δὲ προσήκειν νόμῳ μὲν ὁρίσαι τὸ δίκαιον) (Lys. 2.19).[63]

The connection between *philanthrōpia* and *nomos* is particularly evident in Theseus' address to the Theban Herald, which specifically concerns the divine and Panhellenic *nomos* about the burial of the dead. Theseus states that his war against Thebes is the result of a moral imperative: he deems it right to bury the dead (νεκροὺς δὲ τοὺς θανόντας ... θάψαι δικαιῶ). This reference to justice is coupled with an allusion to Panhellenic *nomos*, which Theseus claims to defend (τὸν Πανελλήνων νόμον σῴζων). Theseus adds that the death of the Seven has repaid the Thebans for any wrongs they may have suffered (εἰ γάρ τι καὶ πεπόνθατ' Ἀργείων ὕπο, τεθνᾶσιν) and that Thebes has no more claims to justice (χἠ δίκη διοίχεται). Theseus then stresses again the Panhellenic character of Theban injustice. He states that the Theban refusal to grant burial to the Seven is not just injuring Argos, but the whole of Greece (δοκεῖς κακουργεῖν Ἄργος οὐ θάπτων νεκρούς; ἥκιστα: πάσης Ἑλλάδος κοινὸν τόδε). The Panhellenic motif is finally combined with a concern for piety and divine *nomos*. Theseus demands the restitution of the dead, whom he wants to bury in accordance with piety (τοὺς ὀλωλότας νεκροὺς θάψαι δὸς ἡμῖν τοῖς θέλουσιν εὐσεβεῖν). Alternatively, he will bury the fallen by force so that nobody will proclaim to the Greeks that the ancient *nomos* of the gods was obliterated when it went to Athens for help (ὡς εἰς ἔμ' ἐλθὼν καὶ πόλιν Πανδίονος νόμος παλαιὸς δαιμόνων διεφθάρη) (Eur. *Supp.* 522–63).[64]

The themes of justice and divine and Panhellenic *nomos* are thus intertwined in Theseus' replies to Aethra and the Theban Herald. Their combination offers a powerful justification for Athens' military intervention and at the same time restates Athenian *philanthrōpia*. Euripides had put Theseus in front of a crossroads that would have been inconceivable at the state funeral for the war dead: the choice between justice and altruism. Only after listening to his mother's advice does the Athenian king conclude that the Argives have already been cleared of their wrongs and deserve to be helped.[65] The divinely sanctioned Panhellenic *nomos* is key in guiding Theseus to his decision. Its power evens out Argive *hybris* and tips the balance of injustice towards the equally hubristic Thebans. Justice and altruism are finally reconciled, and Theseus can perform his customary act of *philanthrōpia*.

The fracture within *philanthrōpia*, however, is not the only conflict between Athenian values in Euripides' *Suppliant Women*. In a play so concerned with appropriate decision-making, Theseus' choice to undertake a

---

[63] Lysias' passage is particulary concerned with *nomos* (νόμῳ ... νόμῳ ... νόμου): see Todd 2007: 229.
[64] As noted by Morwood 2007: 187, divine *nomos* is personified as a suppliant coming to Athens.
[65] This is quite late in the story, if one considers that Lysias reaches the same conclusion in the very first paragraph of his narrative (Lys. 2.7).

just and selfless war could be seen as incompatible with the discursive parameters of the Assembly, which compelled speakers to advise what was advantageous for the city. Theseus' lack of self-interest is particularly evident in the words of the Messenger, who stresses that the victorious Athenian king only demanded the return of the dead despite having the opportunity to sack Thebes (Eur. *Supp.* 723–5). On the other hand, apart from the Chorus's generic reference to the everlasting *charis* that cities derive from pious enterprises (καλὸν δ' ἄγαλμα πόλεσιν εὐσεβὴς πόνος χάριν τ' ἔχει τὰν ἐς αἰεί) (Eur. *Supp.* 373–4), there is surprisingly little discussion of advantage in the first, most clearly deliberative part of the play.[66]

The conflict between *philanthrōpia* and advantage is resolved towards the end of the tragedy, where Theseus, Adrastus and Athena stress the *charis* the Athenians acquired through their intervention. Theseus is the first to reconceptualise the relationship between Athens and Argos in terms of reciprocity. He declares that the corpses of the Seven are a gift from Athens to the Argives (τούτοις ἐγώ σφε καὶ πόλις δωρούμεθα) and asks Adrastus to preserve the memory of this favour (ὑμᾶς δὲ τῶνδε χρὴ χάριν μεμνημένους σῴζειν) (Eur. *Supp.* 1168–70).[67] Adrastus acknowledges the benefactions he has received from the Athenians (ξύνισμεν πάνθ' ὅσ' Ἀργείαν χθόνα δέδρακας ἐσθλὰ δεομένην εὐεργετῶν), promises a *charis* that never grows old (χάριν τ' ἀγήρων ἕξομεν) and states that the Argives owe the Athenians an equal return for their noble deeds (γενναῖα γὰρ παθόντες ὑμᾶς ἀντιδρᾶν ὀφείλομεν) (Eur. *Supp.* 1176–9). Theseus and Adrastus employ the language of reciprocity that characterised deliberative and honorific practice within the Assembly,[68] and indicate the advantageousness of Theseus' decision. Like any public benefactors, the Athenians will receive an appropriate return for their service, and this idea is reinforced by Adrastus' portrayal of the Argives as their debtors.

The expediency of Theseus' policy is explicitly sanctioned by Athena's *ex machina* appearance. The goddess exhorts the Athenian king to do what is beneficial (ἄκουε, Θησεῦ, τούσδ' Ἀθηναίας λόγους, ἃ χρή σε δρᾶσαι, δρῶντα δ' ὠφελεῖν τάδε).[69] This reference to the deliberative principle of advantage

---

[66] Theseus distinguishes between citizens who bring ruin upon the state and those who preserve it (Eur. *Supp.* 229–45), but this digression, although sprung from Adrastus' poor choices, is a generic comment rather than a remark on the expedience of going to war for the sake of the Argives.

[67] A. S. Anderson 2015: 311–14 is right to note the novelty of the burial in Argos but may be going too far when he suggests that the gift of the bones of the Seven to Argos 'puts contemporary Argives in a position of gratitude to the Athenians' at a time when the two cities were negotiating an alliance.

[68] On the language of reciprocity in Athenian deliberative oratory and honorific decrees, see p. 132 with references.

[69] The syntax of the sentence is rather loose and has given rise to different interpretations of the passage; see Collard 1975b: 411; Morwood 2007: 236.

is coupled with the language of reciprocity, as Athena invites Theseus to take an oath from Adrastus in return for the toils endured by the Athenians (ἀντὶ τῶν σῶν καὶ πόλεως μοχθημάτων πρῶτον λάβ' ὅρκον). This will forbid the Argives from ever invading Attic lands and bind them to help the Athenians to repel possible invaders (μήποτ' Ἀργείους χθόνα ἐς τήνδ' ἐποίσειν πολέμιον παντευχίαν, ἄλλων τ' ἰόντων ἐμποδὼν θήσειν δόρυ) (Eur. *Supp.* 1183–95).[70] The terms of the oath imparted by Athena are reminiscent of the technical language of peace treaties and diplomacy,[71] and once again show that Euripides is playing with the audience's familiarity with the discourse of the Assembly. Athena therefore confirms the debt of *charis* established between Adrastus and Theseus as well as the advantageousness of Athenian *philanthrōpia*.

As I have shown, Euripides' *Suppliant Women* played with the values and discourse developed in the institutions of Athenian democracy. The picture of the Athenians' *philanthrōpia* and attitude towards *hybris* produced at the state funeral for the war dead was juxtaposed with the discourse of advantage typical of the Assembly. Just as in the real Athenian community, on the tragic stage these values developed a dynamic interaction that allowed them to coexist. Some degree of ambiguity persisted in the story and was meant to appeal to possible critics of democracy within the audience. Athens, after all, did support the Argives despite their previous *hybris*. Aethra's exhortation to Theseus not to appear a coward and seek glory (Eur. *Supp.* 314–25) could similarly have led Theseus to repeat Adrastus' mistakes.[72] The play's focus on decision-making and religious piety could even have resonated with those Athenians who disapproved of Athens' fortification of the temple of Apollo at Delium in 424 BC. Yet, Athens' victory against Thebes and the establishment of an advantageous bond of *charis* with Argos confirmed the validity of Theseus' actions. Euripides was therefore able to provide his democratic audience with reassuring answers to potential conflicts within Athenian democratic ideology, as he used Argive and Theban *hybris* to dissect and reaffirm Athenian *philanthrōpia* and reconciled *philanthrōpia* with Athenian interests.

THE MYTH OF ADRASTUS IN PROCLES' SPEECH TO THE ASSEMBLY

The myth of Adrastus, which in Euripides' *Suppliant Women* provided a commentary on appropriate decision-making, could also be employed in real

---

[70] The oath has sometimes been seen as an allusion to the alliance between Athens and Argos in 421 BC, but see Mills 1997: 96, who highlights the different character of the historical treaty.

[71] Cf. Thuc. 1.44.1; 5.18.4; 47.2–3; 8.58.3–4; see Zuntz 1955: 74–5; Collard 1975b: 411–12; Morwood 2007: 236.

[72] Hesk 2011: 131.

deliberative settings. This is the case in Xenophon's account of the speech delivered by Procles, an ambassador of the Peloponnesian city of Phlius, to the Athenian Assembly in 369 BC.[73] Whereas Euripides was enabled by the discursive parameters of the dramatic festivals to reconcile Athenian *philanthrōpia* with the interests of the state, Xenophon's passage shows how the discursive parameters of the Assembly conditioned Procles into downplaying Athenian *philanthrōpia* and Theban *hybris* and disregarding the issue of Adrastus' culpability in order to highlight the deliberative principle of advantage.[74]

After their victory at Leuctra in 371 BC, the Thebans made an alliance with the Argives, Arcadians and Eleans, challenging Sparta's dominance in the Peloponnese. The Thebans even freed the territory of Messenia, which had been under Spartan control for centuries, and posed a direct threat to Laconia (Xen. *Hell.* 6.5.22–32; Diod. 15.62–6). In this dire situation, Sparta and her allies sent ambassadors to Athens to request help against the Thebans (Xen. *Hell.* 6.5.33–49).[75] Procles of Phlius was one of the ambassadors who addressed the Athenian Assembly on that occasion, and Xenophon reports his speech in some detail. In accordance with the discursive parameters of the Assembly, the speech focuses on the advantage of the Athenians. Procles opens with a reference to Athens' self-interest: by helping the Spartans, the Athenians would actually be helping themselves, because they would preserve the only obstacle preventing the Thebans from attacking Athens. Procles then insists that it would be more advantageous (συμφορώτερον) for the Athenians to acquire allies against Theban expansionism than to fight Thebes after all potential allies have perished (Xen. *Hell.* 6.5.38–9). He therefore invites the Athenians to help the Spartans and their allies in order to acquire their friendship and put them under an obligation to reciprocate the favour (Xen. *Hell.* 6.5.41–4).

Procles introduces the myth of Adrastus (together with the myth of the Heraclidae) as an example of the sort of benefactions the Athenians should confer on the Spartans to establish an advantageous bond of *charis*. Procles contrasts the Athenians of the past, who won universal admiration by helping all those who were wronged (τοὺς ἀδικουμένους), with those of the present, who are receiving the pleas of the Spartans but also of those same Thebans who at the end of the Peloponnesian War unsuccessfully voted for the destruction of Athens. Procles therefore appeals to Athens' devotion to justice but embeds it in a logic of negative reciprocity: the Thebans have tried to injure

---

[73] Cf. Hdt. 9.27.3, where the Athenians use the myth of Adrastus in their debate with the Tegeans over the leadership of the left wing of the Greek army in Plataea: see Steinbock 2013a: 196–8.
[74] On the reliability of the speeches in Xenophon, see Buckler 1982.
[75] Steinbock 2013a: 200.

the Athenians in the past, but are now requesting their support.[76] The implication, of course, is that the Athenians should reject the Thebans' plea and side with the Spartans. The orator finally recalls the noble deed (καλόν) performed by the Athenian ancestors when they did not let the Seven go unburied in Thebes, and invites the Athenians to perform an even nobler deed (κάλλιον) by not letting the Spartans who are still alive suffer *hybris* (ὑβρισθῆναι) or be destroyed (Xen. *Hell*. 6.5.45–6).[77]

Procles' allusion to the myth of Adrastus well illustrates the values produced in the Assembly. The element of justice within Athenian *philanthrōpia* is toned down. Nothing is said about the legitimacy of Adrastus' campaign against Thebes and its implications for Athens' intervention.[78] It is impossible to determine the mythical variant deployed by the orator, because the issue of Adrastus' culpability was not appropriate to a deliberative setting. Procles does stir the Athenians' pride in their tradition as champions of the wronged, but this reference to justice is incorporated into a broader discourse of reciprocity which focuses on what is advantageous for Athens. This is evident from Procles' allusion to the Thebans' unsuccessful proposal to destroy Athens in 404 BC, which the Athenians are implicitly invited to reciprocate by siding with the Spartans.

Procles' stress on Athens' reciprocal dealings with other communities also undermines Athenian altruism, the other component of *philanthrōpia*. This impression is confirmed by Procles' allusions to the myth of the Heraclidae and to the Spartans' rejection of the Thebans' aforementioned proposal to destroy Athens. Procles tells the Athenians that, although they performed a noble deed (καλοῦ) when they saved the Heraclidae, the founders of Sparta, they should now do something even nobler (κάλλιον) by saving the whole city. He adds that the noblest deed of all (πάντων δὲ κάλλιστον) would be for the Athenians to save the Spartans now at the risk of their own lives, whereas in 404 the Spartans only saved Athens with a vote (Xen. *Hell*. 6.5.47). In both cases, the Athenians are praised for their past deeds and invited to surpass them. Yet, these deeds are not altruistic as much as they are meant to maintain relationships of reciprocity that will ultimately benefit Athens herself.

In the context of the Assembly, unlike at the state funeral, Athenian *philanthrōpia* could therefore be toned down, and was not employed to

---

[76] See Sahlins 1972: 195–6, who describes negative reciprocity as 'the attempt to get something for nothing with impunity'. Justice itself could be conceptualised in terms of reciprocity, specifically as the act of rendering benefits to one's friends and harm to one's enemies: see p. 121.

[77] Steinbock 2013a: 200–1.

[78] Justice was mentioned in the speeches of the Spartan and Corinthian ambassadors in the same debate but only concerning the respect of treaties and international law (Xen. *Hell*. 6.5.36–7), which were under the domain of the Assembly: see Harris 2017: 58.

create an imagined community. As a result, Procles cannot (and need not) use Theban *hybris* as a counterpart to Athenian *philanthrōpia*. Rather than attributing *hybris* to the mythical Thebans for prohibiting the Argives to bury their dead, he stresses how the Thebans of the present are committing *hybris* against the Spartans. The myth is tailored to the present situation and couched in terms of advantage. It elicits an implicit comparison between mythical and historical Thebans that reminds the Athenians of the urgency of the current Theban threat, which, as the orator has already foretold (Xen. *Hell.* 6.5.38–9), may soon become dangerous for Athens herself.[79]

As I have shown, Procles' allusion to the myth of Adrastus is embedded within a chain of noble benefactions that will establish an advantageous bond of *charis* with the Spartans, and the orator significantly closes his speech with an appeal to the Athenians to remember the favours they received from the Spartans and reciprocate them on behalf of Greece (Xen. *Hell.* 6.5.48). Athenian *philanthrōpia* is therefore downplayed in both its components of justice and altruism, and it is not complemented by the Athenians' aversion to *hybris*. The interaction between both values is significantly reduced, and *philanthrōpia* and *hybris* are remodelled according to the principle of advantage typical of the Assembly.

THE MYTH OF ADRASTUS IN A FICTIONAL ASSEMBLY

Isocrates' *Plataicus* deploys the myth of Adrastus in a fictional deliberative setting. The occasion of the speech is provided by the destruction of Plataea by the Thebans in 373 BC, which forced the Plataeans to leave their land and find refuge in Athens (Paus. 9.1.5–8; Diod. 15.46.6).[80] Isocrates' *Plataicus* is imagined to be an address to the Athenian Assembly delivered by a Plataean spokesperson, whose aim is to persuade the Athenians to intervene against Thebes and restore Plataea to its legitimate inhabitants. Whether Isocrates wrote the *Plataicus* for actual delivery by a Plataean representative in front of the Assembly, however, is debated, and it is likely that the speech was rather a pamphlet meant for private circulation.[81] The private nature of the speech allowed Isocrates to

---

[79] One can compare the passage with Procles' allusion to the myth of the Heraclidae, where the orator states that the Athenians checked the *hybris* of Eurystheus (σχόντες τὴν Εὐρυσθέως ὕβριν) (Xen. *Hell.* 6.5.47). Procles may have felt more comfortable mentioning Eurystheus' *hybris* because this did not engender an implicit comparison with present-day Thebes. Procles could have exhorted the Athenians to stop Theban *hybris* just as they once did when they helped Adrastus. Yet, the fact that he did not is further proof that in the Assembly he was not expected to emphasise Athens' aversion to *hybris*.

[80] Steinbock 2013a: 198.

[81] On the nature and aims of Isocrates' *Plataicus*, see Papillon 2004: 228–9; Steinbock 2013a: 198–200.

emphasise the component of justice and minimise the component of altruism within Athenian *philanthrōpia*. For the same reason, the orator could ignore the *hybris* of the mythical Thebans and allude to a version of the myth where Adrastus had led an unjust war of aggression against Thebes.

The private character of Isocrates' *Plataicus* is reflected in the tone of the speech, which does not obey the discursive parameters of the Assembly but mixes deliberative and forensic features. Despite its dramatic setting in the Assembly, the speech includes relatively few references to the deliberative principle of advantage. The argument of advantage is implicit when the speaker warns the Athenians that, if they acquiesce in Thebes' cruel treatment of Plataea, fear of the Thebans will lead the other Greeks to seek the friendship of the Spartans (Isoc. 14.15–16). The speaker disputes the Thebans' claim that their conquest of Plataea is advantageous (συμφέρον) for their allies (including the Athenians themselves) (Isoc. 14.25). He then refutes the view that the Thebans are fighting in defence of Athens and that it would be dangerous if they were to side with Sparta (Isoc. 14.33–8). Finally, the speaker suggests that the Athenians will gain new allies if they go to war against Thebes for the sake of justice and the oaths (Isoc. 14.42–3).

Rather than with what is advantageous for Athens, Isocrates seems to be concerned with what is just. The speaker immediately reminds the Athenians of their role as protectors of the wronged (τοῖς ἀδικουμένοις), and argues that nobody has ever suffered greater injustices than the Plataeans (οὔτε γὰρ ἂν ἀδικώτερον οὐδένας ἡμῶν εὕροιτε). He then invites the Athenians to help the Plataeans and acquire a reputation as the most pious and just (δικαιοτάτους) of all the Greeks (Isoc. 14.1–2).[82] Just as in a forensic setting, justice is omnipresent throughout the speech. The speaker asks whether it is just (δίκαιόν ἐστιν) to inflict punishments (ποιεῖσθαι τὰς τιμωρίας) as cruel and unlawful (ἀνόμους) as those suffered by the Plataeans for their alleged allegiance to Sparta (Isoc. 14.8), and wonders how the Thebans will define what is just (τὸ δίκαιον κρίνοντες) in order to provide a pretext for their own behaviour (Isoc. 14.10). He then compares the past faults of the Plataeans, which they only perpetrated under Spartan compulsion, with the Thebans' terrible injustices (μεγάλων ἀδικημάτων) (Isoc. 14.30).[83] The speech also employs legal language and forensic commonplaces. The speaker rhetorically laments the difficulty of making an adequate accusation against the

---

[82] These references to justice are paired with an appeal to *charis*, as the speaker recalls the Athenians' eagerness to reciprocate benefactions (τοῖς εὐεργέταις μεγίστην χάριν ἀποδιδόντας) and the Plataeans' ancient friendship with them (Isoc. 14.1–2). Unlike Procles' speech in Xenophon, however, Isocrates' *Plataicus* does not suggest that the Athenians would benefit themselves by reciprocating the Plataeans' benefactions.

[83] For other references to justice in the speech, cf. Isoc. 14.25, 35, 40, 42.

crimes of the Thebans (κατηγορῆσαι τῶν Θηβαίοις ἡμαρτημένων), and sets out to prove the Thebans' transgression of the law (τὴν τούτων παρανομίαν) to the best of his ability (ὅπως ἂν δυνώμεθα) (Isoc. 14.4).[84] In typical forensic fashion, he even pleads the Athenians to listen to his words with goodwill (μετ' εὐνοίας ἀκροάσασθαι τῶν λεγομένων) (Isoc. 14.6).[85]

Isocrates' manipulation of the values of *philanthrōpia* and *hybris* in the myth of Adrastus is consistent with the private context and composite nature of the speech. The story is meant to persuade the Athenians that the Plataeans have suffered the greatest injustice and therefore deserve Athens' help more than anybody else. Accordingly, Athenian *philanthrōpia* is reformulated almost exclusively in terms of justice and lawfulness. The speaker complains that it would not be appropriate if the Plataeans, whose city has been unlawfully (ἀνόμως) destroyed, were not to obtain compassion from the Athenians, whereas all those who unjustly suffer misfortune (τῶν παρὰ τὸ δίκαιον δυστυχούντων) receive pity from them. He then recalls how the Athenian ancestors, when the Argives begged them to take up their dead in Thebes, forced the Thebans to take a more lawful decision (βουλεύσασθαι νομιμώτερον) (Isoc. 14.52–3). The unlawful behaviour of the mythical Thebans, who were compelled by the Athenians to deliberate according to *nomos*, thus parallels the historical Thebans' unlawful destruction of Plataea and portrays the Plataeans as suitable recipients of Athens' help.

The speaker also makes a comparison between Argives and Plataeans. He states that the Plataeans have come to Athens concerning more serious and just (πολὺ περὶ μειζόνων καὶ δικαιοτέρων) issues (Isoc. 14.53). Not only does the speaker belittle the seriousness of the Argives' misfortunes,[86] but he even raises issues with the legitimacy of Adrastus' campaign against Thebes.[87] He argues that the Argives supplicated the Athenians after invading the land of others (ἐπὶ τὴν ἀλλοτρίαν στρατεύσαντες), whereas the Plataeans are now supplicating them because they have lost their own (Isoc. 14.54). Isocrates may be implicitly endorsing a version of the myth where Adrastus went to

---

[84] Similar or identical formulas to express modesty are common in forensic speeches: cf. e.g. Lys. 5.1; 19.1; Isae. 4.1; Dem. 20.1. Isocrates alludes again to the Thebans' *paranomia* later in the speech. The speaker states that it would be nobler for the Athenians to force the Thebans to imitate their piety rather than to share in the Thebans' lawlessness (τῆς τούτων παρανομίας) (Isoc. 14.22). The passage is reminiscent of an argument deployed in Demosthenes' *Against Leptines*, where Demosthenes argues that Athens should persuade Leptines to be similar to her rather than the other way round (Dem. 20.14).

[85] For similar appeals to the Athenians' *eunoia* in forensic speeches, cf. e.g. Lys. 19.11; Isae. 2.2, 6.2; Dem. 23.4, 27.3, 34.1; Aeschin. 2.1.

[86] Cf. Isoc 14.53–4, where the speaker argues that losing one's land is much worse than being prevented from burying one's dead.

[87] Gotteland 2001: 202.

war against Thebes despite Polynices' voluntary resignation from the Theban throne. Whether or not this is the case, he clearly depicts the Argive king as guilty of initiating a war of aggression. This is suggested by the expression ἐπὶ τὴν ἀλλοτρίαν στρατεύσαντες. Similar expressions could be employed to portray aggressive and expansionistic policies as unjust. In Lysias' *Funeral Oration*, for example, the Amazons' invasion of Athens is motivated by their unjust desire for the lands of other nations (τῆς ἀλλοτρίας ἀδίκως ἐπιθυμήσασαι) (Lys. 2.6). In an Assembly debate in Xenophon, a Corinthian ambassador similarly compares the behaviour of Sparta and her allies, who have never made campaigns against other cities (ἐπὶ πόλιν τινὰ ἐστρατεύσαμεν) or ravaged the land of other nations (γῆν ἀλλοτρίαν ἐδῃώσαμεν), with the unjust behaviour of the Thebans, who have invaded their lands and seized their properties (Xen. *Hell.* 6.5.37). The speaker of Isocrates' *Plataicus* thus suggests that, since they had initiated an unjust war against Thebes, the Argives were less deserving of Athenian help than the righteous Plataeans.[88]

If the component of justice within Athenian *philanthrōpia* is stressed and exploited to exhort the Athenians to help the Plataeans, little emphasis is placed upon the other component: altruism. Because the speech is imagined to take place in the Assembly, Isocrates does not stress the absence of Athenian interests in going to war against Thebes. Yet, apart from the eternal reputation (δόξαν ἀείμνηστον) that the Athenians are now called to uphold (Isoc. 14.53), he does not mention any advantages deriving from Athens' support to Adrastus. The private nature of the *Plataicus*, in other words, enables Isocrates to limit both the epitaphic value of altruism and the deliberative principle of advantage while keeping the focus on the theme of justice.

Isocrates' choice to focus on justice despite the fictional deliberative setting of the speech also influences the treatment of Theban *hybris*. As already mentioned, the mythical Thebans are accused of not behaving according to *nomos* because they denied burial to the Seven. The speaker, however, never characterises them as guilty of *hybris*. There is no hint that the Thebans were infringing the honour of the dead or the gods, nor is the *nomos* they breached directly described as divine. The speaker thus avoids the impression that the Thebans, by subverting the laws of the gods, overestimated their own honour. This downplaying of Theban *hybris* is consistent with the rhetorical purpose of the passage. Acknowledging the *hybris* of the mythical Thebans would have stressed the seriousness of the injustice suffered by the Argives, which the

---

[88] Steinbock 2013a: 199–200. Cf. Isoc.14.25, where the speaker condemns Thebes' misappropriation of Plataean territory and states that many who have unjustly desired the land of others (πολλοὶ δὴ τῆς ἀλλοτρίας ἀδίκως ἐπιθυμήσαντες) have rightly (δικαίως) imperilled their own. The similarity of the expressions suggests an implicit parallel between the unjust expansionistic behaviour of mythical Argives and historical Thebans.

speaker instead chooses to tone down to emphasise the wrong suffered by the Plataeans.[89]

The private nature of Isocrates' *Plataicus* allows the speaker to mix deliberative and forensic features. Despite the dramatic setting in the Athenian Assembly, the speech appears to be a cross between a request for help and a trial against the Thebans.[90] I have shown that, as a result, the value of *philanthrōpia* is understood almost exclusively in terms of justice and adapted to the case of the Plataeans, while the interaction between *philanthrōpia* and *hybris* is reduced and subordinated to the amplification of the Thebans' current crimes against the Plataeans.

QUESTIONING THEBAN *HYBRIS* IN A PRIVATE CONTEXT

Isocrates provides a different version of the myth of Adrastus in his *Panathenaicus*.[91] The speech purports to be a public oration for performance at the Panathenaea, but it really is a private pamphlet.[92] The private context of the speech enables Isocrates to ignore the issue of the legitimacy of Adrastus' expedition and provide an incomplete picture of Athenian *philanthrōpia*. For the same reason, the orator is able to adopt the peaceful version of the myth and even question Theban *hybris*. The myth of Adrastus is used as an example of Athens' primacy in war. The story comes within a section devoted to the comparison between Athenian and Spartan institutions and their influence over these cities' respective military policies (Isoc. 12.151–98).[93] Isocrates argues that the Spartans did not practise their military skills earlier than the Athenians, nor did they make better use of them (τὴν ἐμπειρίαν τὴν περὶ τὸν πόλεμον οὐ πρότερον ἤσκησαν οὐδ' ἄμεινον ἐχρήσαντο Σπαρτιᾶται τῶν ἡμετέρων) (Isoc. 12.155). He then compares the foreign policy of Sparta (and Athens) after the Persian Wars, which has been aimed at ruling the other Greeks (τῶν μὲν

---

[89] Cf. Isoc. 14.55, where the speaker even states that the prohibition of the burial of the Seven was a greater disgrace for the Thebans than for the Argives.

[90] Cf. Thuc. 3.52–67. When Plataea surrendered to Sparta in 427 BC, the Plataeans had to undergo judgement so that the guilty could be punished according to justice (τούς τε ἀδίκους κολάζειν, παρὰ δίκην δὲ οὐδένα) (Thuc. 3.52.2). Unlike the fictional setting of Isocrates' *Plataicus*, the debate does not take place before a political assembly. Thucydides portrays a trial before five Spartan judges (οἱ ἐκ τῆς Λακεδαίμονος δικασταὶ πέντε ἄνδρες) (Thuc. 3.52.3), and both the speech of the Plataeans and the response of the Thebans accordingly focus mainly on issues of justice and law.

[91] The myth of Adrastus also features in Isocrates' *Panegyricus* (Isoc. 4.54–60) and *Helen* (Isoc. 10.31), but neither is relevant to this discussion of *philanthrōpia* and *hybris*.

[92] On the nature of Isocrates' *Panathenaicus*, see V. J. Gray 1994b; Roth 2003; Papillon 2004: 167–8.

[93] This is consistent with the aim of the whole speech, which praises Athens' benefactions to the Greeks through comparison with Sparta (Isoc. 12.35–41).

Ἑλλήνων ἄρχειν ἀξιοῦσαι), with that of the Athenian ancestors, who resolved to keep away from the Greek cities (τῶν μὲν γὰρ Ἑλληνίδων πόλεων οὕτως αὐτοῖς ἀπέχεσθαι σφόδρα δεδογμένον ἦν) (Isoc. 12.162–3).

Isocrates recalls how Adrastus, unable to recover his dead in Thebes, supplicated the Athenians to intervene and prevent a violation of an ancient custom and ancestral *nomos* (παλαιὸν ἔθος καὶ πάτριον νόμον) established by the gods (ὑπὸ δαιμονίας προστεταγμένῳ δυνάμεως). The Athenians immediately accepted his supplication and sent ambassadors to Thebes. They exhorted the Thebans to take a more pious decision (ὁσιώτερον βουλεύσασθαι) and give a more lawful reply (τὴν ἀπόκρισιν νομιμωτέραν ποιήσασθαι), and made it clear that they would not have allowed them to transgress the common *nomos* of all the Greeks (τὸν νόμον τὸν κοινὸν ἁπάντων τῶν Ἑλλήνων). Not only were the Thebans persuaded to grant the return of the corpses without resorting to war, but they even showed moderation (μετρίως) in making their case with the Athenian ambassadors. Isocrates concludes that the story proves Athens' supremacy in war, because the Thebans yielded to the word of the Athenians more than to the *nomoi* established by the gods (τοῖς νόμοις τοῖς ὑπὸ τοῦ δαιμονίου κατασταθεῖσιν) (Isoc. 12.168–74).

Isocrates' narrative only partially develops the altruistic component of Athenian *philanthrōpia*. The orator introduces the myth of Adrastus alongside Athens' leadership in the Ionian colonisation as an example of the ancestors' use of military skills to benefit the other Greeks. While the ancestors' help to the Ionians is portrayed as their greatest and most universal benefaction (μεῖζον μὲν οὖν εὐεργέτημα τούτου καὶ κοινότερον τοῖς Ἕλλησι γεγενημένον παρὰ τῶν προγόνων τῶν ἡμετέρων οὐκ ἂν δυναίμην ἐξευρεῖν), their intervention on behalf of Adrastus is described as a benefaction more relevant to their attention for war (οἰκειότερον δὲ τῇ περὶ τὸν πόλεμον ἐπιμελείᾳ) (Isoc. 12.164–8). By presenting Athens' help to the Argives as a benefaction, Isocrates thus stresses her altruism. This, however, is the only hint to Athenian altruism in the passage. The orator does stress the Athenians' prompt response to Adrastus' supplication (ὧν ἀκούσας οὐδένα χρόνον ἐπισχὼν ὁ δῆμος ἔπεμψε πρεσβείαν εἰς Θήβας), but nothing is said about their motivations (Isoc. 12.170). Unlike Lysias, for example, Isocrates does not emphasise their lack of self-interest,[94] and the peaceful version of the myth implies that the Athenians did not incur any personal risks for the sake of the Argives.

The other component of Athenian *philanthrōpia*, Athens' devotion to justice, is also only partially developed. Nothing is said about the legitimacy of Adrastus' claims against Thebes and their implications for Athens' intervention. Isocrates simply states that the Argive king wanted to restore Polynices to

---

[94] Cf. Lys. 2.8, which states that the Athenians had no previous enmity with the Thebans and did not wish to create a bond of *charis* with the Argives.

power (κατάγειν βουληθεὶς τὸν Οἰδίπου μὲν υἱὸν αὐτοῦ δὲ κηδεστὴν) (Isoc. 12.169), but the orator does not even hint at the causes of Polynices' enmity with Eteocles. One cannot tell whether Polynices had forfeited the throne voluntarily or suffered an injustice from Eteocles, and therefore whether Adrastus had embarked upon an unjust war. The injustice suffered by the Argives is similarly underdeveloped. Adrastus does appeal to ancient custom and ancestral *nomos* (παλαιὸν ἔθος καὶ πάτριον νόμον) to persuade the Athenians to recover the dead (Isoc. 12.169).[95] The Athenians similarly ask the Thebans to give an answer more in accordance with *nomos* (τὴν ἀπόκρισιν νομιμωτέραν ποιήσασθαι) and to respect the common *nomos* of all the Greeks (τὸν νόμον τὸν κοινὸν ἁπάντων τῶν Ἑλλήνων) (Isoc. 12.170). Yet, Thebes' breach of *nomos* is never explicitly described as an injustice suffered by the Argives,[96] and, as we shall see, it does not reinforce Athenian *philanthrōpia* as much as it stresses the Thebans' fear of Athens as opposed to their disregard for the *nomoi* established by the gods (Isoc. 12.174).

Given the limited emphasis on Athenian altruism and devotion to justice, Isocrates thus provides an underdeveloped picture of Athenian *philanthrōpia*. Theban *hybris* is equally downplayed. Both Adrastus and the Athenians describe the Thebans' actions as violations of the Panhellenic *nomos* about the burial of the dead. Adrastus also stresses the divine origin of this *nomos* (ᾧ πάντες ἄνθρωποι χρώμενοι διατελοῦσιν οὐχ ὡς ὑπ' ἀνθρωπίνης κειμένῳ φύσεως, ἀλλ' ὡς ὑπὸ δαιμονίας προστεταγμένῳ δυνάμεως) (Isoc. 12.169), and the Athenians exhort the Thebans to be more pious in their deliberations (ὁσιώτερον βουλεύσασθαι) (Isoc. 12.170). Yet, these motifs are not exploited in such a way as to imply *hybris*. Unlike Lysias and Euripides, Isocrates never portrays the Thebans as infringing the honour of the gods or the dead, nor does he give the impression that the Thebans are overestimating their own honour.[97] The orator even describes the Thebans as acting with moderation when they made their own case against the Argives in front of the Athenian ambassadors (μετρίως περὶ αὑτῶν τε διαλεχθέντες καὶ τῶν ἐπιστρατευσάντων κατηγορήσαντες), and remarks that their behaviour contrasted with the negative opinion some people hold about them (Isoc. 12.171).

Enabled by the private context of the *Panathenaicus*, Isocrates thus departs from the versions of the myth of Adrastus adopted by Lysias at the state funeral

---

[95] An identical reference to ancient custom and ancestral *nomos* (παλαιὸν ἔθος καὶ πάτριον νόμον) features in Isocrates' narrative of the myth of Adrastus in his *Panegyricus* (Isoc. 4.55). There, the orator deploys the bellicose version of the story to demonstrate Athens' character and power (Isoc. 4.54–9) and propose Athens as the leader of a Panhellenic campaign against Persia.

[96] This is only a matter of emphasis: the Theban breach of *nomos* and the injustice suffered by the Argives are two sides of the same coin, and Isocrates chooses only to stress the first element. Cf. Lys. 2.9–10; Eur. *Supp.* 304–12, 339–41, 524–7.

[97] Cf. Lys. 2.9; Eur. *Supp.* 16–19, 301–2, 741–4.

for the war dead and Euripides at the dramatic festivals. By substituting Theban *hybris* with a more moderate behaviour,[98] Isocrates abandons the image of the Athenians as the just punishers of *hybris*. His justificatory tone towards the Thebans, commonly yet unconvincingly ascribed to his desire to safeguard the Athenians' diplomatic efforts to conclude an anti-Macedonian alliance with Thebes in 339 BC,[99] would have been especially out of place at the state funeral.[100] Isocrates also provides an underdeveloped picture of Athenian *philanthrōpia* that puts only limited emphasis on Athenian altruism and justice but focuses mostly on Athens' support for Panhellenic and divine *nomos*.

Isocrates' treatment of the values of *hybris* and *philanthrōpia* responds to the rhetorical purpose of the passage, which was meant to prove that the Athenians were superior to the Spartans in military power and its use. The peaceful version of the myth of Adrastus allows Isocrates to praise Athens' strength while at the same time depicting the Athenians as abstaining from attacking other Greeks.[101] Coupled with the incomplete picture of Athenian *philanthrōpia* and the downplaying of Theban *hybris*, this version is paradoxically effective in stressing Athenian military power.[102] The Athenians are so powerful that the Thebans will not even risk going to war against them, as shown by Isocrates' conclusion that the Thebans felt compelled to return the dead by the words of the Athenians more than by the *nomoi* set by the gods (ἑλέσθαι μᾶλλον αὐτοὺς ἐμμεῖναι τοῖς λόγοις τοῖς ὑπὸ τῆς πόλεως πεμφθεῖσιν ἢ τοῖς νόμοις τοῖς ὑπὸ τοῦ δαιμονίου καταστταθεῖσιν) (Isoc. 12.173–4). The orator therefore has no interest in highlighting Athenian altruism or the injustice suffered by the Argives as much as he is eager to emphasise the Thebans' breach of Panhellenic and divine *nomos*, and stresses Athens' capacity to induce moderation in the Thebans rather than her aversion for *hybris*.

[98] Gotteland 2001: 209.
[99] See Steinbock 2013a: 201–9 with references. The political interpretation of the passage has been convincingly questioned by V. J. Gray 1994a: esp. 96–100. She rightly notes that Isocrates' depiction of the Thebans is far from flattering, as they only act with moderation under Athenian threat, and a few paragraphs earlier Isocrates had openly criticised Thebes for helping the Persians in Egypt (Isoc. 12.159). Isocrates explicitly justifies his choice of the pacific version over the bellicose version employed in *Panegyricus*. He claims to have written well and expediently (καλῶς γέγραφα καὶ συμφερόντως) and expects to be praised by '[every]one who can understand these things' (τῶν ταῦτα συνιδεῖν ἂν δυνηθέντων) (Isoc. 12.172–3, trans. Papillon). On the difficult interpretation of the expression τῶν ταῦτα συνιδεῖν ἂν δυνηθέντων, see Steinbock 2013a: 202 n. 208.
[100] Cf. Demosthenes' attitude towards the Thebans in his *Funeral Speech*. When describing the disastrous outcome of the Battle of Chaeronea, Demosthenes excuses the Theban and Athenian ranks but blames the defeat on the Theban commanders (Dem. 60.22). At the state funeral, therefore, Demosthenes did not refrain from criticising the Thebans despite the fact that Athens and Thebes were then allies.
[101] V. J. Gray 1994a: 91–2.
[102] V. J. Gray 1994a: 97–8.

CONCLUSIONS

The myth of Adrastus was a potential source of contradictions within Athenian democratic ideology. Different versions of the story disagreed over the causes of Adrastus' expedition. Some implied that the campaign was unjust because Polynices had forfeited the Theban throne voluntarily, while others presented the war as a legitimate reaction to Eteocles' deposition of Polynices. The issue of Adrastus' culpability problematised the consistency between justice and altruism within *philanthrōpia* as well as the relationship between *philanthrōpia* and *hybris*. The choice between the bellicose and peaceful versions of the story could similarly influence the relationship between the selfless component of *philanthrōpia* and the interests of Athens. This chapter has shown that Athenian democratic institutions allowed the Athenians to embrace and solve these contradictions by implementing a dynamic dialogue among different and flexible values.

Athenian *philanthrōpia* was the result of a combination of altruism and devotion to justice. The proportion between the two components was far from fixed but varied based on the discursive parameters of different institutions. At the state funeral for the war dead, altruism and justice were equally emphasised and provided an idealised and coherent image of the Athenians as the selfless champions of the wronged. The Athenians were encouraged to follow in the footsteps of their ancestors, while the orators were expected to provide such an image in order to foster cohesion within the community by appealing to the Athenian value of *philanthrōpia*. The unity of Athenian *philanthrōpia* could be broken at the dramatic festivals, where tragedians were allowed to pit justice against altruism and reconcile them through the actions of the characters on the stage. In the Assembly, orators could downplay both justice and altruism and exploit this mitigated picture of *philanthrōpia* to propose advantageous policies for the community, for example by embedding Athenian *philanthrōpia* into a logic of reciprocity. Other configurations within Athenian *philanthrōpia* were possible in private contexts, which were not influenced by the discursive parameters of democratic institutions. The component of altruism could be disregarded and *philanthrōpia* conceptualised only in terms of justice,[103] or *philanthrōpia* could be almost completely downplayed to praise Athenian power.

The Athenians' *philanthrōpia* was often interconnected with their attitude towards *hybris*. At the state funeral, the Athenians identified with their ancestors' hatred for hubristic people, and the Thebans were the perfect recipients of

---

[103] In principle, this picture of *philanthrōpia* would have been appropriate to the discursive parameters of the lawcourts. What is significant about Isocrates' *Plataicus* is that it adopts such a picture despite purporting to be delivered in the Assembly.

this aversion. The contrast with their *hybris* highlighted Athenian *philanthrōpia* and united the Athenians not only against an external enemy but also against un-Athenian values. The Athenians' attitude towards *hybris* could be problematised at the dramatic festivals, where Athens could be presented with a choice between equally hubristic parties. *Hybris* thus provided tragedians with a tool for dissecting Athenian *philanthrōpia* before reasserting its unity. At the Assembly, the Athenians' hatred for *hybris* did not necessarily complement their *philanthrōpia*. It was not in principle inappropriate to stress Theban *hybris* in such a context, but this value had to be subordinated to Athenian interests. In private context, the absence of institutional constraints made it possible to detach the Athenians' *philanthrōpia* and their attitude towards *hybris* ever further. Orators could tone down or even question Theban *hybris*, with the effect of weakening its impact on Athenian *philanthrōpia*.

CHAPTER 8

Conclusions

This book explored the construction of Athenian democratic ideology through a study of the social memory of Athens' mythical past. I have shown that the ideology of democratic Athens was a fluid set of ideas, values and beliefs shared by the majority of the Athenians as a result of a constant process of ideological practice enacted by both the mass and the elite under the influence of the institutions of the democracy. This view combines the normative aspect and evolving nature of ideology typical of the Marxist tradition with the descriptive aspect and neutral notion of ideology held by the culturalist tradition. It also challenges the Marxist view of Athenian ideological practice as a top-down process (shared by de Ste Croix but notably rejected by Loraux) as well as Ober's bottom-up approach, and demonstrates that Athenian democratic institutions allowed both the mass and the elite to play an active role in the construction of the shared ideas and values of the community.

A series of key features of Athenian democratic ideology have thus emerged, among which its dynamic nature is probably the most notable. The influence of institutions allowed Athenian ideological practice to accommodate multiple and sometimes conflicting values and ideas. As shown in Chapter 5, for example, institutions enabled the Athenians to hold two potentially conflicting values in their dealings with other communities: on the one hand, the importance of reciprocating the favours due to benefactors; on the other, the Athenians' traditional humaneness (*philanthrōpia*), which consisted in acting as the righteous and altruistic champions of the weak. Both values coexisted in Athenian ideological practice but were appropriate to different institutions. In Euripides' *Children of Heracles*, Iolaus thus relies on the significance of reciprocity (*charis*) in Athenian deliberative and honorific practice – which was the domain of the Assembly – to persuade Demophon to defend the Heraclidae in return for Heracles' benefactions to Theseus. Under the influence of the state funeral for the war dead, Lysias' *Funeral Oration* instead denies any reciprocal ties between Athens and the Heraclidae, and describes the Athenian intervention as an act of *philanthrōpia*.

Athenian ideas and values were themselves flexible and tended to adapt dynamically to different institutional settings of the democracy. This is best exemplified by the consistency between the two components of Athenian *philanthrōpia* – justice and altruism – in the myth of Adrastus (Chapter 7). Lysias' *Funeral Oration* implies that Adrastus might have unjustly attacked Thebes, but preserves the legitimacy of Athens' intervention by stating that death had cleared the Argives of their hypothetical wrongs. In the context of the state funeral, Lysias emphasises Athenian *philanthrōpia* as a harmonious combination of justice and altruism and reinforces it through the opposition with Theban *hybris*. Euripides' *Supplicant Women* explicitly discusses Adrastus' faults and portrays both the Argives and the Thebans as guilty of *hybris*. In accordance with the discursive parameters of the dramatic festivals, Euripides uses *hybris* to question the compatibility between justice and altruism within Athenian *philanthrōpia*, which he then restores when he motivates Athenian intervention with an appeal to divine and Panhellenic *nomos*. Procles' address to the Athenian Assembly in Xenophon's *Hellenica* ignores the issue of Adrastus' culpability. The orator downplays Theban *hybris* and both components of Athenian *philanthrōpia*, and incorporates this revised picture of *philanthrōpia* into an advantageous logic of reciprocity compatible with the discursive parameters of the Assembly.

Its dynamic nature also allowed Athenian democratic ideology to evolve and incorporate new ideas and values. This is clearly evidenced by Lysias' introduction of concord (*homonoia*) – a topical value in the aftermath of the democratic restoration – into the epitaphic script of Athenian autochthony (Chapter 4). Funeral speeches usually conceptualise autochthony as collective nobility of birth (*eugeneia*) of the Athenian community. This result is achieved through a standard set of motifs including the opposition between collective and individual, the metaphor of the Athenian community as a family, and the language of legitimacy of birth. Lysias' *Funeral Oration* does not fully develop these motifs. Rather than on *eugeneia*, the orator focuses on *homonoia*, which he characterises as an innate feature of the Athenians due to their autochthonous origins. Both Lysias and the other orators of funeral speeches provide an idealised image of Athens as socially and politically cohesive, but Lysias' innovative account shows that the state funeral could accommodate new ideas that reflected contemporary debates within the *polis*. An institutionalist approach to ideology therefore allows us to look at Athenian ideological practice in the making, and a potential research perspective opened by this book is the development and possible institutionalisation of new ideas and values in Athenian public discourse.[1]

Another important feature of Athenian ideology uncovered in this book is its constructive value. Rather than masking internal conflict or exploitation, ideology had the potential to foster unity and a sense of belonging in the community. This is well illustrated by the integrative function of the state funeral in building an imagined community. Chapter 3 has shown how the casualty lists, by omitting patronymics and demotics of the fallen and arranging their names by tribe, invited onlookers to perceive the dead as equal members of the Athenian community. The same impression is confirmed in the funeral speeches. Their accounts of autochthony, for example, ignore the earthborn kings of Attica – acknowledged in other *loci* of ideological practice, such as the lawcourts – and characterise all Athenians as noble children of their motherland as opposed to the immigrant and illegitimate inhabitants of other *poleis* (Chapter 4). The same oppositional strategy fosters Athenian identity and cohesion in the epitaphic version of the Attic Amazonomachy. Lysias accordingly uses the Amazons as Athens' moral counterpart to provide an idealised image of the Athenians as the righteous punishers of *hybris* (Chapter 6). Ideology in democratic Athens should therefore not be seen as either true or false,[2] nor as essentially aimed at legitimisation within class struggle, but as a necessary element in the political life of a community which was not fundamentally face-to-face.

This book also highlights the normative character of ideology. Public discourse, in other words, did not merely describe but also prescribed and moulded what the Athenians were expected to believe. As showed in Chapter 3, for instance, the orators of funeral speeches frequently urged the Athenians to imitate their ancestors, whose exploits illustrated the values every Athenian was expected to possess, such as *philanthrōpia*, devotion to freedom or aversion to

---

[1] See Christ 2013, who analyses the development of *philanthrōpia* in Athenian public discourse. Christ rightly suggests that *philanthrōpia* was engrained in the institutions of the democracy, but could have done more to highlight how the notion was conceptualised differently in each institution. For example, he argues that Demosthenes uses *philanthrōpia* more often in the lawcourts than in the Assembly because he 'envisions *philanthrōpia* operating more in a domestic context, on which forensic orations tend to focus, than in an interstate one, on which deliberative orations usually center' (206 n. 20). Yet, *philanthrōpia* was not incompatible with the interstate context, as proven by its regular occurrence in the picture of Athenian foreign policy in funeral speeches. The minor role of *philanthrōpia* in the Assembly is rather imputable to its altruistic character, which did not always sit well with the discursive parameters of the Assembly but was appropriate to those of the state funeral.

[2] This does not mean to deny that the shared values and ideas of the Athenians could be exploited by skilled orators: see Barbato 2017: 241–3.

hybris. Finally, my study demonstrates the bidirectional character of Athenian ideological practice. The institutions of the democracy provided both the elite (as orators, playwrights or *chorēgoí*) and the mass (through participation in ritual at the state funeral, voting in the lawcourts and Assembly, providing councillors, clamouring in the Assembly and the theatre or manning choruses at the dramatic festivals) with the means to influence the construction of shared ideas and values through public discourse (Chapter 3). This view moves away from a top-down approach to ideology as imposed on the mass by the dominant classes, but also grants appropriate agency to elite political actors such as the orators. Rather than being passive interpreters of a fixed and superimposed democratic ideology, these played an active and multifaceted role under the influence of different institutions of the democracy and interacted with the masses in creating shared views on justice, public advantage, *philanthrōpia* and other values significant to the community.

This book offers a significant contribution to other fields in the study of Athenian democracy besides ideology. The New Institutionalism adds a further dimension to the traditional institutional analysis of Athenian democracy. It combines the traditional formal description of democratic institutions with the analysis of the relationship between those institutions and the individuals acting within them. As a result, I have shown that the institutions of the democracy tended to condition the political actors who participated in Athenian ideological practice, and that these institutional constraints did not affect private contexts. As a private praise of Athens, for example, Isocrates' *Panegyricus* can disregard Athenian *philanthrōpia* as well as Theseus' private obligation in its account of the myth of the Heraclidae. Rather than highlighting the importance of reciprocating benefactions as such, Isocrates exploits *charis* to stress Athens' unique ability to repay mankind's debt towards Heracles and exalt Athenian power (Chapter 5). Philochorus and Pherecydes similarly attributed the Attic Amazonomachy to Theseus' acquisition of Antiope either as a war prize from Heracles or as a spear-captive during an independent campaign. Writing in private settings, they could portray Theseus as the Amazons' original aggressor and contradict the epitaphic image of Athens' defensive foreign policy (Chapter 6).

Research on Athenian social memory similarly benefited from a new layer of investigation as a result of this study. In addition to exploring what the Athenians remembered, I have analysed the reasons why specific memories were significant to the Athenians in specific contexts. Athenian social memory thus should not be conceived as the sum of separate mnemonic communities, but as a collective process of production of different memories appropriate to different institutional settings. The orators accordingly did not simply pick versions of the past from pre-existing traditions, but actively participated in the creation and dispersion of social memory. This book also contributed to our understanding of Aristotle's classification of rhetoric. The nature of such classification was at the same time descriptive and normative.[3] Viewed from an institutionalist perspective, the descriptive aspect acquires a further level of meaning. My analysis corroborates the view that Aristotle's subdivision of the discipline into three genres was based on the observation of actual oratorical practice,[4] and the presence of clear correspondences between Aristotle's speculation on rhetoric and the institutional structure of Athenian democracy suggests that his classification had an (at least intuitive) institutionalist rationale.[5]

Finally, this book has established a fruitful dialogue with the social and political sciences. My reconciliation of Marxist and culturalist views of ideology meets a scholarly demand in the social sciences for a unified theory of ideology.[6] A prominent attempt in this direction is Teun van Dijk's *Ideology: A Multidisciplinary Approach*, which envisions ideologies as the shared, social beliefs of specific social groups – whose identity and interests they represent – expressed mainly (though not exclusively) through discourse.[7] My picture of Athenian democratic ideology shares some of the features of van Dijk's view of ideologies. I agree that ideology (at least in democratic Athens) is not a purely top-down or bottom-up phenomenon,[8] and my dynamic view of Athenian democratic ideology complements van Dijk's belief that individuals can participate in several ideologies.[9] Yet, while van Dijk sees each ideology as fundamentally coherent,[10] I have shown that Athenian democratic ideology could accommodate potentially contrasting beliefs. By adopting the principles of the New Institutionalism, this book also bridges a gap between ancient history and political science, and shows that institutions are still a valuable tool for the study of Athenian democracy. This methodological realignment can allow Greek historians to ask new and topical questions to the ancient sources. A productive field of investigation could be the influence of ideas on the development of Athenian democratic institutions. This would be especially relevant in the present historical climate, in which traditional ideologies are being challenged or

---

[3] Garver 2009: 13; Pepe 2013: 125–6.
[4] See Pepe 2013: 134; *pace* Kennedy [1991] 2007: 22–3.
[5] The need to connect Aristotle's genres of rhetoric with institutions has been highlighted by Hansen 1989a: 111, Garver 1994: 52–73 and Depew 2013: esp. 319.
[6] See e.g. Ricoeur 1986: 1–18; van Dijk 1998; Chiapello 2003.
[7] See van Dijk 1998: esp. 313–18.
[8] Van Dijk 1998: 174–6.
[9] Van Dijk 1998: 284–90.
[10] Van Dijk 1998: 90–5.

undergoing changes and new ideologies have the potential to influence institutions and policy-making.[11] The institutionalist approach to ideology advocated in this book can thus help ancient historians to attract the interest of social and political scientists, broaden our understanding of Athenian democracy and foster debate on democracy across fields.

---

[11] A prominent example is the increasing popularity and possible institutionalisation of anti-political-establishment ideologies in some contemporary democracies. On anti-political-establishment parties, see Schedler 1996 and Abedi 2004.

Bibliography

Abedi, A. (2004), *Anti-Political Establishment Parties: A Comparative Analysis*, London and New York.
Alcock, S. (2002), *Archaeologies of the Greek Past: Landscapes, Monuments and Memories*, Cambridge.
Allan, W. (2001), *Euripides: Children of Heracles*, Warminster.
Allan, W., and A. Kelly (2013), 'Listening to Many Voices: Greek Tragedy as Popular Art', in A. Marmadoro and J. Hill (eds), *The Author's Voice in Classical and Late Antiquity*, Oxford, pp. 77–122.
Allen, D. S. (2000), *The World of Prometheus: The Politics of Punishing in Democratic Athens*, Princeton.
Althusser, L. [1971] (1984), *Essays on Ideology*, London.
Anderson, A. S. (2015), 'The Seven against Thebes at Eleusis', *ICS* 40/2: 297–318.
Anderson, B. [1983] (2006), *Imagined Communities: Reflections on the Origin and Spread of Nationalism*, London.
Anderson, G. (2003), *The Athenian Experiment: Building an Imagined Political Community in Ancient Attica, 508–490 BC*, Ann Arbor.
Arrington, N. T. (2010), 'The Location of the Athenian Public Cemetery and Its Significance for the Nascent Democracy', *Hesperia* 79/4: 499–539.
Arrington, N. T. (2011), 'Inscribing Defeat: The Commemorative Dynamics of the Athenian Casualty Lists', *Classical Antiquity* 30/2: 179–212.
Arrington, N. T. (2014), *Ashes, Images, and Memories: The Presence of the War Dead in Fifth-Century Athens*, New York.
Assmann, J. (1992), *Das kulturelle Gedächtnis: Schrift, Erinnerung und politische Identität in frühen Hochkulturen*, München.
Avery, H. C. (1971), 'Euripides' Heracleidai', *American Journal of Philology* 92: 539–65.
Azoulay, V. (2004), *Xénophon et les grâces du pouvoir. De la charis au charisme*, Paris.
Azoulay, V. (2009), 'Lycurgue d'Athènes et le passé de la cité: entre neutralisation et instrumentalisation', *Cahiers des études anciennes* 46: 149–80.
Azoulay, V., and P. Ismard (2007), 'Les lieux du politique dans l'Athènes classique. Entre structures institutionnelles, idéologie civique et pratiques sociales', in P. Schmitt Pantel and F. de Polignac (eds), *Athènes et le politique. Dans le sillage de Claude Mossé*, Paris, pp. 271–309.

Badian, E. (1995), 'The Ghost of Empire: Reflections on Athenian Foreign Policy in the Fourth Century BC', in W. Eder (ed.), *Die athenische Demokratie im 4. Jahrhundert v. Chr.: Vollendung oder Verfall einer Verfassungsform?*, Stuttgart, pp. 79–106.

Balot, R. K. (2001), *Greed and Injustice in Classical Athens*, Princeton and Oxford.

Balot, R. K. (2013), 'Epideictic Rhetoric and the Foundations of Politics', *Polis* 30/2: 274–304.

Barbato, M. (2017), 'Using the Past to Shape the Future: Ancestors, Institutions and Ideology in Aeschin. 2.74–8', in E. Franchi and G. Proietti (eds), *Conflict in Communities: Forward-looking Memories in Classical Athens*, Trento, pp. 213–53.

Barber, E. J. W. (1992), 'The Peplos of Athena', in J. Neils (ed.), *Goddess and Polis. The Panathenaic Festival in Ancient Athens*, Hanover, NH and Princeton, pp. 103–17.

Barringer, J. M. (2008), *Art, Myth, and Ritual in Classical Greece*, Cambridge and New York.

Barringer, J. M. (2014), 'Athenian State Monuments for the War Dead: Evidence from a Loutrophoros', in A. Avramidou and D. Demetriou (eds), *Approaching the Ancient Artifact. Representation, Narrative, and Function: A Festschrift in Honor of H. Alan Shapiro*, Berlin and Boston, pp. 153–60.

Battezzato, L. (2003), 'Ospitalità rituale, amicizia e *charis* nell'*Ecuba*', in O. Vox (ed.), *Ricerche euripidee*, Lecce, pp. 13–45.

Bearzot, C. S. (2003), 'Il concetto di «dynasteia» e lo stato ellenistico', in C. Bearzot, F. Landucci Gattinoni and G. Zecchini (eds), *Gli stati territoriali nel mondo antico*, Milano, pp. 21–44.

Bearzot, C. S. (2007), 'Autoctonia, rifiuto della mescolanza, civilizzazione: da Isocrate a Megastene', in T. Gnoli and F. Muccioli (eds), *Incontri tra culture nell'oriente ellenistico e romano*, Milano, pp. 7–28.

Bearzot, C. S. (2015), 'Il tema dell'*homonoia* nell'azione politica di Trasibulo', *Rationes Rerum* 5: 99–116.

Bennett, L. J., and W. B. Tyrrell (1990), 'Sophocles' *Antigone* and Funeral Oratory', *American Journal of Philology* 111/4: 441–56.

Bergemann, J. (1997), *Demos und Thanatos. Untersuchungen zum Wertsystem der Polis im Spiegel der attischen Grabreliefs des 4. Jahrhunderts v. Chr. und der Funktion der gleichzeitigen Grabbauten*, München.

Bers, V. (1985), 'Dikastic *Thorubos*', in P. Cartledge and D. Harvey (eds), *Crux: Essays in Greek History Presented to G. E. M. de Ste Croix on his 75th Birthday*, London, pp. 1–15.

Bers, V. (2003), *The Oratory of Classical Greece: Demosthenes, Speeches 50–59*, Austin.

Bertelli, L. (2001), 'Hecataeus: from Genealogy to Historiography', in N. Luraghi (ed.), *The Historian's Craft in the Age of Herodotus*, Oxford, pp. 67–94.

Bielman, A. (1994), *Retour à la liberté: libération et sauvetage des prisonniers en Grèce ancienne: recueil d'inscriptions honorant des sauveteurs et analyse critique*, Paris.

Blank, T. G. M. (2013), 'Isocrates on paradoxical discourse: an analysis of Helen and Busiris', *Rhetorica* 31: 1–33.

Blank, T. G. M. (2014), *Logos und Praxis: Sparta als politisches Exemplum in den Schriften des Isokrates*, Berlin.

Blok, J. H. (1995), *The Early Amazons: Modern and Ancient Perspectives on a Persistent Myth*, Leiden.

Blok, J. H. (2009), 'Gentrifying Genealogy: On the Genesis of the Athenian Autochthony Myth', in U. Dill and C. Walde (eds), *Antike Mythen. Medien, Transformationen und Konstruktionen*, Berlin and New York, pp. 251–75.

Blok, J. H. (2017), *Citizenship in Classical Athens*, Cambridge.

Blyth, M., O. Helgadottir and W. Kring (2016), 'Ideas and Historical Institutionalism', in O. Fioretos, T. G. Falleti and A. Sheingate (eds), *The Oxford Handbook of Historical Institutionalism*, Oxford, pp. 142–62.

Boardman, J. (1972), 'Herakles, Peisistratos and Sons', *Revue archeologique* 1972/1: 57–72.

Boardman, J. (1975), 'Herakles, Peisistratos and Eleusis', *Journal of Hellenic Studies* 95: 1–12.

Boardman, J. (1982), 'Herakles, Theseus and Amazons', in D. C. Kurtz and B. A. Sparkes (eds), *The Eye of Greece: Studies in the Art of Athens*, Cambridge, pp. 1–28.
Boardman, J. (1989), 'Herakles, Peisistratos and the Unconvinced', *Journal of Hellenic Studies* 109: 158–9.
Boardman, J. (1991), *Greek Sculpture: the Archaic Period; a Handbook*, London.
Boegehold, A. L. (1995), *The Lawcourts at Athens: Sites, Buildings, Equipment, Procedure and Testimonia (The Athenian Agora: Results of Excavations Conducted by the American School of Classical Studies at Athens, Vol. XXVIII)*, Princeton.
Boegehold, A. L. (1996), 'Group and Single Competitions at the Panathenaia', in J. Neils (ed.), *Worshipping Athena: Panathenaia and Parthenon*, Madison, WI, pp. 95–105.
Bosworth, A. B. (2000), 'The Historical Context of Thucydides' Funeral Oration', *Journal of Hellenic Studies* 120: 1–16.
von Bothmer, D. (1957), *Amazons in Greek Art*, Oxford.
Bowie, A. M. (2007), 'Myth in Aristophanes', in R. D. Woodard (ed.), *The Cambridge Companion to Greek Mythology*, Cambridge, pp. 190–209.
Bowie, A. M. (2012), 'Myth and Ritual in Comedy', in G. W. Dobrov (ed.), *Brill's Companion to the Study of Greek Comedy*, Leiden, pp. 143–76.
Bowie, E. L. (1986), 'Early Greek Elegy, Symposium and Public Festival', *Journal of Hellenic Studies* 106: 13–35.
Bowie, E. L. (1993), 'Greek Table-Talk before Plato', *Rhetorica* 11/4: 355–71.
Bowra, C. M. (1964), *Pindar*, Oxford.
Bremmer, J. M. (1987), 'What is a Greek Myth?', in J. M. Bremmer (ed.), *Interpretations of Greek Mythology*, London, pp. 1–9.
Bremmer, J. M. (1997), 'Myth as Propaganda: Athens and Sparta', *Zeitschrift für Papyrologie und Epigraphik* 117: 9–17.
Brommer, F. (1967), *Die Metopen des Parthenon: Katalog und Untersuchung*, Mainz.
Brock, R. (1994), 'The Labour of Women in Classical Athens', *Classical Quarterly* 44: 336–46.
Brock, R. (1998), 'Mythical Polypragmosyne in Athenian Drama and Rhetoric', *Bulletin of the Institute of Classical Studies Suppl.* 71: 227–38.
Buchner, E. (1958), *Der Panegyrikos des Isokrates: eine historisch-philologische Untersuchung*, Wiesbaden.
Buckler, J. (1982), 'Xenophon's Speeches and the Theban Hegemony', *Athenaeum* 60: 180–204.
Budelmann, F. (2012), 'Epinician and the *Symposion*: A Comparison with the *Enkomion*', in C. Carey, R. Rawles and P. Agocs (eds), *Reading the Victory Ode*, Cambridge, pp. 173–90.
Burgess, J. S. (2004–5), 'Performance and the Epic Cycle', *Classical Journal* 100/1: 1–23.
Burian, P. H. (1971), *Suppliant Drama: Studies in the Form and Interpretation of Five Greek Tragedies*, Princeton.
Burian, P. H. (1977), 'Euripides' Heraclidae. An interpretation', *Classical Philology* 72: 1–21.
Cairns, D. L. (1993), *Aidôs: The Psychology and Ethics of Honour and Shame in Ancient Greek Literature*, Oxford.
Cairns, D. L. (1996), '*Hybris*, Dishonour, and Thinking Big', *Journal of Hellenic Studies* 116: 1–32.
Cairns, D. L. (2003), 'The Politics of Envy: Envy and Equality in Ancient Greece', in D. Konstan and K. Rutter (eds), *Envy, Spite, and Jealousy: The Rivalrous Emotions in Ancient Greece*, Edinburgh, pp. 235–52.
Cairns, D. L. (2011), 'Honour and Shame: Modern Controversies and Ancient Values', *Critical Quarterly* 53: 23–41.
Cairns, D. L. (2015), 'Revenge, Punishment, and Justice in Athenian Homicide Law', *Journal of Value Enquiry* 49: 645–65.

Cairns, D. L. (2016a), *Sophocles: Antigone*, London.
Cairns, D. L. (2016b), 'Metaphors for Hope in Archaic and Classical Greek Poetry', in R. R. Caston and R. A. Kaster (eds), *Hope, Joy, and Affection in the Classical World (Festschrift for David Konstan)*, New York, pp. 13–44.
Calame, C. [1990] (1996), *Thésée et l'imaginaire athénien: légende et culte en Grèce antique*, Lausanne.
Calame, C. (2011), 'Myth and Performance on the Athenian Stage: Praxithea, Erechtheus, their Daughters, and the Etiology of Autochthony', *Classical Philology* 106/1: 1–19.
Calame, C. (2013), 'The Dithyramb, a Dionysiac Poetic Form: Genre Rules and Cultic Contexts', in B. Kowalzig and P. J. Wilson (eds), *Dythiramb in Context*, Oxford, pp. 332–52.
Campbell, J. L. (1998), 'Institutional Analysis and the Role of Ideas in Political Economy', *Theory and Society* 27/3: 377–409.
Canevaro, M. (2013a), *The Documents in the Attic Orators: Laws and Decrees in the Public Speeches of the Demosthenic Corpus*, Oxford.
Canevaro, M. (2013b), '*Nomothesia* in Classical Athens: What Sources Should We Believe?', *Classical Quarterly* 63/1: 1–22.
Canevaro, M. (2016a), *Demostene, Contro Leptine. Introduzione, Traduzione e Commento Storico*, Berlin.
Canevaro, M. (2016b), 'The Popular Culture of the Athenian Institutions: "Authorized" Popular Culture and "Unauthorized" Elite Culture in Classical Athens', in L. Grig (ed.), *Locating Popular Culture in the Ancient World*, Cambridge, pp. 39–65.
Canevaro, M. (2017), 'Review of A. Gottesman, *Politics and the Street in Democratic Athens*', *Classical Review* 67/2: 1–3.
Canevaro, M. (2018a), 'Majority Rule vs. Consensus: The Practice of Democratic Deliberation in the Greek *Poleis*', in M. Canevaro, A. Erskine, B. Gray and J. Ober (eds), *Ancient Greek History and Contemporary Social Science*, Edinburgh, pp. 101–56.
Canevaro, M. (2018b), 'The Public Charge for *Hubris* against Slaves: the Honour of the Victim and the Honour of the *Hubristēs*', *Journal of Hellenic Studies* 138: 100–26.
Canevaro, M. (2019), 'Memory, the Orators and the Public in Fourth-Century BC Athens', in L. Castagnoli and P. Ceccarelli (eds), *Greek Memories: Theories and Practices*, Cambridge, pp. 136–57.
Canevaro, M. (forthcoming a), 'Making and Changing Laws in Ancient Athens', in E. M. Harris and M. Canevaro (eds), *Oxford Handbook of Ancient Greek Law*, Oxford (available online).
Canevaro, M. (forthcoming b), 'Social Mobility vs. Societal Stability: Once Again on the Aims and Meaning of Solon's Reforms', in J. Bernhardt and M. Canevaro (eds), *From Homer to Solon: Continuity and Change in Archaic Greek Society*, Leiden.
Canevaro, M., and N. K. Rutter (2015), 'Silver for Syracuse: the Athenian Defeat and the Period of the "Signing Artists"', *Schweizerische Numismatische Rundschau* 93: 5–20.
Canfora, L. (2011), 'L'epitafio in morte di Leostene e la "guerra lamiaca"', *Quaderni di Storia* 37: 5–28.
Carey, C. (1992), *Apollodoros, Against Neaira [Demosthenes] 59*, Warminster.
Carey, C. (1995), 'Rape and Adultery in Athenian Law', *Classical Quarterly* 45/2: 407–17.
Carey, C. (2000), 'Observers of Speeches and Hearers of Action: The Athenian Orators', in O. Taplin (ed.), *Literature in the Greek and Roman Worlds*, Oxford and New York, pp. 192–216.
Carey, C. (2009), 'Genre, Occasion and Performance', in F. Budelmann (ed.), *The Cambridge Companion to Greek Lyric*, Cambridge and New York, pp. 21–38.
Carpenter, T. H. (1991), *Art and Myth in Ancient Greece*, London.
Carrière, J.-C. (1997), 'Les métamorphoses des mythes et la crise de la cité dans la Comédie Ancienne', in P. Thiercy and M. Menu (eds), *Aristophane: la langue, la scène, la cité: actes du colloque de Toulouse 17–19 mars 1994*, Bari, pp. 413–42.

Castriota, D. (1992), *Myth, Ethos and Actuality: Official Art in Fifth-Century BC Athens*, Madison, WI.
Castriota, D. (2005), 'Feminizing the Barbarian and Barbarizing the Feminine: Amazons, Trojans, and Persians in the Stoa Poikile', in J. M. Barringer and J. M. Hurwit (eds), *Periklean Athens and its Legacy: Problems and Perspectives*, Austin, pp. 89–102.
Ceccarelli, P. (2013), *Ancient Greek Letter Writing: A Cultural History (600 BC –150 BC)*, Oxford.
Chiapello, E. (2003), 'Reconciling the Two Principal Meanings of the Notion of Ideology. The Example of the Concept of the Spirit of Capitalism', *European Journal of Social Theory* 6/2: 155–71.
Christ, M. R. (2012), *The Limits of Altruism in Democratic Athens*, Cambridge.
Christ, M. R. (2013), 'Demosthenes on *Philanthropia* as a Democratic Virtue', *Classical Philology* 108/3: 202–22.
Clairmont, C. W. (1983), *Patrios Nomos – Public Burial in Athens During the Fifth and Fourth Centuries BC: The Archaeological, Epigraphic-literary and Historical Evidence, I & II*, Oxford.
Clarke, K. (2008), *Making Time for the Past: Local History and the Polis*, Oxford and New York.
Cobetto Ghiggia, P. (2012), '*Homonoia* e *demokratia* nell'Atene fra V e IV sec. a.C.: un approccio lessicale', in S. Cataldi, E. Bianco and G. Cuniberti (eds), *Salvare le poleis, costruire la concordia, progettare la pace*, Alessandria, pp. 267–79.
Cohen, B. (2012), 'The Non-Greek in Greek Art', in T. J. Smith and D. Plantzos (eds), *A Companion to Greek Art*, Oxford and Malden, MA, pp. 456–79.
Cohen, D. (1984), 'Justice, Interest, and Political Deliberation in Thucydides', *Quaderni Urbinati di Cultura Classica* 16/1: 35–60.
Cohen, D. (1995), *Law, Violence, and Community in Classical Athens*, Cambridge.
Collard, C. (1972), 'The Funeral Oration in Euripides' *Supplices*', *Bulletin of the Institute of Classical Studies* 19/1: 39–53.
Collard, C. (1975a), 'Formal Debates in Euripides' Drama', *Greece & Rome* 22: 58–71.
Collard, C. (1975b), *Euripides: Supplices*, Groningen.
Collard, C., and M. J. Cropp (2008), *Euripides: Fragments*, Cambridge, MA and London.
Connelly, J. B. (1996), 'Parthenon and *Parthenoi*: A Mythological Interpretation of the Parthenon Frieze', *American Journal of Archaeology* 100/1: 53–80.
Connelly, J. B. (2007), *Portrait of a Priestess: Women and Ritual in Ancient Greece*, Princeton and Oxford.
Connor, W. R. (1989), 'City Dionysia and Athenian Democracy', *Classica et Mediaevalia* 40: 7–32.
Cooper, C. (2007), 'Making Irrational Myth Plausible History: Polybian Intertextuality in Plutarch's *Theseus*', *Phoenix* 61/3–4: 212–33.
Cornford, F. M. (1907), *Thucydides Mythistoricus*, London.
Coventry, L. (1989), 'Philosophy and Rhetoric in the *Menexenus*', *Journal of Hellenic Studies* 109: 1–15.
Crawley, R. (1910), *Thucydides. The Peloponnesian War*, New York.
Cropp, M. J. (1988), *Euripides: Electra*, Warminster.
Csapo, E. (2005), *Theories of Mythology*, Oxford and Malden, MA.
Csapo, E. (2007), 'The Men Who Built the Theatres: *Theatropolai*, *Theatronai*, and *Arkhitektones*', in P. J. Wilson (ed.), *The Greek Theatre and Festivals: Documentary Studies*, Oxford, pp. 87–121.
Csapo, E., and M. C. Miller (2007), 'General Introduction', in E. Csapo and M. C. Miller (eds), *The Origins of Theater in Ancient Greece and Beyond: From Ritual to Drama*, Cambridge, pp. 1–38.
Csapo, E., and W. J. Slater (1995), *The Context of Ancient Drama*, Ann Arbor.
Csapo, E., and P. J. Wilson (2014), 'Dramatic Festivals', in H. M. Roisman (ed.), *The Encyclopedia of Greek Tragedy*, Chichester, pp. 292–9.

Culasso Gastaldi, E. (1977), 'L'Amazzonomachia teseica nell'elaborazione propagandistica ateniese', *Atti della Accademia delle Scienze di Torino* 111: 283–96.

Cuniberti, G. (2007), 'Giurare e decretare la *homonoia*: nota a Thuc. VIII 75, 2 e 93, 3', in G. Daverio Rocchi (ed.), *Tra concordia e pace: parole e valori della Grecia antica. Atti della giornata di studio (Milano, 21 ottobre 2005)*, Milano, pp. 39–54.

Currie, B. (2004), 'Reperformance Scenarios for Pindar's Odes', in C. J. Mackie (ed.), *Oral Performance and Its Context*, Leiden and Boston, pp. 49–69.

Daverio Rocchi, G. (2007), 'La concordia: tema culturale, obiettivo politico e virtù civica', in G. Daverio Rocchi (ed.), *Tra concordia e pace: parole e valori della Grecia antica. Atti della giornata di studio (Milano, 21 ottobre 2005)*, Milano, pp. 3–38.

Davis-Kimball, J., L. T. Yablonsky and V. Bashilov (eds) (1995), *Nomads of the Eurasian Steppes in the Early Iron Age*, Berkeley.

Depew, D. J. (2013), 'Why Aristotle Says That Artful Rhetoric Can Happen in Only a Few Venues – and Why We Should Too', *Polis* 30/2: 305–21.

Devambez, P. (1976), 'Les Amazones et l'Orient', *Revue Archéologique* 1976/2: 265–80.

Dickey, E. (2007), *Ancient Greek Scholarship. A Guide to Finding, Reading, and Understanding Scholia, Commentaries, Lexica, and Grammatical Treatises, from Their Beginnings to the Byzantine Period*, Oxford.

Dickie, M. W. (1984), '*Hesychia* and *Hybris* in Pindar', in D. E. Gerber (ed.), *Greek Poetry and Philosophy: Studies in Honour of Leonard Woodbury*, Chico, pp. 83–109.

van Dijk, T. A. (1998), *Ideology: A Multidisciplinary Approach*, London.

Dodds, E. R. (1951), *The Greeks and the Irrational*, Berkeley and Los Angeles.

Dolcetti, P. (2004), *Ferecide di Atene. Testimonianze e frammenti. Introduzione, testo, traduzione e commento*, Alessandria.

Donlan, W. (1998), 'Political Reciprocity in Dark Age Greece: Odysseus and His *Hetairoi*', in C. Gill, N. Postlethwaite and R. Seaford (eds), *Reciprocity in Ancient Greece*, Oxford, pp. 51–71.

Donlan, W. [1980] (1999), *The Aristocratic Ideal and Selected Papers*, Wauconda, IL.

Dover, K. J. (1974), *Greek Popular Morality in the Time of Plato and Aristotle*, Berkeley.

Dowden, K. (1992), *The Uses of Greek Mythology*, London and New York.

Dowden, K. (1997), 'The Amazons: Development and Functions', *Rheinisches Museum* 140: 97–128.

Dumont, L. (1977), *Homo Aequalis: Genèse et épanouissement de l'idéologie économique*, Paris.

Duplouy, A. (2006), *Le prestige des élites: recherches sur les modes de reconnaissance sociale en Grèce entre les Xe et Ve siècles avant J.-C*, Paris.

Eagleton, T. (1991), *Ideology: an Introduction*, London.

Edmunds, L. (2006), *Oedipus*, London.

Emlyn-Jones, C., and W. Preddy (2013), *Plato. Republic, Volume I: Books 1–5*, Cambridge, MA and London.

Erskine, A. (2001), *Troy between Greece and Rome. Local Tradition and Imperial Power*, Oxford.

Esu, A. (2017), 'Divided Power and Eunomia: Deliberative Procedures in Ancient Sparta', *Classical Quarterly* 67/2: 353–73.

Esu, A. (forthcoming), '*Edoxe tei boulei*: Institutional Design and Deliberative Expertise in the Athenian Council', in M. Canevaro and M. Barbato (eds), *The Institutional History of the Greek Polis: New Approaches*, Edinburgh.

Fantham, E., H. P. Foley, N. B. Kampen, S. B. Pomeroy and H. A. Shapiro (1994), *Women in the Classical World: Image and Text*, Oxford.

Faraguna, M. (2009), 'Oralità e scrittura nella prassi giudiziaria ateniese tra V e IV sec. a.C.', in E. M. Harris and G. Thür (eds), *Symposion 2007. Vorträge zur griechischen und hellenistischen Rechtsgeschichte*, Wien, pp. 63–82.

Faraguna, M. (2012), 'Società, amministrazione, diritto: lo statuto giuridico di tombe e *periboloi* nell'Atene classica', in B. Legras and G. Thür (eds), *Symposion 2011. Vorträge zur griechischen und hellenistischen Rechtsgeschichte*, Wien, pp. 165–85.
Fearn, D. (2007), *Bacchylides: Politics, Performance, Poetic Tradition*, Oxford.
Fentress, J., and C. Wickham (1992), *Social Memory*, Oxford.
Feyel, C. (2009), *Dokimasia: la place et le rôle de l'examen préliminaire dans les institutions des cités grecques*, Nancy.
Filonik, J. (2013), 'Athenian Impiety Trials: a Reappraisal', *Dike* 16: 11–96.
Finglass, P. J. (2011), *Sophocles. Ajax*, Cambridge and New York.
Finley, M. I. [1973] (1985), *Democracy Ancient and Modern*, London.
Fisher, N. R. E. (1992), *Hybris: A Study in the Values of Honour and Shame in Ancient Greece*, Warminster.
Fisher, N. R. E. (2000), 'Symposiasts, Fish-Eaters and Flatterers: Social Mobility and Moral Concerns in Old Comedy', in D. Harvey and J. Wilkins (eds), *The Rivals of Aristophanes: Studies in Athenian Old Comedy*, Swansea, pp. 355–96.
Fisher, N. R. E. (2001), *Aeschines: Against Timarchos*, Oxford.
Fisher, N. R. E. (2003), '"Let Envy be Absent": Envy, Liturgies and Reciprocity in Athens', in D. Konstan and K. Rutter (eds), *Envy, Spite and Jealousy: The Rivalrous Emotions in Ancient Greece*, Edinburgh, pp. 181–215.
Fisher, N. R. E. (2011), 'Competitive Delights: The Social Effects of the Expanded Programme of Contests in Post-Kleisthenic Athens', in N. R. E. Fisher and H. van Wees (eds), *Competition in the Ancient World*, Swansea, pp. 175–220.
Flashar, H. (1969), *Der Epitaphios des Perikles: seine Funktion im Geschichtswerk des Thukydides*, Heidelberg.
Forsdyke, S. L. (2012), '"Born from the Earth": The Political Uses of an Athenian Myth', *Journal of Ancient Near Eastern Religions* 12: 119–41.
Fournier, J., and P. Hamon (2007), 'Les orphelins de guerre de Thasos: un nouveau fragment de la stèle des Braves (ca 360–350 av. J.-C.)', *Bulletin de correspondance hellénique* 131/1: 309–81.
Fowler, R. L. (1998), 'Genealogical Thinking, Hesiod's *Catalogue*, and the Creation of the Hellenes', *Proceedings of the Cambridge Philological Society* 44: 1–19.
Fowler, R. L. (1999), 'The Authors Named Pherecydes', *Mnemosyne* 52/1: 1–15.
Fowler, R. L. (2001), 'Early *Historie* and Literacy', in N. Luraghi (ed.), *The Historian's Craft in the Age of Herodotus*, Oxford, pp. 95–115.
Fowler, R. L. (2013), *Early Greek Mythography. Vol. II: Commentary*, Oxford.
Frangeskou, V. (1998–9), 'Tradition and Originality in Some Attic Funeral Orations', *Classical World* 92/4: 315–36.
Frost, F. J. (1984a), 'The Athenian Military before Cleisthenes', *Historia* 33: 283–94.
Frost, F. J. (1984b), 'Plutarch and Theseus', *Classical Bulletin* 60/4: 65–73.
Gantz, T. (1993), *Early Greek myth: a Guide to Literary and Artistic Sources*, Baltimore.
Garver, E. (1994), *Aristotle's Rhetoric: an Art of Character*, Chicago.
Garver, E. (2009), 'Aristotle on the Kinds of Rhetoric', *Rhetorica* 27/1: 1–18.
Garvie, A. F. (2009), *Aeschylus. Persae, with Introduction and Commentary*, Oxford.
Garzya, A. (1956), 'Studi sugli *Eraclidi* di Euripide, I: Il dramma', *Dioniso* 19: 17–40.
Gastaldi, V. (2007), 'Embajadores trágicos: la retórica del κῆρυξ en Heraclidas de Eurípides', *L'Antiquité classique* 76: 39–50.
Geertz, C. (1973), *The Interpretation of Cultures*, New York.
Gehrke, H.-J. (2001), 'Mythos, History, and Collective Identity: Uses of the Past in Ancient Greece and Beyond', in N. Luraghi (ed.), *The Historian's Craft in the Age of Herodotus*, Oxford, pp. 286–313.

Gehrke, H.-J. (2010), 'Greek Representations of the Past', in L. Foxhall, H.-J. Gehrke and N. Luraghi (eds), *Intentional History: Spinning Time in Ancient Greece*, Stuttgart, pp. 15–33.

Gensheimer, M. B. (2017), 'Metaphors for Marathon in the Sculptural Program of the Athenian Treasury at Delphi', *Hesperia* 86/1: 1–42.

Gerber, D. E. (1997), 'General Introduction', in D. E. Gerber (ed.), *A Companion to the Greek Lyric Poets*, Leiden, pp. 1–9.

Gerber, D. E. (1999), *Greek Elegiac Poetry: From the Seventh to the Fifth Centuries BC*, Cambridge, MA.

Giangiulio, M. (2001), 'Constructing the Past: Colonial Traditions and the Writing of History. The Case of Cyrene', in N. Luraghi (ed.), *The Historian's Craft in the Age of Herodotus*, Oxford, pp. 116–37.

Giangiulio, M. (2010), 'Le società ricordano? Paradigmi e problemi della 'memoria collettiva' (a partire da Maurice Halbwachs)', in M. Giangiulio (ed.), *Memorie coloniali*, Roma, pp. 29–43.

Gill, C., N. Postlethwaite and R. Seaford (eds) (1998), *Reciprocity in Ancient Greece*, Oxford.

Godley, A. D. (1920), *Herodotus. The Persian Wars, Volume IV: Books 8–9*, Cambridge, MA.

Goette, H. R. (2007), 'An Archaeological Appendix', in P.J. Wilson (ed.), *The Greek Theatre and Festivals: Documentary Studies*, Oxford, pp. 116–21.

Goette, H. R. (2009), 'Images in the "Demosion Sema"', in O. Palagia (ed.), *Art in Athens during the Peloponnesian War*, Cambridge, pp. 188–206.

Goldhill, S. (1987), 'The Great Dionysia and Civic Ideology', *Journal of Hellenic Studies* 107: 58–76.

Goldhill, S. (1990), 'The Great Dionysia and Civic Ideology', in J. J. Winkler and F. I. Zeitlin (eds), *Nothing to Do with Dionysos? Athenian Drama in Its Social Context*, Princeton, pp. 97–129.

Goldhill, S. (1997), 'The Audience of the Athenian Tragedy', in P. E. Easterling (ed.), *The Cambridge Companion to Greek Tragedy*, Cambridge and New York, pp. 54–68.

Gomme, A. W. (1956), *A Historical Commentary on Thucydides 2: Books II–III*, Oxford.

Gotteland, S. (2001), *Mythe et Rhétorique. Les exemples mythiques dans le discours politique de l'Athènes classique*, Paris.

Gottesman, A. (2014), *Politics and the Street in Democratic Athens*, Cambridge and New York.

Graeber, D. (2011), *Debt: The First 5,000 Years*, New York.

Gray, B. D. (2013), 'The Polis Becomes Humane? *Philanthropia* as a Cardinal Civic Virtue in later Hellenistic Honorific Epigraphy and Historiography', *Studi Ellenistici* 27: 137–62.

Gray, B. D. (2015), *Stasis and Stability: Exile, the Polis, and Political Thought, c. 404–146 BC*, Oxford.

Gray, V. J. (1994a), 'Isocrates' Manipulation of Myth and the Image of Athens, *Panegyricus* 54ff., *Panathenaicus* 168ff.', *Prudentia* 26/1: 83–104.

Gray, V. J. (1994b), 'Images of Sparta: Writer and Audience in Isocrates' *Panathenaicus*', in A. Powell and S. Hodkinson (eds), *The Shadow of Sparta*, London, pp. 223–71.

Griffith, M. (1995), 'Brilliant Dynasts: Power and Politics in the *Oresteia*', *Classical Antiquity* 14/1: 62–129.

Griffith, M. (1998), 'The King and Eye: The Role of the Father in Greek Tragedy', *Proceedings of the Cambridge Philological Society* 44: 20–84.

Griffin, J. (1998), 'The Social Function of Attic Tragedy', *Classical Quarterly* 48/1: 39–61.

Griffin, J. (1999), 'Sophocles and the Democratic City', in J. Griffin (ed.), *Sophocles Revisited: Essays Presented to Sir Hugh Lloyd-Jones*, Oxford, pp. 73–94.

Grethlein, J. (2010), *The Greeks and Their Past: Poetry, Oratory and History in the Fifth Century BCE*, Cambridge.

Halbwachs, M. (1925), *Les cadres sociaux de la mémoire*, Paris.

Halbwachs, M. (1950), *La mémoire collective*, Paris.

Hall, J. M. (1997), *Ethnic Identity in Greek Antiquity*, Cambridge.

Hanink, J. (2013), '*Epitaphioi Mythoi* and Tragedy as Encomium of Athens', *Trends in Classics* 5: 289–317.
Hansen, M. H. (1974), *The Sovereignty of the People's Court in Athens in the fourth century BC and the public action against unconstitutional proposals*, Odense.
Hansen, M. H. (1978), '*Nomos* and *Psephisma* in Fourth-Century Athens', *Greek, Roman, and Byzantine Studies* 19/4: 315–30.
Hansen, M. H. (1979), 'How often did the Athenian *Dicasteria* Meet?', *Greek, Roman, and Byzantine Studies* 20/3: 243–6.
Hansen, M. H. (1983), *The Athenian Ecclesia. A Collection of Articles 1976–1983*, Copenhagen.
Hansen, M. H. (1985), *Demography and Democracy: The Number of Athenian Citizens in the Fourth Century BC*, Herning.
Hansen, M. H. (1987), *The Athenian Assembly in the Age of Demosthenes*, Oxford.
Hansen, M. H. (1989a), 'On the Importance of Institutions in an Analysis of Athenian Democracy', *Classica et Mediaevalia* 40: 107–13.
Hansen, M. H. (1989b), *The Athenian Ecclesia II. A Collection of Articles 1983–89*, Copenhagen.
Hansen, M. H. (1990), 'Review of J. Ober, *Mass and Elite in Democratic Athens*', *Classical Review* 40: 348–56.
Hansen, M. H. [1991] (1999), *Athenian Democracy in the Age of Demosthenes: Structure, Principles and Ideology*, Bristol.
Harding, P. (2008), *The Story of Athens. The Fragments of the Local Chronicles of Attika*, London.
Hardwick, L. (1990), 'Ancient Amazons – Heroes, Outsiders or Women?', *Greece & Rome* 37/1: 14–36.
Harris, E. M. (1990), 'Did the Athenians Regard Seduction as a Worse Crime Than Rape?', *Classical Quarterly* 40/2: 370–7.
Harris, E. M. (1992), 'Pericles' Praise of Athenian Democracy: Thucydides 2.37.1', *Harvard Studies in Classical Philology* 94: 157–67.
Harris, E. M. (2000), 'The Authenticity of Andocides' *De Pace*: A Subversive Essay', in P. Flensted-Jensen, T. H. Nielsen and L. Rubinstein (eds), *Polis & Politics: Studies in Ancient Greek History Presented to Mogens Herman Hansen on his Sixtieth Birthday*, Copenhagen, pp. 479–506.
Harris, E. M. (2006), *Democracy and the Rule of Law in Classical Athens. Essays on Law, Society, and Politics*, Cambridge.
Harris, E. M. (2010), 'Introduction', in E. M. Harris, D. F. Leão and P. J. Rhodes (eds), *Law and Drama in Ancient Greece*, London, pp. 1–24.
Harris, E. M. (2013a), 'How to Address the Athenian Assembly: Rhetoric and Political Tactics in the Debate about Mytilene (Thuc. 3.37–50)', *Classical Quarterly* 63: 94–109.
Harris, E. M. (2013b), *The Rule of Law in Action*, Oxford.
Harris, E. M. (2013c), 'The Plaint in Athenian Law and Legal Procedure', in M. Faraguna (ed.), *Archives and Archival Documents in Ancient Societies*, Trieste, pp. 143–62.
Harris, E. M. (2016a), 'Alcibiades, the Ancestors, Liturgies, and the Etiquette of Addressing the Athenian Assembly', in V. Liotakis and S. Farrington (eds), *The Art of History: Literary Perspectives on Greek and Roman Historiography*, Berlin and Boston, pp. 145–55.
Harris, E. M (2016b), 'From Democracy to the Rule of Law? Constitutional Change in Athens during the Fifth and Fourth Centuries BCE', in C. Tiersch (ed.), *Die athenische Demokratie im 4. Jh.: Zwischen Modernisierung und Tradition*, Stuttgart, pp. 73–88.
Harris, E. M. (2017), 'Rhetoric and Politics', in M. J. MacDonald (ed.), *The Oxford Handbook of Rhetorical Studies*, Oxford and New York, pp. 53–62.
Harris, E. M. (2018), 'Herodotus and the Social Contexts of Memory in Ancient Greece: The Individual Historian and his Community', in Z. Archibald and J. Haywood (eds), *The Power of Individual and Community in Ancient Athens and Beyond: Essays in Honour of John K. Davies*, Swansea, pp. 79–113.

Harris, E. M. (2019), 'Aeschylus' Eumenides. The Role of the Areopagus, the Rule of Law and Political Discourse in Attic Tragedy', in A. Markantonatos and E. Volonaki (eds), *Poet and Orator: A Symbiotic Relationship in Democratic Athens*, Berlin, pp. 389–419.

Harris, E. M., D. F. Leão and P. J. Rhodes (eds) (2010), *Law and Drama in Ancient Greece*, London.

Harrison, A. R. W. (1971), *The Law of Athens. Vol. II: Procedure*, Oxford.

Harrison, E. B. (1966), 'The Composition of the Amazonomachy on the Shield of Athena Parthenos', *Hesperia* 35: 107–33.

Harrison, T. (1997), 'Herodotus and the Ancient Greek Idea of Rape', in S. Deacy and K. Pierce (eds), *Rape in Antiquity*, London, pp. 185–208.

Havelock, E. A. (1978), *The Greek Concept of Justice: From its Shadow in Homer to its Substance in Plato*, Cambridge, MA.

Hay, C. (2001), 'The "Crisis" of Keynesianism and the Rise of Neoliberalism in Britain: an Ideational Institutionalist Approach', in J. L. Campbell and O. Pedersen (eds), *The Rise of Neoliberalism and Institutional Analysis*, Princeton, pp. 193–218.

Hay, C. (2006), 'Constructivist Institutionalism', in R. A. W. Rhodes, S. Binder and B. Rockman (eds), *The Oxford Handbook of Political Institutions*, Oxford, pp. 56–74.

Henrichs, A. (1994–5), '"Why Should I Dance?": Choral Self-Referentiality in Greek Tragedy', *Arion* 3/1: 56–111.

Herman, G. (2006), *Morality and Behaviour in Democratic Athens: A Social History*, Cambridge.

Herrman, J. S. (2008), 'The Authenticity of the Demosthenic *Funeral Oration*', *Acta Antiqua Academiae Scientiarum Hungaricae* 48: 171–8.

Herrman, J. S. (2009), *Hyperides. Funeral Oration*, New York.

Hesk, J. (2011), 'Euripidean *Euboulia* and the Problem of "Tragic Politics"', in D. M. Carter (ed.), *Why Athens? A Reappraisal of Tragic Politics*, Oxford, pp. 119–44.

Hesk, J. (2013), 'Leadership and Individuality in the Athenian Funeral Orations', *Bulletin of the Institute of Classical Studies* 56/1: 49–65.

Hobden, F. (2013), *The Symposion in Ancient Greek Society and Thought*, Cambridge.

Hornblower, S. (1991), *A Commentary on Thucydides. Vol. I: Books I–III*, Oxford.

Hurwit, J. M. (1999), *The Athenian Acropolis. History, Mythology, and Archaeology from the Neolithic Era to the Present*, Cambridge.

Hurwit, J. M. (2004), *The Acropolis in the Age of Pericles*, Cambridge.

Jacoby, F. (1944), '*Patrios Nomos*. State Burial in Athens and the Public Cemetery in the Kerameikos', *Journal of Hellenic Studies* 64: 37–66.

Jacoby, F. (1949), *Atthis. The Local Chronicles of Ancient Athens*, Oxford.

Jameson, F. (2009), *Valences of the Dialectic*, London.

Jameson, M. (2005), 'The Family of Herakles in Attica', in L. Rowlings and H. Bowden (eds), *Herakles and Hercules: Exploring a Graeco-Roman Divinity*, Swansea, pp. 15–36.

Jones, C. P. (1999), *Kinship Diplomacy in the Ancient World*, Cambridge, MA.

Käppel, L. (2000), 'Bakchylides und das System der schorlyrischen Gattungen im 5. Jh. v. Chr.', in A. Bagordo and B. Zimmermann (eds), *Bakchylides: 100 Jahre nach seiner Wiederentdeckung*, München, pp. 11–27.

Kahn, C. H. (1963), 'Plato's Funeral Oration: The Motive of the *Menexenus*', *Classical Philology* 58: 220–34.

Kakridis, J. T. (1961), *Der Thukydideische Epitaphios: ein stilistischer Kommentar*, München.

Kapparis, K. (1999), *Apollodoros 'Against Neaira' [D 59]*, Berlin.

Kasimis, D. (2013), 'The Tragedy of Blood-Based Membership: Secrecy and the Politics of Immigration in Euripides' *Ion*', *Political Theory* 41: 231–56.

Kennedy, G. A. [1991] (2007), *Aristotle. On Rhetoric: a Theory of Civic Discourse*, Oxford and New York.

Kirk, G. S. (1970), *Myth, its Meaning and Functions in Ancient and Other Cultures*, Cambridge.
Kirk, G. S. (1985), *The Iliad: A Commentary. Volume 1, Books 1–4*, Cambridge.
Kirk, G. S. (1990), *The Iliad: A Commentary. Volume 2, Books 5–8*, Cambridge.
Konstan, D. (2001), *Pity Transformed*, London.
Konstan, D. (2005), 'Pity and Politics', in R. H. Sternberg (ed.), *Pity and Power in Ancient Athens*, Cambridge, pp. 48–66.
Konstan, D. (2006), *The Emotions of the Ancient Greeks: Studies in Aristotle and Classical Literature*, Toronto.
Konstantinou, A. (2015), 'Tradition and Innovation in Greek Tragedy's Mythological Exempla', *Classical Quarterly* 65/2: 476–88.
Kosmopoulou, A. (2001), 'Working Women: Female Professionals on Classical Attic Gravestones', *Annual of the British School at Athens* 96: 281–319.
Kovacs, D. (1994), *Euripides: Cyclops; Alcestis; Medea*, Cambridge, MA.
Kovacs, D. (1995), *Euripides: Children of Heracles; Hippolytus; Andromache; Hecuba*, Cambridge, MA.
Kowalzig, B., and P. J. Wilson (2013), 'Introduction: The World of Dithyramb', in B. Kowalzig and P. J. Wilson (eds), *Dithyramb in Context*, Oxford, pp. 1–28.
Kron, U. (1976), *Die zehn attischen Phylenheroen: Geschichte, Mythos, Kult und Darstellungen*, Berlin.
Kurke, L. (1991), *The Traffic in Praise. Pindar and the Poetics of Social Economy*, Ithaca.
Kyle, D. G. (1992), 'The Panathenaic Games: Sacred and Civic Athletics', in J. Neils (ed.), *Goddess and Polis. The Panathenaic Festival in Ancient Athens*, Hanover, NH and Princeton, pp. 77–101.
Kyriakou, P. (2006), *A Commentary on Euripides' Iphigenia in Tauris*, Berlin.
Lamb, W. R. M. (1930), *Lysias*, Cambridge, MA.
Lambert, S. D. (2011), 'What Was the Point of Inscribed Honorific Decrees in Classical Athens', in S. D. Lambert (ed.), *Sociable Man: Essays in Ancient Greek Social Behaviour in Honour of Nick Fisher*, Swansea, pp. 193–214.
Lambert, S. D. (2012), *Inscribed Athenian Laws and Decrees 352/1–322/1 BC. Epigraphical Essays*, Leiden and Boston.
Lambert, S. D. (2018), *Inscribed Athenian Laws and Decrees in the Age of Demosthenes: Historical Essays*, Leiden and Boston.
Langdon, M. K. (2015), 'Herders' Graffiti', in A. P. Matthaiou and N. Papazarkadas (eds), *ΑΕΩΝ: Studies in Honor of Ronald S. Stroud*, Athens, pp. 49–58.
Lanni, A. M. (2006), *Law and Justice in the Courts of Classical Athens*, Cambridge and New York.
Lanni, A. M. (2016), *Law and Order in Ancient Athens*, Cambridge and New York.
Lape, S. (2010), *Race and Citizen Identity in the Classical Athenian Democracy*, Cambridge.
Leão, D. F. (2010), 'The Legal Horizon of the *Oresteia*: the Crime of Homicide and the Founding of the Areopagus', in E. M. Harris, D. F. Leão and P. J. Rhodes (eds), *Law and Drama in Ancient Greece*, London, pp. 39–60.
Leão, D. F. (2012), 'The Myth of Autochthony, Athenian Citizenship and the Right of *Enktesis*: a Legal Approach to Euripides' *Ion*', in B. Legras and G. Thür (eds), *Symposion 2011. Vorträge zur griechischen und hellenistischen Rechtsgeschichte*, Wien, pp. 135–52.
Leão, D. F., and M. do Céu Fialho (2008), *Plutarco. Vidas Paralelas – Teseu e Rómulo*, Coimbra.
Lee, K. H. (1997), *Euripides: Ion*, Warminster.
Lévi-Strauss, C. [1958] (1963), *Structural Anthropology*, trans. C. Jacobson, New York.
Liddel, P. (2007), *Civic Obligation and Individual Liberty in Ancient Athens*, Oxford and New York.
Lissarrague, F. (2001), *Greek Vases: the Athenians and Their Images*, New York.
Lloyd, M. (1992), *The Agon in Euripides*, Oxford.
Lloyd-Jones, H. (1996), *Sophocles: Fragments*, Cambridge, MA and London.

Longo, O. (2000), *Tucidide. Epitafio di Pericle per i caduti del primo anno di guerra*, Venezia.
Loraux, N. (1979), 'L'autochtonie: Une topique athénienne: le mythe dans l'espace civique', *Annales. Économies, Sociétés, Civilisations* 34: 3–26.
Loraux, N. (1981), *L'invention d'Athènes: Histoire de l'oraison funèbre dans la cité classique*, Paris.
Loraux, N. [1981] (1993), *The Children of Athena: Athenian Ideas about Citizenship and the Division between the Sexes*, trans. C. Levine, Princeton.
Loraux, N. [1996] (2000), *Born of the Earth: Myth and Politics in Athens*, trans. S. Stewart, Ithaca.
Loraux, N. [1997] (2002), *The Divided City: on Memory and Forgetting in Ancient Athens*, trans. C. Pache and J. Fort, New York.
Low, P. (2003), 'Remembering War in Fifth-Century Greece: Ideologies, Societies, and Commemoration beyond Democratic Athens', *World Archaeology* 35/1: 98–111.
Low, P. (2007), *Interstate Relations in Classical Greece. Morality and Power*, Cambridge.
Low, P. (2010), 'Commemoration of the War Dead in Classical Athens: Remembering Defeat and Victory', in D. M. Pritchard (ed.), *War, Democracy and Culture in Classical Athens*, Cambridge, pp. 341–58.
Low, P. (2012), 'The Monuments to the War Dead in Classical Athens: Form, Contexts, Meanings', in P. Low, G. J. Oliver and P. J. Rhodes (eds), *Cultures of Commemoration: War Memorials, Ancient and Modern*, Oxford, pp. 13–39.
Lowndes, V., and M. Roberts (2013), *Why Institutions Matter. The New Institutionalism in Political Science*, Basingstoke.
Luraghi, N. (2008), *The Ancient Messenians. Constructions of Ethnicity and Memory*, Cambridge.
Luraghi, N. (2010), 'The Demos as Narrator: Public Honors and the Construction of Future and Past', in L. Foxhall, H.-J. Gehrke, and N. Luraghi (eds), *Intentional History: Spinning Time*, Stuttgart, pp. 247–63.
Luraghi, N. (2014), 'Ephorus in Context: The Return of the Heraclidae and Fourth-century Peloponnesian Politics', in G. Parmeggiani (ed.), *Between Thucydides and Polybius: The Golden Age of Greek Historiography*, Cambridge, MA and London, pp. 133–51.
Lynch, K. M. (2011), *The Symposium in Context: Pottery from a Late Archaic House near the Athenian Agora*, Athens.
Lynch, K. M. (2013), 'Drinking and Dining', in T. J. Smith and D. Plantzos (eds), *A Companion to Greek Art*, Oxford and Malden, MA, pp. 531–41.
Ma, J. (2009), 'The City as Memory', in G. Boys-Stones, B. Graziosi and P. Vasunia (eds), *The Oxford Handbook of Hellenic Studies*, Oxford, pp. 248–59.
MacDowell, D. M. (1976), 'Hybris in Athens', *Greece & Rome* 23/1: 14–31.
MacDowell, D. M. (2000), *Demosthenes: On the False Embassy (Oration 19)*, Oxford and New York.
MacDowell, D. M. (2009), *Demosthenes the Orator*, Oxford and New York.
Mack, W. (2015), *Proxeny and Polis: Institutional Networks in the Ancient Greek World*, Oxford.
Mack, W. (2018), 'Vox Populi, Vox Deorum? Athenian Document Reliefs and the Theologies of Public Inscription', *Annual of the British School at Athens* 113: 365–98.
Mackenzie, M. M. (1981), *Plato on Punishment*, Berkeley and Los Angeles.
Macleod, C. W. (1978), 'Reason and Necessity. Thucydides III 9–14, 37–48', *Journal of Hellenic Studies* 98: 64–78.
Maehler, H. (2004), *Bacchylides: a Selection*, Cambridge.
Malkin, I. (1994), *Myth and Territory in the Spartan Mediterranean*, Cambridge and New York.
Mann, C. (2007), *Die Demagogen und das Volk. Zur politischen Kommunikation im Athen des 5. Jahrhunderts v. Chr. (Klio, Beiträge zur Alten Geschichte, Beihefte, Neue Folge Band 13)*, Berlin.

Mannheim, K. [1929] (1936), *Ideology and Utopia: An Introduction to the Sociology of Knowledge*, trans. L. Wirth and E. Shils, London.
March, J. G., and J. P. Olsen (1984), 'The New Institutionalism: Organizational Factors in Political Life', *The American Political Science Review* 78/3: 734–49.
March, J. G., and J. P. Olsen (2006), 'Elaborating the "New Institutionalism"', in R. A. W. Rhodes, S. A. Binder and B. A. Rockman (eds), *The Oxford Handbook of Political Institutions*, Oxford, pp. 3–20.
Marincola, J. (2010), 'Speeches in Classical Historiography', in J. Marincola (ed.), *A Companion to Greek and Roman Historiography*, Chichester, pp. 294–324.
Martin, G. (2018), *Euripides, Ion. Edition and Commentary*, Berlin.
Martin, R. P. (1989), *The Language of Heroes: Speech and Performance in the Iliad*, Ithaca.
Marx, K., and F. Engels [1932] (1938), *The German Ideology*, trans. W. Lough and C. P. Magill, London.
Mayor, A. (2014), *The Amazons: Lives and Legends of Warrior Women across the Ancient World*, Princeton.
Mendelsohn, D. (2002), *Gender and the City in Euripides' Political Plays*, Oxford.
Meyer, R. E., K. Sahlin, M. J. Ventresca and P. Walgenbach (2009), 'Ideology and Institutions: Introduction', in R. E. Meyer, K. Sahlin, M. J. Ventresca and P. Walgenbach (eds), *Institutions and Ideology*, Bingley, pp. 1–15.
Millett, P. (1998), 'The Rhetoric of Reciprocity in Classical Athens', in C. Gill, N. Postlethwaite and R. Seaford (eds), *Reciprocity in Ancient Greece*, Oxford, pp. 227–53.
Mills, S. (1997), *Theseus, Tragedy, and the Athenian Empire*, Oxford and New York.
Mirhady, D. C., and Y. L. Too (2000), *The Oratory of Classical Greece: Isocrates. I*, Austin.
Missiou, A. (1998), 'Reciprocal Generosity in the Foreign Affairs of Fifth-Century Athens and Sparta', in C. Gill, N. Postlethwaite and R. Seaford (eds), *Reciprocity in Ancient Greece*, Oxford, pp. 181–97.
Missiou, A. (2011), *Literacy and Democracy in Fifth-Century Athens*, Cambridge and New York.
Mitchell, L. G. (1997), *Greeks Bearing Gifts: The Public Use of Private Relationships in the Greek World, 435–323 BC*, Cambridge.
Monoson, S. S. (1994), 'Citizen as Erastes: Erotic Imagery and the Idea of Reciprocity in the Periclean Funeral Oration', *Political Theory* 22/2: 253–76.
Monoson, S. S. (1998), 'Remembering Pericles: The Political and Theoretical Import of Plato's *Menexenus*', *Political Theory* 26/4: 489–513.
Morris, I. (1992), *Death-Ritual and Social Structure in Classical Antiquity*, Cambridge and New York.
Morris, I. (1994), 'Everyman's Grave', in A. L. Boegehold and A. D. Scafuro (eds), *Athenian Identity and Civic Ideology*, Baltimore, pp. 67–101.
Morrison, A. D. (2007), *Performances and Audiences in Pindar's Victory Odes*, London.
Morwood, J. (2007), *Euripides. Suppliant Women*, Oxford.
Morwood, J. (2012), 'Euripides' *Suppliant Women*, Theseus and Athenocentrism', *Mnemosyne* 65: 552–64.
Murray, O. (1990a), 'Sympotic History', in O. Murray (ed.), *Sympotica: a Symposium on the Symposion*, Oxford, pp. 3–13.
Murray, O. (1990b), 'The Affair of the Mysteries: Democracy and the Drinking Group', in O. Murray (ed.), *Sympotica: a Symposium on the Symposion*, Oxford, pp. 149–61
Murray, O. [1980] (1993), *Early Greece*, Cambridge, MA.
Mylonas, G. E. (1975), *Τὸ δυτικὸν νεκροταφεῖον τῆς Ἐλευσῖνος* II, Athens.
Nagy, G. (2002), *Plato's Rhapsody and Homer's Music: the Poetics of the Panathenaic Festival in Classical Athens*, Cambridge, MA and London.
Naiden, F. S. (2006), *Ancient Supplication*, Oxford and New York.
Naiden, F. S. (2016), 'Contagious Ἀσέβεια', *Classical Quarterly* 66/1: 59–74.

Neer, R. (2004), 'The Athenian Treasury at Delphi and the Material of Politics', *Classical Antiquity* 23/1: 63–93.
Neils, J. (1992), 'The Panathenaia: An Introduction', in J. Neils (ed.), *Goddess and Polis. The Panathenaic Festival in Ancient Athens*, Hanover, NH and Princeton, pp. 13–27.
Neils, J. (2001), *The Parthenon Frieze*, Cambridge.
Nervegna, S. (2007), 'Staging Scenes or Plays? Theatrical Revivals of "Old" Greek Drama in Antiquity', *Zeitschrift für Papyrologie und Epigraphik* 162: 14–42.
Norlin, G. (1929), *Isocrates. On the Peace. Areopagiticus. Against the Sophists. Antidosis. Panathenaicus*, Cambridge, MA.
Nouhaud, M. (1982), *L'utilisation de l'histoire par les orateurs attiques*, Paris.
Ober, J. (1989a), *Mass and Elite in Democratic Athens. Rhetoric, Ideology, and the Power of the People*, Princeton.
Ober, J. (1989b), 'Review of M. H. Hansen, *The Athenian Assembly in the Age of Demosthenes*', *Classical Philology* 84: 322–34.
Ober, J. (1998), *Political Dissent in Democratic Athens: Intellectual Critics of Popular Rule*, Princeton.
Ober, J. (2008), *Democracy and Knowledge: Innovation and Learning in Classical Athens*, Princeton.
Ober, J. (2016), 'Mass and Elite Revisited', in R. Evans (ed.), *Mass and Elite in the Greek and Roman World: From Sparta to Late Antiquity*, London, pp. 1–10.
Ogden, D. (1996), *Greek Bastardy in the Classical and Hellenistic Periods*, Oxford.
Olson, D. (2002), *Aristophanes. Acharnians. Edited with Introduction and Commentary*, Oxford.
Osborne, M. J. (1983), *Naturalization in Athens. Volumes III and IV (Verhandelingen van de koninglijke Academie voor Wetenschapen, Letteren en Schone Kunsten van België)*, Bruxelles.
Osborne, R. (1985), *Demos: The Discovery of Classical Attika*, Cambridge.
Ostwald, M. (1986), *From Popular Sovereignty to the Sovereignty of the Law. Law, Society and Politics in Fifth-Century Athens*, Berkeley.
Pàmias i Massana, J. (2008), *Ferecides d'Atenes, Històries. Vol. I–II. Introducció, edició crítica, traducció i notes*, Barcelona.
Papillon, T. L. (2004), *The Oratory of Classical Greece: Isocrates II*, Austin.
Pappas, N., and M. Zelcer (2015), *Politics and Philosophy in Plato's Menexenus: Education and Rhetoric, Myth and History*, London and New York.
Pariente, A. (1992), 'Le monument argien des *Sept contre Thèbes*', in M. Piérart (ed.), *Polydipsion Argos: Argos de la fin des palais mycéniens à la constitution de l'état classique*, Athens, pp. 195–229.
Parke, H. W. (1977), *Festivals of the Athenians*, London.
Parker, R. C. T. (1987), 'Myths of Early Athens', in J. Bremmer (ed.), *Interpretations of Greek Mythology*, London, pp. 187–214.
Parker, R. C. T. (1996a), *Athenian Religion*, Oxford.
Parker, R. C. T. (1996b), 'Chthonian Gods', in S. Hornblower and A. Spawforth (eds), *Oxford Classical Dictionary*, 3rd edn, Oxford, pp. 329–30.
Parker, R.C. T. [1983] (1996c), *Miasma. Pollution and Purification in Early Greek Religion*, Oxford.
Parker, R. C. T. (1998), *Cleomenes on the Acropolis: An Inaugural Lecture Delivered before the University of Oxford on 12 May 1997*, Oxford.
Parker, R. C. T. (2005), *Polytheism and Society at Athens*, Oxford.
Patterson, C. (2006), '"Citizen Cemeteries" in Classical Athens?', *Classical Quarterly* 56: 48–56.
Pébarthe, C. (2006), *Cité, démocratie et écriture. Histoire de l'alphabétisation d'Athènes à l'époque classique*, Paris.
Pelling, C. (2002), *Plutarch and History*, London.
Pelling, C. (2009), 'Bringing Autochthony Up-to-Date: Herodotus and Thucydides', *Classical World* 102: 471–83.

Pepe, C. (2013), *The Genres of Rhetorical Speeches in Greek and Roman Antiquity*, Leiden.
Petrovic, A. (2016), 'Casualty Lists in Performance: Name Catalogues and Greek Verse-Inscriptions', in E. Sistakou and A. Rengakos (eds), *Dialect, Diction, and Style in Greek Literary and Inscribed Epigram*, Berlin, pp. 361–90.
Petruzziello, L. (2009), *Epitafio per i caduti del primo anno della guerra lamiaca: PLit. Lond. 133v. Iperide; introd., testo critico, trad. e commento*, Pisa.
Pickard-Cambridge, A. W. (1927), *Dithyramb, Tragedy and Comedy*, Oxford.
Pickard-Cambridge, A. W. (1946), *The Theatre of Dionysus in Athens*, Oxford.
Pickard-Cambridge, A. W. [1953] (1968), *The Dramatic Festivals at Athens*, 2nd edn rev. J. Gould and D. M. Lewis, Oxford.
Pierrot, A. (2015), 'Who were the *Eupatrids* in Archaic Athens?', in N. R. E. Fisher and H. van Wees (eds), *'Aristocracy' in Antiquity: Redefining Greek and Roman Elites*, Swansea, pp. 147–68.
Piovan, D. (2011), *Memoria e oblio della Guerra civile. Strategie giudiziarie e racconto del passato in Lisia*, Pisa.
Podlecki, A. J. (1966), *The Political Background of Aeschylean Tragedy*, Ann Arbor.
Podlecki, A. J. (1971), 'Cimon, Skyros and "Theseus' Bones"', *Journal of Hellenic Studies* 91: 141–3.
Pope, M. (1986), 'Athenian Festival Judges. Seven, Five, or However Many', *Classical Quarterly* 36: 322–6.
Postlethwaite, N. (1998), 'Akhilleus and Agamemnon: Generalized Reciprocity', in C. Gill, N. Postlethwaite and R. Seaford (eds), *Reciprocity in Ancient Greece*, Oxford, pp. 93–104.
Prinz, K. (1997), *Epitaphios Logos. Struktur, Funktion und Bedeutung der Bestattungsreden im Athen des 5. Und 4. Jahrhunderts*, Frankfurt am Main.
Pritchard, D. M. (1996), 'Thucydides and the Tradition of the Athenian Funeral Oration', *Ancient History* 26/2: 137–50.
Pritchard, D. M. (2004), 'Kleisthenes, Participation and the Dithyrambic Contests of Late Archaic and Classical Athens', *Phoenix* 58: 208–28.
Pritchard, D. M. (2014), 'The Position of Attic Women in Democratic Athens', *Greece & Rome* 61/2: 174–93.
Pritchett, W. K. (1985), *The Greek State at War, IV*, Berkeley and Los Angeles.
Proietti, G. (2012), 'Memoria collettiva e identità etnica: nuovi paradigmi teorico-metodologici nella ricerca storica', in E. Franchi and G. Proietti (eds), *Forme della memoria e dinamiche identitarie dell'antichità greco-romana*, Trento, pp. 13–41.
Proietti, G. (2013), 'The Marathon Epitaph from Eua-Loukou: Some Notes about Its Text and Historical Context', *Zeitschrift für Papyrologie und Epigraphik* 185: 24–30.
Race, W. H. (1997), *Pindar. Nemean Odes. Isthmian Odes. Fragments*, Cambridge, MA.
Rhodes, P. J. (1972), *The Athenian Boule*, Oxford.
Rhodes, P. J. (1981), *A Commentary on the Aristotelian Athenaion Politeia*, Oxford.
Rhodes, P. J. (2003), 'Nothing to Do with Democracy: Athenian Drama and the *Polis*', *Journal of Hellenic Studies* 123: 104–19.
Rhodes, P. J. (2004), 'Keeping to the Point', in E. M. Harris and L. Rubinstein (eds), *The Law and the Courts in Ancient Greece*, London, pp. 137–58.
Rhodes, P. J. (2016), 'Demagogues and *Demos* in Athens', *Polis* 33: 243–64.
Rhodes, P. J., and D. M. Lewis (1997), *The Decrees of Greek City-States*, Oxford.
Ricoeur, P. (1986), *Lectures on Ideology and Utopia*, New York.
de Romilly, J. (1972), 'Vocabulaire et propagande ou les premiers emplois du mot ὁμόνοια', in A. Ernout (éd.), *Mélanges de linguistique et de philologie grecques offerts à P. Chantraine*, Paris, pp. 199–209.
de Romilly, J. (1979), *La douceur dans la pensée grecque*, Paris.

Rose, P. W. (2006), 'Divorcing Ideology from Marxism and Marxism from Ideology: Some Problems', *Arethusa* 39/1: 101–36.

Rose, P. W. (2012), *Class in Archaic Greece*, Cambridge.

Roselli, D. K. (2011), *Theater of the People. Spectators and Society in Ancient Athens*, Austin.

Rösler, W. (1990), '*Mnemosyne* in the *Symposion*', in O. Murray (ed.), *Sympotica: a Symposium on the Symposion*, Oxford, pp. 230–7.

Rosivach, V. J. (1987), 'Autochthony and the Athenians', *Classical Quarterly* 37: 294–306.

Roth, P. (2003), *Der Panathenaikos des Isokrates: Übersetzung und Kommentar*, München.

Rubinstein, L. (1993), *Adoption in IV. Century Athens*, Copenhagen.

Rutherford, I. (2011), 'Singing Myth: Pindar', in K. Dowden and N. Livingstone (eds), *A Companion to Greek Mythology*, Oxford, pp. 107–23.

Sahlins, M. D. (1972), *Stone Age Economics*, Chicago.

Sanders, E. (2014), *Envy and Jealousy in Classical Athens: A Socio-Psychological Approach*, Oxford and New York.

Saunders, T. J. (1991), *Plato's Penal Code: Tradition, Controversy, and Reform in Greek Penology*, Oxford.

Saxonhouse, A. W. (1986), 'Myths and the Origins of Cities: Reflections on the Autochthony Theme in Euripides' *Ion*', in J. P. Euben (ed.), *Greek Tragedy and Political Theory*, Berkeley and Los Angeles, pp. 252–73.

Schedler, A. (1996), 'Anti-Political Establishment Parties', *Party Politics* 2/3: 291–312.

Schmidt, V. A. (2002), *The Futures of European Capitalism*, Oxford.

Schmidt, V. A. (2006), 'Give Peace a Chance: Reconciling the Four (not Three) New Institutionalisms in Political Science', presented at *Annu. Meet. Am. Polit. Sci. Assoc.*, Philadelphia.

Schmidt, V. A. (2008), 'Discursive Institutionalism: The Explanatory Power of Ideas and Discourse', *Annual Review of Political Science* 11: 303–26.

Schmidt, V. A. (2010), 'Taking Ideas and Discourse Seriously: Explaining Change Through Discursive Institutionalism as the Fourth "New Institutionalism"', *European Political Science Review* 2/1: 1–25.

Schwinge, E.-R. (1992), 'Griechische Tragödie: das Problem ihrer Zeitlichkeit', *Antike und Abendland* 38: 48–66.

Scullion, S. (2002), 'Tragic Dates', *Classical Quarterly* 52/1: 81–101.

Scully, S. E. (1973), *Philia and Charis in Euripidean Tragedy*, PhD dissertation, University of Toronto.

Seaford, R. (1994), *Reciprocity and Ritual: Homer and Tragedy in the Developing City-State*, Oxford and New York.

Seaford, R. (1998), 'Introduction', in C. Gill, N. Postlethwaite and R. Seaford (eds), *Reciprocity in Ancient Greece*, Oxford, pp. 1–11.

Shapiro, H. A. (1983), 'Amazons, Thracians, and Scythians', *Greek, Roman, and Byzantine Studies* 24/2: 105–14.

Shapiro, H. A. (1992), '*Mousikoi Agones*: Music and Poetry at the Panathenaia', in J. Neils (ed.), *Goddess and Polis. The Panathenaic Festival in Ancient Athens*, Hanover, NH and Princeton, pp. 53–75.

Shapiro, H. A. (1998), 'Autochthony and the Visual Arts in Fifth-Century Athens', in D. Boedeker and K. A. Raaflaub (eds), *Democracy, Empire and the Arts in Fifth-Century Athens*, Cambridge, MA and London, pp. 127–52.

Shear, J. L. (2001), *Polis and Panathenaia: The History and Development of Athena's Festival*, PhD dissertation, University of Pennsylvania.

Shear, J. L. (2011), *Polis and Revolution: Responding to Oligarchy in Classical Athens*, Cambridge.

Shear, J. L. (2013), 'Their Memories Will Never Grow Old: The Politics of Remembrance in the Athenian Funeral Orations', *Classical Quarterly* 63/2: 511–36.
Simonton, M. (2017), *Classical Greek Oligarchy: A Political History*, Princeton and Oxford.
Sobak, R. (2015), 'Sokrates among the Shoemakers', *Hesperia* 84/4: 669–712.
Sommerstein, A. H. (1997), 'The Theatre Audience, the *Demos*, and the *Suppliants* of Aeschylus', in C. Pelling (ed.), *Greek Tragedy and the Historian*, Oxford, pp. 63–80.
Sommerstein, A. H. (2008), *Aeschylus: Fragments*, Cambridge, MA.
Sommerstein, A. H. (2009), *Aeschylus: Oresteia. Agamemnon. Libation-Bearers*, Cambridge, MA.
Sommerstein, A. H. (2010), *Aeschylean Tragedy*, London.
Sourvinou-Inwood, C. (2011), *Athenian Myths and Festivals: Erechtheus, Plynteria, Panathenaia, Dionysia*, ed. R. C. T. Parker, Oxford.
Stansbury-O'Donnell, M. D. (2005), 'The Painting Program in the *Stoa Poikile*', in J. M. Barringer and J. M. Hurwit (eds), *Periklean Athens and its Legacy: Problems and Perspectives*, Austin, pp. 73–87.
de Ste Croix, G. E. M. (1981), *The Class Struggle in the Ancient Greek World from the Archaic Age to the Arab Conquest*, London.
Steinbock, B. (2013a), *Social Memory in Athenian Public Discourse*, Ann Arbor.
Steinbock, B. (2013b), 'Contesting the Lessons from the Past: Aeschines' Use of Social Memory', *Transactions of the American Philological Association* 143: 65–103.
Stewart, A. (1995), 'Imag(in)ing the Other: Amazons and Ethnicity in Fifth-Century Athens', *Poetics Today* 16/4: 571–97.
Stewart, E. (2017), *Greek Tragedy on the Move: The Birth of a Panhellenic Art Form c. 500–300 BC*, Oxford.
Storey, I. C. (2008), *Euripides: Suppliant Women*, London.
Stoupa, C. (1997), 'Ὁδός Σαλαμίνος 35', *Archaiologikon Deltion* 52/B1: 52–6.
Stupperich, R. (1977), *Staatsbegräbnis und Privatgrabmal im klassischen Athen*, Münster.
Tacon, J. (2001), 'Ecclesiastic *Thorubos*: Interventions, Interruptions, and Popular Involvement in the Athenian Assembly', *Greece & Rome* 48: 173–92.
Taylor, C. (2017), *Poverty, Wealth, and Well-Being: Experiencing Penia in Democratic Athens*, Oxford.
Taylor, C., and K. Vlassopoulos (eds) (2015), *Communities and Networks in the Ancient Greek World*, Oxford.
Tentori Montalto, M. (2014), 'La stele dei caduti della tribù Erechtheis dalla villa di Erode Attico a Loukou – Eva Kynourias (SEG LVI 430)', *Zeitschrift für Papyrologie und Epigraphik* 192: 34–44.
Thériault, G. (1996), *Le culte d'Homonoia dans les cités grecques*, Québec.
Theunissen, M. (2000), *Pindar: Menschenlos und Wende der Zeit*, München.
Thomas, R. (1989), *Oral Tradition and Written Record in Classical Athens*, Cambridge and New York.
Thomas, R. (2016), 'Performance, Audience Participation and the Dynamics of Fourth-Century Assembly and Jury-Courts of Athens', in C. Tiersch (ed.), *Athenische Demokratie im 4. Jh.: Zwischen Modernisierung und Tradition*, Stuttgart, pp. 89–107.
Thomas, R. (2019), *Polis Histories, Collective Memories and the Greek World*, Cambridge.
Thompson, H. A. (1982), 'The Pnyx in Models', *Hesperia Supplements* 19: 133–47 and 224–7.
Thompson, H. A., and R. E. Wycherley (1972), *The Agora of Athens: The History, Shape and Uses of an Ancient City Center (The Athenian Agora: Results of Excavations Conducted by the American School of Classical Studies at Athens, Vol. XIV)*, Princeton.
Thompson, J. B. (1990), *Ideology and Modern Culture: Critical Social Theory in the Era of Mass Communication*, Cambridge.

Thür, G. (2008), 'The Principle of Fairness in Athenian Legal Procedure: Thoughts on the *Echinos* and *Enklema*', *Dike* 11: 51–74.
Tober, D. (2017), 'Greek Local Historiography and its Audiences', *Classical Quarterly* 67/2: 420–84.
Todd, S. C. (2007), *A Commentary on Lysias*, Oxford and New York.
Too, Y. L. (1995), *The Rhetoric of Identity in Isocrates: Text, Power, Pedagogy*, Cambridge.
Townsend, R. F. (1995), *The East Side of the Agora: The Remains Beneath the Stoa of Attalos (The Athenian Agora: Results of Excavations Conducted by the American School of Classical Studies at Athens, Vol. XXVII)*, Princeton.
Tracy, S. V. (2007), 'Games at the lesser Panathenaia?', in O. Palagia and A. Choremi-Spetsieri (eds), *The Panathenaic Games: Proceedings of an International Conference held at the University of Athens, May 11–12, 2004*, Oxford, pp. 53–7.
Trevett, J. (1990), 'History in [Demosthenes] 59', *Classical Quarterly* 40: 407–20.
Trevett, J. (1992), *Apollodoros, the Son of Pasion*, Oxford.
Trivigno, F. V. (2009), 'The Rhetoric of Parody in Plato's *Menexenus*', *Philosophy and Rhetoric* 42: 29–58.
Tsitsiridis, S. (1998), *Platons Menexenos: Einleitung, Text und Kommentar*, Stuttgart.
Tyrrell, W. B. (1984), *Amazons. A Study in Athenian Mythmaking*, Baltimore.
Tyrrell, W. B., and F. S. Brown (1991), *Athenian Myths and Institutions: Words in Action*, Oxford and New York.
Tzanetou, A. (2012), *City of Suppliants: Tragedy and the Athenian Empire*, Austin.
Usher, S. (1990), *Isocrates: Panegyricus and To Nicocles*, Warminster.
Vansina, J. (1985), *Oral Tradition as History*, Madison, WI.
Veness, R. (2002), 'Investing the Barbarian? The Dress of Amazons in Athenian Art', in L. Llewellyn-Jones (ed.), *Women's Dress in the Ancient Greek World*, Swansea, pp. 95–110.
Vernant, J.-P. [1974] (1988), *Myth and Society in Ancient Greece*, trans. J. Lloyd, New York.
Veyne, P. [1983] (1988), *Did the Greeks Believe in their Myths? An Essay on the Constitutive Imagination*, trans. P. Wissing, Chicago.
Vickers, M. J. (2008), *Sophocles and Alcibiades: Athenian Politics in Ancient Greek Literature*, Stocksfield.
Vlassopoulos, K. (2007), 'Free Spaces: Identity, Experience and Democracy in Classical Athens', *Classical Quarterly* 57/1: 33–52.
Walbank, F. W. (1985), *Selected Papers: Studies in Greek and Roman History and Historiography*, Cambridge.
Walcot, P. (1978), *Envy and the Greeks: A Study of Human Behaviour*, Warminster.
Walker, H. J. (1995), *Theseus and Athens*, Oxford and New York.
Wallace, R. W. (1989), *The Areopagus Council to 307 BC*, Baltimore and London.
Wallace, R. W. (1997), 'Poet, Public, and "Theatrocracy": Audience Performance in Classical Athens', in L. Edmunds and R. W. Wallace (eds), *Poet, Public, and Performance in Ancient Greece*, Baltimore and London, pp. 97–111.
Walsh, G. B. (1978), 'The Rhetoric of Birthright and Race in Euripides' *Ion*', *Hermes* 106: 301–15.
Walters, K. R. (1980), 'Rhetoric as Ritual: The Semiotics of the Attic Funeral Oration', *Florilegium* 2: 1–27.
Węcowski, M. (2014), *The Rise of the Greek Aristocratic Banquet*, Oxford.
van Wees, H. (1998), 'The Law of Gratitude: Reciprocity in Anthropological Theory', in C. Gill, N. Postlethwaite and R. Seaford (eds), *Reciprocity in Ancient Greece*, Oxford, pp. 13–49.
van Wees, H. (2000), 'Megara's Mafiosi: Timocracy and Violence in Theognis', in R. Brock and S. Hodkinson (eds), *Alternatives to Athens: Varieties of Political Organisation and Community in Ancient Greece*, Oxford, pp. 52–67.

van Wees, H. (2013), *Ships and Silver, Taxes and Tribute: A Fiscal History of Archaic Athens*, London.
van Wees, H., and N. R. E. Fisher (2015), 'The Trouble with "Aristocracy"', in N. R. E. Fisher and H. van Wees (eds), *'Aristocracy' in Antiquity. Redefining Greek and Roman Elites*, Swansea, pp. 1–57.
West, M. L. (1989), 'The Early Chronology of Attic Tragedy', *Classical Quarterly* 39: 251–4.
Westwood, G. (2017), 'The Orator and the Ghost: Performing the Past in Fourth-Century Athens', in S. Papaioannou, A. Serafim and B. da Vela (eds), *The Theatre of Justice. Aspects of Performance in Greco-Roman Oratory and Rhetoric*, Leiden, pp. 57–74.
Westwood, G. (2018), 'Views on the Past', in G. Martin (ed.), *The Oxford Handbook of Demosthenes*, Oxford, pp. 179–90.
Whitehead, D. (1977), *The Ideology of the Athenian Metic*, Cambridge.
Whitehead, D. (1983), 'Competitive Outlay and Community Profit: ΦΙΛΟΤΙΜΙΑ in Democratic Athens', *Classica et Mediaevalia* 34: 55–74.
Wilkins, J. (1993), *Euripides: Heraclidae*, Oxford.
Wilson, J. (1982), 'What Does Thucydides Claim for His Speeches?', *Phoenix* 36/2: 95–103.
Wilson, P. J. (2000), *The Athenian Institution of the Khoregia*, Cambridge.
Winnington-Ingram, R. P. (1948), 'Clytemnestra and the Vote of Athena', *Journal of Hellenic Studies* 68: 130–47.
Wolpert, A. (2002), *Remembering Defeat: Civil War and Civic Memory in Ancient Athens*, Baltimore.
Worthington, I. (2003), 'The Authorship of the Demosthenic *Epitaphios*', *Museum Helveticum* 60: 152–7.
Worthington, I., C. Cooper and E. M. Harris (2001), *The Oratory of Classical Greece: Dinarchus, Hyperides, and Lycurgus*, Austin.
Yunis, H. (2001), *Demosthenes: On the Crown*, Cambridge.
Zaccarini, M. (2015), 'The Return of Theseus to Athens: A Case Study in Layered Tradition and Reception', *Histos* 9: 174–98.
Zaccarini, M. (2018), 'The Fate of the Lawgiver: The Invention of the Reforms of Ephialtes and the *Patrios Politeia*', *Historia* 67/4: 495–512.
Zeitlin, F. I. (1978), 'The Dynamics of Misogyny: Myth and Mythmaking in the *Oresteia*', *Arethusa* 11/1: 149–84.
Zeitlin, F. I. (1990), 'Thebes: Theater of Self and Society in Athenian Drama', in J. J. Winkler and F. I. Zeitlin (eds), *Nothing to Do with Dionysos? Athenian Drama in Its Social Context*, Princeton, pp. 130–67.
Zimmermann, B. (1992), *Dithyrambos: Geschichte einer Gattung*, Göttingen.
Ziolkowski, J. E. (1981), *Thucydides and the Tradition of Funeral Speeches at Athens*, New York.
Zuntz, G. (1955), *The Political Plays of Euripides*, Manchester.

Index Locorum

Literary sources

Aelian
VH 2.13: 27, 80

Aeschines
1.19–20: 45
1.80–4: 72n55
1.143: 54
1.154: 66
1.157: 27
1.166–70: 67
2.1: 207n85
2.31: 47
2.72: 46
2.74–8: 48, 71
2.74–7: 16
2.75–6: 125
3.6: 66
3.177–82: 68
3.191: 48

Aeschylus
Ag. 10–11: 164
535–6: 86
1069–71: 164
1377–8: 164
1432–3: 164
1440: 172
Cho. 984–90: 78
Eum. 625–30: 164n97
685–90: 32n18, 146, 148, 162
Pers. 234: 166n102
362: 163
745–6: 159
749–50: 157n67, 161

803–8: 160
805–22: 191
809–12: 160n83
820–2: 160
908–1076: 161
Sept. 609–14: 198n56
778–84: 55
TrGF 53a–54: 184, 193n36
73b–75a: 117
77: 117

Alcaeus
fr. 348 Voigt: 92

Andocides
1.2: 66
1.73: 101n77
1.75: 45
1.76: 101n77

Androtion
FGrHist 324 F 1: 52
F 2: 36, 52
F 4b: 52

Antiphon
1.3–4: 188

Apollodorus
Epitome
1.16–17: 164n99
Library
2.5.9: 145

2.8: 115n1
3.14.2: 164n97

Archilochus
fr. 120 West: 34
fr. 225 West: 92

Aristophanes
Ach. 1–25: 46
504–6: 26
524–9: 173n126
Av. 1377–1409: 35
Eccl. 1140–3: 80
Lys. 399–401: 155
425: 155
507–20: 155
658–9: 155
676–9: 155
781–828: 34n20
1128–32: 130
Nub. 1047–70: 34n20
1135: 131n65
1355–8: 50
Ran. 727–33: 94
757–8: 79
Thesm. 295–372: 69n48
Vesp. 1108–9: 42

Aristotle
Eth. Nic. 1107a8–12: 162
1108a35–b6: 163
1124a26–b6: 190
1130b–31a: 70n50
1167b17–1168a27: 137n83

INDEX LOCORUM 241

Poet. 1453a2–6: 122n31
Pol. 1255a6–7: 172n120
1273b35–74a5: 42
1274a8–9: 43
1275a6: 97n65
1275a22–33: 42, 45
1281b: 80
1291b14–30: 95
1326a17–25: 111
Rh. 1354a22–3: 66n37
1358b21–8: 15, 66, 70
1358b22: 128
1360b: 95
1375b30: 83n4
1378b23–35: 150, 152
1386b11–12: 163n89, 163n94

[Aristotle]
Ath. Pol. 3.6: 43
7.4: 74
8.4: 45
9.1: 42
14.4: 115
19.3: 50, 92n41
21.3: 44
27.3–4: 43
41.2: 42, 45
43.2: 45
43.3–6: 46
53.3: 43
57.3: 43
57.4: 43, 43n49
58.1: 60
60.3: 43
62.2: 43
62.3: 72
63–4: 43
63.3: 42–3
67.1: 66
68.1: 43

Armenidas
FGrHist 378 F 6: 183

Athenaeus
14.653d: 92n40

Bacchylides
15–20: 35
15: 37n29

Bion of Proconnesus
FGrHist 332 T 1: 173n122
T 2: 173n122
F 2: 173n122

Callinus
fr. 1.12–13 West: 93

Cicero
Fin. 5.1.1–5.2.5: 39n35

Cleidemus
FGrHist 323 F 17: 51
F 18: 51, 146
F 19: 52

Demon
FGrHist 327 F 5: 51

Demosthenes
1.8–9: 71
1.14–15: 71
2.24: 71
3.24: 64n30
6.5: 70
8.1: 70
8.41–2: 64n30
8.60: 64n30
9.24–5: 64n30
9.29: 129
9.74: 17n81
14.32: 129
16.1–3: 70
16.4–5: 71
16.9: 124
16.10: 124
16.14–15: 124
16.16–17: 125
16.17: 132
16.32: 124
18.66–8: 17n81
18.95–101: 17n81
18.121: 66
18.180: 27
18.187: 47n63, 140n89
18.231: 125
18.265: 79
18.285: 40
19.1: 67
19.15–16: 16
19.16: 125
19.17–23: 72n55
19.17: 125
19.70: 69n48
19.112–13: 72n55
19.123: 46
19.337: 79
20.1: 207n84
20.10: 122, 155
20.14: 207n84
20.25: 155
20.43–4: 122
20.55: 123
20.64: 122
20.81: 122
20.109: 124
20.110: 101n77
20.141: 122
20.156–8: 131
20.156: 122
21.10: 27n7
21.48–9: 123

21.56–60: 79
21.143: 95
21.144–7: 95
21.148–50: 126
21.154–9: 67
21.196: 163
21.226: 79
22.77: 101n77
23.4: 207n85
23.53: 173n124
23.66: 164n97
23.156: 123
23.196–203: 68n44
23.204–6: 17n81
24.22: 43
24.24: 123
24.45–6: 46
24.48: 73
24.51–2: 126
24.65: 129n53
24.149–51: 43n47
24.185: 101n77
24.192–3: 126
24.201: 129n53
27.3: 207n85
28.18: 164
34.1: 207n85
36.41: 131n65
45.17: 42
45.33: 131n65
45.50: 66
45.78: 97n65
51: 47n64
51.7–10: 76
54.3–9: 95n56
54.13–14: 95
54.17: 95
57.35: 154
60: 64n28
60.3: 97
60.4: 88, 89, 97
60.5: 89n30, 97n66
60.6: 16n80
60.7–8: 153
60.7: 63, 139, 161n86
60.8–9: 118
60.8: 53, 134, 146, 153n48, 179n139, 185, 191
60.10–11: 60, 139
60.10: 64
60.13: 60
60.22: 62n25, 212n100
60.26: 62
60.27–31: 41, 62
60.27: 8n29
60.28: 119, 153n48
60.36: 60

[Demosthenes]
7.38: 131
44.34: 97n65

44.39: 97n65
59.1–15: 109n101
59.1: 188
59.4: 74
59.16: 109n102
59.52–3: 109n104
59.52: 42
59.64–71: 110n17
59.72: 109
59.73: 110
59.74: 90, 110
59.75: 110, 111
59.76: 110
59.85–7: 110n107
59.87: 110n107
59.89–90: 46
59.94–107: 68
59.122: 154

Dinarchus
1.14–15: 68
1.109–10: 17n81
2.14: 69n48
2.16: 69n48

Dio Chrysostomus
52.14: 54

Diodorus Siculus
4.16: 145, 171n117
4.28: 147, 165n101
4.57–8: 115n1
15.46.6: 205
15.62–6: 203

Diogenes Laertius
1.57: 37

Dionysius of Halicarnassus
Ant. Rom. 1.8.3: 51
Thuc. 6–7: 51

[Eratosthenes]
Cat. 13: 27

Etymologicum Magnum
s.v. Ἱππία: 184

Eupolis
fr. 384 K.-A.: 94

Euripides
Bacch. 820: 163n90
El. 35–8: 94
253: 94
362–3: 94
367–90: 94
551: 94n53
1258–62: 164n97
Hec. 122: 84n10
Heracl. 134–252: 127

134–43: 128
137–8: 138
142–3: 138
144–6: 128
147–52: 128
153–78: 128
153–7: 138
154: 128
175–8: 128
184–90: 130
187–90: 138
191–201: 130
194–5: 138
197–8: 138
207–13: 130
215–22: 78, 118, 127
215–20: 130
215–17: 145, 171n117
218–19: 175n132
226–31: 130
240–1: 131, 133
242: 138
243–6: 138
253–4: 138
253: 138
286–7: 138
329–32: 139n88
333–4: 133
337–41: 199
849–50: 127n44
1030–1: 127n44
HF 348–435: 32n18
408–18: 145
1336–7: 133
Ion 15–20: 87
20–1: 105
29–30: 87, 105
237–40: 105
267–74: 87, 90n34, 105
289–92: 105
464–5: 199
542: 87, 90n34, 105n90, 107
579–80: 106
589–92: 107
589–90: 87, 90n34
634–40: 199
670–5: 107
673–5: 87, 90n34
723–30: 199
735–7: 90n34
999–1000: 87, 90n34, 105
1056–7: 106n93
1058–60: 106, 106n93
1144–5: 145
1463–7: 90n34, 107
1465–7: 87, 105
1540–1: 106
1561–2: 106
1575–94: 108n99
1601–3: 107
Med. 248–51: 154

Orest. 244: 130n60
453: 130n60
Phoen. 55–80: 182
79–80: 196
159–60: 183n6
439–42: 196
1427–59: 55
Supp. 16–19: 198n59, 211n97
131–54: 195
148: 197n55
155–61: 196
195–219: 197
219–49: 195
220–1: 197
222–5: 197
229–45: 201n66
229–31: 197
230–1: 197
235: 197
286–364: 194
297–364: 195
301–2: 198, 211n97
304–12: 198, 211n96
314–25: 202
373–4: 201
377–80: 139n88
399–462: 194
339–41: 211n96
399: 199n60
409–25: 77
494–505: 198
496–9: 199n61
511–12: 198
522–63: 200
524–7: 211n96
723–5: 201
737–44: 199n62
741–4: 211n97
754–9: 184
825–7: 198n56
857–917: 194n42
928–31: 195n46
955–89: 194
1165–75: 184n11
1167–79: 136n80
1183–95: 202
Tro. 28–9: 172
31: 84n10
130–7: 177
766–73: 177
864–8: 177
987–1001: 149n28, 177
1036–41: 177
1168–70: 177
1176–9: 201
TrGF 61b: 94
228–46: 116n5
334.1–2: 163n90
360: 87
370: 88
448a–59: 116n5

481.9–11: 108n99
495.40–3: 94
541: 55
545a.9–12: 55
728–40: 116n5
741a–51a: 116n5

Gorgias (DK)
B 5a–6: 39, 64n28
B 6: 63

Harpocration
s.v. παράβυστον: 42

Hecataeus
FGrHist 1 F 1: 19
F 30: 117

Hellanicus
FGrHist 4 F 98: 182
F 161: 86n16
F 166: 145, 149n24
F 167: 146
FGrHist 323a F 1: 52
F 2: 36, 52
F 14: 51
F 16a: 51
F 17a–c: 51
F 18–20: 52
F 22a–b: 52

Herodorus of Pontus
FGrHist 31 F 25a: 145, 149n24

Herodotus
1.1–6: 18
1.1–4: 173
1.4.1–2: 177
1.5.2: 177
1.23: 35
1.56.2: 87
1.60: 115
1.171–2: 86
2.23: 17
2.45: 17
2.113–15: 177n136
3.142: 92
4.110–16: 145n6, 154
4.114.3: 154
5.57: 49n71
5.72.3: 116
6.59: 131n65
7.5–16: 151
7.8a–8b: 151
7.8a.2: 159
7.8b: 159
7.8b.1: 159
7.8b.2: 160
7.8c: 151, 191
7.8c.1–2: 159
7.8c.3: 159, 160

7.9–9c: 151
7.10e: 151
7.16a.2: 151
7.94: 108n99
7.150: 130
7.161.3: 87
8.44: 108n99
8.55.1: 83n3
8.73.1: 86
8.77: 156
8.109.3: 191
9.26–7: 47n66
9.27: 117
9.27.3: 184, 185, 203n73
9.27.4: 146
9.73.2: 86n19
9.76.1–2: 172

Hesiod
WD 321–4: 129n52
349–50: 123
351: 123
Cat. fr. 9: 108n99
fr. 10(a).20–4: 108n99

Homer
Il. 1.12–21: 174
1.92–100: 174
2.546–51: 83, 83n4
2.553–5: 83n4
2.557–8: 83n4
3.182–90: 144
4.376–98: 182
5.253: 92n40
5.801–8: 182
6.145–211: 91
6.171–86: 144
6.191: 91n38
6.292: 91n35
6.381–2: 17n84
6.490–3: 155n61
7.123–8: 91
9.431: 17n84
9.443: 17n84
10.285–90: 182
11.785–7: 54
14.112–14: 91
14.114: 183
Od. 7.77–81: 83
11.235: 91n35
11.271–80: 55
22.227: 91n35

Homeric Hymn to Aphrodite
94: 92

Hyperides
6: 64n28
6.5: 63, 139, 199
6.7: 88, 89, 98
6.10: 65

6.14: 137
6.20: 153n48
6.32: 62
6.37–8: 60, 62
6.37: 119

Ion of Chios
fr. 29 West: 84n10

Isaeus
2.2: 207n85
2.47: 67
3.61: 97n65
4.1: 207n84
5.6: 97n65
6.2: 207n85
9.26: 129n53

Isocrates
4.18: 141
4.23–5: 88
4.23–4: 87
4.29: 123
4.53: 167
4.54–9: 19, 53, 118, 185, 209n91,
    211n95
4.55: 211n95
4.56: 120, 132, 140, 141
4.57: 141
4.60: 142
4.61–3: 141
4.62: 141
4.64–5: 142
4.66–70: 20, 148
4.66–72: 18
4.66–7: 165
4.66: 166
4.67: 166
4.68: 165, 166
4.71: 166
4.184: 163
5.33–4: 118
5.53–5: 156
8.42–4: 64n30
8.64–6: 64n30
8.85–8: 64n30
10.19: 175n131
10.21: 175n131
10.31: 118, 185, 209n91
12.35–41: 209n93
12.35: 176
12.39–41: 176
12.124–6: 88
12.126: 89n29
12.151–98: 209
12.155: 209
12.159: 212n99
12.162–3: 210
12.168–74: 19, 53, 185, 186, 210
12.168–9: 34n21, 53n84
12.169: 211

12.170: 210, 211
12.171: 211
12.172–3: 212n99
12.173–4: 212
12.174: 211
12.178: 101n77
12.188: 176
12.189: 176
12.193–5: 176
12.193: 20, 145, 149, 175, 176
12.194: 118
12.196: 149, 178
12.239–40: 178n137
12.265: 178n137
14.1–2: 206, 206n82
14.4: 207
14.6: 207
14.8: 206
14.10: 206
14.15–16: 206
14.22: 207n84
14.25: 206, 206n83, 208
14.30: 206
14.33–8: 206
14.35: 206n83
14.40: 206n83
14.42–3: 206
14.42: 206n83
14.52–3: 207
14.53–5: 53n85, 185, 186, 207n86
14.53: 207, 208
14.54: 207
14.55: 209n89
15.4: 163
15.13: 163
15.142–3: 163
16.25: 93
18.4: 67
18.52–7: 67
18.58–67: 68
18.67: 131

Istrus
FGrHist 334 F 10: 52
F 14: 52n82
F 27: 52

Lycurgus
1.41: 88, 107n98
1.83–130: 68
1.98–101: 88

Lysias
1.6–8: 154
2.3: 16n80, 62
2.3–47: 18
2.4–6: 20, 146, 148, 152
2.4: 153
2.5: 65n31, 136, 155, 156, 163
2.6: 157, 158, 208
2.7–10: 53, 185, 186, 187
2.7: 187, 190, 200n65
2.8: 136, 187, 188, 190, 192, 210n94
2.9–10: 211n96
2.9: 189, 191, 192, 211n97
2.10: 138n87, 184, 188, 192
2.11–16: 118, 134
2.11: 189n23
2.12: 135, 136, 138, 138n86, 138n87
2.13: 135, 138
2.14: 138, 138n86, 138n87, 153n48, 155
2.15: 135
2.16: 135, 138n86
2.17: 88, 89, 100, 139, 157
2.18: 62, 89n32, 100
2.19: 200
2.20: 64, 89n32, 100, 102
2.21: 65n31, 159, 160
2.22: 63, 138n87, 166n102
2.23: 136
2.24: 89n32, 102
2.27: 159, 160
2.29–30: 129n53
2.33: 64n27
2.42: 60, 64n27
2.43: 89n32, 100, 102n83
2.44: 64n27, 135
2.47: 65, 65n33
2.52: 60
2.55–7: 64n27
2.55–6: 65
2.55: 65n33
2.56: 65n32
2.57: 65n33
2.58–60: 62
2.60: 64n27
2.61: 62, 63, 135n75, 138n87
2.63: 89n32, 102
2.65: 102
2.67–8: 63
2.67: 138n87
2.69: 62
2.75: 136
2.80: 60
3.6: 154
5.1: 207n84
6.47: 135n75
9.1: 67
12.38: 67
12.43: 49
13.2: 135n75
13.69: 135n75
14.1: 135
14.25: 49
15.9: 66
16: 47n64
16.3–5: 73n61
16.13–18: 75
18.16: 129n53
18.17–19: 101n77
19.1: 207n84
19.11: 207n85
22.7: 67
23.3: 8n32
24: 47n64
24.1: 73
24.25–6: 76
24.25: 73
25.20: 101n77
25.27: 101n77
26: 47n64
26.1: 75
26.5: 73n61, 75
26.9–10: 73n61
26.9: 75
26.11: 43
26.13: 75
26.15: 75
26.16–18: 73n61
31: 47n64
31.1: 74
31.1–2: 75
31.5–7: 75
31.7–9: 76
31.26: 75
31.34: 75
34.3: 93

[Lysias]
6.29: 74
6.33: 74

Mimnermus
fr. 9 West: 50

Pausanias
1.2.1: 145, 149n25, 149n27, 172n121, 176n133, 178n138
1.15.2: 146
1.17.2: 146
1.21.4: 164n97
1.22.6: 55
1.28.8: 42
1.29.3–15: 39n35, 59
1.29.4: 39n35, 59n11
1.30.4: 184
1.39.2: 184
1.44.10: 127n44
2.18.7–8: 115n1
3.1.5: 115n1
4.3.3–8: 115n1
7.1.2–5: 108n99
7.2.7: 148n20
8.2.1: 36
9.1.5–8: 205
9.18.1–3: 183n4
9.29.4: 50

INDEX LOCORUM 245

Phanodemus
FGrHist 325 F 4: 52
F 27: 52

Pherecydes
FGrHist 3 F 2: 93
F 15: 153n49
F 84: 117
F 96: 182
F 151: 145, 149
F 152: 149, 174

Philochorus
FGrHist 328 F 3: 52
F 8–9: 52
F 8: 36
F 10: 52
F 11: 52
F 13: 52
F 17a–c: 51
F 18a–c: 52
F 20c: 52
F 93–8: 52
F 105–6: 52
F 110: 52, 145, 149
F 111: 51
F 112: 184
F 113: 184

Philostratus
Imag. 1.15.1–5: 49
VS 2.22: 39n35

Phocylides
fr. 3 West: 93

Photius
Lex. s.v. Παναθήναια: 36
s.v. ἐφέται: 43

Pindar
Isthm. 2.19–20: 84
Nem. 9.23–5: 53, 183
11.44–8: 156
Ol. 1.75–111: 51
6.12–17: 53, 183, 194n42
Pyth. 1.50–7: 51
1.50–3: 55
2.20–30: 51
6.28–46: 51
7.9–12: 84
7.17–18: 163
8.71–2: 163
9.79–83: 117n8, 127n44
Fragments ffr. 70–86a Maehler: 35
fr. 172 Maehler: 145
fr. 174 Maehler: 145
fr. 175 Maehler: 145, 149n25, 172n121, 178n138

Plato
Alcib. I 104a–c, 112c: 49n71
Lach. 179a–80b: 48
Leg. 659b–c: 80
700a–01b: 80
700a–01a: 35
876b: 79
887c–d: 49n72
Lysis 205b–e: 49n71
Menex. 234c–35c: 42
237a: 98
237b1–c6: 88, 89
237b: 98
237c: 98
237e: 88, 89n31, 98n68
238b–39a: 62
238d: 99
238e–239a: 88, 89, 99
239a–b: 153, 189
239b: 53, 118, 134, 146, 179n139, 185
240d–e: 62
240e: 64
241e: 137
242c: 137
242e6–243a7: 62
243c–d: 62
244a3–6: 60
244b–c: 137
244e–45a: 63, 139
245c6–d6: 88, 89n31, 99n70
246b–c: 62
248e: 62
249b3–6: 60
Prt. 319b5–c8: 72n55
Resp. 331d–32d: 121
377b–83c: 49
468a–b: 172n120
492b–c: 72n55, 79
Symp. 179b–80b: 51, 54
180a: 19
Tht. 174e–75a: 49
Ti. 21b: 37

[Plato]
Hipparch. 228b4–c3: 27

Plutarch
Comp. Thes. Rom. 6.1: 174
Dem. 21.2: 40
Per. 8.6: 40n37
13.5–6: 37
28.3–5: 40n37
Sol. 8.2: 45
19.1: 43, 45
24.2: 97n65
30.1: 45
Thes. 2.1: 172
24.3: 36
26–8: 170
26: 145

26.1: 145, 149, 171
26.2: 173n122
27.2: 146
27.3–4: 146
28.1: 146
29.1: 172
29.2: 172
29.4–5: 53, 184, 193n36
29.4: 184
31.4: 172
32.2: 173, 174n130
34.1: 172n119

[Plutarch]
X orat. 842a: 27

PMG
893–6: 50
907: 50, 92

Pollux
Onom. 8.33: 42
8.125: 43, 43n49

Polybius
9.1.2–5: 51

Proclus
Chr. 175–81: 145
211–13: 55
277–303: 176n133

scholia ad Aelius Aristides
1.362: 36

scholia ad Aristophanes
Pax 905–7: 74
Plut. 953: 79
Vesp. 88: 43
300: 43

scholia ad Homer
Il. 2.553–5 (schol. A): 83n4
24.804 (schol. T): 145

scholia ad Pindar
Nem. 5.89: 149, 171, 174
Pyth. 9.82: 117n8

scholia ad Plato
Prm. 127a: 36

scholia ad Sophocles
OC 712: 184

scholia ad Thucydides
2.34.5 (schol. ABFGc$_2$): 39

Simonides
fr. 11 West: 50

Solon
fr. 4.5–16 West: 157

Sophocles
Aj. 202: 86
1069–72: 94
1091–2: 191
1093–6: 94
1129–31: 190
Ant. 21–5: 191
37–8: 94
66–7: 198
76–7: 190
175–91: 78
567–81: 78
615–24: 156
640–80: 78
734–9: 78
OC 1066: 84
1292–8: 182
OT 1237–64: 55
1265–79: 55
Trach. 417: 172

Stesichorus
PMGF 222b: 182

Strabo
8.6.19: 127n44
9.1.10: 83n4
9.2.11: 184n9

Suda
s.v. Ἄρειος πάγος: 164n97
s.v. Παναθήναια: 36
s.v. Σοφοκλῆς: 79

Thebaid
frr. 2–3 Bernabé: 182
frr. 7–8 Bernabé: 183

Theognis
183–92: 92
429–38: 92

Thespis
TrGF 1 T 1–2: 26

Thucydides
1.2.5–6: 87
1.2.6: 88
1.9.2: 117n8
1.21.1: 17
1.22.4: 51
1.24.3: 111
1.35: 128
1.35.5–36.3: 71
1.38–40: 128
1.44.1: 202n71
1.71.4: 130
1.73.2: 47

1.75–7: 64n29
1.144.4: 71
2.26.4: 42n44
2.34–46: 40
2.34.2–6: 39
2.34.8: 42n44
2.36.1–3: 16n80
2.36.1: 87, 90n33
2.36.2–3: 64n29
2.37.1: 61, 99n72
2.37.2–3: 99n73
2.37.3–38.1: 62
2.37.3: 139
2.40.4: 137
2.40.5: 137n83, 139
2.41.3: 64n29
2.43.1: 62
2.45.2: 153n53, 154
2.62–4: 64n29
2.103.1: 172
3.36–49: 70, 121, 129n55
3.37–40: 64n29
3.38.2: 129
3.39.2–3: 122
3.40.4: 122
3.44–8: 64n29
3.44.4: 70, 122
3.47.5: 122
3.52–67: 209n90
3.52.2: 209n90
3.52.3: 209n90
3.63.4: 132
3.70.1: 174
3.82.5–6: 49
3.113.5: 131
4.28.1: 72n55
4.40.2: 172
4.90–100: 194
5.18.4: 202n71
5.39.2–3: 174
5.42.1: 174
5.44.3: 131
5.47.2–3: 202n71
5.85: 129
5.89–99: 64n29
5.89: 129
5.93: 129
6.2.2: 86
6.10–11: 64n29
6.17–18: 64n29
6.17.7: 71
6.18.2: 71
7.77.3: 163
8.54.4: 49
8.58.3–4: 202n71
8.72: 46
8.75.2: 101n77
8.93.3: 101n77

Tyrtaeus
fr. 2.12–15 West: 50, 115

fr. 5 West: 50
fr. 11.1 West: 115
fr. 19.8 West: 115

Xenophanes
fr. 1.19–24 West: 50

Xenophon
Cyr. 3.1.39: 163n90
7.5.73: 172n120
Hell. 2.4.40: 129
3.5.10–15: 64n30, 65n33
3.5.16: 132
6.5.22–32: 203
6.5.33–49: 203
6.5.36–7: 204n78
6.5.37: 208
6.5.38–9: 203, 205
6.5.41–4: 203
6.5.45–6: 185, 186, 204
6.5.46–8: 47, 53
6.5.47: 204, 205n79
6.5.48: 116, 205
Mem. 1.1.18: 74
Oec. 3.10–12: 154
7.22–3: 154
7.24–5: 154
7.35–6: 154

INSCRIPTIONS

IG I²
186–7: 27

IG I³
104.13–19: 43
104.19: 43n49
105.34: 45
258bis: 27
503/504: 61, 61n21
972: 117n10
1144.34: 59
1144.118: 59
1144.139: 59
1147: 59, 60n15
1147.5: 59
1162: 59, 60n15
1162.4: 59
1162.45–8: 61
1162.96: 59
1163.34–41: 61
1166: 59
1166.2: 59
1179.10–13: 61
1183: 59
1186.108: 59
1191: 59
1193bis: 59

IG II²
103: 46
196.11–14: 122n30
380: 27
389: 46
391.10–12: 122n30
392.1–3: 122n30
456: 27
1178: 27
1182: 27
1183.36: 27
1186: 27
1198: 27
1200: 27
1202: 27
1496.70: 27
1612.111: 64n30
1612.122: 64n30
1618.110: 64n30
1629.771: 64n30
1629.845: 64n30
1631.133: 64n30
1631.202: 64n30
1641.25–33: 42
1646.12: 42
1670.34–5: 42
2318: 26
2320: 26
2323 a: 26
3090: 27
3092: 27
3093: 27
3094: 27
3095: 27
3099: 27
3100: 27
3106: 27
3108: 27
3109: 27
5221: 59
5222: 59
5225: 61

IG II³, 1
306.13–14: 122n30
378.17–20: 122n30
451: 132
452.11–16: 122n30
475.9–14: 122n30

IG VII
1888: 60n16

IG XII, 5
444.17–18: 36

IPrien
37.107–23: 51

Miletos
27.5–12: 51

SEG
19.149: 74n65

General Index

Achilles and Patroclus, 19, 44, 51, 54
Acropolis, 36, 37–8
Adrastus
　culpability of, 187–8, 195–6, 204, 207–8
　flight to Athens, 183–4
　help to Polynices, 182–3
　hybris of, 196–8
　recovery of the Seven (bellicose version), 53, 184–5, 186–7, 193, 207
　recovery of the Seven (peaceful version), 53, 184, 193n36, 210
advantage, 15, 69–71, 74–6, 128, 200–2, 203, 206
Aeschines, 16–17, 125
Aeschylus' *Eumenides*, 162, 164n97
Aethra, 172n119, 193, 194, 198–9
Agora, 37, 38, 42, 45
aidōs see respect
alien *see* foreign, foreigner
Allan, W. and Kelly, A., 77–8
Althusser, L., 4; *see also* ideology
altruism *see* humaneness
Amazons
　Attic Amazonomachy, 32n18, 33, 145–7, 162, 174–5, 176–7
　as anti-Athenians, 158, 161, 179
　in the figurative arts, 145n5, 145n9, 146, 158–9, 158n72, 167–70
　gender status of, 144, 153–5, 164
　and Heracles, 145, 171
　hybris of, 148, 154–7, 161, 178, 179
　and Persians, 145, 158–61
　at Troy, 144–5
　see also Antiope; imperialism
Anderson, B. *see* imagined community
Anthesteria (festival), 109–10, 114
Antiope
　abducted by Theseus, 148–9, 162, 165–6, 167–8, 173n122, 174
　elopement with Theseus, 149, 168–9, 176–7
　legitimately acquired by Theseus, 148, 171–3
　role in the Attic Amazonomachy, 146–7
　see also Amazons
Apollodorus' *Against Neaera*
　authorship, 109n101
　documents in, 109n102, 109n104, 110n107
　outline of the case, 109
archē see imperialism
Areopagus
　in Aeschylus' *Eumenides*, 162, 165
　eligibility and size, 43
　origin of name, 164n97
　procedure, 43
　reform of Ephialtes, 164n97
aristocratic ideology, 9–10
　democratisation of, 96, 137n83
Aristotle, 218–19
　on deliberative rhetoric, 15, 69–70
　on forensic rhetoric, 15, 66
　on *hybris*, 150–1, 152, 189–90
asebeia see impiety
Assembly
　attendance, 46
　curse and prayer, 69n48
　discursive parameters, 15, 69–71, 80, 200–1, 203
　eligibility, 46
　frequency of sessions, 46
　historical allusions, 71
　meeting place, 45–6
　myths at the, 47
　pay, 46
　powers, 69
　quorum, 46
　types of sessions, 46
Athena, 36, 82–3, 104, 105, 107, 108, 115, 162, 167, 201–2
Athenian ancestors, 16–17, 62, 125
Atthidographers, 51–2
Attic Amazonomachy *see* Amazons

autochthony
    of Attic kings, 82–4, 105, 110–11, 114
    and cohesion, 96, 97–9, 100–3, 113
    complete notion of, 82, 87–9, 103, 113
    and concord (*homonoia*), 99n73, 101–3, 114
    and equality, 99, 106
    and exclusiveness, 106–7, 109–13, 114
    as indigenous nature, 86–7
    and justice, 99–100
    metaphor of the family, 97–9, 100, 106, 107–8, 113–14
    and nobility of birth, 88, 97, 100, 103, 105–6, 113

Basilinna *see* King Archon
Boardman, J., 115, 116
boulē see Council of the Five Hundred
bouleutērion see Council of the Five Hundred

Cairns, D., 152
charis see reciprocity
children of Heracles *see* Heraclidae
Cimon
    and the Painted Stoa, 146
    and Theseus, 119, 134, 139
citizen, citizenship, 6–7, 87, 88–9
    marriage with non-citizens, 109–10, 112
    naturalisation, 97n65
civil war, 7n30, 13–14, 101
collective memory *see* social memory
concord *see* autochthony
Council of the Five Hundred
    Bouleutic Oath, 74–5
    composition, 45, 72–3
    discursive parameters, 72–6, 80–1
    eligibility, 45
    frequency of sessions, 45
    historical allusions, 75–6
    meeting place, 45
    myths at the, 47
    origins, 43–4
    pay, 45
    powers, 74
    prytaneis, 45
Creusa
    conflict with Ion, 107, 108
    earthborn origin, 105
    see also Euripides' *Ion*

decree
    decree proposers, 72n53
    distinction from law, 69
    see also honour
democratic restoration, 102–3, 114, 216
    Amnesty, 13, 67, 89n32, 101–2
dēmos see mass
dēmosion sēma see State funeral for the war dead
Demosthenes' *Funeral Speech*, 40
    authenticity, 40n39
dikaion, to see justice
dikastērion see lawcourt
Dionysus, 33, 34n20; *see also* dithyramb; dramatic festivals
diplomacy (language of), 130, 132, 202n71

dithyramb
    contests, 26, 27, 37
    history and characteristics, 34–5
    name, 34
    themes, 35
dokimasia, 74–6
doxa see reputation
dramatic festivals
    attendance, 28, 77
    choruses, 78–80
    discursive parameters, 16, 76–80, 81, 108, 133, 139, 162, 164–5, 179–80, 194–5, 202
    Great Dionysia, 25–6
    judges, 77, 79–80
    Lenaea, 26–7
    myths at the, 29–34
    number of plays, 27–8
    performances of old plays, 26, 29
    pre-play ceremonies, 77
    Rural Dionysia, 27
    subversive nature of tragedy, 76–7
    Theatre of Dionysus, 28
    Theoric Fund, 28n14
    see also dithyramb

ekklēsia see Assembly
ekklēsiai kyriai see Assembly
ekklēsiai nomimoi see Assembly
ekklēsiai synklētoi, 46n62; *see also* Assembly
elite, ideological agency, 3, 61–5, 68–9, 71–2, 73–4, 79, 218
elpis see hope
Empire *see* imperialism
envy *see* phthonos
ephetai, 43n49; *see also* homicide courts
epinician poetry, 50–1, 53
epitaphios logos see funeral oration
equality, 59–60, 61–2; *see also* autochthony
Erechtheus
    as ancestor of the Athenians, 83, 84–6
    earthborn nature, 82–3
    and Eumolpus, 38n31, 87–8
    identity with Erichthonius, 82n2, 83–4
    as tribal hero, 89n29
Erichthonius
    birth, 83–4
    founder of the Panathenaea, 36
    see also Erechtheus
Eteocles *see* Adrastus; Oedipus; Seven against Thebes
eugeneia see nobility of birth
Eupatrids, 92n41; *see also* nobility of birth
Euripides' *Children of Heracles*
    plot, 126–7
    rhetoric in, 127n45
    see also Heraclidae
Euripides' *Ion*
    dating, 108n99
    and Hellenic genealogy, 108n99
    plot, 104
    subversive readings of, 104n89, 108n100
    Xuthus' critique of autochthony, 107

Euripides' *Suppliant Women*
    dating, 194
    interpretation, 193n37, 194
    plot, 193
Eurystheus, 116–17, 141–2

face-to-face society, 7–8, 15, 58, 73; *see also* imagined community
family tradition, 48–9
    family defence, 48n70
    myths transmitted through, 49
Finley, M., 6; *see also* ideology
Fisher, N., 150–2
foreign, foreigner, 79, 88, 98, 106–7
freedom, 61–2, 63–4
funeral oration
    catalogue of exploits, 62–4
    depiction of democracy, 61–2
    extant speeches, 39–40
    and individuality, 60
    influence on Athenians, 41–2
    myths in, 40–1
    structure, 58n6
    see also Loraux, N.; State funeral for the war dead

gain, 128–9, 138
Geertz, C., 5; *see also* ideology
Gigantomachy, 36, 37, 56
Goldhill, S., 76–7
Gorgias' *Funeral Speech*, 39–40, 60
Gotteland, S., 20

Hansen, M., 72, 73
hegemony *see* imperialism
hēliaia see lawcourt
helping paradigm *see* humaneness
Heracles
    and the Amazons, 145, 147
    in Attic vase painting, 115
    and Pisistratus, 115, 116
    and Theseus, 118, 130–1, 132–3, 134–5, 141, 142
    see also Heraclidae
Heraclidae
    Athenian defence of the, 116–18, 126–7, 133–4, 140
    return of the, 115, 116
Hippolyta *see* Antiope
history *see* Assembly; Council of the Five Hundred; lawcourt; myth
homicide courts, 43; *see also* Areopagus; *ephetai*
homonoia see autochthony
honour, 135–6, 187n17, 190, 191–2
    honorific decrees, 122, 132
    see also hybris
hope, 155–6, 159–60
humaneness, 63–5, 122–3, 128, 138–9, 142–3, 213, 217n1
    and altruism, 63–4, 123–4, 139, 141, 188–9, 204, 208, 210
    exclusively Athenian, 124–5, 188
    helping paradigm (international relations), 124, 125, 158
    and justice, 124–5, 126, 138–9, 187–8, 199–200, 203–4, 207, 210–11
    and reciprocity, 123–4, 125
hybris
    in Athenian law, 150, 173
    behavioural aspect of, 151–2, 197
    dispositional aspect of, 152, 197
    and honour, 150–1, 152
    of the Persians, 159–61
    and rape, 173
    and religion, 149–50, 190–1, 196–7
    see also Amazons; Thebes, Thebans; thinking big
Hyperides' *Funeral Speech*, 40

identity, 12n54, 15, 49, 65–6, 82, 87, 98n67, 103, 217, 219
ideology
    bidirectional nature, 3, 66, 81, 218, 219
    constructive function, 3, 7–8, 14–15, 21, 58–60, 61–6, 81, 103, 217
    culturalist view of, 5, 8–9, 21, 215
    definition, 2–3
    descriptive aspect, 7–8
    dynamic nature, 3, 14, 21, 81, 103, 114, 185–6, 213–14, 215–17
    in the Enlightenment, 3
    Marxist view of, 3–4, 5–6, 7, 21, 215
    normative aspect, 63–5, 81, 217–18
    see also aristocratic ideology; elite; mass; orator
imagined community, 7–8, 58
imperialism
    of the Amazons, 155, 156, 159, 160, 166
    Athenian attitudes to, 64n30
    Athenian Empire, 7, 64–5, 71
    of the Persians, 159, 160
impiety, 190–1, 192, 194
indignation *see phthonos*
institution *see* New Institutionalism
Iolaus, 117n8, 126–7, 130–1
Ion, 104, 107; *see also* Creusa; Euripides' *Ion*
Isocrates' *Panathenaicus*
    nature and purpose, 176, 178n137, 209–10, 212
    depiction of the Thebans, 211, 212
Isocrates' *Panegyricus*
    nature, 140, 165
    purpose, 141–2, 165, 166–7
Isocrates' *Plataicus*, 205–6

justice, 15, 63, 66, 67–8, 74–6, 99–100, 112–13, 138–9, 157–8, 178, 187–8, 206–7
    corrective, 70, 75
    distributive, 70n50, 75
    see also humaneness; reciprocity

kerdos see gain
King Archon, 109–10, 111–12
    wife of (Basilinna), 110
kinship (in diplomacy), 128n48, 130, 195–6
kyklioi choroi see dithyramb

law
    distinction from decree, 66

GENERAL INDEX   251

international, 128, 204n78
nomos on burial, 189, 190, 192, 198–200, 211
see also lawcourt
lawcourt
   allocation to panels, 43
   character evidence, 67–8
   discursive parameters, 15, 67–9, 80, 112–13
   eligibility, 42–3
   frequency of sessions, 44
   Heliastic Oath, 43, 66–7
   historical allusions, 68
   meeting places, 42
   myths at the, 44
   origins, 42
   pay, 43
   size of panels, 43
   see also Areopagus; *ephetai*; homicide courts
Leosthenes, 40, 60, 62, 137
literacy see social memory
Loraux, N.
   on ideology, 1, 3, 7–8, 21, 58, 64n30
   on Theseus, 118–19
Lysias' *Funeral Oration*
   authenticity, 40
   dating, 40, 101n76

Marathon (Battle of), 59n10, 61n21, 62, 64, 102, 136, 146n13, 158
Marx, K. and Engels, F., 3–4; see also ideology
mass, ideological agency, 3, 60–1, 68–9, 71–2, 74, 79–80, 218
mega phronein see thinking big
moicheia see seduction
myth
   Athenians' knowledge of, 32–4, 38, 41–2, 44, 47–8, 52–3, 56
   definition, 17–18
   Greek attitudes to, 18–19
   and history, 17–19
   multiple versions, 19, 52–6
   relevance to ideology, 19–20

Neaera, 109; see also Apollodorus' *Against Neaera*
New Institutionalism, 2, 10–12, 218, 219–20
   and ancient Greek history, 11–12
   definition of institution, 10
   and ideas, 10–11
nobility of birth
   in archaic Greece, 91–3
   aristocratic, 93, 94–5, 96, 105–6, 113
   collective, 95–6, 97–9, 100, 103, 113
   in democratic Athens, 93–6
   in Homer, 91
   moral value of, 92–3
   see also autochthony
nomos see law

Ober, J.
   on the Council of the Five Hundred, 73
   on ideology, 1–2, 3, 7–10, 21
   on orators, 9

Oedipus, 55, 182, 195; see also Adrastus
orator
   role in ideological practice, 9, 61–5, 68–9, 71–2, 218–19
   use of the past, 38–9, 68, 71, 75–6

Panathenaea
   athletic competitions, 36–7
   Great Panathenaea, 36
   musical contests, 37
   myths at the, 37–8
   rhapsodic competitions, 37
   Small Panathenaea, 36
   see also dithyramb; Erichthonius; Theseus
Parthenon frieze, 38n31
Pericles, citizenship law, 87–8, 197n55; see also Thucydides
Phano (daughter of Neaera), 109–10; see also Apollodorus' *Against Neaera*
Pherecydes, 170
philanthrōpia see humaneness
Philochorus, 170; see also Atthidographers
Philoctetes, 33, 54–5
phthonos
   as envy, 148, 162–3, 164
   of the gods (*phthonos theōn*), 163
   as indignation, 148, 163–4
Plato's *Menexenus*, 40
Plutarch' *Life of Theseus*, 171, 174n130
Pnyx see Assembly
Polynices see Adrastus; Oedipus; Seven against Thebes
punishment see *timōria*

rape
   in Athenian law, 173, 177
   as cause of war, 173
reciprocity, 121–2, 130–1, 133, 134–7, 141, 201–2, 203–5
   and Athenian identity, 122, 142–3
   balanced, 121, 125, 137n85
   generalised, 121, 123
   and honorific decrees, 122, 132, 142–3
   and justice, 121–2
   negative, 121, 203–4
   and *philanthrōpia*, 120, 123
   vocabulary of, 131–3, 140–1
reputation, 155, 156
respect, 135–6, 138
revenge see *timōria*
Rosivach, V., 82, 86

Ste Croix, G. E. M. de, 5–6; see also ideology
seduction, 149, 175–6, 177–8
   in Athenian law, 170n113, 173, 177
Seven against Thebes
   burial in Thebes, 53, 183
   burial place in Attica, 184, 193
   causes of Argive expedition, 182, 195–6, 210–11
   see also Adrastus

Shear, J., 60–1
slavery
    and *hybris*, 123, 150n33, 156, 159
    and ideology, 5–6
social memory, 12–14, 12n54, 218–19
    and institutions, 14–17
    and literacy, 12n56, 13
    mnemonic communities, 12–13
Sparta, Spartans, 115, 116, 125, 141, 203
stasis see civil war
State funeral for the war dead
    casualty lists, 58, 59–60
    collective status, 59–60
    discursive parameters, 15, 58–66, 80, 103, 139–40, 161, 179, 192–3
    figural reliefs, 61
    funerary epigrams, 61
    and individuality, 58–9, 60
    public burial ground, 39n35
    rituals, 60–1
    see also funeral oration; Loraux, N.; Thucydides
Steinbock, B., 13
supplication, 117, 126, 130n58, 210
    rejection of, 189n24, 193, 195
    suppliant drama, 127n46, 193n37
sympheron, to see advantage
symposium, 49–51
    and history, 49–50
    and myth, 50–1
synoecism *see* Theseus

Thebes, Thebans, 203–4, 205–6
    as anti-Athenians, 192–3
    hybris of, 189–92, 198–9, 204–5, 208–9, 211

Theseus
    absence from *epitaphios logos*, 118–19, 134, 158, 179
    and Adrastus, 195, 196–7
    and Cimon, 119
    founder of the Panathenaea, 36
    and Heracles, 118, 130–1, 132–3, 134–5, 141, 142
    synoecism, 111–12
    and women, 170n112, 172–3, 174, 175n131
    see also Antiope
thinking big, 151–2, 197; *see also hybris*; Xerxes
Thirty Tyrants, 14n64, 73, 76, 102, 114; *see also* democratic restoration
Thomas, R., 12–13; *see also* family tradition
thorybos, 72, 196n52
Thucydides
    Melian Dialogue, 129
    Mytilenean Debate, 70, 121–2
    Pericles' funeral oration, 40, 42n44, 60
    speeches, 40n37
    on the State funeral for the war dead, 39
timōria, 187–8, 192
tragedy *see* dramatic festivals

Whitehead, D., 6–7; *see also* ideology
Wolpert, A., 13–14
women
    and politics, 154–5
    role, 154
    seclusion, 154
    and war, 154–5
    see also Amazons

Xenophon, speeches, 203n74
Xerxes, 151–2, 159–61
Xuthus *see* Euripides' *Ion*

EU representative:
Easy Access System Europe
Mustamäe tee 50, 10621 Tallinn, Estonia
Gpsr.requests@easproject.com

www.ingramcontent.com/pod-product-compliance
Lightning Source LLC
Chambersburg PA
CBHW071831230426
43672CB00013B/2810